The Work of Revision

The Work of Revision

Hannah Sullivan

Harvard University Press

Cambridge, Massachusetts · London, England

2013

Library of Congress Cataloging-in-Publication Data

Sullivan, Hannah, 1979-
The work of revision / Hannah Sullivan.
pages cm
Includes bibliographical references and index.
ISBN 978-0-674-07312-8 (alk. paper)
1. American literature—20th century—Criticism, Textual.   2. English literature—20th
century—Criticism, Textual.   3. Modernism (Literature)—English-speaking countries.
4. Intertextuality.   5. Authorship.   6. Editing.   I. Title.
PS221.S86 2013
810.9'005—dc23   2012042986

To Ian

Contents

Introduction   1

1   Textual Criticism, the History of Revision,
and Genetic Reading   13

2   Henry James's Perfectionism:
Problems of Substitution   62

3   Excision and Textual Waste   101

4   Joyce and the Illogic of Addition   147

5   "I Am Dead":
Autobiography Revisited   193

6   Revision, Late Modernism,
and Digital Texts   237

Notes   271

Works Cited   315

Acknowledgments   339

Index   341

The Work of Revision

Introduction

Dencombe was a passionate corrector, a fingerer of style; the last thing he ever arrived at was a form final for himself. His ideal would have been to publish secretly, and then, on the published text, treat himself to the terrified revise, sacrificing always a first edition and beginning for posterity and even for the collectors, poor dears, with a second.

Henry James, "The Middle Years," 1893/ 1895/ 1909

EARLY TWENTY-FIRST-CENTURY WRITERS believe in revision, in the second chances that self-editing allows. Novelists and poets draw attention to their habit of revising; college and school composition classes emphasize that "good writing always involves revision"; and academic work usually appears in print only after going through a process of "revise and resubmit."[1] MFA programs may not claim to teach students how to write well, but they usually do claim to teach "deep revision," or "the all-important revision process," and prospective applicants are encouraged to discuss their "work with revision."[2] The most successful contemporary writers are not necessarily required to revise to see their work into print, but they still continue to emphasize the intensity and commitment of their revisionary practice. Joyce Carol Oates tells an interviewer, "I revise all the time, everyday. I revise every page, all the time";[3] Michael Cunningham, "I revise constantly, as I go along and then again after I've finished a first draft. Few of my novels contain a single sentence that closely resembles the sentence I first set down";[4] Charles Simic, "Even published poems I won't leave alone. I very rarely get it

1

right in one go. Mostly I revise endlessly."[5] In each of these statements, durative adverbs, "constantly," "everyday," "all the time," suggest that the revision process could, and perhaps should, continue indefinitely. In their fervent commitment to continued process rather than completed product, these descriptions threaten to become paradoxical. How can a writer look at and rewrite every page of a text at once? And what would cause an endless, Sisyphean process of revision to stop, enabling publication?

In contemporary literary culture, revision has become synonymous with critical rereading or even intelligent writing. Curiously, in acquiring this symbolic value, it has come to mean less, as well as more, than literal self-editing. The novelist Monica Ali, for example, describes her own revisionary work as both different from and exclusive of textual alteration: "I revise constantly, every day I revise, and revise, although I don't always change a great deal."[6] If minimal revision suggests careless or commercial writing, poised for quick success in the market, heavy and intensive revision has become an indicator of authorial integrity and the difficulty and seriousness of the revised artwork. It is rare to find a writer who claims not to revise, or even one who asks if the process might have diminishing returns. In his best-selling *How to Write*, Alastair Fowler speaks for his generation with a rather unpleasant metaphor: "excessive revision is rarer than hen's teeth with gold fillings."[7]

In *The Work of Revision*, I argue that the association of revision and literary value is the legacy of high modernism and the print culture that nourished it. Modernist writers revised overtly, passionately, and at many points in the lifespan of their texts. They used revision, an action that implies retrospection, not for stylistic tidying-up but to *make it new* through large-scale transformations of length, structure, perspective, and genre. When Joyce abandoned the Bildungsroman *Stephen Hero*, for example, and began again with the same material and a spottier, more impressionistic focalization in *A Portrait of the Artist as a Young Man*, he was revising both his own first draft attempt and, by extension, a set of inherited literary conventions. Where *Ulysses*, Pound's *Cantos*, and Proust's *À la recherche* grew beyond their authors' original designs through acts of repeated addition, *The Waste Land*, many Imagist poems, Hemingway's prose written on the principle of the iceberg, and Marianne Moore's postpublication omissions were motivated by a stern commitment to excision by reduction of a long first draft. In this respect, non-substitutive revision became a way to iterate toward styles of minimalism and maximalism—to novels and poems that breach inherited conventions of form and length. It also enabled writers to discover many of the stylistic features that we associate with modernism. Pound's and Eliot's cuts to *The Waste Land* drafts produced a faster proliferation of perspectives and historical moments; the consequence of Joyce's indefatigably self-delighting extensions to "Ithaca" was a showcase of parodic parataxis. In revising the "Time Passes" section of *To the Lighthouse*, Woolf moved away from traditional free indirect discourse and towards a more pictorial, objective form of elegy. In the 1926 typescript, Mrs. Ramsay's death is a stray, reported thought in Mrs. McNab's muddled mind "(She had died very sudden at the end, they said)." In the first book edition, the square brackets coldly remove sentiment and confusion, "[Mr. Ramsay, stumbling along a passage one dark morning, stretched his arms out, but Mrs. Ramsay having died rather suddenly the night before, his arms, though stretched out, remained empty.]"[8]

In turning to revision as a major method of composition—an experimental tool comparable to collage in painting or deviations from classical tonality in music—modernist writers had to overcome the nineteenth-century preference for writing that was, or at least seemed to be, spontaneous. Romantic poetics tended to imagine the text existing in its fullest form in the past, in pre-linguistic shape, and even the first rendition on paper as already a transcription of waning imagination. Revision was, consequently, a threat to a work's organic unity and freshness. We see this anxiety in Browning's fury on reading Tennyson's revised 1842 poems, "The alterations are insane. *Whatever* is touched is spoiled" and, before that, in Keats's belief that "if Poetry comes not as naturally as leaves to a tree it had better not come at all."[9] In the twentieth century, the future-oriented avant-garde turned around this teleology, so that the ideal text could be imagined as existing just out of grasp, like Mr. Ramsay's longed-for letter *R*. Often, the process of reaching it seemed arduous and painful. James felt smothered by the New York Edition and the "voluminosities of Proof" to be read and corrected;[10] Woolf repeatedly described the agony of "intense correction" of proofs, and she labeled more than one of her novels as "interminable";[11] Yeats's "textual restlessness," to borrow Warwick Gould's eloquent phrase, persisted throughout his life as he sought a final form that would be "something intended, complete."[12] James even revised a description of a fictional writer's compositional process between the nineteenth and twentieth centuries. In 1893, Dencombe meditates on the pleasure afforded by his newly published book: "if the achievement had been real, however, the process had been manful enough." This reading was retained for the revised 1895 first book edition but, for the sixteenth volume of the New York Edition in 1909, "manful enough" became "painful enough."[13] James's own obsessive work on the New York Edition puts him at home among the modernists, but in cagily refusing to admit that his revision *was* rewriting he remained Victorian. In the preface to *The Golden Bowl*, he described his successful frustration of the "grand air with which the term Revision had somehow, to my imagination, carried itself" by returning the word to its etymological meaning: "To revise is to see, or to look over, again— which means in the case of a written thing neither more nor less than to re-read it." This is pretty much the opposite of Monica Ali's position. Where she uses the culturally loaded term *revision* to describe rereading before publication without significant change, James frames the activity of substantial and perhaps unnecessary postpublication rewriting as *mere* rereading.

Revision is sometimes understood to mean only textual change or fluidity, but it also implies the possibility of a text being fixed in some material form. It points to the balance between what changes and what stays the same and, accordingly, is a powerful trope for a literary period often described as "Janus-faced," looking forward and back. In his study of poetic allusion, Christopher Ricks has shown that allusions are prone to self-enactment, to being "self-delightingly about allusion," and that poets allude when they are thinking thematically about borrowing, theft, haunting, reminiscence.[14] Revision is subject to the same logic. Even Pound's slogan "make it new," "the most frequently repeated quip of the early twentieth century," was itself borrowed;[15] in *Canto* 53, Pound explains that he found it on the bath-tub of the Emperor Tching.[16] In fact, the textual history is even more complicated than that: "Pound's phrase . . . is a translation (from French) of a translation (from Manchuan or Mongolian Chinese) of a translation (from twelfth-century neo-Confucian Chinese) of a text of greater antiquity than the earliest parts of the Hebrew Bible."[17]

One of the general questions that this book asks is: "how are a text's thematic or formal concerns linked to its genesis"? To date, literary criticism has not given a good account of this connection. Although we understand that form and content are themselves related in complex, mutually sustaining ways, we tend to assume that a text's coming-to-be is either irrelevant to what it is, or connected in a quite arbitrary fashion. But it is not in fact true that all genres, or forms, or kinds of writing come to be with equal ease, and it is certainly the case that different methods of revision create distinct formal effects. In modernist writing, genetic complexity is often allied to—even, produced by—a thematic interest in complicated geneses. Certainly, many of the most heavily revised modernist poems and novels—Pound's early *Cantos*, Moore's "Poetry," the Dante section of "Little Gidding; Proust's *À la recherche du temps perdu*, Joyce's *Portrait*, Woolf's *The Years*—take the sinuous passage of time as their very subject. As T. S. Eliot eventually (after revision) wrote in "Gerontion," "History has many cunning passages, contrived corridors."[18]

The aims of modernist revision might have been largely aesthetic—a feeling toward new forms and styles—but the practice was significantly enabled by technological improvements in the publishing process, including cheaper typesetting and storing and the invention of the personal typewriter, and by a culture of patronage that allowed for multiple sendings of proof and a relative lack of concern for economic profit. Technological opportunity and patronage are linked in a peculiar way, in the inverse logic familiar from Bourdieu's "winner loses" model.[19] On the one hand, it became much easier to mark out and transmit the desire for revision: writers who owned typewriters could make and circulate neat copies of their work quickly in carbon copy, and publishers using typesetting machines were more willing to issue proofs of entire novels. On the other hand, revision still had a substantial cost. Unlike in digital environments, where a new file can be uploaded to Amazon for free, pulping a first edition to make way for a second or rewriting a novel in proof required a significant commitment of time and money. As a result, writers found themselves inhabiting a situation where revision was both tantalizingly possible and off-puttingly expensive. I argue that this friction between possibility and constraint was an important motivator for experimental writers to continue revising. By doing so, they acquired symbolic capital for their work even as they delayed its completion and circulation as a commodity in the market. *Ulysses,* as so often in arguments about modernism, provides a prime example.[20] Joyce had finished the episodes up to and including "Nausicaa" in a satisfying enough way to permit their publication in *The Little Review* between 1918 and 1920, and he would have continued to serialize the novel if the magazine hadn't been prosecuted for obscenity in 1920. Nevertheless, when the time came for book publication, he insisted on his publisher Darantiere issuing several different kinds of wide-margined proofs, and he continued to rewrite the novel, particularly its later episodes, substantially on these pages through a process of addition and accretion.

Joyce's habit of making very late-stage revisions on proof didn't only protract and delay the appearance of *Ulysses*; it also led to error and textual instability in the published text. The textual difficulty of Pound's *Cantos,* published and revised over fifty-five years, is even more serious and, as Lawrence Rainey and others have argued, a critical edition or even an annotated variorum seems currently unimaginable.[21] In some cases, this textual instability or "fluidity," to borrow John Bryant's more positive term, is a direct consequence of authorial revision, both before and after initial publication.[22] In other cases, as Christine Froula's work on Pound has shown, the modernist practice of revision coexisted with unusual attitudes toward textual authority and accuracy, including a relative openness to error and fallibility in its printed transmission.[23] Textual instability has traditionally been the unfortunate result of corruption or interpolation during the course of transmission by errant scribes or copyists. Why would modernist authors welcome it? In the case of post-publication revision, one answer is that variance provides a way to forfend against simple mechanical reproduction. It is another strategy for removing a text from the normal market economy and for labeling it as a special *kind* of product. In Pound's case, for example, the issuing of new *Cantos* in limited, physically deluxe, formats provided a way to preserve the work's auratic value and the possibility of direct communication with an elite audience.

Modernism coincided with the development of English as a university discipline and, as the period progressed, authors became increasingly conscious of preserving their drafts to sell to university collections, to publish in facsimile editions, or simply to provide material for scholarship. Auden wittily observed, "God! How careless and downright incompetent I used to be. . . . The revisions will be a gift to any anal-minded American Ph.D. student."[24] They set down their maxims about composition in forms new for the early twentieth century: interviews on radio, television, and for journals such as the *Paris Review,* addresses to university audiences of English students, and in self-reflexive autobiographies. James's aversion to "large loose baggy monsters," Hemingway's iceberg principle and general commitment to "show, don't tell," Pound's precepts for Imagism, and Eliot's observation that "no verse is free for the man who wants to do a good job" began as highly specific compositional maxims, with immediate polemical purposes.[25] Over time, however, these ideas became domesticated in college classrooms and composition manuals into a catchall writing advice, so we can trace a direct line from Pound's "direct treatment of the 'thing'" (1913) to Hemingway's macho boast about rewriting the end of *A Farewell to Arms,* made in his 1956 *Paris Review* interview, to Nabokov's "My pencils outlast their erasers" (1966), Capote's "I believe more in the scissors than I do the pencil" (1985), and John Irving's tersely antiromantic dismissal of inspiration, "The value is in how many times you can redo something" (2005).[26] Mark McGurl has even argued that "the value of craft as represented by the practice of multiple revision" is the central value of the period he terms "the program era."[27]

Despite the power and persistence of these edicts about how to compose, writers in the second half of the twentieth century found themselves writing in materially very different forms from the high modernists. When Pound boasted in the "Homage to Sextus Propertius" (1917) that "we have kept our erasers in order," he was obviously, although peculiarly, modernizing a Roman poet who did not write in pencil. Reflecting on the material book culture of *his* day, Propertius had written "*exactus tenui pumice versus eat,*" a request for the book of verses to go out into the world in fine shape, smoothed down neatly by pumice stone.[28]

In 1966, on the other hand, Nabokov was being relatively old-fashioned in continuing to draft in longhand (pen and pencil on index cards); by the 1950s, most writers—from the ageing modernists (Pound, Hemingway) to young Beat poets, were composing straight onto the typewriter. The modernist period itself was one of transition, in which writers tended to see their work in a wider range of formats than either their nineteenth-century predecessors or, more surprisingly, contemporary writers. Austen, Dickens, and Tennyson worked in manuscript until the moment of "bon à tirer"; writers in the digital age see their work in something closely resembling its final printed form from the first draft in Microsoft Word. They may correct proof electronically and, increasingly, the final form itself is designed to be an ebook. By contrast, all the writers whom I study in detail continued to draft in longhand before transferring to typescript for a fair copy or second draft, from typescript to proof before a magazine publication or first book edition, and then from one proof format to another in the case of subsequent editions. Until the postwar period, very few writers typed straight on to a machine. The classic document of modernist revision is therefore a typed or proof page—a materially intermediate document, neither manuscript nor print—with extensive manuscript scrawls, cross-outs, and speech bubbles inserting large portions of new text. The very existence of this visually intermediate stage seems to have been a better spur to rewriting than either a homogenous manuscript or homogenous digital culture. Counter-intuitively, being able to see texts *fixed* in many visually different forms seems to promote textual fluidity (as anyone who has had the experience of discovering mistakes in proof can attest).

Both those who advocate revision and those who denigrate it tend to assume that it works in the same way for all writers at all points in time, regardless of medium. My approach in this book is historicist and comparative. First-draft composition can take place in many different ways, but revision requires interacting with something that is already achieved in material form. In this respect, revising is more influenced by writing technology and medium than initial composition. It is markedly easier to revise in some medial formats than others—a galley proof is easier to emend than an oral poem (which is never really fixed in the first place) or a stone inscription (which can only be erased with great difficulty). Freud's mystic writing pad, providing both a receptive surface that can be used repeatedly *and* the capacity to retain permanent traces, would be a useful tool for a writer who wanted to revise heavily, for, in a dialectical way, the possibility of revision is premised on the possibility of both textual flux and textual fixity.[29] Revision is possible to the extent that a writing medium resembles a chalkboard, but it is also only necessary because of the danger of a text becoming fixed in a particular, undesired form. In his essay "The Word Processor," Jacques Derrida explained that moving from a typewriter to this new technology produced a different kind of writing, "a desubstantialized substance, more fluid, lighter, and so closer to speech."[30] In digital environments where revision has become almost free, and where there is no real danger of a work becoming fixed in a single, imperfect form, Dencombe's act of "passionate correction" may be losing its urgency.

In chapter 1 I discuss the theoretical and historical foundations for my work in more detail. Revision is not a very important topic in traditional textual criticism, which developed to address the problems of scribal corruption over many centuries and in situations where we do not usually have authorial autographs. After delineating three basic kinds of revision, and distinguishing intentional revision from corruption, I provide a brief history of the period since romanticism; this is the period of English literature for which original manuscripts tend to survive. How and why did the historical avant-garde turn around the romantic preference for spontaneity, first thoughts, and organic form? What effect did new technologies of writing and printing have on writers' ability to make changes in the early twentieth century? In the final part of the chapter, I provide a brief history of textual criticism in the period after modernism.

My work is indebted to an eclectic range of textual traditions, not all easily consonant with each other, including Anglo-American editing based on "final intention"; the social-text criticism of Jerome McGann and George Bornstein; French genetic criticism; and the comparative genetic criticism practiced by Geert Lernout and Dirk Van Hulle at the University of Antwerp. In general, methods in textual criticism tend to develop as practical attempts to solve particular problems: stemmatics comes from Lachmann's work on Lucretius and the Greek New Testament; the Greg-Bowers-Tanselle line of criticism originated in the study of Renaissance printed books, and genetic criticism began serendipitously in the 1970s to deal with nineteenth-century manuscripts acquired by the Bibliothèque Nationale. These principles are sometimes formalized into theories on the basis of (more or less articulated) philosophical premises, which may themselves be explicit or germane in general literary criticism: that authorial intention is knowable or unknowable, singular or shared, rational or unconscious, and hermeneutically determinative or irrelevant. My own preference is for a historically attentive, comparative reading of manuscript materials and edition histories. This practice happens—and perhaps ought—to fall short of a theorizable routine.

Chapter 2 discusses Henry James's practice of revision from the 1870s until the very end of his career, focusing particularly on the period after the New York Edition. Philip Horne's *Henry James and Revision: The New York Edition* (1990) is the standard study. I have found Horne's work valuable, but I read James as a less idiosyncratic author than Horne does. Earlier in his career, James's practice of revision was primarily substitutive but, after the failure of the New York Edition, and as dictation to a typist completely replaced longhand drafting, I argue that he became a more accretive, additive writer. Setting the tale "The Middle Years" (1893) against the unfinished and posthumously published volume of autobiography *The Middle Years* (1917) provides one way to trace this change. I provide a detailed reading of the kinds of revisions that James made to both texts, looking at the short story in magazine, first book, and New York Edition texts, and at the Houghton typescript of *The Middle Years,* with James's manuscript corrections.

The third and fourth chapters examine the high modernist interest in non-substitutive forms of revision. In chapter 3 I focus on "radical excision," beginning with Pound's manifesto for Imagism, and then looking in some detail at the cuts made to *The Waste Land* and *The Sun Also Rises.* Pound developed this strategy of composition in the 1910s to produce effects of concentration and focus, "direct treatment of the 'thing' "; over time, excision also became identified with broader cultural and technological preferences for efficiency, hygiene, and rapidity. When recent critics praise Pound for "cutting the 'waste' from *The Waste Land,*"[31] they are, indirectly, still subscribing to a Poundian aesthetic legacy, "in art economy is always beauty," "good writing is writing that is perfectly controlled."[32] In fact, *The Waste Land* was produced through a seesaw act of compositional counterpoint: Eliot began additively, conjoining short drafts into an elaborate montage, before submitting the long 1921 draft to Pound's excisive blue pencil.

In chapter 4, I explore the opposite style of revision by accretion or extension. Where excision produces ellipsis and asks the reader to perform syntactic work, extension tends to overdescription and the flat "and and and" of parataxis. I argue that the revisions to *Ulysses* cluster in two main categories. When Joyce added more to the earlier, Bloom-focused chapters, it was often with the effect of enriching and elaborating Bloom's perceiving consciousness; he does more "wondering" about other characters, or his cat, and the narrative flickers more between external observation and internal analysis. In the later episodes addition works differently, producing long paratactic lists whose tonal and rhetorical mood is hard to place. Gerty's fantasies about her "dreamhusband" become more pathetically elongated and stylized with the addition of manufactured words; the narrator of "Eumaeus" more long-windedly boring; "Ithaca's" long lists still more parodically excessive. At the close of this chapter, I suggest that Joyce's two kinds of too-muchness, which might be categorized as adding more *within* and *outside* a focalizing consciousness, have important afterlives in contemporary writing.[33] As in the chapter on excision, I link modernist spareness and excess to the postwar styles of literary "minimalism" and "maximalism."

Chapter 5 explores the relationship between genetic process and genre. Here I am following a suggestion made by Philippe Lejeune, who asks if "generic specificities" govern the process of composition, and then argues that autobiography has "a different relationship to its avant-textes than do texts of fiction, poetry, or thought."[34] One of the difficulties of writing an autobiography is making an end, for, as Paul de Man has argued, its governing trope is "prosopopoeia," a voice speaking from beyond the grave. This means that writers tend to leave autobiographies unfinished, although revised, at their death; this was true for Darwin, Wordsworth, Trollope, and J. S. Mill. Alternatively, writers such as Nabokov or Robert Graves, who do publish in their lifetime, often find themselves returning to produce revised second editions. As primary examples, I discuss the histories of three texts spanning the period from

1895 to 1940: these are Leslie Stephen's *Mausoleum Book,* Joyce's *A Portrait of the Artist as a Young Man,* and Woolf's "A Sketch of the Past." Why do all three turn into diaries? How do their authors' attitudes toward revision differ? I look in particular detail at "A Sketch," which represents Woolf's final attempt to write the twin traumas of her childhood—the death of her mother and half-sister, Stella. In the 1927 novel *To the Lighthouse,* these deaths had been bracketed off and framed as closed, but "A Sketch" reopens old wounds. If Woolf's need to keep writing about the same topics is an example of a repetition compulsion, the compulsion remained unresolved at her death.

In chapter 6—a coda—I ask what has happened to the practice of revision after the period of high modernism. In the postwar period, as literary value has become closely correlated with "revisedness," authors have become more open and even self-advertising about their practice. At the same time, in genetic readings of W. H. Auden, Allen Ginsberg, and David Foster Wallace, I diagnose a return to substitution as the primary tool of textual change.

CHAPTER 1

Textual Criticism,
the History of Revision,
and Genetic Reading

T HE PROBLEM OF TEXTUAL VARIATION is as old as writing and
copying, and the study of it, according to David Greetham, is "the
most ancient of scholarly activities in the West," predating the early literary criticism of Plato and Aristotle.[1] Authorial revision is one of the reasons for the same work to exist in multiple forms, each with a claim to *be*
the work itself. Despite this, revision has not historically been of great
concern to textual critics. Why so? One important reason is that the principles of English textual criticism were developed from classical studies,
where scholars are primarily concerned with scribal copying and corruption, and then adapted to the specific problem of early modern printed
books, where errors of transmission are again more palpably problematic
than authorial changes of mind. As Jerome McGann points out in his
1983 *Critique of Modern Textual Criticism,* these methods were not especially well suited to recent periods where the critic "actually possesses
the 'lost originals' which the classical critic is forced to hypothesize,"
and where intentional variation rather than unintentional corruption is
the most important question.[2] In addition, literary critics of nineteenth-
and twentieth-century materials—where revision very often *is* a central
problem—have tended to be less interested in textual issues than medi-
evalists and early modernists. The various forms of anti-intentionalism

advocated by the New Critics and then post-structuralism were undoubtedly also harmful, leading to an unbridgeable gulf between final intentionalist editing and a practice of criticism certain that "it is language which speaks, not the author."[3]

In this first chapter, I briefly outline the history of revision before and during the twentieth century. Authors' methods of composition are subtly linked to the way they think about the poetics of writing, so this is both a practical and an intellectual history. Not all writers practice exactly as they preach on the topic of revision, but these discontinuities can themselves be of interest. Available writing and printing methods have a more direct effect on whether and how a writer can revise, and I discuss the economic and technological basis for modernist rewriting in some detail. I will have more to say at the end of the chapter about the development of New Bibliography, social-text editing, and French *critique génétique* in the twentieth-century university, and about the way in which this study navigates between different approaches.

In everyday speech, we use the word *revision* without very much thought, often in ways that extend its literal meaning: she revised for an exam, learned revisionist history, had revision surgery. Literary critics who are not specifically interested in textual issues speak of Woolf's "revision" of "Conrad,"[4] "history,"[5] "her father's biographies,"[6] "conventional biographical modes,"[7] and "the stereotypical Victorian gender plot."[8] In this book I am concerned with revision in its more basic sense of postcompositional change. In his study of the romantic period, Zachary Leader terms this "revision proper."[9]

How is *revision proper* to be defined? Linguists sometimes speak of a related phenomenon called conversational repair, "the attempt made by participants in a conversation to make good (repair) a real or imagined deficiency in the interaction (e.g. a mishearing or misunderstanding)."[10] This kind of alteration, made in real time, and in direct response to an auditor's actual or perceived misunderstanding bears a close resemblance to revisions made *currente calamo,* with a running pen. On a typewriter or computer, we "repair" texts when we immediately correct a spelling mistake or slip, either by writing the new word *next* so it visibly supersedes the mistake, or by pressing backspace and writing over it. At some points in this study I draw attention to these kinds of revision, but they are not my focus. *The Work of Revision* is instead a study of laborious, belated, even otiose changes, made without reference to the linguistic "felicity" or basic communicability of the original version. Often these kinds of revision are surprising and unique. No copy editor or helpful friend would be likely to suggest them. For example, when Joyce reread his description of Bloom looking at his cat in the first set of *Ulysses* page proofs, he saw, "She blinked up out of her avid eyes" and "Then he went to the dresser, poured milk on a saucer and set it slowly on the floor."[11] He then decided to insert more specificity, including two brilliant but unpredictable compound adjectives, so the cat looks from "avid, shameclosing eyes," the milk is "warmbubbled," and poured from "the jug Hanlon's milkman had just filled for him." He also deleted "for her" in "set it for her slowly on the floor"; this had been the reading published in 1918 in *The Little Review*.[12]

Between *The Little Review* and the 1922 first book edition, Joyce deletes two words and adds twelve, so the passage as a whole is ten words longer. This represents the general tendency of his revisions in *Ulysses*: to extend. It also represents a basic property of modernist revision: to alter length. At the simplest level, we can say that a revising writer has three choices: a) to add material, so the final version is longer than the first draft, b) to delete, so it is shorter, and c) to substitute, producing a first and final draft of similar length. Here a writer might swap out a line-ending, part of speech, or character description for another, without changing the basic overall structure and shape. (Transposition or cutting and pasting would be a subset of substitution.)

Some writers are particularly prone to one form of revision. In more basic cases, this may emerge as a need to correct problems or stylistic tics in first draft composition. Mimi Schwartz, who has taught composition for many years, has argued that student writers should cultivate an awareness of intrinsic tendencies toward "overwriting" or "underwriting" so that they can correct the habit when they revise. Using another metaphor from speech, she argues that overwriters resemble "effusive speakers" who "start by writing out as many words as possible until the 'right' ones appear" and who must learn to condense; while underwriters are "like taciturn speakers" who begin with only a scaffold of words which must then be filled in."[13] Substitutive revision, which allows for more local refinement, often below the level of the whole sentence, is less dramatic than radical excision or extension. In this study, I argue that the first two kinds of revision are particularly and unusually prevalent in the period we call "high modernism," and that they actually produce some of the difficulties and stylistic patterns we recognize *as* modernist. Is Joyce's original description of the cat underwritten? If his extensions between first and second publication are correcting deficiencies in the original version, it seems reasonable to say that these deficiencies were palpable only to him. He is a self-diagnosed underwriter rather than a "true" underwriter, just as Hemingway was a self-diagnosed rather than an actual overwriter.

Modernist texts present many different kinds of editorial difficulties, including (although not limited to) the following. How do we compare the value of historical, documented texts to the "ideal" versions that a writer intended? In the case of *Ulysses,* for example, should we read the text of the 1922 first-book edition (e.g., in Jeri Johnson's edition for *Oxford World's Classics*) or Gabler's synoptic text? If a text has been revised after first publication, which of the historically actual texts is more valuable? If it has been suppressed by an author, should we read it or eschew it? And even if we have decided to read genetically, across versions, how should the different textual strata or variants be represented? This problem is particularly acute *because* of modernist texts' propensity to shrink or expand. A facing-page edition is a good way of displaying substitutive revisions: at least, it is a good way of representing the maximal difference between versions. For example, Ernest de Selincourt's 1926 edition of the 1805 and 1850 *Prelude*—published in the middle of the modernist period—is an attractive and easily navigable way of showing Wordsworth's revisions, which tend to be local and lexical, rather than structural. The 1805–1806 text is printed on the verso pages, faced by the 1850 text (the only text of the *Prelude* known before this edition) on the recto. One page of text is sometimes a couple of lines longer than the other but, by and large, the two versions keep pace with each other; the differences are to be found *within* individual sentences and verse paragraphs. As an example, compare these two descriptions of a cottage on Lake Windermere, from the second book of the poem:

Upon the Eastern Shore of
    Windermere,
	Midway on long Winander's
	    eastern shore

Above the crescent of a pleasant
    Bay,
	Within the crescent of a
	    pleasant bay,

There stood an Inn, no
    homely-featured Shed,
	A tavern stood: no homely-
	    featured house

Brother of the surrounding
    Cottages,
	Primeval like its neighbouring
	    cottages,

But 'twas a splendid place . . .
    (1805)
	But 'twas a splendid place . . .
	    (1850)[14]

In both versions, the description begins with geographical location on the "eastern shore" of Lake Windermere, and ends with a description of the "splendid" tavern's lack of kinship with its humble surroundings. Even though he is writing in blank verse, Wordsworth makes these changes within quite fixed parameters and often by substituting a word for a near synonym: the preposition "above" becomes "within," a "Shed" a "house," "surrounding," "neighbouring," and "Brother of" the adjectival "Primeval like."

Hypertext editions and programs such as Juxta (a tool developed for automatic collation of text-files on the computer) can give us access to more numerical textual states than a printed book, but they still function through a left-right, compare-and-contrast logic. They work best when the two textual states being compared are formally quite similar. Because writers in the high modernist period tended to revise structurally, by significant deletion or extension, a facing-page model is less effective—in fact, it may be completely ineffective. Gabler's synoptic edition of *Ulysses* uses diacritic markers to show on the verso pages when material in the final, 1922 novel was added, but it does not intuitively facilitate a reading of an original shorter version: the reader has to work to reproduce the version of "Calypso" that *The Little Review* readers saw in 1918. The problem is equally vexing for texts that have been dramatically cut. Marianne Moore remembered discussing with her editor what to do about the original, longer version of "Poetry" in her *Complete Poems* and his solution: "Mr. Kennebeck said, 'Oh no. But I think some people are going to complain if you leave the whole thing out.' But then he said, 'Well I thought of this: How would it be if we had an appendix and put that in the back, together with the other things you have reduced to nothing?' "[15] Moore adopted this solution but, of course, it is itself imperfect—a dyadic representation of the textual history of a poem that existed and was published in more than two versions.

A secondary kind of revision takes place across boundaries, retaining some aspect of the original expression, but altering the category label under which it can be defined. This is the kind of revision that G. Thomas Tanselle described in 1976 as vertical rather than horizontal: it "aims at altering the purpose, direction, or character of a work, thus attempting to make a different sort of work out of it" and not "intensifying, refining, or improving the work as then conceived (whether or not it succeeds in doing so), thus altering the work in degree but not in kind."[16] In the first kind of revision, the two (or more) versions can be understood as tokens of a type—two instances of the novel *The American* by Henry James, or "Poetry" by Marianne Moore. In the second case, however, we are dealing with two separate types. Virginia Woolf's repeated descriptions of her mother's death across a range of genres and forms—in private diary entries, the novel or quasi-novel *To The Lighthouse,* and the late, posthumously published "A Sketch of the Past"— share and develop particular images (the Homeric or Virgilian trope of the mourner reaching out for a vanished shade) and recycle verbal and syntactic structures, but they are not versions of the same thing; in fact, each of the individual items in this kind of revisionary series might have itself been revised several times. Other examples of this type of revision, which I term *extrinsic,* would be the relation between *Stephen Hero* and *A Portrait of the Artist as a Young Man,* or the novel-essay *The Pargiters* and the novel *The Years.* It is not strictly true to describe *Stephen Hero,* as Wayne Booth does, as "that earlier, windier version of *Portrait*": the two have a filial relationship rather than one of direct descent on a family tree, and the earliest proper version of *Portrait* was Joyce's manuscript of it.[17] The failed, cut-short branch of the tree may, nonetheless, help to illuminate the genetic sequence of the completed and published text.

A Brief History: Revision and the Textual Stemma

Textual criticism began in the ancient world as a method of identifying the correct form for works that already existed in multiple and divergent copies. By the third century BC, Alexandrian editors had begun to lay down basic principles and methods for editing the work of earlier authors, particularly Homer. They tried systematically to sort out the best and worst manuscripts, to identify patterns of conjugational and declensional regularity and to emend texts to follow them (marking or "athetizing" those lines that seemed spurious), to remove narrative inconsistencies, and they wrote commentaries explaining their work.[18] These basic activities—recension followed by emendation, and accompanied by commentary—have remained central to classical textual criticism to the present. In 1921, for example, in an enjoyably grouchy speech, A. E. Housman said that "textual criticism is a science, and, since it comprises recension and emendation, it is also an art. It is the science of discovering error in texts and the art of removing it."[19] By emphasizing the creative and speculative aspects of textual criticism, Housman was writing against the influence of Lachmannian stemmatics, which had begun to ossify by the late nineteenth century into a rigid procedure for sorting surviving manuscripts into family trees and for labeling these as good and bad. On the other hand, even if Housman's textual critic is "much more like a dog hunting for fleas" than "Newton investigating the motions of the planets," he is still firmly bent on discovering the truth: the single, correct reading that a text assumed before corruption by scribes and copyists who might be malicious or simply "sleepy or illiterate or drunk."

In its traditional form, textual criticism was a method for dealing with textual variation consequent on transmission. Its primary concern was corruption, not revision, and its aim was to produce an eclectic "best" text from the many surviving documents. In this situation, textual variation is something that exists in the present, at the end of a stemma; at its head, before the process of transmission begins, a single, ideal version can then be hypostasized. This ideal may never actually be reachable but, as Jerome McGann explains, it functions as a *terminus ad quem*

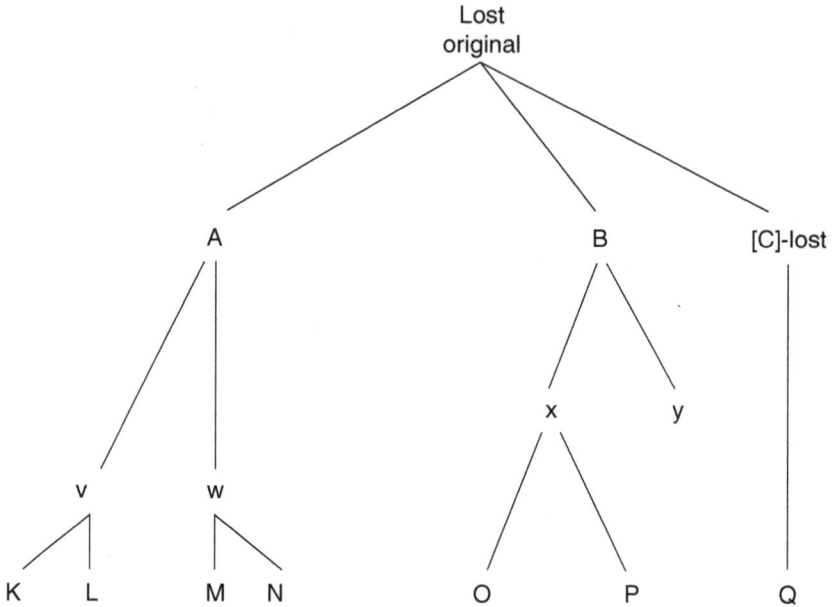

Figure 1a: Schematic representation of a traditional textual stemma.

enabling the critic "to isolate and remove accumulated error."[20] The basic methods of the discipline were developed first for the classics and the Bible, but they proved easily extensible to textual situations in vernacular languages that presented similar bodies of evidence: multiple, variously corrupt textual versions, all of which postdated the original author—perhaps by many centuries. This was already clear by the eighteenth century. To Pope, for example, it seemed that the text of Shakespeare's plays had existed in its most correct form only prior to the printing of the first Quarto and Folio, and before "arbitrary additions, expunctions, transpositions of scenes and lines, confusions of character and persons . . . corruptions of innumerable passages . . . and wrong corrections—again" could be introduced; for his rival, Theobald, "*Shakespeare's* Case has in great Measure resembled That of a corrupt *Classic;* and consequently the Method of Cure was likewise to bear a Resemblance."[21]

When authors consciously revise their work, either before or after publication, they produce textual stemmas of a different shape. The images shown are hypothetical representations of a traditional stemma, branching outward and downward from a lost original; on the right, we

Notebook

Manuscript draft

Typescript draft 1   Typescript draft 2

Proofs for
magazine   Proof set 2

Proof set 3

Magazine   First book
publication   edition

Second book edition

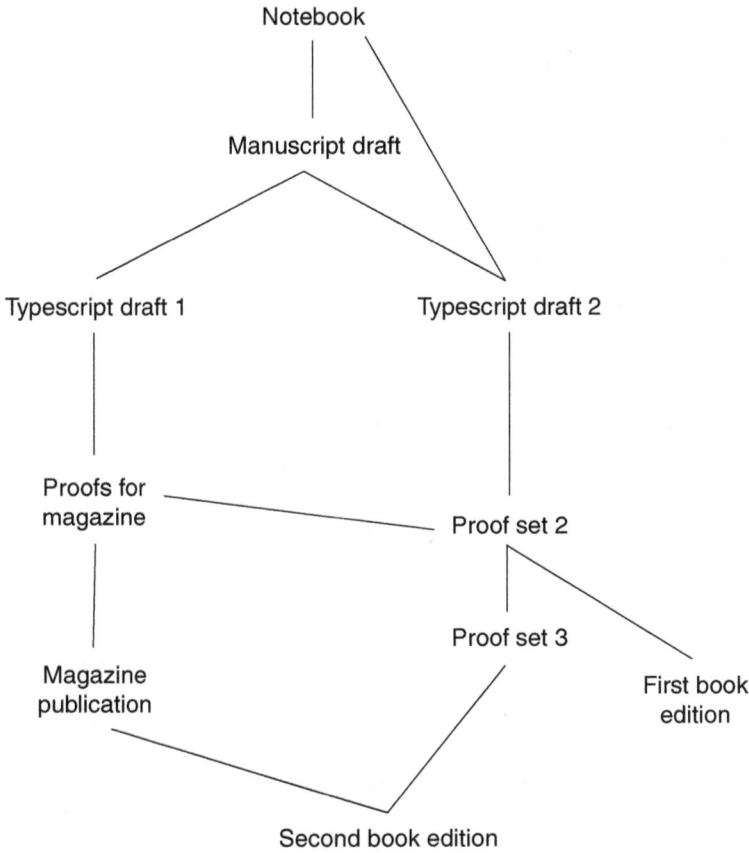

Figure 1b: Schematic representation of the complex genesis of a modernist text across mixed media.

see the situation common during the modernist period, where later stages may loop back to earlier ones and where manuscript and typescript exist alongside one another, sometimes with equal authority or finality. For many modern authors, textual variation exists not in the present but in the past, in the manuscripts or typescripts that precede a single, printed final form. In this respect, both the textual stemma and its teleology are inverted: now the "best" text is the single finally intended version, while the archive contains records of the various false starts and alternative possibilities that preceded it.

The study of revision is less directly purposive than traditional textual editing; it is descriptive rather than normative, and deals with multiple actual intentions rather than a single possible one. A subset of the works I discuss raise issues of both kinds, being both genetically interesting and editorially problematic, but in many cases my examples present no great difficulty to a traditional textual critic asking "which text should we read?" Christine Froula's 1977 dissertation on Pound's *Cantos*, revised in 1984 as *Style and Error in Pound's Cantos*, provides both a genetic text of *Canto* IV and a detailed discussion of its editorial problems, which result from errors of transmission and "errors and divergences made by Pound himself" as he manipulated his sources.[22] *Ulysses* is another text with a complicated publication history that led to nonauthorial error being introduced from the first publication. On the other hand, the 434-line poem beginning "April is the cruellest month" that Eliot published in 1922 simply *is The Waste Land*. The thousand lines or so of draft materials, beginning "First we had a couple of feelers down at Tom's place," are of interpretive, rather than editorial, interest; we know that they were not Eliot's final intention for the poem, and no one would suggest reprinting them *as* the 1922 poem. Some of the cases I discuss are slightly more complicated; there are three different published texts of some Henry James tales, for example, and two or more published versions of many Auden poems. But, once again, no one would suggest using these materials to produce a conflated best text; each represents an author's intention at a certain moment in time, and each has historical interest of its own. Auden himself seems to have recognized this when he allowed the poem "September 1, 1939" to continue appearing in anthologies of 1930s poetry (as indicative of a fossilized, historical intention) while banishing it from his own collected editions (representing his current sensibilities).[23]

I claim in this book that writers in the modernist period revised more than their predecessors in several senses: more frequently, at more points in the lifespan of the text, more structurally and experimentally (rather than through lexical substitution alone), and more self-consciously, often leaving traces of the revision in the final product. The individual chapters address more precisely the questions of length-transformation and self-consciousness. What about *more frequently?* A simple but important objection might run: "Isn't it simply the case that more evidence, more documents, survive for the early twentieth century than for earlier periods?"

The amount of evidence documenting revision does indeed increase over time. But this fact is intimately related—not extrinsic—to the fact that authors were revising more. In periods where paper was more expensive, and publication more of an event, writers were more likely to content themselves with one draft. During the eighteenth and nineteenth century, manuscripts "were destroyed in the normal course of things once their text was set in type," preventing retroactive collation; and authors before the twentieth century were likely to see at most one sending of proof.[24] Texts such as *Pamela,* which was heavily and elaborately revised, often had unusual publishing histories. Richardson was a master printer before he began to write fiction and, because he was self-publishing, he was able to revise, reprint, and remarket the book in very sophisticated ways: this was the process that William Warner terms "the *Pamela* media event."[25] The enormous amount of paper evidence that survives from the early twentieth century—authorial notebooks, manuscripts, typescripts and copies; galley and page proofs; marked-up editions; computer printouts—is not only the result of better preservation; it is also illustrative of paper becoming cheaper, and new ways of composing that made revision easier and more likely.

Without direct evidence of its existence, revision is an uncertain and often even an uninteresting topic for textual discussion. The debates about the relationship between the Folio and Quarto versions of *King Lear* illustrate how difficult it is to prove that revision *rather than* corruption is the best explanation for textual change without direct evidence. Traditionally, the Folio and Quarto printings were imagined to represent variously corrupt versions of the (now lost) authorial manuscript.[26] In the 1980s the situation turned around when Gary Taylor and Michael Warren suggested that the Folio and Quarto texts of *King Lear* were in fact serially related, on a single stemma, and that the 1623 Folio was a substantial, Shakespearean revision of the 1608 *Quarto.* As Zachary Lesser argues, "new revisionists have shown that many of the features that were once taken as signs of textual corruption could as easily be evidence of authorial revision."[27] This argument gained substantial traction: Stephen Orgel's Pelican edition (2000), Stanley Wells's Oxford (2008), Jay Halio's Cambridge (2005), and Rene Weis's Longman (1993) all forgo the traditional conflated text for either a single main text or facing page versions of the Folio and Quarto. The new revisionism could, in principle, be extended to any number of early texts where no authorial autograph survives. At the same time it has to remain speculative: if we have no external proof that Shakespeare didn't revise, we also have no direct proof that he did. The bold excision of the mock-trial scene between the Folio and Quarto texts of *King Lear* might be reasonably construed as purposive authorial change; so too the alteration to Lear's opening speech, "Meantime we will express our darker purposes," where the Folio renders us a firmer, more regal king, who outlines his intentions in a deliberate and logical manner.[28] At the same time, an uncomfortably large amount of the textual variation consists of words that *look* very similar on the page. Does it really make sense that Shakespeare would have revised "pottage" to "porridge," "ruffle" to "rustle," "possesses" to "professes," "lanched" to "latched" and so on? If he did, he was not only guided to an unusual degree by aural constraints in making semantic change, but for a difficult word he often chose a more familiar one. The idea that scribes tend to introduce easier readings into a tradition is one of the most venerable maxims of textual criticism, *lectio difficilior potior.*[29] Therefore these minimal verbal changes would argue for textual corruption or external intervention rather than purposive revision. Authorial revision often looks more metaphoric and unexpected, as when Henry James turned "he lived once more into his story and was drawn down" into "he dived once more into his story," pulling the suboceanic metaphor further back in the sentence.[30] Where corruption produces easier readings, revision often leads to more difficult ones.

Original authorial autographs are necessary to prove that textual variation can be attributed to revision rather than corruption, and so revision only becomes a significant textual problem once they begin to survive. This has happened at surprisingly different historical moments in different European countries. In Italy, where important manuscripts including Boccaccio's *Decameron* survive from the medieval period, the genetic study of "variantistica" has long been an important part of textual scholarship.[31] Just as Alexandrian textual scholars were stimulated by the texts of Homer that came down to them, and the New Bibliographers by specific problems in English Renaissance drama, Italian textual criticism grew up to take account of authorial revision. If Shakespeare's manuscripts had survived, English textual criticism would undoubtedly have taken on a very different appearance from the beginning. The difference between substantives and accidentals in printed books might have seemed less important than it did to the early-twentieth-century New Bibliographers and, assuming that the manuscripts showed traces of authorial correction, revision would have been an important problem in establishing a text.[32] The American critic Fredson Bowers described his own aim as being to "strip the veil of print" away from a text, and thereby to recover "the lost manuscript which served as printer's copy."[33] This rather idealistic statement implies that finding the lost manuscript—were that possible—would put an end to further textual discussions, and it assumes that the manuscript would be an unproblematic and unaltered fair copy. But this is naïve, as Ben Jonson recognized when he laughed at ignorant actors for saying, as a form of praise, that "whatsoever he penned, he never blotted out a line."[34] If Shakespeare's manuscripts did survive, blotted lines and all, Renaissance textual criticism would have been completely different from the beginning.

Romanticism and Modern Manuscripts

The romantic period is the first moment in English literature where revision becomes a common problem—common in the sense of being a pervasive editorial and textual critical challenge, problematic not only for scholars of romanticism, but for the revising writers themselves. Just before this—over the course of the eighteenth century—the meaning of the word *revision* had shifted slightly, from retroactive change made by *anyone* (including the kinds of changes we would call edits or interpolations) to change made by the original author. This change in itself coincided with important developments in the history of authorship. For Foucault, the rise of systems of ownership and copyright in the eighteenth century led to the development of an "author-function" to regulate, group, and commodify texts. We might say that revision—the possibility of returning to a text to reregulate and control it—is one part of this emergent ethic.

In seventeenth- and eighteenth-century print culture, new editions of earlier authors were often described as *revisions* rather than *editions*. Samuel Johnson might have been using the word in a modern sense when he told Boswell, "I am engaging in a very great work, the revision of my Dictionary," but he used it in its more traditional sense in this quip: "I was many years ago so shocked by Cordelia's death, that I know not whether I ever endured to read again the last scenes of the play till I undertook to revise them as an editor."[35] His dictionary itself defined revision only as "review."[36] This was consistent with the earliest meaning of the word, which, after being adopted from French in the seventeenth century, was used to refer to a wide range of textual processes. In 1611, for example, John Cotgrave defined the word in his *English Treasury of Wit and Language:* "*Revision,* a reuision, reuise, reuiew, reexamination, looking ouer againe."[37] Note that this definition makes no specification about authorial intention or, even, about rewriting. Revision, to begin with, was simply to see or look over again. It is this primary, *literal* meaning that Henry James, disingenuously, tried to reestablish in his exquisitely controlling and magisterially rewritten New York Edition. Modern scholarship of works written in the seventeenth and eighteenth centuries sometimes continues to use "revision" where nineteenth- and twentieth-century critics would prefer "editing" or "interpolation." In her excellent recent study of Richard Bentley, for example, Kristine Haugen refers quite frequently to Bentley's "bold textual revisions" of Horace and Manilius, as well as—most infamously—Milton.

Bentley's 1732 edition of *Paradise Lost* was premised on the belief that Milton had almost no supervisory control over early editions, and that the intervention of a corrupt editor/friend made these radically faulty. The latter conjecture seemed to Dr. Johnson "rash and groundless, if he thought it true; and vile and pernicious, if, as is said, he in private allowed it to be false."[38] Either way, Bentley used the myth as a justification for introducing more than eight hundred conjectural emendations into the poem and seventy deletions. Readers since the eighteenth century have unanimously agreed that the edition is a wild failure but, from a historicist perspective, we might equally see it as a staging-point in this history of thinking *about* revision. What is not often remarked is that Bentley's justification for his work was not merely corruption. He also blames Milton for not having done a better job of revising. In a quasi-legal argument, he "charges" the poet for "want of his Revisal of the Whole": "And yet a further Misfortune befell this noble Poem, which must be laid to the Author's Charge, though he may fairly plead *Not Guilty;* and had he had his Eye-sight, he would have prevented all Complaints. There are some Inconsistencies in the System and Plan of his Poem, for want of his Revisal of the Whole before its Publication."[39] Where earlier editors had assumed that corruption was the fault of anyone other than the original author, Bentley lays at least some of the perceived textual problems of *Paradise Lost* at Milton's own door. In doing so, he makes one of the first claims that revision is a *necessary* component of successful composition, and that it is something different from editorial intervention or corruption. By the 1790s, Edmond Malone was able to make the point much more explicitly in the preface to his edition of Shakespeare: in fact, he presents the distinction as something obvious and commonly understood. "It is well known to those who are conversant with the business of the press, that, (unless when the authour corrects and revises his own works,) as editions of books are multiplied, their errours are multiplied also; and consequently that every such edition is more or less correct, as it approaches nearer to or is more distant from the first."[40] The parenthetical "unless" here is important, distinguishing the negative teleology of corruption, where later versions are *worse* than the original, from the potentially ameliorative process of revision, where later versions might be more correct—even better.

Just as in the modernist period, new ideas about revision in the late eighteenth and early nineteenth century developed alongside practical changes in the printing and publishing process. Cheaper and more widely available paper for drafting, more careful proofreading at the printers' and by editors, the chance to see second and subsequent editions through the press as the reading public grew, and the possibility of auditing work in periodicals before book form meant that authors had more opportunities to revise than ever before. Keats, for example, swapped out a line in "On First Looking into Chapman's Homer" between its first appearance in the left-wing *Examiner* and subsequent book publication, while *Lyrical Ballads* appeared in four revised editions after the first publication of 1878; revisions were made to individual poems, to the overall contents, and to the preface, first added in 1800.[41] William St. Clair has shown that publishers at this period actively encouraged authors to revise for second and subsequent editions to bolster a sense of excitement about the work and to increase profits. In some cases, they even "pretended to editions which had never actually existed," so there seems to have been a first and fourth edition of Byron's *Lara,* but no second or third.[42] Changes in copyright law over the eighteenth century gave a further spur to revision. In 1710, the right to continue printing a work had belonged indefinitely to the publisher; after 1774, perpetual copyright was abandoned in Britain. This was intended to bolster the "Liberty of the Press" and allow ideas to disseminate more easily.[43] One of its side effects was that revising authors in the later decades of the eighteenth century could often claim new copyrights over their altered work and, when they did so, this brought substantial financial benefits.

While making postpublication revisions to circulating work, authors also began to preserve the drafts and working papers that showed the traces of earlier stages in the genetic process. This was undoubtedly the result of new, more visionary ideas about what an author *was.* Rough papers started to seem like independently valuable records of the workings of an individual mind rather than disposable chaff, useful only as prompts for a printed book.[44] Austen provides a kind of interstitial example. Some of the pages of *Persuasion* survive in authorial holograph (and have recently been digitized), but they did so only because they were *not* published in the posthumous first edition of 1818. So, although Austen herself appears not to have made a great effort to keep her papers, she quickly became the kind of modern celebrity-author whose rough work was valuable enough to be carefully preserved, and successive generations of her family kept hold of the pages until 1925, when they were sold to the British Museum. Keats's manuscripts, showing traces of the writing and revision process, have come down to us because he preserved them and gave them away, and also because of the posthumous cult that quickly grew around him. The genetic critic Laurent Jenny has noted that at this period, "from the end of the eighteenth century," manuscripts lost their communicative and distributive function to become instead "the personal trace of an individual creation."[45] He continues by arguing that genetic criticism itself pertains quite specifically to a period that begins here and ends at some point "a bit before 'our time' when the widespread use of word processors relegated the draft to oblivion."

It is in the early nineteenth century that we also find the first systematic thinking about revision: in particular, the first strong arguments against it. In *A Defence of Poetry*, written in 1821 and published posthumously in 1840, Shelley famously claimed that "the mind in creation is as a fading coal, which some invisible influence, like an inconstant wind, awakens to transitory brightness."[46] Siting artistic genesis in the mind rather than on the page, in the past rather than the present, this is a model where second thoughts can only ever weaken the primacy of original inspiration. Coleridge provided a more practical example when he described the writing of "Kubla Khan" as the rendering of a dream vision, "if that indeed can be called composition in which all the images rose up before him as *things* . . . without any sensation or consciousness of effort."[47] After being interrupted by the notorious person from Porlock—"a byword for Philistine intrusion on genius"[48]—he could recollect only "some vague and dim recollection of the general purport of the vision," and felt himself consequently unable to finish the poem in a satisfactory way. Byron provided an objection to revision of a slightly different kind, associating it with a socially degrading professionalism and preferring, at least in public, to present his own writing process as casual and unstudied.[49] In an 1820 letter he compared himself to a tiger able to leap forth only once: "I am like the tyger (in poesy) if I miss my first Spring—I go growling back to my Jungle.—There is no second.—I can't correct—I can't—and I won't."[50] In addition to these aesthetic reasons, which reflect a transition from an artisanal to a creative-genius model of authorship, there may, as William St Clair suggests, have been a simple shift in fashions in the publishing industry.[51] After a heyday of advertising books on the basis of their numerical novelty (Byron's *Poems on his Domestic Circumstances* reached its twenty-third edition), publishers "went to the other extreme" and printed revised work without mentioning that it had been altered; of course, in doing this, they were also helping to market a new concept of the author as a spontaneous, visionary genius.

Many of the romantics did more reworking than they or their publishers liked to pretend: in this regard, as I suggested in the introduction, the literary culture of the early nineteenth century was a mirror image of our own, where the pedagogic institutions of creative writing make it difficult for writers to claim that they don't revise. One example would be the letter in which Keats formulated his grand axiom of naturalness and compared poetry to leaves on a tree. It began and ended rather bathetically by its own stated standards, with questions about the placement of commas and an explanation of "one or two alterations" found necessary in *Endymion*. Another great romantic legend is the familiar story about the genesis of "Chapman's Homer": Cowden Clarke found the poem on his breakfast table, after he and Keats rapturously perused the book all night; Keats had walked home at dawn and scribbled it down. The swift revision in manuscript of "low-browed" to "deep-browed" needn't argue against the primacy of sudden inspiration, but the swapping out of line seven between magazine and first book publication shows that the poem as we have it was the product of mature deliberation. This tension between the romantic poets' disdain for second chances and the careful reworking that they practiced has been the subject of fine studies by Jack Stillinger and Zachary Leader. Leader examines "the manner in which revision calls into question and complicates Romantic attitudes to authorship" (1), focusing on the tension between theory and practice. Stillinger juxtaposes Coleridge as an inveterate reviser and Keats as a poet who, at least within bounds, practiced what he preached. "But where Keats's creative activity on a poem stopped at that [initial] point, and the work was more or less finished once and for all, with Coleridge there was a series of subsequent stages in which Coleridge the poet metamorphosed into Coleridge the critic, as if someone else had written his poems."[52] Wordsworth's *Prelude*, which was not published in his lifetime, has some genetic similarities to the big ongoing projects of modernist poetry, such as Auden's *Collected Poems;* given that it is an autobiographical account of the growth of the poet's mind, it is perhaps not surprising that the account wanted alteration as the poet himself aged and changed. (The intrinsically revisionary nature of autobiography as a mode is something I come back to in chapter 5.) Nonetheless, Wordsworth was more penitent and guarded than modernist writers about describing the work of ongoing revision. The gentle irony of "The Middle Years" stems from Dencombe's reluctance to label his already-published and circulating book finished. By contrast, Wordsworth claimed as early as 1814 in the preface to *The Excursion* that the *Prelude* was a completed speech act: "That Work, addressed to a dear Friend, most distinguished for his knowledge and genius . . . has been long finished."[53] It is *The Recluse,* which Wordsworth thought about for fifty years but never completed, and of which *The Excursion* was supposed to be one part, that more closely resembles a work such as Pound's *Cantos:* both were intended to be published piecemeal and devoutly wished-for, but their ends or final form remained impossible to discern from any individual staging-point.

The romantic creed of antirevisionism, premised on a belief in inspiration, spontaneity, and organic form, persisted for most of the nineteenth century. Browning was so irritated by Tennyson's 1842 revisions that he described the poet as mentally ill, "There is some woeful mental infirmity in the man—he was months buried in correcting the press of the last volume, and in that time began spoiling the new poems (in proof) as hard as he could."[54] It crops up again in 1900, when an anonymous periodical writer criticized the "malady of revision" spreading among ambitious young writers by referring back to the keywords of romantic poetics: "When my friend spends weeks upon a sonnet,—that sometimes he cannot get published,—I fail in convincing him that in all probability he has hammered the life out of it entirely, and that its chances were far better in the rather fiery chaos of its first state; it was alive at least."[55] He ends by suggesting that the "slaves of revision" should correct themselves by hanging one of Landor's midcentury sayings over their desks: "Though hemp and flax and cotton are the stronger for being threshed, verses and intellects certainly are not."[56]

This recourse to metaphors of organic form illustrates the enduring impact of romantic aesthetics, but there were, in addition, good economic reasons why the book industry in the nineteenth century was inhospitable to revision. Before the introduction of stereotype in England in the 1810s, it had cost publishers only as much to print new, or substantially revised, books as to reprint old ones. In either case, they had to handset the type from scratch and its high fixed cost meant that usually only a few pages were printed at a time. The new technology allowed them to store each page of type permanently on metal plates, produced by pouring molten metal into a plaster mold. As William St Clair explains, this "altered the balance of economic incentives between publishing new titles and reprinting existing titles" because it was now much cheaper to reprint a book from the plates than to set new type.[57] As a result publishers had stronger disincentives than before for allowing authorial revision and texts tended to stay "fixed" in their plate form for a long time, even when those plates contained errors. It is this technology that leads, at the other end of the century, to Dencombe's fiscally ruinous and proto-modern desire to sacrifice the first edition of his work by *replacing* the book already in collectors' libraries with a new edition containing an altered text. By implication, he is suggesting that his publishers—who have only just sent him a copy of his recently published novel—should throw away the metal plates that they had invested in producing and start over again.

Modernist Poetics

Modernist writers who wanted to revise had to navigate two legacies from the nineteenth century, a romantic disdain for second thoughts, and a printing culture that made revising costly. I will come in a moment to some of the quite practical and specific technological issues that early-twentieth-century revisers faced. First, we might note that high modernism flipped over the poles in arguments about the rights and wrongs of revision. Sometimes, in making this inversion so neatly, its theorists seem to be laboring under a palpable anxiety of influence, privileging labor over spontaneity, last thoughts over first thoughts, machine art over organic form, and futurism over nostalgia. The notion that modernism has an ambivalent relationship to romanticism in general is not new. Edmund Wilson expressed this proposition elegantly in the opening of his 1931 study of modern literature, *Axel's Castle:* "the movement of which in our own day we are witnessing the mature development is not merely a degeneration or an elaboration of Romanticism, but rather a counterpart to it, a second flood of the same tide."[58] What I want to emphasize are the specific consequences of this ambivalence for textual thought and, as a result, genetic and book history.

Where the romantics had shied away from revision in case it diminished the primacy of an original vision, the future-oriented avant-garde fantasized about the voyage out rather than the return home, about discovery rather than anamnesis.[59] This is the reason that the ageing Dencombe bewails his lack of "a second age, an extension," and the source of the young Pound's cheerful reminder to William Carlos Williams, "remember that a man's real work is *what he is going to do,* not what is behind him. Avanti e coraggio!"[60] The preference for future over past time, for the text-to-come rather than the one achieved, is observable even at a bibliographic level, in tentative titles that propose themselves merely as staging points: *Work in Progress, A Draft of XVI Cantos* and *Draft of XXX Cantos,* "Notes Toward a Supreme Fiction," and "Part of a Novel, Part of a Poem, Part of a Play." Organic metaphors of spoiling (like a foodstuff going bad), threshing, or overcooking assume that texts have a natural and correct way to develop, but modernist writers often represent textual genesis as mechanical or a perverse alternative to organic form. Pound's verses "Sage Homme," which Eliot considered using as a preface to *The Waste Land,* describe the poem's coming-to-being as the bizarre consequence of male pregnancy, "A Man their Mother was,/ A Muse their Sire."[61] Henry James provided another rather repellent image when he described his earliest texts as "wizened" and "grizzled" children: young because they were the "first-born of my progeny," old because they had aged poorly.

In addition, where romantic and Victorian writers tended to think about revision as adornment or encrustation—this is also a common figure for a manuscript corrupted and weathered by time—modernist poetics figured it as a way of getting below the surface to the passionate heart of the matter. This is apparent as early as 1909, in James's peculiar description in the preface to *The Golden Bowl* of revising as breaking through, rather than merely recovering, old ground: "It was, all sensibly, as if the clear matter being still there, even as a shining expanse of snow spread over a plain, my exploring tread, for application to it, had quite unlearned the old pace and found itself naturally falling into another, which might sometimes indeed more or less agree with the original tracks, but might most often, or very nearly, break the surface in other places."[62] The original version is introduced as a pure surface, a field of snow marked out by tracks. Revision then becomes not only a second navigation over the field but also a way of penetrating into it, of turning a flat surface into a three-dimensional model.[63] This disruptive, changeful metaphor is, of course, a much more accurate description of James's own work for the New York Edition than his statement that revision is merely rereading. As Julie Rivkin has noted, the description of the snowy field is a visually appropriate metaphor for the wide-margined pages that Macmillan had produced for James to revise upon: the snowy expanse is very much like the white paper, and those footprints the alphabetical characters of a particular passage.[64] Of course, if James had been *only* rereading, he would not have needed these special sheets; he could have read any published edition of his work. We see the same focus in Hemingway's iceberg principle and Pound's use of mining as a metaphor for Imagism. He described the process of finding the hard nugget of an image as follows: "If a man owned mines in South Africa he would know that his labourers dug up a good deal of mud and an occasional jewel, looking rather like the mud about it."[65] Rather than being simply a mild improvement, the revised text is accordingly represented as *deeper* and more fundamental than the original version. This fits with a general tendency in modernist thought—Fredric Jameson has termed it the "depth model"—to prefer the latent to the manifest.[66]

Virginia Woolf's reaction to the "Lycidas" manuscript provides a simple but vivid example of the gulf between romantic and modernist thinking about revision. In a *Room of One's Own,* she remembers that "Lamb wrote how it shocked him to think it possible that any word in *Lycidas* could have been different from what it is. To think of Milton changing the words in that poem seemed to him a sort of sacrilege." In his 1820 essay "Oxford at the Vacation," Charles Lamb had written of his preference for print over manuscript, textual fixity over variation: "There is something to me repugnant, at any time, in written hand. The text never seems determinate. Print settles it. I had thought of the Lycidas as of a full-grown beauty—as springing up with all its parts absolute—till, in an evil hour, I was shown the original written copy of it, together with the other minor poems of its author, in the Library of Trinity, kept like some treasure to be proud of. . . . How it staggered me to see the fine things in their ore! interlined, corrected! as if their words were mortal, alterable, displaceable, at pleasure! as if they might have been otherwise, and just as good!"[67] In conclusion, Lamb vows strictly to avert his eyes from the sight of artistic process. Valuing the unfinished as a kind of treasure seems not only misguided to him but morally repugnant and a bleak illustration of human imperfection. In the age of mechanical reproduction, we may have learned to allocate a cult value to the original, valuing the single interlined manuscript rather than the (many possible) printed books containing the final text, but for Lamb seeing the original strips the finished work of its aura. "I will never go into the workshop of any great artist again, nor desire a sight of his picture, till it is fairly off the easel; no, not if Raphael were to be alive again, and painting another Galatea." Woolf's mission into the library of Trinity is, of course, a failure—this is central to the feminist politics of the essay—and a "deprecating, silvery, kindly gentleman" tells her regretfully that "ladies are only admitted to the Library if accompanied by a Fellow of the College." In spirit, though, she is a geneticist, amusing herself by "guessing which word it could have been that Milton had altered, and why." She also considers looking at the manuscript of Thackeray's novel *Esmond,* to see if the eighteenth-century style (which she finds affected) was natural to Thackeray, and whether his alterations—she assumes as a matter of course that they must exist—were "for the benefit of the style or of the sense."

As several critics have noted, *A Room of One's Own* (based on lectures that Woolf had given at Cambridge) was itself heavily revised. Susan Gubar explains, "the drafty *Women & Fiction* lets us watch Woolf cutting and inserting, stopping and starting, reworking scenes over and over again with various phrasings."[68] Writers may not always practice as they preach where revision is concerned, but it is obviously much easier to revise heavily—particularly after publication or airing material in front of an audience as a lecture—for those whose poetics encourage or even prescribe it. Lamb did occasionally make small changes to his London Magazine essays before their book publication as *Essays of Elia* but, by and large, he was opposed to revising his own work.[69] In addition, writers who are completely comfortable with the fact of their own revision are often happy to leave traces of the genetic process inside their texts rather than trying, at all costs, to fashion one single, final, and completely perfect version. Self-revealing revision of this kind is particularly noticeable in the later modernist period. Andrew Kappel points out that, earlier in her career, Marianne Moore tended to "close up the holes she created by cutting material" and to restore the seamlessness of her texts, while later she begins "to let the seams show."[70] This comes over clearly in the editorial arrangement of the 1966 *Complete Poems*. There the much-reduced version of "Poetry" (a thing that the speaker has always claimed to "dislike") does not so much attempt to supersede the original version of the poem as to produce a dialogue with it, and Moore in fact chose to print the 1951 "Original Version" in her notes, as if to make sure that readers would not forget that it had once been other. Both Christine Froula and Jerome McGann have eloquently shown how, on a much larger scale, Pound attached value to the "historicity" of the *Cantos,* whose meaning he saw as produced not in spite of but through the complicated history of genesis and publication.[71] He wrote in a 1937 letter, "When I get to end, pattern *ought* to be discoverable," and this pattern in turn was going to be discovered not only by moving forward in a straight line from earlier to later poems, but by looping back and revising the earliest *Cantos* to take account of the later ones. Rather than moving in a melioristic way to a single, far-off textual form, modernist writing often loops back on itself in this way, returning to an apparently early stage of its genesis just at the moment when it seems about to be completed.

Modernist Print Culture

However attractive "passionate correction" might have been in theory to modernist writers, they would not have been able to revise so heavily in practice without certain enabling conditions. In the nineteenth century, it was rare for authors to view their complete work in proof before first publication and, even when they did so, they usually had to travel to London to see the proofs and then could make changes only within a strictly limited time frame. Simon Eliot explains that "the form and content of a novel would be fixed as it went along, and the beginning could not be corrected in the light of the end," and he links this in turn to certain structural and formal features in the Victorian novel.[72] "The 'loose baggy monsters' of the mid-Victorian period that James so disparaged were a product of the available technology, just as his own were." As a result, most late-stage revision took place not on the proofs and not, as we have seen, between simple reprintings, but during the elapse of time between significant format change: either between serial publication and an initial, expensive three-decker edition, or between a first edition and a cheaper reset one. Thackeray, for example, rewrote chapters of *Vanity Fair* between its appearance in serial and the 1848 first edition; and he revised the text again for the 1853 cheap edition to remove reference to the illustrations (which were not reprinted).[73] George Eliot revised the second, rather dour, ending of *Middlemarch* for the 1874 cheap edition after it distressed her readers. Some poets lucky enough to see their work in multiple editions also made retroactive revision although, compared to the multiple postpublication revisions of twentieth-century poets such as Auden and Moore, this practice seems minimal. Tennyson revised many of his 1833 poems before republication in 1842, but he then left alone their texts for the rest of his life. Others rejected the chance to make any changes after a first edition. Swinburne, for example, complained in 1875 about the idea that he might make revisions or corrections to a republished edition of *Atalanta in Calydon*. "I suppose others are not expected to re-revise every word of the text in every fresh edition of every one of their works? it would be a dog's life to lead—worse than a galley-slave's."[74] His attitude here is reminiscent of Byron's, and he sees the possibility of continued revision as mere drudgery rather than an opportunity for artistic improvement. It is very difficult to imagine a modernist poet who would make the same complaint.

After Ottmar Mergenthaler's invention of linotype in 1886 and the introduction of monotype the following year, a machine could set type automatically—either a line at a time, or from a perforated paper sheet. Most importantly, once printing was finished, the cast lines of type were simply melted down and the lead reused. Contemporary estimates claimed that the linotype was four- and monotype five-times faster than hand-setting of type.[75] The relative ease of resetting and reprinting a whole book meant that, for the first time, publishers were willing to provide writers with proofs of their entire book; nor was it any longer so financially prudent to store a text for many years on plates in a single fixed version. Proof pages—as much as first manuscripts or even typescripts—turned out to be an important revision site for modernist writers. Joseph Conrad frequently asked publishers to send him more than one set of galley proofs; Faulkner found *Sanctuary* "so badly written" and "cheaply approached" when he reread it in galleys that he "tore the galleys down and rewrote the book";[76] D. H. Lawrence revised *Sons and Lovers* in galleys after it had already been substantially altered by Edward Garnett and his printer's reader; and both Hemingway and Fitzgerald made the practice of extensive rewriting after receiving proofs a normal part of a novel's composition. In his *Paris Review* interview, Hemingway enumerated the different stages in the publication process as opportunities for change, "The last chance is in the proofs. You're grateful for these different chances."[77]

During the early twentieth century, most books went through the following stages: manuscript, typescript, galley proof, revised proof, page proof, first edition. The first set of galley proofs with wide margins for correction and annotation was sent back to authors to be collated against their original manuscript or, increasingly, their typescript. (By the early twentieth century many publishers were only willing to consider submissions presented in typescripts.)[78] The authorially corrected—or revised— galleys, now known as "foul proofs" were then used to set a second set of proofs. A publisher's in-house reader usually compared the "revised proofs" or "revises" carefully against the foul proofs; they were used in turn to produce page proofs. Page proofs were the most difficult of all to correct and, as one 1916 handbook points out, they were "supposed to contain no errors."[79] As a matter of courtesy, publishers would usually send them back to the author along with the foul proofs for final review, but they strongly discouraged substantial changes at this point. The final stage involved casting the page proofs as "plate proofs" at the foundry. These proofs were marked by a distinctive black rule around the edge of the page from metal guards, as if to forbid further alteration. And, indeed, publishers asked authors to make no changes at this stage except the removal of a gross error. In 1904 Ruskin's editors described the habit of rewriting in proof as "the greatest of literary vices"—at least, from the publishers' perspective.[80]

The important point about this multistage process is that it stimulated, rather than merely enabled, the act of revision. This is perhaps just human perversity, but many modernist writers seemed to find that the more potential final forms they saw their work in the less satisfactorily *final* any of these versions turned out to be. Joyce's interleaving of more and more material on the placard and page proofs of "Ithaca" is one peculiar and celebrated example. Why should proofs prompt changes? One answer is a that visual difference—seeing the same words in a new form—promotes the kind of self-critical, self-disowning reread-ing that promotes revision. In 1919, Paul Valéry described this kind of revisionary rereading as forgetful, self-critical, and distanced, almost as if the author were reading someone else's writing: "Relire, donc, relire après oubli—*se* relire, sans ombre de tendresse, sans paternité; avec froi-deur at acuité critique."[81] The modernist period was rich in opportuni-ties for reading after forgetting, because mixed technology produced a high degree of visual defamiliarization. Today, most of us compose on the computer in Microsoft Word and even our most provisional drafts are clearly paginated, legible sheets, with standardized characters and spacing. We have become self-publishers of a kind, and the first printout is not so very different from the final book. By contrast, we might com-pare the first printed text of *The Waste Land* in the *Criterion* or *Dial* to the documents preserved in the facsimile edition: Eliot's neatly written, calligraphic autographed version of "Death by Water," the crabbed, un-even, heavily overwritten draft of "London, the swarming life you kill and breed," and a mixture of "good" neat typescripts and messier, error-filled ones, with phrases blocked out xxxx. During the year that he and then Pound worked on *The Waste Land,* both poets were exposed to the poem in a wide array of visually different forms.

The other important technology promoting visual difference was the typewriter. All of the writers that I study before 1950 continued to draft by hand. The consequence was exposure, from an early stage, to two visually very different forms of text. Manuscript became a place for free-wheeling fast composition; typescript, which was scarcer, a space for correction and revision. Ezra Pound was showing the material preju-dices of his day when he wrote on the manuscript of *The Waste Land,* "Bad—but can't attack until I get typescript." W. H. Auden made a similar point when he spoke of the disliked typewriter as an aid to the removal of "defects" from a poem: "Much as I loathe the typewriter, I must admit that it is a help in self-criticism. Typescript is so impersonal and hideous to look at that, if I type out a poem, I immediately see defects which I missed when I looked through it in manuscript."[82] The point isn't that typewriters show error in a way that longhand cannot; it's that by transferring a text from one visual medium into another, one sees it anew, afresh. Auden continued by commenting that the "severest test" of someone else's work was to copy it from type into longhand, a process that would again ensure that "the slightest defect will reveal itself."

In a normal or model writing process, at least from the point of view of the publisher, a writer would fix something close to a final form in manuscript and typescript revisions, and proof would be a place only for minor changes. Many early-twentieth-century writers learned to type themselves or employed cheap typists, so penciling in changes on typescript was not much more expensive than making them on a manuscript. Making them on proof did, however, remain somewhat costly. A handbook for college writers published in 1914 has a section devoted specifically to the problem of "Author's Changes," and begins by staging the argument between pro-revision writers and their editors and cost-sensitive publishers as a dialogue: "Should an Editor ask (1) 'Why are an author's changes so expensive?' the printer might ask (2) 'Why need they be considered necessary?' "[83] Some contracts stipulated that the cost of revision should be capped at 10 percent or less of the total publishing cost.[84] The publishing industry, in other words, repeatedly discouraged revision in proof as an inefficient, wasteful habit: the handbook advises that "a few hours of careful and final editing will save *time*, *money* and *ill* feeling." To see why the high modernists so often flouted this rule, returning to an *early* stage in the genetic process at a late stage in the publication process, we need to understand something about the perverse market economy of modernism.

The question of modernism's relationship to the market has been heavily debated in the last two decades. The traditional view, following the polemics of the historical avant-garde, was one of extreme hostility; as Terry Eagleton put it, the modernist text "holds out by the skin of its teeth against those social forces which would degrade it to an exchangeable object." The power and inherent instability of this argument was pointed out by Andreas Huyssen in 1986: on the one hand the "opposition between modernism and mass culture has remained amazingly resilient over the decades," but on the other "modernism's insistence on the autonomy of the art work, its obsessive hostility to mass culture, its

radical separation from the culture of everyday life, and its programmatic distance from political, economic, and social concerns was always
challenged as soon as it arose."[85] A host of recent critics, including Paul
Delany, Kevin Dettmar, Timothy Materer, Mark Morrisson, Lawrence
Rainey, and Jennifer Wicke, among others, have reconsidered the relationship between "high" modernism and "low" commercial culture, by
showing how subtly modernist writers positioned their work within the
marketplace.[86] Lawrence Rainey puts it most clearly when he argues that
modernist art wants to become "a commodity of a special sort," impli-
cated in a network of patronage and investment that is separate from "the
exigencies of immediate consumption prevalent within the larger cultural economy."[87]

Revision became technologically much easier in the 1890s, but during
that decade many of the central institutions of publishing, including the
circulating library, the three-volume novel, and the weekly review began
to collapse, and profits in the publishing industry became less predictable and certain.[88] When Henry James began revising for the New York
Edition in 1906, he hoped that it would be a financial success, a consolation for his failure in the theater and also for the increasing difficulty he
was experiencing in serializing his fiction.[89] In fact the edition was a
failure, giving its unhappy creator a sense "of literature being for me,
somehow, ever only an *expensive* job."[90] It also illustrated a basic economic truth about revision: authors usually care more about revised versions than their readers do, and the time cost in meticulously reworking
an already achieved text is rarely recouped in economic terms. Instead,
following Bourdieu, we might say that the commercial cost of revision
for the publisher is translated into symbolic capital for the author.[91] By
revising excessively, long after a book was apparently finished, writers
were able to display disdain for a commercial notion of efficiency. But, in
many ways, their habit of revision accords with Rainey's view of the art
object as a "commodity of a special sort" rather than an anticommodity.
Publishers wanted to reduce labor costs and printing costs, to increase
the speed by which a book could be brought to market, and to minimize
the possibility of introducing error across the different stages; Joyce's
reworking of *Ulysses,* by contrast, was slow, expensive, and error-
producing. On the other hand, it was not the case that the modernists

showed no interest in efficiency. Instead, they sublated efficiency from an economic goal into an aesthetic one, producing texts that communicated through "rare compression," with as few wasted words as possible. Efficiency in the final product was achieved by sacrificing efficiency of process. In the chapter on excision, I discuss Pound's aversion to textual waste as a kind of self-conscious perversion of the economic and industrial goals of the "Anti-Waste" movement that developed after World War I.

The patrons who funded modernism found pleasure, even glory, in being able to support compositional habits that conventional publishers despaired of. In her 1956 memoir *Shakespeare and Company,* Sylvia Beach remembered that she was warned by Darantiere "that I was going to have a lot of extra expense with these proofs," and that "he suggested that I call Joyce's attention to the danger of going beyond my depth; perhaps his appetite for proofs might be curbed."[92] Here, in a series of metonyms, both the difficulty and the profundity of the final product are tied to the depth of the patron's pocket, and Joyce's desire to produce a masterpiece is the same as his appetite for spending inexhaustibly on proofs. Beach continues by narrating her triumphant denial of this sensible advice for, unlike a "real" publisher, she needs to pay no attention to financial profit. "But no, I wouldn't hear of such a thing. *Ulysses* was to be as Joyce wished, in every respect. I wouldn't advise 'real' publishers to follow my example, nor authors to follow Joyce's. It would be the death of publishing. My case was different. It seemed natural to me that the efforts and sacrifices on my part should be proportionate to the greatness of the work I was publishing." As if absorbing some of Joyce's own fetish for proofs, Beach interleaved this description with a facsimile image of a heavily written over page from the "Cyclops" episode showing, among other things, the scrawled addition of extra names of "Irish heroes and heroines of antiquity." She subtitled it "Page of proof of the first edition of *ULYSSES* with changes by the author." Despite this frenetic activity, some of Joyce's very last second thoughts, such as Molly's "what I never had," still had to be delivered to Darantiere by telephone; others, including the name "Borus Hupinkoff," which Joyce wanted inserted into the list of foreign delegates in "Cyclops," arrived just too late, and were marked with a rueful "trop tard" by the printers.[93] As

Paul Delany argues, "to use up seven years for *Ulysses* and sixteen for *Finnegans Wake* was not a commercial rate of literary production."[94] Without the generous income provided by Harriet Shaw Weaver, and Sylvia Beach's publishing subsidies, "Joyce would have had to write more numerous but simpler books, as commercial novelists have always had to do."

Joyce was heavily reliant on the work of his typists, printers, and patrons, and never used the typewriter to produce new creative work. Derek Attridge has suggested that he found the typewriter (and the fountain pen) to interfere with the proximate relation "between body and words on the page that traditional pens and pencils gave him."[95] This was relatively old-fashioned. Most major writers in this period took a more self-directed approach to controlling the publication and dissemination of their work. Virginia and Leonard Woolf purchased a small handpress in 1917; within a few years the Hogarth Press has become an important force in British avant-garde publishing, printing Woolf's own *Jacob's Room* in 1922 and the first British book edition of *The Waste Land* in 1923. In *Three Guineas,* Woolf explained that cheap new technology made a home-run press financially possible, and that it in turn enabled an unparalleled intellectual freedom: "Still, Madam, the private printing press is an actual fact, and not beyond the reach of a moderate income. Typewriters and duplicators are actual facts and even cheaper. By using these cheap and so far unforbidden instruments you can at once rid yourself of the pressure of boards, policies, and editors."[96] Because the Woolfs were using a publishing technology that was commercially outmoded by the twentieth century, the books they produced at the Hogarth Press also had a different look and feel from their mainstream equivalents. They drew attention to this in a positive way with bright paper covers and illustrations produced from woodcuts by Vanessa Bell and Dora Carrington. In doing so, they were participating, almost by accident, in a tradition stretching back to the late nineteenth century; Jerome McGann has described the "explosion of fine-press publishing" represented by presses such as Kelmscott, Cuala, Doves, and Eragny as part of a reaction against the very technologies of linotype and monotype that I have been discussing. Virginia Woolf self-published all of her own works after *Night and Day*—perhaps not coincidentally, that novel and its predecessor, both published by Duckworth, are usually regarded as not yet, or not quite, modernist. Other writers, such as Yeats, moved between smaller and larger presses. In *Black Riders,* McGann details Yeats's adoption of a three-tier format, where periodical or anthology publication was followed by "publication in two distinct book formats: the private press Dun Emer/Cuala format, and the commercial Macmillan format."[97] Like Pound, who also published in more and less commercial formats, he tended to use the space between these different bibliographic contexts to make changes to the linguistic code of his poems.

As Rainey's work has shown, the inverted economy of modernism was fragile, unstable, and short-lived: a "momentary equivocation" between resistance and capitulation to commodification.[98] In the earlier part of the modernist period, wealthy patrons and collectors were able to fund writers' revisionary habits with ease. In the 1930s, as capital started to dry up, the "uneasy synthesis" between writers and investors broke down. T. S. Eliot's *Criterion,* which had begun by publishing *The Waste Land,* folded in January 1939. By the time *Finnegans Wake* was published in 1939, Joyce had spent the entire £21,000 that Harriet Shaw Weaver had given him between 1919 and 1923, and saw few possibilities of persuading a wealthy benefactor to settle a similar amount on him again. He had also produced an incredible amount of unused textual material. By one recent estimate, the *Finnegans Wake* archive, which represents only the surviving pages, stands at 25,000 pages: this is forty times longer than the book itself.[99] Virginia Woolf had delighted in the 1920s that she was the only woman in England free to say what she liked, but after selling her share of the Hogarth Press to John Lehmann in 1938, she lost a certain degree of guaranteed control over the publishing process. This seems to have influenced her decision to give up on "Pointz Hall" or *Between the Acts* before putting the draft through her usual process of intense revision, and may also account for the self-conscious provisionality of "A Sketch of the Past." Not only is the memoir an unimportant, self-pleasuring digression from the real work of writing a biography of Roger Fry, but it turns up at odd moments of dead time, frequently in the form of waste paper: "I have just found this sheaf of notes, thrown away into my waste-paper basket. I had been tidying up."[100] When Woolf died in 1941, her husband found that she had literally turned her writing room into revisionary waste, as if giving up on the possibility that any production would be a text's publishable final form. Looking for her last essay on Mrs. Thrale, he found among the "immense numbers of typewritten sheets lying about her room," "several revisions of [it] in the waste-paper-basket."[101] As the basic institutions of modernism—the little magazines (or the fairly long-lasting ones, including Eliot's *Criterion*), independent publishing houses, structures of patronage and distribution—began to collapse for good, compulsive but expensive revision became harder to support. I will come in more detail in the final chapter to the additional impact of new technologies, including word processing and then the personal computer. Functioning more like an infinitely erasable slate than a piece of paper, to borrow Freud's terminology from "The Mystic Writing Pad," the computer has made the cost of revision effectively free but also makes it harder to preserve its material traces.

The New Bibliography and Intentionalism

In the final part of this chapter, I provide a brief history of four dominant methods of thinking about revision in the period since modernism: New Criticism; the Greg-Bowers-Tanselle school of final-intentionalist editing; sociological approaches including social-text editing; and genetic criticism, principally as practiced in Paris at the Institut des Textes et Manuscrits Modernes. My aim is more historical than evaluative; I have found useful tools and methods for reading revision in all of these places and will say something of my own comparative approach at the end.

Modernism is the first literary period that existed alongside or even in the university, and it is symbiotically related to the early discipline of English. Louis Menand and Lawrence Rainey warn, however, against assimilating New Criticism and modernist writing too closely, as if the former "were merely a more systematic, more philosophical, or more academic articulation of formalist undercurrents within modernism."[102] One of the major differences between avant-garde experiment and its reception centers, in fact, around the question of autonomy and intention; this in turn has important consequences for thinking about revision.

How to reconcile Joyce's imperious claim that he had put into *Ulysses* "so many enigmas and puzzles that it will keep the professors busy for centuries arguing over what I meant" with the strong anti-intentionalism of New Criticism?[103] The seed or origin of this difference might be traced back to the *Egoist,* which published T. S. Eliot's argument in support of artistic impersonality under the masthead of being "An Individualist Review." To push further at the gap: why did the New Critics pay so little attention to textual questions and variation when contemporary writers were producing texts of great genetic and revisionary complexity? In addition, what was the relationship between New Criticism—as a critical practice that disavowed inquiries into intention—and the work in the 1920s and 1930s of the New Bibliographers, who aimed resolutely to recover it? Textual questions had traditionally been fundamental to all forms of literary study, but during the early twentieth century editing and criticism diverged in British and American English departments, leading to a gulf between literary and textual theory that has persisted up to the present.[104]

Wimsatt and Beardsley's 1946 essay "The Intentional Fallacy" formalized a position that was already dominant among literary critics, and it remains a useful touchstone for understanding the hostility of midcentury literary critics to questions about what an author meant. They argued, with unusual philosophical clarity, that authorial intention was "neither available nor desirable" as a metric for interpretation.[105] Their argument is both in tune with the theory of artistic impersonality advocated by T. S. Eliot and perhaps a response to the continued presence— the long lives—of modernist authors. Traditionally, literary interpretation had focused on the dead; now critics had to deal with the possibility that, at least in principle, a living author might reply to a question such as "Did you have Donne in mind when you wrote 'I have heard the mermaids singing, each to each?' " with a firm answer. In fact, Eliot himself proved reluctant to answer questions of this sort and was, in this respect, a rather satisfying object of study for anti-intentionalists. When he was asked what he meant by the line "Lady, three white leopards sat under a juniper tree," he refused to paraphrase and answered simply, "I mean, 'Lady, three white leopards sat under a juniper tree.' "[106] One wonders if his strangely elusive presence as an interpreter of his own work had something to do with its success and canonization during the 1940s and 1950s. If Eliot *had* answered letters about what "Prufrock" or *The Waste Land* meant and if, as is quite likely, these answers had been informative and critically acute, then he would have removed much of the pleasure and value of his difficult poetry for literary critics. In this respect, although his poetry and critical essays are closely linked, the double-act's triumph rests on the essays' complete evasion of explicit self-exegesis.

Wimsatt and Beardsley recognize that revision—where an author returns to a text, reasserting his or her presence—poses unique problems for anti-intentionalism. Verbal commands such as "omit" or "stet" or a direct line drawn through a paragraph show intention very clearly. And doesn't the fact that publishers are able to interpret and follow through these commands even when, as in the case of *Ulysses,* they are confusingly multiple, indicate that there is nothing genuinely oblique about them?[107] Some critics have suggested that genetic or revised texts require a "special poetics," in which "authorial intention plays a more important and less problematic role than it ordinarily does in literary criticism,"[108] but this begs the question: don't all texts have a genesis? Might not all texts have been revised? Wimsatt and Beardsley conclude by fudging their original definition of intention. "There is a sense in which an author, by revision, may better achieve his original intention. But it is a very abstract sense. He intended to write a better work, or a better work of a certain kind, and now has done it. But it follows that his former concrete intention was not his intention. 'He's the man we were in search of, that's true,' says Hardy's rustic constable, 'and yet he's not the man we were in search of. For the man we were in search of was not the man we wanted.' " (5)

A "concrete intention" (a term which Wimsatt and Beardsley don't define, and which they don't use elsewhere) seems to be nothing more than "what the author in fact achieved." Once again, Eliot is a model case. He played along with this game by displaying no interest at all in the genetic documents that he had produced. In the case of *The Waste Land* manuscript, he might even have presented dissemination by ignoring requests from the curator of the New York Public Library for a meeting in the early 1960s, after the manuscript had reappeared.

In a brilliant piece of bibliographic acuity, D. F. McKenzie showed that "The Intentional Fallacy" itself opens with a misquotation. Its authors had not delved carefully into the text that they were quoting and ended up printing a reading that provided pleasing, but unwarranted, support for their own position. "Wimsatt and Beardsley say that Congreve 'wrote' the following scenes, but Congreve was a deliberate craftsman. He said he '*wrought*' them."[109] This problem is not unique in midcentury criticism for, as Hershel Parker archly comments, New Criticism "thrived when the professor could make a career from writing about a few paperback novels or collections of short stories which he (and increasingly she) carried to the beach at summer."[110] This is due in part to the success and expansion of English as a discipline. Professors working in new universities without research libraries did not always have access to early editions; over time, they also tended to lack the training to make bibliographic scholarship possible. Textual criticism became a dowdy subset of literary criticism in the Anglo-American academy.[111]

I. A. Richards provides another cautionary tale. He worked at a university with excellent libraries, but had not been trained in literary or textual studies. His 1929 book *Practical Criticism* gives very little information about any of the passages selected for criticism—this is its famous gambit—but in omitting bibliographic information as a pedagogic device it also furnishes up inaccurate texts. Richards therefore placed himself in the rather awkward position of criticizing his students for misreading texts (hermeneutically) that were themselves already misprinted. Hopkins's "Spring and Fall," for example, is printed with a notable omission (lines 3 and 4 of the original poem) and with the neologism "unleaving" in line 2 altered to "unleafing." Richards probably set the text from Robert Bridges's 1916 *Spirit of Man* anthology, where the poem appears without a title and with an ellipsis to show the omission of lines 3–4, rather than following the first published version (1893), Bridges's own 1918 edition of Hopkins, or the guidance of the surviving manuscripts. The short version of the poem omits the syntactically awkward parenthetical question "Leaves, like the things of man, you/ With your fresh thoughts care for, can you?" and, in doing so, tones down the poem's slightly acidic interrogation. By omitting both the couplet and Bridges's ellipsis, Richards provided his readers with a substantially different poem from the one that Hopkins wrote. In the end, he is doubly cavalier about intention, ignoring first Hopkins's own words, including the perfect rhyme "grieving"/ "unleaving," and then Bridges's editorial signal.

It is one of the more complete ironies of literary history that this anti-intentionalist mode of literary appreciation also coincided with the fiercely intentionalist editorial practices of the New Bibliographers. The mainstream of English editorial thought at this period—represented in the work of McKerrow, Greg and Pollard in Britain, and later Bowers and Tanselle in the United States—was strongly committed to final rather than early or medial intention. The procedures of this method of editing were developed primarily for English Renaissance texts and above all for Shakespeare. In his first rule of editing, Greg, citing McKerrow, defined the task as follows: "to present the text, so far as the available evidence permits, in the form in which we may suppose that it would have stood in a fair copy, made by the author himself, of the work as he finally intended it."[112] According to this method, the first printed edition of a work would *already* have introduced unwanted alterations into the text, understood to have reached its finest form in a "postulated" (not necessarily actual) fair copy. In selecting a copy-text, Bowers also recommended using "that document on the family tree that is closest to the ultimate authority of the lost manuscript, since only this document preserves the accidentals in their purest extant form." He then allowed that an editor could introduce substantive (i.e., semantic/verbal) alterations from later revised or altered editions. In some respects, this method of editing—which privileges individual intention over all other factors—is in tune with the willful, disciplined authority that modernist writers tried to retain over their texts. Auden, for example, who was constantly revising and updating his past poetry to accord with current feeling found a sympathetic editor in Edward Mendelson. In an essay on Auden's revisions, Mendelson claims to find the modernist gothic tower—his term— "more realistic" than the romantic fading coal as a model of composition. His posthumous edition of Auden's *Collected Poems* works this out in practice by simply printing "all the poems that W. H. Auden wished to preserve," which were by no means all the poems he had published, "in a text that represents his final revisions."[113] Intentionalist editing was not so well-tuned to the beliefs of twentieth-century literary criticism. Several generations were in the peculiar position of pursuing anti-intentionalist readings in texts that had been assembled carefully to preserve the "initial purity" of the text and an author's intention.[114] This was true not only for the first generation of anti-intentionalists, the New Critics, but for poststructuralists committed to even more thorough-going versions of the position. For example, Hans Walter Gabler has argued that revision is only controlled in a secondary way by "an author's intuition, intelligence, judgement and taste," and that "in a primary respect, it is controlled, since it is engendered, by the text's—the written, but, as yet unrevised, text's—potentials to mean, and (indeed) to signify."[115] This stronger version of anti-intentionalism—familiar and dispersed through many kinds of literary criticism since the 1970s—is premised on the Saussurian idea that linguistic signification is *never* determined by intention but only by the system of language itself.[116] It leads to the position articulated most clearly in genetic criticism where texts are said to "write themselves" rather than be written.

Weaker Versions of Intention: Social Texts and Genetic Criticism

The Greg-Bowers-Tanselle school of editing takes a very firm view on authorial intention, seeing it as something firm, individual, conscious, and, in principle, fully knowable. Its challengers in the second half of the twentieth century have usually taken a view of intention that is weaker and less monolithic. For our purposes, two directions are of particular interest: in Britain and America, the "social-text editing" of McGann, Shillingsburg, and Bornstein, among others, which argues that intention is spread out across different participants; and French critique génétique, which understands intention as a less conscious and controlled process. In working with a weaker view of intention these different groups of scholars laid the ground for a long-overdue rapprochement between textual studies and general literary criticism.[117]

The early 1980s saw several attempts—not all in the same field—to propose a more collaborative and sociological model of literary production. In 1983 Jerome McGann published his *Critique of Modern Textual*

Criticism, which questioned the realism of the idea that authors work in splendid isolation, showing that they in fact often rely heavily on family members, friends, editors, and publishers to make certain kinds of correction or alteration before publication.[118] Social-text editing asks us to pay attention to "nonauthorial textual determinants," and to abandon the idea that meaning was fixed ideally by a single individual at some single past moment. The previous year, the intellectual historian Robert Darnton published a model for a "communications circuit," aiming to be "a general model for the way that books come into being and spread through society."[119] The circuit, based on Darnton's research into the eighteenth-century French book trade, depicts books traveling from an author to a reader via a host of other agents: printers, shippers, even smugglers. Its influence and success, particularly among book historians, is illustrated by the number of modifications that other scholars have proposed: in 2007, Darnton reflected, "Every once in a while since then I receive a copy of another model that someone has proposed to substitute for mine. The pile of diagrams has reached an impressive height—and a good thing, too, because it is helpful for researchers to produce schematic pictures of their subject."[120] All of the connections in the circuit are depicted as strong black lines except for the final link, connecting the reader back to the author, which is a broken line. In 1985, D. F. McKenzie turned attention to the sociology of literature and the role of material form in determining meaning in his Panizzi lectures; they were published the following year as *Bibliography and the Sociology of Texts.* He had tried out some of these ideas in earlier essays from the 1970s, leading Jerome McGann humbly to conclude, "I see my own work as a critical pursuit of McKenzie's ideas."[121]

This sociological turn focused attention away from a single ideal text, produced as the final intention of an individual genius, and toward the multiple historical versions that exist. McKenzie put the argument in favor of versioning rather than final intentionalism like this: "Where an author revised a text, and two or more versions of it happen to survive, each of these can be said to have its own distinct structure, making it a different text. Each embodies a quite different intention. It follows therefore that, since any single version will have its own historical identity, not only for its author but for the particular market of readers who bought and read it, we cannot invoke the idea of one unified intention which the

editor must serve."[122] Variorum or versioning editions had been published before the 1980s. Ernest de Selincourt's 1926 facing-page edition
of the 1805 and 1850 *Prelude* is one important example. What was new in
the 1980s was the historicist belief that all texts are of independent interest and therefore that all are potentially worth reproducing as distinct
versions. De Selincourt himself showed an implicit preference for the
freshness of the young Wordsworth over "later excrescences of a manner
less pure, at times even meretricious, which are out of key with the spirit
in which the poem was first conceived and executed."[123] In this respect,
his edition was not simply presenting two texts of equal historical interest, neither of which had been printed in the poet's lifetime, but an implicit argument in favor of the earlier version.

Social-text editing has proved particularly useful for thinking about
the way that bibliographic code determines meaning, and it may be in
part responsible for the flurry of interest in modernist little magazines in
the 1990s and 2000s. George Bornstein's *Material Modernism,* with its
close-up focus on the semantics of bibliographic form—the magazine
page, the limited edition, the trade edition—is one excellent example. It
has helped critics to see the important role played by patrons and
editors—often women—in the modernist project, and to understand the
canny ways in which authors navigated the literary marketplace. Lawrence Rainey's discussion in *Institutions of Modernism* of Eliot's placing
of *The Waste Land* uses ideas that began in editorial theory to refine the
old-fashioned perception that "high" modernism took a position of aloof
hostility to a mass market.

The weaker, less author-centric view of intention developed by
McKenzie and McGann was undoubtedly a reaction to the extreme emphasis on "final intention" in traditional textual editing; it was perhaps
an inevitable dialectical response within the discipline. Other changes
in method in textual studies happen more serendipitously, as an attempt
to explain new bodies of material evidence.

Genetic criticism began quite suddenly in France in the 1960s and
1970s, as a response to new manuscript acquisitions by the Bibliothèque
Nationale. Louis Hay, who had been working on a thesis on Heine, peti-
tioned the French government to acquire his manuscripts when they
became available; "it is hardly surprising," van Vliet comments, "that

the heirs of this Jewish author, banned from German literature by the Nazis, should prefer to sell his manuscripts to the French state rather than to a library in the town in which he was born."[124] The library had no German conservator available to classify them once they arrived, so Hay took a sabbatical from his job at the Sorbonne and helped to establish a small research group to examine them.[125] Some financial support was forthcoming from the Centre National de la Recherche Scientifique (CNRS). In 1974, two more teams were added, on Zola and Proust, and the group as a whole became first the Centre d'Analyse des Manuscrits and then, in 1982, the more formal institution the Institut des Textes et Manuscrits Modernes. The early proponents of genetic criticism had grown up during the heyday of poststructuralism, and they brought to their work on manuscripts a post-Barthesian suspicion of the sway of the author. In his early and influential book *Le texte et l'avant-texte* (1972), Jean-Bellemin Noel explained that his aim was "to show to what extent poems *write themselves* despite, or even against, authors who believe they are implementing their writerly craft."[126] His later work makes repeated use of psychoanalytic readings to understand the unconscious of the text, seeing genetic processes as a repression, writing cure, or repetition compulsion. The advantage of this method of reading manuscripts is that it does not require a rational, controlling author to steward a text ever onward toward its ideal, publishable form. On the other hand, the periphrases that genetic critics sometimes find to *avoid* mentioning authorial intention can seem cumbersome and even evasive: "texts' coming to be," "places of disruption," "a change on the intertextual front," or "the genetic text of *To the Lighthouse*" rather than "Woolf's revisions to *To the Lighthouse*." In addition, as Susan Stanford Friedman has shown in her work on H.D., it is difficult to decide whether the text represses or analyzes itself. She explains that while "earlier versions of the text can be read vertically as the textual unconscious of the horizontal narrative in the published text," revision can also function as a form of self-analysis "in which the earliest versions are the most disguised, with each repetition bringing the writer closer to the repressed content that needs to be remembered."[127] In some respects, the psychoanalytic focus of early genetic criticism sits at odds with its funding by the French center for scientific research. In their introduction to *Genetic Criticism:*

Texts and Avant-Textes (2004), Daniel Ferrer and Michael Groden explain that this brought the new discipline back to earth and "encouraged an early interest in computer-assisted genetic editions and hypertexts, and it also helped facilitate studies of the material aspects of manuscripts, such as papers and watermarks, and authors' 'hands' " (9). Laurent Jenny agrees that "the vast deciphering and archival work necessary to its goal" lends genetic criticism a privileged status when compared to "solitary, artisanal, and unverifiable critical work."[128]

French genetic criticism did not begin to have much of an effect on Anglo-American scholars until the early 1990s. An early article by Frank Bowman in 1990 introduced some of its basic terms, "avant-texte" (which he translated as "foretext"), "brouillon," and "rature" into English.[129] In 1994, more influentially, Almuth Grésillon and Antoine Compagnon organized a conference at Columbia University on the new method. They printed some of the papers the following year in *Romanic Review,* accompanied by an introduction by Comagnon that posed the basic, and still relevant, question, "is genetic criticism not primarily and effectively the institutional legitimation of a research group at the CNRS?"[130] Two years later, *Yale French Studies* published a *Drafts* issue, which contained articles by Edward Mendelson and Christine Froula, as well as the French critics Pierre-Marc de Biasi, Daniel Ferrer, Gérard Genette, Louis Hay, and Laurent Jenny. But it was not until the publication in 2004 of the introductory *Genetic Criticism* by Deppman, Ferrer, and Groden that the method became widely known among literary critics who were not textual specialists, or taught alongside other branches of theory in graduate seminars.

In the meantime, as the bibliography of this book makes clear, genetic work was happening independently—sometimes on a less theorized basis—across the United States. The groundwork was laid in the 1960s and 1970s, when libraries began to see original manuscript collections, even of recent or living authors, as an attractive source of institutional prestige. Between 1957 and 1964, John Gordan, who was the first curator of the Berg Collection in New York, acquired Virginia Woolf's papers, including diaries, letters, and manuscripts of many of her novels, as well as valuable manuscripts by Auden and, most notoriously, the original drafts of *The Waste Land,* presumed lost.[131] The Ransom library in

Texas, founded in 1957, underwent a period of "explosive growth" in the 1960s and 1970s and acquired papers and manuscripts by Pound, Cummings, Hemingway, Steinbeck, and Yeats, among others.[132]

As in France, the presence of writers' papers—an Everest to climb—stimulated scholarly interest in analyzing them. After Ezra Pound's death in 1972, the Beinecke library at Yale acquired his correspondence and manuscripts. This led to focused doctoral studies of the genesis of the *Cantos* by Ronald Bush and Christine Froula, both of whom have remained interested in genetic process. Froula explains in her 1984 book *To Write Paradise*, "the availability of these papers opened up exciting new possibilities for studying *The Cantos* . . . in this case the 'nature' of the thing seemed particularly to invite the kind of explanation that a study of its origins as traced in the manuscripts Pound had accumulated in composing it would make possible."[133] Sometimes competitive acquisition policies—the effect of a free market—led to collections being split up, so while most of Sylvia Beach's papers went to Princeton, the manuscripts that Joyce had given her were sold to Buffalo. In the case of *Ulysses,* the notesheets went to the British Library; the holograph manuscript to the Rosenbach library in Philadelphia; and the first placard proofs to Harvard; while other important Joyce collections were formed at Cornell, Yale, and the National University of Ireland. The significant geographic dispersal of these archives mean that English-language scholars have and will continue to have a more difficult time doing genetic work than their colleagues in Paris, where intellectual life is more centralized.

One way to make manuscript collections more widely available is to publish them in facsimile or, now, online. Indeed, the 1970s was a golden age of facsimile reproduction for modernist authors: Valerie Eliot's facsimile of *The Waste Land* came out in 1971; Phillip Herring's edition of Joyce's *Ulysses* notesheets was published in 1972, followed by Clive Driver's facsimile of the Rosenbach manuscript in 1975; in 1977, Mark Schorer produced a facsimile of the *Sons and Lovers* manuscript; and Louise DeSalvo introduced the first version of *The Voyage Out* in 1980.[134] Most impressive and ambitious of all was the multivolume *James Joyce Archive*, published in 63 volumes between 1977 and 1979. Michael Groden, who directed its publication, also produced one of the first genetic studies of Joyce, *Ulysses in Progress,* in 1977. The great advantage of the James Joyce Archive facsimile was that it reunited related documents that had been geographically dispersed, but it was produced in only 250 copies and priced at $5,000.[135] Very few libraries now have a complete copy.

The collection and republication of this material made the close study of modernist composition and revision possible. It also suggested new directions for editorial work. After the publication of his controversial synoptic edition of *Ulysses* in 1984, Hans Walter Gabler admitted that it "could not have been realized without the *James Joyce Archive,*" which he called a "publisher's gift to Joyce studies."[136] The debates around the rights and wrongs of this edition—which reached the front page of the *New York Times*—also drew attention back to basic questions in an unfashionable field of literary study. Unfortunately, many of the other editions and facsimiles published during the 1970s and beyond languished on the library shelves—unable to make much impact on the field of modernism during its preoccupation with high theory. Writers themselves were more alert. As I discuss in the final chapter, Allen Ginsberg decided to self-publish a facsimile edition of "Howl" after the model of *The Waste Land;* in doing so, he made certain claims about the genetic complexity and literary value of his own work. One of the recuperative aims of *The Work of Revision* is to make fair and evenhanded use of this astonishingly rich material.

Conclusion and Methodological Implications

When I began this project, I planned to yoke together the methods of genetic criticism and social-text editing to provide an account of modernist rewriting that would attend equally to all points in the lifespan of the text—from marginal revisions on an early draft to changes made in proof and marks made on published books as pointers to a new edition. To a limited extent this has been possible, but it is not really true that the work of genetic criticism precedes textual criticism temporally, in the way that an architect's sketches come before planning permission. Christine Froula's work on genesis and error in Pound's *Cantos* illustrates one dimension of the problem; her 1984 book *To Write Paradise* devotes the first half to establishing a genetic text of the Fourth Canto, and the second to discussing the publication history of the poem, reversing the order of her 1977 dissertation. Arguments might be made for both arrangements. Composition precedes publication temporally, but readers almost always come to know a final or edited text before delving into its genesis and in this respect editing may be said to take epistemological precedence.

My view of intention is closer to that of traditional textual criticism than genetic criticism, but the outcome of my work is not intended to be editorial and I focus on early and medial intentions as much as final ones. In other words, I believe that in many cases an author's intention to revise is knowable, rational, and explicable, but I am not trying to claim any one textual state as superior *in principle* to the others; nor do I believe that early and late stages are *necessarily* connected in a teleological or even causational way. In some cases, despite having a knowable and explicable intention to produce a certain form or effect, authors' creative processes misfire and produce something else entirely that might, in turn, be a failure or serendipitously brilliant. Some of Joyce's revisions to *Ulysses* have this quality of happy coincidence, as intention is moderated by accident.

Both traditional final-intentionalist editing and genetic criticism are prone to making teleological claims about works' improvement toward a final goal, or their degeneration from a point of origin, as if all textual processes were internally motivated by a text that writes itself. It is always tempting to narrativize the revision process rather than remaining content with a series of fossilized historical intentions, but I try to avoid statements of the form: "There is something peculiar in the way his text corrupts itself: the freshness of earlier versions is dimmed by scruples and qualifications" (Hartman on Wordsworth) or "the manuscript of *The Waste Land* embodied a desire for Pound's curative arrival" (Koestenbaum on Eliot).[137] Both kinds of teleology, when pressed too hard or turned from a best-fit interpretation into a general rule, can ossify into reductive claims about literary value. I believe that discussion of *The Waste Land* drafts, for example, has been silenced rather than stimulated by the common judgment "weaker throughout than the final version" (Richard Ellmann), while the genetic tendency to "consider the final work to be a destruction and . . . valorize the point of departure" (Lejeune) leads to interpretations that ignore the final text and process of publication, and the role of bibliographic code in determining meaning.[138] In his recent study *I Do I Undo I Redo: The Textual Genesis of Modernist Selves,* Finn Fordham points to the difficult gap between Anglo-American and continental methodologies. He argues that by "keeping a tight focus on the avant-textes, genetic criticism does not often see the relevance of specific socio-economic networks around or, more vaguely, ahead of the text," and consequently that it ignores the way that expectations about eventual publication shape first draft composition.[139]

One of the important lessons of the McGann-Darnton sociological turn is that revisions are sometimes motivated from without, by censorship or collaboration, or simply by an unpredictable opportunity to republish. I try to be attentive to the role of collaborators and editors in shaping meaning; in the next chapter, for example, both Theodora Bosanquet and Percy Lubbock turn out to be important participants in the textual arrangement and publication of Henry James's final works. On the other hand, many of the modernist writers I study—beginning with the figure of James as the master—were unusually willful and controlling about the state of their texts. Their authorial behaviors and attitudes do not sit comfortably with either the geneticist's belief that an author is simply a mere conduit through which language can pass, or with the social editor's belief that authorship is inherently collaborative. Henry James asserted the "muffled majesty" of his own authorship by refusing the help and interference of others, and he became visibly angry with those who suggested that his revision process might be excessive. In 1906, for example, Edmund Gosse advised James against undertaking the massive overhauling of his earlier work for the New York Edition, comparing it to dribbling new wine into old bottles: "Henry James was conscious, I think, of the arguments which might be brought against this reckless revision, but he rejected them with violence."[140] The aesthetic of textual recklessness persists in the generation of the high modernists and becomes linked to the very nature of avant-garde experiment: its unexpectedness. Who would have encouraged Joyce to keep extending the boring, paratactic lists of "Ithaca," or suggested that Pound overhaul the Pisan *Cantos* to produce a "requiem for Italian fascism"?[141]

In some cases I have found critics who focus heavily on bibliographic coding to be insufficiently alert to the egoism and isolation of modernist authorship. More simply, they often downplay the fact of revision. George Bornstein, for example, explains quite simply that his reading of Yeats's poem "When You Are Old" emphasizes "not the minor changes in the linguistic code but the enormous impact of the bibliographic one."[142] So too, in his analysis of Keats's sonnet "On First Looking into Chapman's Homer," he makes a fascinating argument about the intersection between the left, class-conscious politics of the *Examiner* and Keats's self-professed ignorance of Greek, but then has nothing to say about the linguistic change between the two magazines and first book version. Can the bibliographic code explain why Keats swapped out line 7, "Yet I could never judge what men could mean" for "Yet did I never breathe its pure serene" before the first book publication? Perhaps the reason is purely formal, motivated by the internal sound-chamber of the rhyme. One answer, given as early as 1817 by H. Buxton Forman, was that Keats was stung by Leigh Hunt's identification of "one incorrect rhyme" in the poem: "The only disputable rhyme is that of 'mean' and 'demesne,' and that is got rid of by the revision."[143] If this is true, the change also has something to do with class-conscious anxieties about verbal correctness, but these were not created or allayed simply by available publication formats.

Both Dirk Van Hulle and Geert Lernout have called for more work within "the fairly unexplored field of comparative genetic criticism" and I try to contribute to this field. The dispersal of English and American writers' archives over multiple UK and US institutions makes it practically very difficult for Anglo-American scholars to work with more than one body of textual materials. In Paris, the Bibliothèque Nationale acts as a central focus for manuscript study, but research funding is handed out on a scientific model and has encouraged the formation at ITEM of collaborative teams, each working on a single author. One way to work toward a comparative genetic criticism is to do a certain amount of what, following Franco Moretti's coinage, we might call "distant genetic reading." Distance, he argues, is a basic condition of knowledge and the more ambitious a comparative project is, the less possible it will be to pursue it through the traditional, even reverential focus on a small number of texts.[144] Moretti is writing in response to the New Criticism's focus on a small canon, but we can equally extend his argument to the (in one sense necessary) tendency of editors to go deeper and deeper into the textual problems of a single writer or even text. In some cases, then, I rely on editors or critics of authors whom I don't study to provide detailed information about their revisionary practice (Simon Gatrell on Hardy, e.g., or Christine Cano on Proust).

In general my approach is practical rather than theoretical, and I use methods borrowed from different schools and critics as they fit the occasion. Reflecting on the difference between these approaches—at times it moves toward incommensurability—has, nonetheless, proved a salutary activity. Schools of textual study tend to arise as best-fit methods for interpreting particular bodies of evidence and they only later become formalized as theories or injunctions: "search for an author's fair copy of his work in its final state"; "all texts are collaborative"; "many texts exist within any text."[145] History has shown that it is easy to overextend these principles into rigid, general theories that fail to explain the nature of material different from those for which they were formulated. Theorists of textual process draw their theories inferentially from material evidence, but they often overlook the fact that the body of material in which they specialize—medieval manuscripts of Latin poetry, seventeenth-century printed editions of plays—is not constitutive of the textual condition in general. As McGann showed us in the 1980s, the classical critic's stemma does not work well for the era of modern manuscripts—from, roughly, the mid-eighteenth century to the mid-twentieth. In the digital period, we might ask whether the notion of revision from one discrete version to the next continues to have as much purchase as it did in the early twentieth century, when works migrated across a large number of visually and materially different forms. In the final chapter, I will return to this question and suggest that revision is a feature of print culture—of a publishing world in which texts are "fixed" at discrete moments in time.[146] In this respect, authorial revision may be considered not only a figure for modernism, but a textual process closely tied to modernity itself. In the future, we might well find ourselves revising not more, because technology enables us to do so, but much less, because it also makes revision pointless. For now, though, I would like to step back from the digital age and return to the period that I claim is the high-water mark of—perhaps already also a valediction to—the sovereign, revising author.

CHAPTER 2

Henry James's Perfectionism:
Problems of Substitution

H ENRY JAMES WAS CONSTITUTIONALLY disposed to revision and to thinking about revision. In the preface to *The Golden Bowl*, he disingenuously figured it as something simple: "To revise is to see, or to look over, again—which means in the case of a written thing neither more nor less than to re-read it"; elsewhere, it is reliving, reexposure to a past self, even an autoerotic act of self-pleasuring.[1] He revised from the very beginning of his career until the end, but his practice of postcompositional change altered while working on his final books, none of which was finished.

The argument of this chapter is that James's delicate habit of verbal substitution prefigured the modernist obsession with length-altering revision in important respects. He showed that the novel and even the short story were forms of sufficient value to merit rereading and reworking; and he revised for himself, rather than in response to others' criticisms or the demands of the market. At the same time, James's revisions for the majority of his career were also limited in scope and scale. Whenever he was given a bibliographic opportunity to revise he took it, but he did not revise without the promise of republication, and he usually contained individual revisions to a word or short phrase. One of his complaints about playwriting was that it required working with the "foul fiend Excision" close at hand;[2] unlike Pound, Stein, or Hemingway, he saw no virtue in excision as a route to effects of textual economy. He believed that critical rereading would make his texts better versions of themselves, rather than different works, and this commitment to textual "betterment" was underpinned by a more general theory of history.

During the 1890s he also began to worry at an idealistic, future-oriented teleology of textual "final form" in his descriptions of writers revising. "The Middle Years," first published in 1893, is the best example. Its writer–hero longs for but never feels he fully achieves "a form final for himself" (181), and he immediately returns to his newly published book to revise it. The postpositive position of the adjective emphasizes the negative aspects of finality and, at the end of the tale, Dencombe dies without finishing the work of revision. His practice of rewriting also frustrates his great admirer and reader, Doctor Hugh, who keeps insisting that the interpretive "second chance" Dencombe longs for is in fact the province of readers, not writers: "The second chance has been the public's—the chance to find the point of view, to pick up the pearl" (195). As in some of the other stories of writers and artists from the 1890s, the birth of the reader has to be achieved quite literally at the cost of the death of the author.

At the same time, and as if disobeying the lessons of "The Middle Years," James revised it twice after its first publication. Michael Anesko claims that "James's own career can be read as the best revision of this tale, for in preparing his texts for the New York Edition, he got what Dencombe is denied."[3] I would put it the other way round. In his representation of a fictional "passionate corrector" (181), James was able to voice anxieties about the value and purpose of postpublication revision that he did not address in his own case until the very end of his life. Can it ever be completed? Do readers care? Is it a waste of limited energies and resources? Is it an unhealthy psychological compulsion or limitation?

It was not until the 1910s, after the relative failure of the New York Edition, after switching from writing by hand to dictation to a typist as a method of composition, and as he began to question the idea that history itself had any arc of "making for or meaning," that James gave up on his passion for substitutive revision.[4] Some of the reasons for James's change of practice are highly personal, but his shifting attitudes toward textual change are also indicative of a broader shift in early-twentieth-century culture. By setting the 1893 tale "The Middle Years" against the unfinished and posthumously published memoir, *The Middle Years,* we can begin to narrate the shift from Victorian to modernist practices of rewriting. I suggest that James was unable to complete *The Middle Years,* *The Ivory Tower* (begun early in 1914), or *The Sense of the Past* (begun in 1900, and taken up again in 1914 to distract himself from the outbreak of war), because he had lost faith in one form of composition, and was unable—at the age of seventy—to develop another.[5]

"Revived (not revised!)"

The New York Edition of 1907–1909 is such an ambitious and peculiar monument to revision that James's critics have found it hard to look beyond it. James was convinced that it would secure his financial success, but its preparation quickly became onerous, "a task of the most arduous sort," smothering its author "like an enormous feather-bed" with "voluminosities of Proof" to be read and corrected.[6] Its publication was even more of a disappointment. James was to remain adamant that the new versions of his texts were an improvement over the earlier ones, and recognized a certain "reality and an honour" in the fact of the edition's existence, but he was also deeply disappointed by its commercial failure, finding it a cause of humiliation and despair.[7] Most studies, including Philip Horne's excellent *Henry James and Revision: The New York Edition,* have focused primarily on James's methods of reworking his early novels for this final, collected form. Horne notes that "after the *NYE* James did not abandon revision," but his discussion of James's practice of composition in the closing years of his life is fairly brief; he also provides no sustained discussion of the way that James revised his work in the nineteenth century.[8]

In fact, James's "re-seeing" for the New York Edition was only the—arguably perverse—extension of a habit of postpublication revision that he had been developing since the beginning of his career. Until 1897, when he employed his first typist, all of James's novels and tales were written by hand.[9] He does not seem ever to have been a great manuscript redrafter. Many of these documents were "ruthlessly burned," but the manuscript of *The Europeans*, preserved by chance in the *Atlantic Monthly*'s archives, has been published in facsimile. Leon Edel notes in his introduction that it is not a fair copy; James wrote "too much and too rapidly to allow himself this luxury," and he comments that it shows "the spontaneities of James's invention."[10] Indeed, the handwritten draft is remarkably close to the serial and then the first book edition. There is about one *currente calamo* revision per handwritten page, and most are trivial corrections or additions of small modifiers. After his work was rendered to print, it was a different story. We know that James "made many revisions" to the *Bostonians* between its 1885–1886 publication in *Century Magazine* and the 1886 three-volume Macmillan edition;[11] that he made more than twelve hundred changes to the serialized *The Old Things* (the title being one) before the first book editions of *The Spoils of Poynton*;[12] and that his first work of fiction *Watch and Ward* only appeared in book form seven years after serial publication, with the note, "It has now been minutely revised, and has received many verbal alterations."[13] Even his anxiety in the preface *to The Golden* Bowl about the very term *revision* and its "grand air" has antecedents: the preface to his 1885 *Stories Revived* explains that these stories "have been in every case minutely revised and corrected—many passages being wholly rewritten," but for the title James preferred the organic "revived" to the textual "revised." In 1885 he told Benjamin Ticknor that the forthcoming volume was to be called " 'Stories Revived' (not *revised!*)."[14]

James's postpublication revisions were mostly local substitutions, operating at the level of the word or phrase rather than the sentence. Indeed, they are so apparently insignificant taken each by each that attempts to narrate a general teleology of change have tended to flounder. At the same time, the sheer number of changes made, and the consistency of the practice, seem to require explanation. If not trying to shift his work in a particular direction, why did James revise so intently? Looking at the multiple texts of "A Passionate Pilgrim," Albert Gegenheimer notes "beneficent omission," a sharpening of "pictorial" description, increased geographic vagueness, and the disappearance of foreign terms.[15] But the logic is never general. Gegenheimer argues that James dramatically improved his description of the narrator going in to dinner, "having dreamed of lamb and spinach and a *charlotte-russe*," by replacing *"charlotte-russe"* with *"salade de saison"*—but the final term of the menu is still restaurant French. Critics have often tried to argue that James revises with a clear aim, and that he was iterating toward predefined representational goals. In an essay on *The Portrait of a Lady,* for example, Anthony Mazzella claims that "of the thousands of changes, the most significant concern characterization," and that James revised to give us a "new Isabel."[16]

This style of argument requires picking one or two revisions from many and labeling them "the most significant." In fact, the complete list of variants for *The Portrait of a Lady* suggests not so much a clear thematic goal, a reconception of the novel, as a set of new stylistic habits. Keeping the structure, dramatic action, and length of his work essentially the same, James altered the details; looking steadfastly at the work as a *type,* he was content to generate more tokens. His own description of the unchanging diegetic worlds of his fiction was "substance," and he repeatedly claimed that his aim was "a mere revision of surface and expression."[17] One analogy would be someone refilming from different angles an unchanging series of acted scenes, keeping the object of mimesis constant while altering the medium. Another would be translation, where early and late versions are understood as renderings of a (lost, ideal) source text into different into slightly different English vernaculars. In the first book edition of *The American,* for example, we come across the following description of Newman's response to Veronese's painting of the marriage-feast of Cana: "Wearied as he was he found the picture entertaining; it had an illusion for him; it satisfied his conception, which was ambitious, of what a splendid banquet should be."[18] Picking up the New York Edition is like picking up a foreign language novel rendered into English by a different, but equally competent translator, "Weary as he was, his spirit went out to the picture; it had an illusion for him; it satisfied his conception, which was strenuous, of what a splendid banquet should be."[19]

James's revising pen hovered longer over some parts of speech than others; direct speech, speech introductions, adjectives, and adverbial modifiers are labile and often modified, sometimes in predictable patterns, but more often in ways that seem almost random. For example, we find a general tendency to move toward the contracted forms in direct speech; in the opening pages of *The Portrait of a Lady*, for example, we have "you would" shortened to "you'd," "I am" to "I'm," "I have never" to "I've never."[20] Speech introductions are also often replaced, but sometimes in oscillating patterns, so in the same pages we have "declared" changed to "returned" and two pages later to "replied"; "said" to "replied," but then the apparently preferred reciprocal form "rejoined" turned back into "declared." Adjectives and adverbial modifiers also shift in these descriptions, in less predictable ways, so "Pansy answered" becomes "Pansy unreservedly answered," and "she cried with a discordant laugh" becomes "she discordantly laughed". This is part of a general fragility or impermanence in adjectives, seen in other parts of sentences, too: so "willowy" and "spare" replace "thin" in descriptions of Isabel; Warburton becomes "nice" instead of "good" to both Isabel and Ralph in an early conversation but, later, when faced with the prospect of marrying him, Isabel finds his system of life "stiff and stupid" instead of "heavy and rigid."

Unlike Pound's excisions, or Joyce's accretions, or Woolf's migrations, James's revisions before and up to the New York Edition are easy to represent on a facing-page edition. This is a consequence of the way that James went about revising. When he reread his earlier fiction for the New York Edition, he was working on texts that had already been achieved as material books and then turned *back* into proofs; and the speech bubbles with which he prompted changes more often contain one or two words than a whole sentence. The image below shows the first book edition and New York Edition texts of *The American* laid side-by-side and collated in Juxta. The white page is heavily shaded, showing variation between the two versions, and yet they also keep pace with each other: the lines connecting divergences are mostly straight, and don't fan open (the pattern produced by addition), or point to a closed V (excision). Note how many of the contractions and speech introductions are altered: "You are" becomes "You're," the longer, participle clause "said . . . throwing out his hands" becomes "threw up his hands"; and the everyday phrase "you have already made me lively" becomes the

The American 1877.txt

"Oh yes, I should like to learn French," Newman went on, with democratic confidingness. "Hang me if I should ever have thought of it! I took for granted it was impossible. But if you learned my language, why shouldn't I learn yours?" and his frank, friendly laugh drew the sting from the jest. "Only, if we are going to converse, you know, you must think of something cheerful to converse about."

"You are very good, sir; I am overcome!" said M. Nioche, throwing out his hands. "But you have cheerfulness and happiness for two!"

"Oh no," said Newman more seriously. "You must be bright and lively; that's part of the bargain."

M. Nioche bowed, with his hand on his heart. "Very well, sir; you have already made me lively."

"Come and bring me my picture then; I will pay you for it, and we will talk about that. That will be a cheerful subject!"

The American NYE.txt

"Oh yes, I should like to converse with elegance," Newman went on, giving his friends the benefit of any vagueness. "Hang me if I should ever have thought of it! I seemed to feel it too far off. But you've brought it quite near, and if you could catch on at all to our grand language - that of Shakespeare and Milton and Holy Writ - why shouldn't I catch on to yours?" His frank, friendly laugh drew the sting from the jest. "Only, if we 're going to converse, you know, you must think of something cheerful to converse about."

"You're very good, sir; I'm overcome!" And M. Nioche threw up his hands. "But you've cheerfulness and happiness for two!"

"Oh no," said Newman more seriously. "You must be bright and lively; that's part of the bargain."

M. Nioche bowed with his hand on his heart. "Very well, sir; you've struck up a tune I could almost dance to!"

"Come and bring me my picture then; I'll pay you for it, and we 'll talk about that. That will be a cheerful subject!"

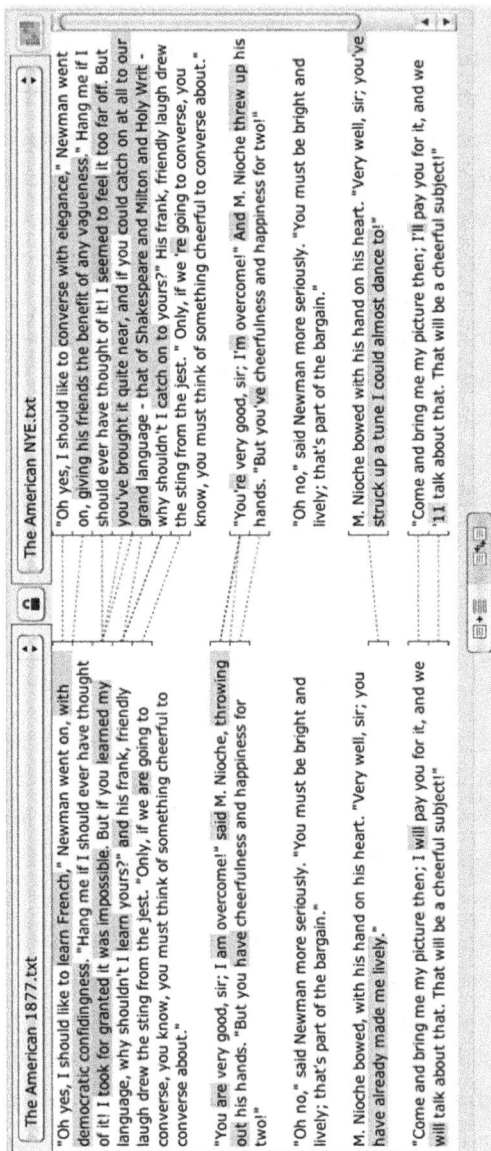

Figure 2: 1877 and 1908 versions of Henry James's novel *The American*, laid side-by-side in Juxta.

(perhaps less idiomatic) idiom, "You've struck up a tune I could dance to." At some points James becomes more abstruse or sophisticated, as when "learn French" is altered to "converse with elegance," and some revisions are introduced by necessity, to take account of what is already altered. "Democratic confidingness" might work to describe the honest simplicity of "learn French," but the narrator needs "giving to his friends the benefit of any vagueness" to explain Newman's less specific desire to "converse."

This points to a second, more subtle aspect of James's lifelong revisionary practice. As well as bearing more heavily in revising on some parts of speech, he also had a tendency to turn literal descriptions into metaphors or to extend already figurative language in a more defamiliarizing direction in later versions. Changing "replied" to "said" is one thing, but if this were the only kind of alteration James made, we would have to judge his work on revision a peculiar but unimportant compulsion. But then we find a flat description of Ralph's being reconciled to poor health by "a certain fund of indolence that he possessed," a simple banking metaphor, rendered into a bizarre tuck-box image. Now he is consoled by "a secret hoard of indifference—like a thick cake a fond old nurse might have slipped into his outfit."[21] Later in the same passage, the completely literal "the truth was that he had simply accepted the situation" becomes the memorably melodramatic "his serenity was but the array of wild flowers niched in his ruin." I do not read this, as F. O. Matthiessen did in one of the first study's of James's revisions as merely an "elaborate" and "lambent" visual image; in fact, the metaphoric picture is hard to see.[22] The same tendency is at work in an important passage in chapter 26, as Isabel meditates on Osmond and, implicitly, on marriage. Having in the 1881 text admired his ideas with a rather stale metaphor (mind: sharp blade), "There was such a fine intellectual intention in what he said, and the movement of his wit was like that of a quick-flashing blade," she comes in the New York Edition to something of baroque complexity.[23] Now, in a metaphor that seems unconsciously to perceive Osmond's grasping coldness, his ideas are "old polished knobs and heads and handles, of precious substance, that could be fitted if necessary to new walking-sticks—not switches plucked in destitution from the common tree and then too elegantly waved about."

These divagating revisions produce effects that verge on parody, often by mixing different types of figurative language. Having begun metaphorically by mapping Osmond's ideas to polished knobs, James veers away in two separate metonymies; first, through adjacency, he links the knobs to the walking-sticks that they could adorn, and then provides a temporal, causal account: these sticks are ornamental and static, not common, cheap switches plucked by laborers from trees. The effect is to emphasize Osmond's conservatism, his snobbery, his fondness for artistic arrangement, and his rigidity. If we accept this elongated Jamesian thought *as* Isabel's, then our reading of the novel as a whole needs slight readjustment. Isabel is not marrying Osmond because she thinks he is sharp, and is deluded about everything else; she is choosing to marry someone whose essential and disastrous qualities are, at least subconsciously, perceived from the beginning.

Several writers have fancied their hand at parodying the elaborate, long-winded and curiously unidiomatic prose style of the ageing James, but it proves difficult to do so accurately. Max Beerbohm turned his hand to rendering "The Death of the Lion" (1895) into James's extreme late style by a process curiously similar to James's own process of revision; in his copy of *Terminations* he wrote " 'Don't you beautifully see that I just can't?' were the words the young woman opposed to my first appeal that she after all so very well might."[24] James of course did *not* revise "The Death of the Lion" so far as this, but the awkwardness of the loosely placed adverb "beautifully" is reminiscent of the revision "too elegantly" that he did make in *The Portrait of a Lady*. W. H. Auden did an even better job in the rendition of "Caliban to the Audience" at the end of "The Sea and the Mirror": in particular, he captures the artistically hesitant James of the New York Edition prefaces, and his metaphoric weirdness. The repeated combination of words of travelling and tracking and the language of virtue, facility, and fortune creates the exquisitely cloudy sense of a profundity just out of grasp. "Such are the alternative routes, the facile glad-handed highway or the virtuous averted track, by which the human effort to make its own fortune arrives all eager at its abruptly dreadful end. I have tried—the opportunity was not to be neglected—to raise the admonitory forefinger, to ring the alarming bell, but with so little confidence of producing the right result, so certain that the open eye and attentive ear will always interpret any sight and any sound to their advantage, every rebuff as a consolation, every prohibition as a rescue."[25] In fact, he was so satisfied with this rendition that he was subsequently to name it his proudest poetic accomplishment.[26]

Passionate Correction and "The Middle Years"

James retained remarkable faith in substitutive, postpublication revision until after the disaster of the New York Edition, but he had explored some of its problems as early as 1893 in the tale "The Middle Years." Its hero is a writer who has an obsessive need to keep revising. Dencombe's problem is not that he can't bring his fiction into print, but that he can't leave it alone once it has been published. At the moment when he should be beginning a new work, he finds himself rereading, and then revising, the one "just out."

This inability to stop has led to painful temporal disjunctions in Dencombe's life. He is decidedly past his own "middle years" but, "hindered and retarded by experience," his last novel bears that title.

> The result produced in his little book was somehow a result beyond his conscious intention: it was as if he had planted his genius, had trusted his method, and they had grown up and flowered with this sweetness. If the achievement had been real, however, the process had been manful enough. What he saw so intensely to-day, what he felt as a nail driven in, was that only now, at the very last, had he come into possession. His development had been abnormally slow, almost grotesquely gradual. He had been hindered and retarded by experience, and for long periods had only groped his way. It had taken too much of his life to produce too little of his art. The art had come, but it had come after everything else. At such a rate a first existence was too short—long enough only to collect material; so that to fructify, to use the material, one must have a second age, an extension. This extension was what poor Dencombe sighed for. As he turned the last leaves of his volume he murmured: "Ah for another go!—ah for a better chance!" (172–173)

For Leon Edel, who borrowed the title for the fourth volume of his biography of James, the title suggests "the 'middle' span of an individual's life—from the late twenties to the late fifties," but Dencombe behaves like a much older man, a man who has "outlived." We learn toward the end of the tale that he has survived not only his wife, dead in childbirth, but also his son, carried off by typhoid at school and, in this respect, his family life has the same genetic disorder as his writings.[27] One possible reading is that Dencombe has in fact been so traumatized by these twin losses that he is unable to move—or write—beyond them, and so he has become arrested in, fixated on, his own middle years. I will return to revision as a response to trauma, a kind of repetition compulsion, in discussing Woolf—also doubly bereaved—in chapter 5.

A decade earlier, James had Isabel Archer turn over the same ambiguous phrase as she contemplates the balance between the past "time of her folly" and "the quick vague shadow of a long future": "Then the middle years wrapped her about again and the grey curtain of her indifference closed her in."[28] In 1914, as he began his third volume of autobiography, James reached for the title again. Given that Dencombe dies before he can revise his book to his satisfaction, the choice was an ominous one. Was James aware that, like his fictional hero, he was never going to be able to get past his "middle years," and that the project of writing a full autobiography was therefore futile? Did he suspect that this would be the last work that he began? The coincidence has been little remarked and never explained, despite the fact that James never otherwise reused a title.

From the beginning, James seems to have associated the phrase "the middle years" not with the apex of human life, its prime, but with a Yeatsian vision of the balance between life and death, the "waste of breath" of both past and future time. Isabel figures her own middle years as smothering passivity and mental indifference, while Dencombe faces a more specifically textual kind of "choosing not choosing."[29] In his 1893 tale, James depicts the revising novelist stranded like Buridan's ass between an already achieved first draft and an imagined ideal version. He described a similar tug-of-war in the preface to *The Golden Bowl*, when analyzing his own habits of revision. If the revision of texts composed in the (more or less distant) past begins with a desire to see "the buried, the latent life of a past composition vibrate, at renewal of touch," hope of reanimation has to be balanced against the fear of textual fixity, "no activ-

ity." Over time, the phrase becomes shorthand for the hopes and disappointments of revision in its broadest sense.

"The Middle Years" considers the relationship between textual and
human lifespans, and it does so by contrasting an old man and a younger
one, a writer and a reader. The novelist Dencombe is convalescing on a
Bournemouth bench when he catches sight of Doctor Hugh for the first
time. He holds his latest novel unopened on his lap, finding more enjoy-
ment in the scene around him. Doctor Hugh, by contrast, is neglecting
his party—composed of a fat and sickly Countess and her humble
companion—because he is absorbed in his own book. Punning on the
link between the bright look of the book and the pleasure Dencombe receives from seeing it being read, the *Scribner's Magazine* version of the
story prints "which, as Dencombe could perceive even at a distance, had
a cover intensely red." For the first book publication, "intensely" became the more designing "alluringly" (168).

From the beginning, the two men are presented as pairing halves.
Dencombe is bored of his own work, and finds the "lingering, credu-
lous, absorbed" young man "an object of envy to an observer from
whose connection with literature all such artlessness had faded" (168).
He is also an invalid, in need of the solicitous care that Doctor Hugh is
providing to the Countess. When Dencombe does finally open his own
book, his behavior as a reader mirrors Doctor Hugh's guileless enthusiasm; in a peculiarly satisfying way, he is absorbed by both his own text
and, metonymically, by himself, the material object of his own book.
"He read his own prose, he turned his own leaves, and had, as he sat
there with the spring sunshine on the page, an emotion peculiar and
intense. His career was over, no doubt, but it was over, after all, with
that" (171).

The two men are actually reading the *same* book—it happens to have
the same title as the tale that we are also reading—but the dance of authorial and readerly misrecognition plays out slowly. First, there is a fusing of perspectives: Dencombe realizes that Doctor Hugh has recognized another copy of *The Middle Years,* but its material form—dust
jacket, crimson cover, the markers between the closed pages—cannot
give away the intimacy of the author's relation to it. It is "alluringly red,"
but not yet alluringly *read,* and Doctor Hugh mistakes Dencombe as a

rival reviewer. Only when the covers are opened—and the text is revealed—will the true situation be apparent.

> He had taken up, as it lay on the bench, Dencombe's copy instead of his own, and his neighbour immediately guessed the reason of his start. Doctor Hugh looked grave an instant; then he said: "I see you've been altering the text!" Dencombe was a passionate corrector, a fingerer of style; the last thing he ever arrived at was a form final for himself. His ideal would have been to publish secretly, and then, on the published text, treat himself to the terrified revise, sacrificing always a first edition and beginning for posterity and even for the collectors, poor dears, with a second. This morning in "The Middle Years," his pencil had pricked a dozen lights. (181)

This is a remarkable description of the problems that postpublication revision engenders. Dencombe threatens to alienate his readers, publishers, and even the collectors of his work by restricting its dissemination. His continual revision also has a more personal cost. Although it begins as a "treat," as a private, passionate act of self-pleasuring, the pleasure quickly sours and "treat" modulates into "terrified." The first edition has to be sacrificed for the second, and perhaps the second for the third. The very notion of "a form final for himself"—which begins as a useful *terminus,* as something to iterate toward—can also be menacing, representing a state of textual perfection that will never be achieved.

Dencombe's identity as author is revealed at almost the exact midpoint of this tale about middles and endings, and it is proved not by his possession of the novel, but by his corrections to it. Doctor Hugh "looks grave an instant" and the guilty author provides a mirror: he is first "amused at the effect of the young man's reproach," then changes color "for an instant," then catches sight of Doctor Hugh's "mystified eyes" as he falls himself into an equally mystifying faint. As H. L. Jackson has shown, readerly marginalia cannot always be easily distinguished from "'authorial revisions,' 'owner's signature,' 'typographical corrections,' and so on."[30] In that case, how is Doctor Hugh able to recognize Dencombe's marks as the sign of authorial correction rather than readerly enthusiasm? The Victorian stereotype of the bad reader is very often someone who writes too *much* on a text. Thackeray, for example, envisages the unsympathetic reader of *Vanity Fair* sitting in an armchair at his club, "rather flushed with his joint of mutton and half pint of wine" as he takes out a pencil "scoring under the words 'foolish, twaddling,' etc. and adding to them his own remark of 'quite true.' "[31] Dencombe, by contrast, is a "passionate corrector, a fingerer of style." Curiously, W. B. Yeats was later to style his own practice of poetic revision in rather Jamesian terms; he told John Berryman "I never revise now . . . but in the interests of a more passionate syntax."[32]

Driven by a proto-modernist desire for concision and "rare compression," Dencombe seems also to have developed a decidedly modern strategy for producing it. The strange metaphor of "pricking lights" refers to marking up changes for future correction, but it also carries intimations of aggression: "to prick" is normally "to pierce," "to poke," "to wound," or "to hurt."[33] If reading notes supplement an author's text through forms of exegesis, digression, repetition, and appreciation, authorial marginalia—would *centralia* be the more accurate term?—remove existing text and provide substitutes. This is the kind of revision that James himself undertook when he marked up earlier versions of his novels for the New York Edition, covering the printed text with balloons, wavy lines, crossings out, and substitutions.

These "dozen lights" are, at any rate, sufficient to bring the game of misplaced identity to a close. The identity of the author is revealed—his hand is forced—by the literal marks left by the hand on the printed page. In "The Middle Years," revision is both coterminous with authorship and its remaining trace or visible sign. For Dencombe, it is also a source of deep embarrassment and shame. In this sense, there is a tight parallel between the revision and the characters' reaction to it—the blush. If revision is both cause, effect, and sign of writing, so blushing can be understood as both the cause, effect, and sign of embarrassment. For Darwin, writing twenty years before James, "blushing is the most peculiar and most human of all expressions," partly because its origins are psychosomatic; it is not something that can be willed or stimulated by physical means.[34] In fact, "blushing is not only involuntary; but the wish to restrain it, by leading to self-attention, actually increases the tendency." According to this account, blushing is closely associated with mental confusion and also with states of "shyness, shame, and modesty; the essential element in all being self-attention."[35]

The tension between authorial and readerly wants, or between thrift and proliferation, is not resolved at the end of the tale. Critics such as Julie Rivkin and John Carlos Rowe, who have read the tale as an essentially benign tale of homoerotic wish-fulfillment, assume that both men have their desires gratified. Rivkin argues: "As a supplement, Doctor Hugh completes Dencombe's deficiency, ministering to both his bodily life and his text . . . Not surprisingly, this exchange is able to provide for Dencombe's *The Middle Years* what it does for James's 'The Middle Years'—closure, an end to the interminable need to revise."[36] I do not find the same closural relief at the ending of the tale. To begin with, it ends tragically; Dencombe hopes that Doctor Hugh will cure him, but medical attention seems to be the last thing on the doctor's mind. When he returns from London, it is to prove himself as a writer in his own right, "He had returned because he was anxious and for the pleasure of flourishing the great review of 'The Middle Years.' Here at least was something adequate" (194). He explains that he has sacrificed the possibility of a large inheritance for the promise of art: "I chose to accept, whatever they might be, the consequences of my infatuation . . . A fortune be hanged!" It is at this point that Dencombe makes his famous and impassioned speech, "Our doubt is our passion and our passion is our task . . ." to which Doctor Hugh briefly responds.

"The Middle Years" also evades closure at a formal level, as the rhetorical mastery of Dencombe's famous speech cedes to readerly doubt. "Dencombe lay taking this in; then he gathered strength to speak once more. "A second chance—*that's* the delusion. There never was to be but one. We work in the dark—we do what we can—we give what we have. Our doubt is our passion and our passion is our task. The rest is the madness of art" (197). The riddling beauty of these last words lies in their rhetorical control. The three five-syllable phrases have the same metrical shape (all scanned as an iamb and an anapaest), and this enforces the anaphoric rise of the "Wes," working rather like Churchill's even more rhetorical ascension, "We shall not flag or fail. . . . We shall never surrender." And then, in the next sentence, we find doubt transformed into passion—both suffering and delight—and passion retransformed chiastically into "our task," before, finally, the sound echo of "task" and the concluding "art." In Philip Roth's novel *The Ghost Writer,* the Dencombe-like writer Lonoff has typed these important and compelling words out on a card in his study and pinned it to the wall as a kind of motto.[37] Joyce Carol Oates reads the final words as a "moment of epiphany" that "would seem, in the surpassing beauty of its language, to have generated the diaphanous fiction that surrounds it."[38]

Doctor Hugh does not respond with either aesthetic admiration or the mute respect that last words ought to compel, and he undermines the triumph of Dencombe's speech with "subtle," even sophistical argument.

> "If you've doubted, if you've despaired, you've always 'done' it," his visitor subtly argued.
>
> "We've done something or other," Dencombe conceded.
>
> "Something or other is everything. It's the feasible. It's *you.*" (198)

By choosing to reply to Dencombe, rather than allowing the author to have his last words, Doctor Hugh is continuing a pattern of behavior evident from the beginning of the tale. His unwillingness to let Dencombe's speech stand is, specifically, a form of readerly arrogation that was evident in his review of *The Middle Years*. At one level, this "great review" is laudatory, but it is also an attempt to substitute readerly for authorial determination of meaning. Not only an "acclamation," it is also "a critical attempt to place the author in the niche he had fairly won"—that is, to control, judge, and determine Dencombe's reputation from an alternative perspective. Dencombe, obsessed with the fantasy of retaining control over his published texts, is less pleased with this review than Doctor Hugh expects: he "accepted and submitted; he made neither objection nor inquiry, for old complications had returned and he had had two atrocious days" (194).

As his health continues to deteriorate, the author begins to give up the only hope that we have seen him entertain—that of the extension or second chance. Doctor Hugh's response is unexpected and hardly professional, directing attention to the survival of Dencombe's literary corpus rather than the imminent demise of his physical body. "At this the young man stared; then he exclaimed: 'Why, it has come to pass—it has come to pass! The second chance has been the public's—the chance to find the point of view, to pick up the pearl!'" (197) Dencombe, addicted until the end to the hope of revisionary completion, believes that the real value of his work resides in what he has not yet done: "the pearl is the unwritten—the pearl is the unalloyed, the *rest,* the lost." By this model, literary glory is not something that can be bequeathed and inherited—it is only a metaphysical ideal, a *terminus ad quem.* For Doctor Hugh, however, the pearl is quite clearly a material object and, like the narrator of *The Aspern Papers,* he is willing to sacrifice a significant amount of money to "pick it up." This is a tremendously competitive and fraught depiction of interchange between reader and writer. As in some of the other "stories of writers and artists" from the 1890s, first gathered as a group in 1944 by F. O. Matthiessen, the birth of the reader has to be achieved quite literally at the cost of the death of the author.

The final dialogue of the tale does not remove the "interminable need to revise"; it merely frustrates Dencombe's opportunity to do so, illustrating that it will always be impossible to complete an "interminable" process within the quickly terminated span of human life. It is an argument against revision on practical grounds and also an illustration of the antagonistic relationship between authorial revision and textual dissemination or, to put it more boldly, between reading and writing. In the preface to the New York Edition of *The Golden Bowl,* James would imply that revision was a simpler task than it at first seemed: "To revise is to see, or to look over, again—which means in the case of a written thing neither more nor less than to re-read it."[39] If his difficulty in preparing that edition suggests that the definition is inadequate, the ending of "The Middle Years" shows precisely how it is disingenuous. Rereading takes as its premise a fixed, stable text, capable of unfixed and altering interpretations, but rewriting destabilizes and unfixes a text. Postpublication revision promises to allow the writer to repossess a text once it has begun circulating in the public sphere, and, therefore, to "re-fix" meaning at the point of origins. By becoming his own best (and only) reader, Dencombe short-circuits normal models of literary communication.[40] One might describe this as an extreme example of authorial "thrift," preventing the "proliferation of meaning" by rerouting meaning back to the author.[41] At the same time, Dencombe's desire to substitute authorial revision for new readings leads to decreased rather than increased textual stability. His "ideal" is squarely oriented toward future generations, "sacrificing always a first edition and beginning for posterity and even for the collectors, poor dears, with a second." But working toward this ideal in fact means generating more and more versions, each with an increasingly weak claim to be the *thing itself.* This is a very old problem in Idealism. In the dialogue named after him, Plato has Parmenides put forward an objection to the theory of Forms that exploits what Gregory Vlastos has called "the prize product of Greek logical virtuosity"—the infinite regress.[42] The only way to bridge the gap between the imperfect achieved text and the "pearl" or ideal is to produce a third version, and that engenders a fourth, and so on.

Instead of one, possibly imperfect, tale called "The Middle Years," James ended up with three, and a long list of textual variants. The title made its first outing in *Scribner's Magazine* in 1893, where the tale ran to eleven pages, preceded by Thomas Hardy's short story "The Fiddler of the Reels," and followed by a saccharine etching of domestic life. It was republished in *Terminations* in 1895, a volume whose own title subtly inflects our sense of the interplay between middle and ending, middle age and old age. Finally it appeared in the fifteenth volume of the New York Edition in 1909. In each of these cases, James's pencil seems to have pricked rather more than "a dozen" lights in rereading: there are about three textual variations per page between the 1893 and 1909 texts. In this sense, "The Middle Years" can be understood to refer to a *surplus* of authorial intentions and texts rather than a single, chronologically fixed, textual act. Accordingly, at a genetic level, the title is not so much proof of "an end to the interminable need to revise" as of the very real possibility of continuing to do so.

As if worrying at the tension between writerly and readerly determinations of meaning, many of James's own revisions to the tale are focused on elaborating the relationship between Dencombe and Doctor Hugh. In the first magazine publication, for example, Dencombe's dying words had been delivered in response to an attempt at encouragement from the "bristling young doctor":

> "You're a great success!" said Doctor Hugh, putting into his voice the ring of all young cheer. (1893)[43]

In *Terminations,* James chose a phrase that exaggerates the intense, perhaps even homoerotic, admiration marking the bond between dying author and young reader.

> "You're a great success!" said Doctor Hugh, putting into his young
> voice the ring of a marriage-bell. (1895, 197)

For Joyce Carol Oates, this "deliberate, pointed" choice of simile is a revelation of the story's buried theme—"this strange marriage of artist and 'greatest admirer'" (262). She does not comment on the fact that the phrase was added only after revision. And yet, there is something doubly pointed about the way that the text's genetic history quarrels with its thematic content, laying bare its "buried theme" only after a revisionary hand has passed over it. Is there not something too deliberate, even insincere, about the affections that Doctor Hugh "puts" into his voice? Another change made for the New York Edition also casts this "strange marriage" in a dark light. Originally, Dencombe had been depressed by Doctor Hugh's thorough, but not purposeful, inability to understand the meaning of his novel:

> The baffled celebrity wondered then who in the world *would* guess
> it: he was amused once more at the thoroughness with which an in-
> tention could be missed. (1893)

In 1895, "the thoroughness" became "the fine, full way" (189). Finally, by the New York Edition the reader's failure to grasp authorial meaning has become a matter of much more perverse misprision.

> He was amused once more at the diffused massive weight that could
> be thrown into the missing of an intention. (1909)[44]

Dencombe's sense of his own achievement as a writer is also diminished in the second version of the tale. Originally he replied to Doctor Hugh's "subtle argument" by saying:

> "We've done *something,*" Dencombe conceded.
>   "*Something* is all. It's the feasible. It's *you!*" (1893)

This concession is already uncertain—Dencombe does not believe that he had done what he could, but only, as the dictionary has it, "some unspecified or indeterminate thing."[45] Two years later, this sense of indeterminacy was greatly increased by James's revision:

> "We've done something or other," Dencombe conceded.
> "Something or other is everything. It's the feasible. It's *you!*"

The addition of "other" provides a final example of this tale's propensity to doubling. Like Miles Standish, in Longfellow's best-selling poem of the 1850s, Dencombe has achieved only an entirely unnamable "something-or-other."

> So he won the day, the battle of something-or-other.
> That's what I always say; if you wish a thing to be well done,
> You must do it yourself, you must not leave it to others![46]

The addition of the second indefinite adjective might also be read as an alternative allegory for the bewildering and sometimes intensifying second chances that revision can provide: to revise something is to make it more indeterminate, harder to name, more *other*.

Other revisions have less determinate results, and seem, in fact, to be more of a case of "revision for its own sake," a self-enabling production of textual difference. Here, as elsewhere, James is fond of making revisions that aurally recall the original word choice: this process includes the replacement of words by homophones, and by words that differ slightly in sound but have completely different meanings. This is normally a strategy of substitution more closely associated with poetry than prose, and perhaps with metaphor than metonymy. For example, Dencombe's joy at rereading his own work had originally been described as a type of re-*living*.

> He lived once more into his story and was drawn down, as by a siren's hand, to where, in the dim underworld of fiction, great silent subjects loom. (1893)

In the 1895 text, James replaced "great" by an adjective with a similar central vowel sound—"strange"—thereby increasing the uncanny sibilance of the final phrase, and mimetically creating some of the very "strangeness" that the word introduces. In the New York Edition, he made one further change to the sentence, replacing "lived" with its orthographic minimal pair, "dived." Whether or not the final version is an improvement, it is noticeable that the revision can be regarded as *already* implicit in the previous version: it seems to be produced both by the suggestion of minimal difference, and by the elaborate metaphor of a suboceanic fictional world that the 1895 text had contained. A similar, and rather poignant, example is provided a few sentences later as Dencombe reviews his own talent, emphasizing that "only now, at the very last, had he come into possession." The two first versions tell us that "If the achievement had been real, however, the process had been manful enough." Perhaps overcome by the arduous task of preparing the New York Edition itself, James edited this sentence in 1909 to read, "If the achievement had been real, however, the process had been painful enough."

If "The Middle Years" warns that postpublication revision frustrates readers and becomes futile (leading potentially to infinite regress), why did James not take its lessons more seriously? One early review of the New York Edition cites a reader crying, "It's a falsification of history!" and the process troubled even James's friends and supporters. In a posthumous essay, Edmund Gosse recalls making a criticism of this "reckless revision" directly and receiving a violent response. His unease is subtly underpinned by a romantic commitment to organic form: note how metaphors of natural growth and development are set up against ones drawn from commercial practice.

> I thought—I dare say I was quite mistaken—that the whole perspective of Henry James's work, the evidence of his development and evolution, his historical growth, were confused and belied by this wholesale tampering with the original text. Accordingly, I exclaimed against such dribbling of new wine into old bottles. This was after dinner, as we sat alone in the garden-room. All that Henry James—though I confess, with a darkened countenance—said at the time was "The only alternative would have been to put the vile thing"—that is to say the graceful tale of Roderick Hudson—"behind the fire and have done with it!" [47]

James's first response might have been dismissal, but the criticism obviously troubled him. The next morning, Gosse continues, he found James "somber and taciturn" at the breakfast table, complaining of a sleepless night: " 'Slept!' he answered with dreary emphasis. Was I likely to sleep when my brain was tortured with all the cruel—and—to put it plainly to you—monstrous insinuations which you had brought forward against my proper, my necessary, my absolutely inevitable corrections of the disgraceful and disreputable style of *Roderick Hudson*?" Nine years later, James was forced to admit that the objection had some force; in an awkward letter, he described to Gosse how poorly the edition had sold. Rather than serving as a complete set of his collected works, it was a "poor old rather truncated edition, in fact entirely frustrated one," illustrating the impossibility of gathering a life's work up into a single monument.[48] With weary self-depreciation, he claimed that his attempt at completeness had come to have "the grotesque likeness for me of a sort of miniature Ozymandias of Egypt ('look on my *works*, ye mighty, and despair!')."[49] Although James continued to insist that his revision of his earlier fiction had solved certain artistic problems "very effectively," and that it was "so intimately and interestingly revised" he was frustrated by the lack of attention paid to the new versions of his work. His readership, as if composed of Doctor Hughs, turned out to prefer new performances to renovations.

Revision After the New York Edition

Most of the other writers that I discuss in this book—Eliot, Joyce, Woolf—revised much more heavily than James at the prepublication stage, and much less (if at all) after book publication had been achieved. We might wonder: why did James not revise his fiction from the 1870s–1890s more carefully *before* first publication? The answer to this is primarily technological. James always preferred to make corrections and alterations to his work rendered in the "fierce legibility of type" rather than his own handwriting. Before 1897, this was possible only at a late stage in the publication process or even after a first printing. But once he began dictating to a typist, he could compose in the mornings and read over and revise the typescript in the afternoons. Instead of having to

wait for months or even years to begin the process of "passionate correction," it could take place almost immediately, and before the work as a
whole was complete. In a letter from 1902, he claimed that the very "value
of that process [dictation]" lay in "its help to do over and over, for which
it is extremely adapted."[50] Critics have wondered how James's dramatic,
late shift of compositional method changed his style, sometimes attributing the tortuous elaboration of the "late late style" to its orality. For Leon
Edel, dictation led to "the ultimate perfection of his verbal music";[51]
more recently, Sarah Campbell has explored the peculiarities of James's
speech, suggesting that his "intricate, astonishing, and fluent sentences"
were built upon a stutter.[52] I would suggest that the stylistic change
might also be a product of a different engagement with the work as
script.

James delighted in his new method of composition, and he made full
use of it. But because he was now revising at a much earlier stage, it
started taking him longer to finish first versions. In 1900, he had to delay
sending off the last bit of copy of *The Sacred Fount* for "reproduction
with embodied new inspired last touches" because he was still trying to
"finish & super-finish it."[53] Two and a half months after his deadline
for *The Golden Bowl* had passed, James was writing to his brother William, "I have been pressing hard toward the finish of a long book, still
unfinished . . . which I am doing with such perfection that every inch is
done over and over; which makes it come expensive in the matter of
time."[54] In fact, the belief that "perfection"—true "finish"—was now
within his grasp seems to have encouraged him to return to his earlier
works, and give them the same treatment. The possibility of making *The
Golden Bowl* perfect from its first printing also opened up the option of
remaking all of his earlier books in the image of *The Golden Bowl*. Once
he began work on the New York Edition, he soon found that "the revision, the re-manipulation, as I may call it, of *The American* and *Roderick
Hudson* is demanding of me, I find, extreme (and very interesting) deliberation."[55] James handled the wide-margined pages of his earlier novels,
which his agent, James B. Pinker had pasted up for him from published
versions, in much the same way that he treated the typescripts that Bosanquet produced each day. By subjecting his earlier work to a process of
revisionary scrutiny that had not been available earlier in his career, he

was able to bring the earlier work closer to the later novels: the revised version of *The American* was, he boasted, "in as perfect form as that of the Golden Bowl."[56] *The Golden Bowl* itself required very little amendment for the New York Edition, as James notes in his preface. This is not only because it was more recent, but because it had already been heavily revised. In the first chapter of *The Golden Bowl,* James's substantive revisions account for only 0.1 percent of the text; in the case of *The American,* first published some thirty years earlier, more than 6 percent of the original text was revised.[57] Most of the changes made to *The Golden Bowl* are changes to accidentals, like "anyone" to "any one" or "connection" to "connexion."

One way to define James's late style—the style supremely manifest in *Wings of the Dove* and *The Golden Bowl,* and flickeringly present in revised versions of the earlier novels—is to focus not on its oral (rather than written) qualities but its higher genetic complexity (its greater revisedness). Its propensity to metaphoric divagation, in particular, seems to be directly linked to the process of thinking for a second time. These metaphors often come not in the initial fervour of composition but later, on rereading, and are added in speech bubbles on either fresh, unpublished typescript *or* on wide-margined proof.

When he began using a typist in 1897, James became a more passionate drafter and prewriter. After the failure of the New York Edition in 1909, he continued to dictate and revise dictation, but he also largely gave up on postpublication revision. Instead of relying primarily on stylistic substitution while keeping the "content" fixed, he became a more experimental, additive, accretive writer. The composition of his last works—*The Outcry* (extended from an unperformed and unpublished play), *The Sense of the Past, The Ivory Tower,* and three volumes of autobiography—was tortuous in a new way.[58] No longer attempting to confine his work within conventional bibliographic forms and lengths, James started adding more and more, working like younger writers of the 1910s. Some of his bizarre habits of extension might even be called Joycean.

Compression had always been a problem. Dencombe may aim for a "rare compression" in his own writing, but James explained in the preface to the sixteenth volume of the New York Edition that in writing "The Middle Years," he had struggled to an exceptional degree to keep "compression rich," and that this was necessitated by *Scribner's* strictly prescribed word limit. The sinuous sentence enacts the maddened frustration it describes: "To get it right was to squeeze my subject into the five or six thousand words I had been invited to make it consist of—it consists, in fact, should the curious care to know, of some 5500—and I scarce perhaps recall another case, with the exception I shall presently name, in which my struggle to keep compression rich, if not, better still, to keep accretions compressed, betrayed for me such community with the anxious effort of some warden of the insane engaged at a critical moment in making fast a victim's straitjacket" (v). A tendency to add becomes rendered here not as parataxis ("and . . . and . . . and . . .") but as syntactic subordination, so that each additional breath ("with the exception . . . ," "if not, better still . . .") not only lengthens but convolutes the sentence.

This was James's natural manner of speech, his linguistic habitus, brilliantly parodied by Virginia Woolf in another sentence of roiling nested clauses. "My dear Virginia, they tell me—they tell me—they tell me— that you—as indeed being your fathers daughter nay your grandfathers grandchild—the descendant I may say of a century—of a century—of quill pens and ink—ink—ink pots, yes, yes, yes, they tell me—ahm m m—that you, that you, that you *write* in short."[59] In the 1910s, the combination of composing through dictation and no longer attempting to place work within publishers' tight word limits allowed James to give addition full rein. Theodora Bosanquet notes in her study *Henry James at Work* that "he was well aware that the manual labour of writing was his best aid to a desired brevity."[60] During the period that she worked for him, James wrote his plays—the most necessarily "compressed" genre—by hand. He allowed himself "a little more freedom" with short stories, "dictating them from his written draft and expanding them as he went to an extent which inevitably defeated his original purpose." Novels and autobiography were entirely dictated, and dictation led to loosely packed prose.

James's new accretive style of composition is illustrated by three of his final productions: the unpublished and unfinished novels *The Sense of the Past* and *The Ivory Tower*, which were produced alongside an extensive process of ruminative prewriting; the successful novel *The Outcry*, which was adapted from a play script by retaining the dialogue and padding it out with another thirty thousand words of pure description; and the unfinished autobiography *The Middle Years,* which was both a "spillover" from an autobiographical project that refused to be contained in a single volume, and itself extended through typescript accretion. All of these works show a refusal to be bound, to be "squeezed in."

When James had turned *The American* into a play in 1890, he followed his earlier habit of privileging content over form, of seeing an action again while allowing its expression to alter. When he turned *The Outcry* into a novel in 1911, he did the opposite: showing a marked attachment to his earlier words, he kept the dialogue almost perfectly intact (occasionally restoring lines that had been cut from the play typescript after consultation with the producer), and gave imaginative expression to the setting, and the characters' appearances and tones of voice. The play of *The Outcry,* which James wrote in 1909, was commissioned by Charles Forhman's repertory company but never performed. Its subject was the public outcry over the Duke of Norfolk's plan to sell a painting that he owned, but which was housed in the National Gallery. When James fictionalized it, moving from a more compressed to a looser form, he called for an early version of typescript (before the producer's extensive cuts had been made) and then redictated it with long expository paragraphs of descriptive addition. So a curt stage direction to the butler, "*(Exit BANKS to the left.),*" became "With which, his duty majestically performed, he retired to the quarter—that of the main access to the spacious centre of the house—from which he had ushered the visitor." The second line spoken in the play, after the butler has ushered two characters in, is Lord John's greeting "I luckily find *you* at least, Lady Sandgate—they tell me Theign's off somewhere." In the novel, James interposed several paragraphs between the first and second line of dialogue, describing the "ample apertures" and "stately stone outworks" of the house, Lady Sandgate's modernity and intelligence ("almost clever enough to be vulgar") and Lord John's manner of speech. At other points the novel considers the action from multiple perspectives and a longer temporal horizon:

Lord John: I luckily find *you* at least, Lady Sandgate—they	Lord John addressed her as with a significant manner that he

tell me Theign's off somewhere.	might have had—that of a lack of need, or even of interest, for any explanation about herself: it would have been clear that he was apt to discriminate with sharpness among possible claims on his attention. "I luckily find *you* at least, Lady Sandgate—they tell me Theign's off somewhere."
Lady Sandgate: Only in the Park . . .	She replied as with the general habit, on her side, of bland reassurance; it mostly had easier consequences—for herself—than the perhaps more showy creation of alarm. "Only off in the park . . ."

The Outcry turned out to be a modest best seller, restoring James's income after the disaster of the revised New York Edition. James left his other three late prose works, *The Sense of the Past, The Ivory Tower,* and *The Middle Years,* unfinished at his death. They were published posthumously in 1917 by his executor, Percy Lubbock.

Lubbock's prefaces, and some of his editorial decisions, implied that all three works had been left unfinished by accident, and that James would have completed them if he had lived longer. In fact, James chose to abandon each of his final three works in 1914, more than two years before his death. Why did he abandon each in turn? One possibility is that as his method of composition and revision changed, and as prewriting and tentative dictation replaced the correction of already published work, James lost the ability to "finish." Until the mid-1890s, when James found that periodical publication had become "practically closed," he would usually commit to and begin publication before getting to the last page of a novel, and so was effectively compelled to get to the last page.[61] Once these constraints were removed, the difficulty of "finish" in the genetic sense (the last item in a series) became the more literal problem of finishing (completing).

James began *The Ivory Tower* in the summer of 1914, laid it aside two days after the outbreak of war to begin the third volume of his autobiography, and then laid *The Middle Years* aside in turn in December without reaching a narrative or thematic end to return to *The Sense of the Past*. This novel had already been laid aside in 1900 after "intrinsic difficulties" had mastered its author, and it again proved impossible to complete.[62] In his editions of the two novels, Lubbock made up for the missing pages—the incompletion—by printing multiple "pages of preliminary notes" that James had dictated as preparatory material. He implies that this was the writer's usual practice, but in these remarkably digressive, hesitant, troubled notes, I think we can discern some of the reasons why James's method of "finishing" had started to fail. Lubbock wrote, "It was Henry James's constant practice, before beginning a novel, to test and explore, in a written or dictated sketch of this kind, the possibilities of the idea which he had in mind. Such a sketch was in no way a first draft of the novel . . . The notes, having served their purpose, would not be referred to again, and were invariably destroyed when the book was finished."[63] The smoothness of tone here betrays the very real editorial *choices* that have been made. If the notes were invariably destroyed when a book was finished, and if Lubbock's aim was to complete a task that James did not live to see done, then why publish them?

Percy Lubbock justified printing these peculiar fragments by reference back to James's tale from the 1890s, "The Death of the Lion": "If justification were needed for the decision to publish this 'overflow' it might be found in Paraday's last injunction to his friend: 'Print it as it stands—beautifully.'" Today Lubbock is commonly regarded as a sensitive disciple of James, whose own *Craft of Fiction* mediated between the delicate complexity of James's theory of the novel and the demands of a growing mass market for literary criticism.[64] And yet, this was a rather unhappy choice of quotation, an example of the "diffused massive weight that could be thrown into the missing of an intention." For in the earlier tale, Paraday's command is never fulfilled; the "inédit" has been lost in mysterious circumstances, perhaps "wantonly destroyed," perhaps through "some hazard of a blind hand."[65] Although the exact events remain mysterious, there is a strong suspicion that editorial negligence might have played a part—perhaps even that the editor has lost the text himself.

Where the preface to *The Golden Bowl* had emphasized the necessity of "seeing again," implying that true textual polish was achieved through a derivative process of second sight, the dictated sketches for James's final novels dwell frequently on the problem of seeing in the first place. Looking through a glass darkly, the anxious author keeps trying to discern something shadowy or hidden. One of the most common phrases is "I seem to see": in *The Sense of the Past*, James tells us that "The more I get into my drama itself the more magnificent, upon my word, I seem to see it and feel it"; in the notes to *The Ivory Tower*, the phrase occurs eleven times as, for example, when he "seems to see it [the action] as going to the end" in New York, before wondering if he shouldn't after all "manage to treat myself to some happy and helpful mise-en-scéne or exploitation of my memory of (say) California."[66] In their indirection and sense of compositional difficulty, these notes bear little resemblance to his earlier habit of fleshing out the "germ" of a story. They are primarily a meditation on the problems of "completeness" and the dangers of "splendid economy." "Of course I can but reflect that to bring this splendid economy off it must have been practiced up *to* VII with the most intense and immense art: the scheme I have already sketched for I and II leaving me therewith but III, IV, V, and VI to arrive at the completeness of preparation for VII, which carries in its bosom the completeness of preparation for VIII—this last, by a like grand law, carrying in *its* pocket the completeness of preparation for IX and X. But why not? Who's afraid?"[67]

Ezra Pound, already deeply committed to the aesthetic of efficiency, picked this out in his essay "The Notes to 'The Ivory Tower,'" noticing, "we see the author . . . most anxious to get all the sections fitted in with the greatest economy, a sort of crux of his excitement and anxiety."[68] It seems as if in *spirit* James's late, diffuse musings were aesthetically confluent with the ambitions of a younger generation of writers. Certainly— and this is a bitter irony in James's career—his last, posthumously published books were much more commercially successful than the New York Edition had been. They were also well reviewed. The publishers admitted in the advertisements that they were unfinished, but then went on to promote them by reference to their genetic interest: "The novels are unfinished, but printed with each is a sketch outlining the complete story. These sketches are of unique literary interest, since they disclose the methods of work of one of the greatest masters of his craft."[69] The two novels sold well enough for Collins to issue a reprinted edition two months after the first edition. One reason may be that they *look* modern by the standards of 1917, and they wear their genetic problems openly: the books are slender and self-consciously provisional, not a single block of text, but a multilayered mix of preface, text, and notes.

The Houghton Typescript of *The Middle Years*

If "The Middle Years" had thematized revision in its most literal sense, the autobiographical fragment *The Middle Years* is more generally about the problem of "seeing again." As the fifth chapter will make clearer, there is an intrinsic link between autobiography as an aspectual mode and re-vision as a writing process; as Georges Gusdorf has put it, autobiography begins as a second reading of life experience, a "final chance to win back what has been lost."[70] Percy Lubbock's preface to his 1917 edition states that the chapters begun in 1914 "were laid aside for other work toward the end of the year and were not revised by the author."[71] The-odora Bosanquet's note on the preserved Houghton typescript con-curs: "The original dictated typescript was not revised by Mr. Henry James except in so far as it was his usual habit to revise as he went along."[72] This sentence is itself rather Jamesian in its indirection. The typescript is revised in the normal sense of having been read over and altered after dictation; it is a revised draft, but not a finished or super-finished one.

Besides the base layer of type, we can see corrections of three kinds: typed cancellations and additions of text, including XXX over a mistaken word or phrase; black pen corrections made in James's own distinctively bad hand; and a mixture of red ink and pencil markings, apparently in a different hand. The typed cancellations and corrections were presum-ably made by Theodora Bosanquet on the spot, either because she had made a typing mistake or because James immediately corrected himself after dictating to her. The manuscript corrections were made at some later point, not quite as James "went along," but within a few hours, days, or weeks of the original composition. The base layer of typescript, for example, contains the phrase "c'est le temps qui fait le chanson" as a way of invoking the "sincerity" of Victorian London compared to the skepticism of the modern city. Realizing that she had misheard or mistyped, Theodora Bosanquet crossed out "temps" and replaced it with "ton." Later "la," the correctly gendered form of the article, was written above "le." Lubbock's edition prints the end stage of these changes, "c'est la ton qui fait la chanson," or "it's the tone that makes the music."

When Lubbock prepared the typescript for publication he marked it up. Red crayon marks are used to indicate the "marking of the paragraphs"—which Lubbock's preface admits he undertook—and sometimes they make more substantive corrections. James claimed to have been in his "twenty fifth year" when he arrived in England, but Lubbock altered this on both the typescript and in the printed text to the factually correct "twenty-sixth." Strangely, *Scribner's Magazine* published an excerpted version in October and November 1917 without this correction and with different paragraphing. Both the Collins and Scribner's book versions contain Lubbock's changes.

The most hermeneutically significant decision that Lubbock made was to end *The Middle Years* with an ellipsis. James's last mark was a period. The final page of the typescript describes a visit to Lady Waterford's house in Northumberland. As so often in this text, James seems less interested in precise recall of particulars than in succumbing to what he variously terms the "flush," "the waiting array," or the "bristle" of old memories; as Virginia Woolf's review noted, the book is a "superb act of thanksgiving" for a vanished aristocratic world.[73] After telling us that she and her kind "had indeed had their innings," he remembers that "later on a few days spent at a house in Northumberland did wonders to round off my view; the place . . . fairly bristled, it might be said, with coloured designs from her brush" (599).[74] Lubbock prints instead, "with coloured designs from her brush . . ." as if to suggest a dying hand trailing across the page. The ellipsis implies that James would have finished the book if he had lived longer, and it provides a subtle justification for Lubbock's decision to publish it.

Lubbock's edition suggests that James had, but was unable to execute, a final intention for *The Middle Years*. I would suggest that the problems of completion were more structural than circumstantial. First, like many autobiographers, James has problems marking time, moving forward. As the first sentence notes, this record is "meandering," and diegetic time moves so slowly that by the third volume of autobiography James has only just got to his late twenties. Second, the process of revision adds a further layer of complexity and digression. Instead of making things clearer, James's postcompositional changes tend to darken already muddy waters. Simple vocabulary items are replaced with the complex, and very often a surprising periphrasis replaces some initially straightforward piece of syntax.

The general tendency of James's own revisions is toward addition and semantic complexity; Bosanquet's and Lubbock's markings fortify clarity and structural integrity. The process of reminiscence had originally been described as "a quantity that divided itself somehow into the double line of its elements"; James then crossed out "line" by hand and wrote the much more unusual "muster" above it (550). "A perfect bower" becomes "the most embowered retreat"; "the evening" is changed to "the revelational evening"; "horrible" becomes "monstrous"; "implication," "intimation"; even "all wonderings" cannot be left alone, ending up as the jangling "all worryings and wonderings." Sometimes, as earlier in his career, changes appear to be motivated by sound rather than sense, although this could also be a consequence of Bosanquet's aural mishearings. In the first draft, Mrs. Greville "knew no law but that of innocent and exquisite adoration"; in the corrected version, "adoration" is changed to the rather different "aberration." Tennyson, who disappointed James by not being as "pale and penetrating" as his young admirer had hoped, was originally found to be simply not himself: "These were considerations of which I recall the pressure, at the same time that I fear I have no account of them to give after they have fairly faced the full demonstration that Tennyson was not Tennysonian" (587). But inserted above the original text is a correction in type. James seems immediately to have decided that "full demonstration" required another qualifying adjective, and picked the following: "the full demonstrous demonstration that Tennyson was not Tennysonian."

the sense of that quality in the texture of his verse, which had ap-

pealed all along by its most inward principle to one's taste, and had

by the same stroke shown with what a force of lyric energy and sin-

cerity the kind of beauty so engaged for could be associated. Was it

that I had preconceived him in that light as pale and penetrating, as

emphasising
in every aspect the fact that he was fastidious ? was it that I had

supposed him more fastidious than really could have been — at the

best for that effect ? was it that the grace of the man couldn't,

by my measure, but march somehow with the grace of the poet, given

a perfection of this grace ? was it in fine that style of a par-

ticular kind, when so highly developed, seemed logically to leave

no room for other quite contradictious kinds ? These were consider-

ations of which I recall the pressure, at the same time that I fear

I have no account of them to give after they have fairly faced the

the monstrous
full, demonstration that Tennyson was not Tennysonian. The desperate

sequel to that was that he thereby changed one's own state too, one's

beguiled, one's aesthetic; for what could this strange apprehension

do but reduce the Tennysonian amount altogether ? It dried up, to

Figures 3a and 3b: Houghton typescript of *The Middle Years*.

in Carlton House Terrace,
an exhibition of Lady Waterford's paintings held, under the roof of

a friend of the artist,   and, as it enriched the hour also to be able

to feel, a friend, one of the most generously gracious, of my own;

during which the reflection that "they" had indeed had their innings,

and were still splendidly using for the purpose the very fag-end of

the waning time, mixed itself for me with all the "wonderful colour"

framed and arrayed,
  that blazed from the walls of the kindly great room, lent for the

                                                    chorus
advantage of a charity, and lost itself in the general ××××× of

immense comparison and tender
  ×××× consecration.   Later on a few days spent at a house of the

greatest beauty and interest in Northumberland did wonders to round

off my view; the place, occupied for the time by genial tenants,

                    family of Lady Waterford's husband
belonged to the ×××××××××××× and fairly bristled, it might be

said, with coloured designs from her brush.

"Demonstrous" is not a word recorded in any dictionary and it obviously puzzled Lubbock, who crossed it out in heavy red crayon, and replaced it with, "the full, the monstrous demonstration that Tennyson was not Tennysonian." This might be another example of Theodora Bosanquet mishearing James's meaning—"the monstrous" could easily be confused with "de-monstrous." And yet Bosanquet was a meticulous grammarian, unlikely to choose a nonce word instead of the obvious one. James also chose not to make a correction by hand, although he did alter other material in the same passage. It seems more likely that this neologism was intended: despite not being defined in the dictionary, *demonstrous* does have some semantic load, combining rather wittily the notions both of demonstration and monstrosity. In this particular passage, it might be suggested that its function is, in fact, to play on the gap between the sign and its referent that the second phrase confirms: Tennyson is Tennyson, but he is not Tennysonian; a demonstration both points something out *(de-monstrare)* and reveals what is monstrous about it *(monstrum,* literally "an omen"). In either case, Lubbock's crayon change has the effect of preferring the *lectio facilior.*

Lubbock finished James's text off by simplifying it; James failed to finish his own work because his method of composition—long-winded dictation followed by accretive revision—tended to sublime complexity. In the following passage, which could stand in thematic metonymy for the text as a whole, James is concerned with the difficulty of recovering lost time. Lubbock's edition reads: "To return at all across the years to the gates of the paradise of the first larger initiations is to be ever so tempted to pass them, to push in again . . . In speaking of my earliest renewal of the vision of Europe, if I may give so grand a name to a scarce more than merely enlarged and uplifted gape, I have, I confess, truly to jerk myself over the ground, to wrench myself with violence from memories and images, stages and phases and branching arms, that catch and hold me as I pass them by" (551). In the typescript, Lubbock's red crayon makes a series of changes that fortify readability and logical progression, marking off the beginning and end of the passage, and changing a past perfect "had" to a perfect "has," thereby increasing the sense that James is engaged with the present moment and hopeful for the future ("a seed . . . the harvest of which . . . has even yet not all been gathered"). James's changes, by contrast, tend to increasing hesitancy and equivocation. Originally, he had written "to return across the years . . . is to be," but he later added the negative adverbial modifier "at all," implying that the recovery of lost time may be futile or impossible. Indeed, throughout this passage language itself is on the verge of rupture, as James figures the intellectual process of memory in bodily terms—to remember is to "jerk" and "wrench," the ghosts of the past are described as the snagging branches of trees. Images of the body in pain seem to be something that James was revising toward. Originally, the typescript records only, "if I may give so grand a name to a matter," but James appears immediately to have corrected himself, scoring out "matter" and replacing it with the bizarre "scarce more than merely enlarged and uplifted gape." He also changed the agency in this sentence: no longer do the images "pass," in a mechanical and passive act of memory, but "I pass them by." The subjective version was added by hand. Why make such a small grammatical change? At one level, the language of struggle, capture, and violence mimetically emphasizes the difficulty of James's project. *The Middle Years* is a theoretical meditation on the "hazards" and "traps" of revisiting the past, as well as an attempt at autobiography and, as Tony Tanner observes, there is often a helpless passivity about the attempt: "Certainly, his mode of remembering, searching for lost time, is the reverse of aggressive or predatory; James does not give even the impression of rummaging around much."[75]

1914 and the End of Meliorism

This functional failure of language in *The Middle Years* is part of James's despairing response to the outbreak of war in August 1914. His letters from this period, described by Leon Edel as "among the most eloquent of his life," show an astonishing degree of prescience; from the beginning, James realizes that the war has reconstituted the shape of history. The day after Britain entered the conflict, he wrote to Howard Sturgis: "The plunge of civilization into this abyss of blood and darkness by the wanton feat of those 2 infamous autocrats is a thing that so gives away the whole long age during which we have supposed the world to be, with whatever abatement, gradually bettering, that to have to take it all now for what the treacherous years were all the while really making for and *meaning* is too tragic for any words."[76] As Paul Fussell has shown, the liberal belief in historical progress or meliorism was one of the first casualties of the 1914–1918 war. For James, the disillusionment was sudden and profound. Three days after writing this letter, he abandoned *The Ivory Tower* and started work on *The Middle Years*, an event recalled baldly in Theodora Bosanquet's diary: "Wet. H.J. started 'The Middle Years'—another autobiographical volume."[77]

On October 8, as James was in the middle of dictating *The Middle Years,* he told Edmund Gosse that "I was struck dumb, like most of us all, ten weeks ago, and you will perhaps have noted that consistently dumb I have remained."[78] Literally this is untrue, but in the text's endlessly repeated echo chamber of gaping, "lapses and gaps," incapacity and failure, we can read a similar refusal to "make for and mean," to fit old words to a new situation. Writing to William Roughead the previous month, James referred to the outbreak of war as a historical puzzle— something akin to the tricky intentions concealed in Vereker's or Dencombe's work: "I never _wanted_ to live on to see the collapse of so many fond faiths, which makes all the past, with this hideous card all the while up its sleeve, seem now a long treachery, an unthinkable humbug."[79] In a letter written to Rhoda Broughton six days after war was declared, he suggested that the conflict had unraveled the very web of history, providing a poignant *anti*-revisionary story of its own. Dwelling, as many later writers were to do, on the English countryside's "loveliness of light, and summer grace," now placed in ironic juxtaposition with the "unthinkable massacre and misery" coming to France and Belgium, James explains that history is no longer a predictable organic process.[80] "The tide that bore us along was then all the while moving to *this* as its grand Niagara—yet what a blessing we didn't know it. It seems to me to *undo* everything, everything that was ours, in the most horrible retroactive way—but I avert my face from the monstrous scene."

Tennyson is not Tennysonian; what seemed to be "betterment" turned out to be deterioration. As a result, James's task of reminiscence is doubly complicated, requiring not only the remembering of past time, but the reinterpretation of old material in light of a new understanding of historical process. The first page of *The Middle Years* begins with a ring of Housman, prompted perhaps by the crowds of young men going off to the front: "youth is an army, the whole battalion of our faculties and our freshnesses, our passions and our illusions, on a considerably reluctant march into the enemy's country, the country of the general lost freshness" (547). As soon as it is uttered, however, this elaborate metaphor seems to fail, and it is replaced with a more static image. If youth isn't an army, then it is "a book in several volumes"—not, as we might expect, the first volume in the series, but the one that remains open. And yet the possibility of one volume remaining open is premised on another having already closed with a "clap of its covers": it is envisaged, perhaps, as the "middle" part of the (already old-fashioned) triple-decker format. The double metaphoric flourish is immediately troubling, for how can something be both an army and a book at the same time? In one sense, the metaphors cancel each other out by their dissonance; in another, they share a commonality of *aspect*. Both begin with an image of freshness, and end with that freshness already soured: a book is never read for the first time; the march into enemy country is a journey into already discovered ground. Similarly, it seems that meaning is never freshly possible, either because it can be deciphered only in "horrible" retrospect or because it is inherently unbearable.

James's sense that the world was "gradually bettering" was premised on a set of beliefs about teleology and historical process, and in turn suggests certain views about textual composition. Meliorism implies that the world will be more fully realized at some future point than at the past or the present moment, and that an orderly process of development will lead from past to future time. Translated into the realm of textual composition, it resembles Dencombe's initial belief in "final form": a novel or other artwork exists most perfectly and fully in the not-yet-achieved future, and can be slowly iterated toward through successive acts of revision. In other words, a meliorist view of history is akin to a belief in revision as positive iteration: as David Greetham explains, it prefers the teleological attractions of the finished product to a Romantic originary moment.[81] To borrow a model used by Edward Mendelson in an essay on Auden's revisions, it imagines the text as a "gothic tower" rather than a "fading coal."[82]

One of the critiques that has been leveled against Whig history is that it is prone to taking conceptual shortcuts, ignoring the "twists and turns" of the actual evidence (to borrow Herbert Butterfield's term) in its enthusiasm for progressive narratives.[83] In the autumn and winter of 1914, James found himself facing "the wreck of our belief that through the long years we had seen civilization grow and the worst become impossible."[84] In such circumstances, a compositional practice premised on the idea of gradual improvement over time and through discrete textual stages—from dictation, to typescript, to proof, to first and subsequent published editions—began to break down. Without the possibility of accounting more satisfactorily for "lapses and gaps" in the future, James gave up on his project of remembering the past altogether. He stopped work on *The Middle Years* in December 1914 without reaching a narrative or thematic end and returned to *The Sense of the Past*.

The ellipsis with which Lubbock concluded *The Middle Years* suggests that the published text is only part of an unfinished, but intended and imagined, whole. In an important sense it is a Jamesian ellipsis, in that it is poignantly self-aware of the difficulties of achieving "final form" within the limits of a human lifespan, and it is precisely the sort of final punctuation mark that James's writer heroes from the 1890s might have imagined for themselves. It has been my intention to suggest that "late late," or post-1914, James had a different sense of the reasons why texts might remain incomplete or fragmentary. In "The Middle Years" revision becomes a problem only by accident, because of the imbalance between Dencombe's ambitions and his "reasserted strength"; by 1914, revision is by definition a problem. Convinced of the modern, even modernist, belief that a gross discontinuity separates the present from the past, James struggled thematically to represent the 1870s except as "lapses and gaps," and compositionally with the purpose of doing so. Two months after he had stopped working on the book, he reached for the language of an emergent modernism: "the subject-matter of one's effort has become *itself* utterly treacherous and false—its relation to reality utterly given away and smashed."[85] It would be up to the next generation to make sense of this "smashing and crashing" and, as Virginia Woolf explained, a "season of failures and fragments" was to be expected first.[86]

CHAPTER 3

Excision and Textual Waste

I N THE PREFACES to the New York Edition, James repeatedly meditates on his problems achieving compression and keeping his unruly
subject matter contained. At some points he presents himself as helpless
before "the expansive, the explosive principle in one's material," constantly wary of "its characteristic space-hunger and space-cunning."[1] In
the 1908 preface to *The Tragic Muse,* he talks with more control of his
"delight in a deep-breathing economy and an organic form" and he criti-
cizes the classic nineteenth-century realist novel for resembling a picture
without adequate composition. The examples he gives are *The New-
comes, Les trois mousequetaires,* and *War and Peace:* "but what do such
large loose baggy monsters, with their queer elements of the accidental
and the arbitrary, artistically *mean?*"[2]

During the decade that followed the publication of that edition, writers of many kinds became anxious about the balance between textual
economy and textual waste. In the next two chapters, I suggest that they
found diametrically opposed ways to deal with it. Proust found that À *la
recherche* was infinitely extensible—he could always produce one volume more. (In this respect, his reader's report from 1912 is prescient, as
Christine Cano observes, "écrire vingt volumes est aussi normal que de
s'arrêter à un ou à deux").[3] And Joyce found that the episodes of *Ulysses*

provided an ideal framework for inside-out addition, so that new ideas or old notebook phrases could be interleaved on typescript and proof into a preordained structure. I discuss Joyce's problems with adding material in the next chapter. In this chapter I consider the opposite strategy—radical excision. This kind of revision begins with a first draft of "normal" length and compression, and then attempts to produce supercharged effects through removing connecting material, adjectives, fillers, and abstraction. If additive revision tries to incorporate everything into a text, even to "contain history" (borrowing Pound's description of his own expanding *Cantos*), excision aims for the charged fragment over the ordered whole, syntactic ellipsis rather than elaboration, and often the removal, rather than the proliferation, of individual perceiving consciousness.[4]

The pitiless concision of this style made it particularly useful to writers who were trying to elegize or memorialize the war dead. *The Waste Land,* which I discuss later in this chapter as the excisive work par excellence derives much of its mysteriously somber tone from the deletion of explanatory material: "I read, much of the night, and go south in the winter"; "I too awaited the expected guest." At the same time, Eliot himself was not prone to cutting as he revised: it remains a curious fact of literary history that he invited Pound and his blue pencil to have their way with *The Waste Land.* In his 1926 novel *The Sun Also Rises,* Ernest Hemingway also used excision and a form of submerging of material to produce an elegiac, epigonal mood. Jake's war-wound, which is never fully explained, lurks in the background of the plot as the sad, pointless explanation for his ennui and inability to form a relation with Brett. By shearing away the contextual frames that tell us who is speaking, or how two images are to be related, excisive revisers leave interpretive gaps that the reader has to fill.

The genealogy of literary "minimalism," often associated with working-class subjects and what Mark McGurl has depicted as "a form of resistance to the self-assertive blare of modern American gigantism," is rarely traced back further than Hemingway; often, in fact, minimalism is assumed to be a purely postwar style.[5] And yet its techniques are directly related to the style of deletion developed in London in the second decade of the twentieth century. The *New Yorker*'s recent publication of the original version of Raymond Carver's short story "Beginners" has shown that his own brand of concision was produced editorially. Gordon Lish cut the manuscript (published in 1981 as "What We Talk About When We Talk About Love") by more than half, and other stories by up to 70 percent.[6] When Samuel Beckett self-translated his plays from French into English, and also when he revised them in response to performance, he deleted more than he added. For Beckett, revision became an opportunity to delete not only words and stage directions but also people and things from an increasingly bleak landscape. Unlike James's elaborate process of reseeing old matter or even Hemingway's submersion of unnecessary detail, it had diegetic as well as formal consequences. In *Krapp's Last Tape*, the people at the wine house where the thirty-nine-year-old Krapp drinks were erased from later versions, leaving "hardly a soul," while the Russian clowns Bim and Bom were deleted from the drafts of both *Endgame* and *Waiting for Godot*.[7]

Imagism and "The Thing"

Imagism as a movement in English poetry was far more important than the small body of work that the Imagist poets actually produced; for T. S. Eliot, in 1953, it was the "point de repère" and the "starting-point" of modern poetry, and a seismic shift that he missed out on, "I was not there."[8] I want to suggest that its importance was in showing that particular writing protocols lead, almost automatically, to certain aesthetic effects. In particular, it showed a route through deletion to a particular kind of excised compression.

First, a note of caution: I am not suggesting that excision is the only route to minimalism. Some writers are able to achieve brevity or condensation from the beginning. Emily Dickinson's poetry has been repeatedly described as riddling, lean, and elliptical, "the verbal equivalent of *sfumato*," a form of "revoked . . . referentiality."[9] As Sharon Cameron's work has shown, the poetry raises substantial genetic and ontological questions—about what constitutes a lyric, for example, and about how Dickinson intended individual poems to be bound together. On the other hand, there is no evidence at all that Dickinson produced her short, formally rather monotonous poems through excision. Most of

the observable variation in her manuscripts relates to spacing and linea-
tion, or small verbal substitutions. For example, "I'll tell you how the
sun rose," which is usually printed now as a single block, was originally
copied out in four quatrains. In "This world is not conclusion," the
original ending was "Narcotics cannot still the Mouse -/ That nibbles at
the soul-," but the homely image was swapped out for the less winsome
"Narcotics cannot still the Tooth."[10] *Dubliners,* which Joyce completed
in 1907 and published in 1914, showed the early modernists some of the
possibilities and virtues of concision in prose. Where did this come
from? Joyce rather pointedly claimed never to have read Chekhov, but
the minimal plots presented flatly, with little discursive commentary,
seem to owe something to both Chekhov's and Flaubert's experiments
in the late nineteenth century. From what we know of Joyce's revision
process, however, he did not produce a style of scrupulous meanness by
cutting back more discursive and conventional first drafts.[11] In fact,
many of his alterations were small acts of substitution or addition aimed
at changing narratorial perspective and focus, or pointing up the themes
of the collection as a whole. For example, the first version of "The Sisters," published in *The Irish Homestead* in 1904, is a straightforward
description of the pull of a sickroom: "Three nights in succession I had
found myself in Great Britain Street at that hour, as if by Providence."
The paragraph that Joyce replaced it with in 1906 has the narrator assume a greater degree of control, "There was no hope for him this time:
it was the third stroke. Night after night I had passed the house (it was vacation time) and studied the lighted square of the window." And then the
following sentences chime associatively across the book's major themes:
"Every night as I gazed up at the window I said softly to myself the word
paralysis. It had always sounded strangely in my ears, like the word gnomon in the Euclid and the word simony in the Catechism." In the revised manuscript, Joyce underlined "paralysis," "gnomon," and "simony."
The length of the book as a whole also increased over time: Joyce added
"Araby" and "Grace" to the ten stories in the 1904 manuscript in 1905,
before sending the book for publication, then "Two Gallants" and "A
Little Cloud" in 1906, and in early 1907, "The Dead."[12]

This kind of minimalism *ab ovo* is not what I want to discuss. It is
fundamentally different from the aesthetic effects produced by removing

material. Rudyard Kipling comments on the difference in his posthumously published autobiography, *Something of Myself,* and he expresses a preference for his own work when shortened rather than written short. "A tale from which pieces have been raked out is like a fire that has been poked. One does not know that the operation has been performed, but every one feels the effect. Note, though, that the excised stuff must have been honestly written for inclusion. I found that when, to save trouble, I 'wrote short' *ab initio* much salt went out of the work." This was written more than twenty years after Pound's manifestos for Imagism, but it expresses some of the stylistic commitments—in particular a preference for a *reduced,* dieted-down style rather than intrinsic brevity. In Pound's case, the link between the charged effect of ellipsis and the use of a blue pencil seems to have been almost an accidental discovery. In her 1979 memoir *End to Torment,* H. D. remembers how it happened, and how she acquired her own status as the foundational "Imagiste." She and Pound were in the British Museum tearoom looking over her draft of "Hermes of the Ways," when he suddenly took out his pencil and cut most of it: he "scratched 'H. D. Imagiste' . . . at the bottom of a typed sheet, now slashed with his creative pencil, 'Cut this out, shorten this line.'"[13] Shortly afterward, Pound sent the short final version to Harriet Monroe at *Poetry* magazine with a note that explained, "It is in the laconic speech of the Imagistes . . . Objective—no slither—direct—no excess of adjectives. etc."[14] Through this apparently chance act of alteration, Pound discovered a way of producing the "laconic" and brief speech that his poetics had already demanded. However seriously we take Imagism as an aesthetic program—it has been called the first avant-garde in English writing, the first "anti *avant-garde*," and a "red herring"—this story illustrates that, from the very beginning, it united three disparate things.[15] A Callimachean preference for short texts over long ones was married to an observational insistence on exactitude and directness. In turn, a particular writing method was prescribed for achieving these aims—deletion. "Excess of adjectives" may be allowed in the first draft, but surplus material must be winnowed before the final version.

H. D.'s poem appeared in the January 1913 issue of *Poetry*. The March issue of the magazine was almost entirely devoted to the new movement;

it contained Pound's own poem "In a Station of the Metro," widely regarded as Imagism's enabling text, his article "A Few Don'ts by an Imagiste," and a definitional piece by F. S. Flint, "Imagisme," which was
produced after conversation with Pound. Flint's article included the following succinct statement of the movement's aesthetic aims:

1. Direct treatment of the "thing," whether subjective or objective.
2. To use absolutely no word that did not contribute to the
   presentation.
3. As regarding rhythm: to compose in sequence of the musical
   phrase, not in sequence of a metronome.[16]

Pound's "Don'ts" insisted that these rules were not to be regarded as
"dogma" ("never consider anything as dogma") but as the useful profit
of "long contemplation." In his own article he reinforced many of Flint's
points, with a particular emphasis once again on the balance between
length and brevity, complexity and immediacy. He begins by defining
an image as something that can be communicated at lightning speed, but
which is nevertheless "complex." "An 'Image' is that which presents an
intellectual and emotional complex in an instant of time." Like a zip file,
the Imagist poem allows for maximally efficient transfer of material between writer and reader. The poet reduces an experience or emotion to
a single image, and the reader unlocks the image in turn to reactivate the
plenitude of original experience.

In an ideal world, there seems to be no reason why the poet should
not produce an Imagist poem at once. But almost all the descriptions we
have of the genesis of actual Imagist poems emphasizes that they resulted from an inefficient, reductive writing process. "In a Station of the
Metro"—the best-known of all of them—is an excellent example. In his
1914 "Vorticism" essay, Pound explained how the idea came to him in
1911: "Three years ago in Paris I got out of a 'metro' train at La Con-
corde, and saw suddenly a beautiful face, and then another and another,
and then a beautiful child's face, and then another beautiful woman, and
I tried all that day to find words for what this had meant to me, and I
could not find any words that seemed to me worthy, or as lovely as that
sudden emotion."[17] Unable to able to transform this perception immedi-

ately into a satisfying form, Pound began by writing a thirty-line poem, but destroyed it because it was a "work of second intensity." He continues: "Six months later I made a poem half that length; a year later I made the following *hokku*-like sentence:— The apparition of these faces in the crowd:/ Petals, on a wet, black bough."[18]

The final version of Pound's haiku is one verb short of a complete sentence. It suggests a variety of poignant and lyrical connections between faces in the crowd and petals on a tree, but lacks both a definitive copula and a spatial or temporal location.[19] What is the force of the deictic "these"? Who is speaking? In the early long version of the poem, these questions might well have been answered, with the crowd specified as Parisian and the observer as an outsider emerging from a metro train. The condensed final version is indeterminate. Revision has worked rhetorically as a form of ellipsis, omitting the logical stages of normal syntax and creating what Daniel Albright has described as a "deleted picture": "stern modes of omission hope to create a feeling of pregnancy of meaning."[20] The only link between the urban world of line 1 and the Japanese garden imagery of line 2 is a sense of fleeting temporality: faces appear but are then blurred with others in a crowd; petals bloom briefly on a bough, but then wither under the rain that has dampened it. Beneath the two-part metrical structure of the haiku is a four-part logical structure, where each line introduces a beautiful image ("the apparition of these faces," "petals") and then gestures to the fadeout ("in the crowd," "on a wet, black bough"). The subtlety and delicacy of this configuration is, according to Pound's account, the result of an intensifying process that allows the writer to separate the valuable from the dross, the jewel from the mud.

H. D.'s Imagist poems make use of the same syntactic structures. Metaphors tend to be created appositively, without the use of the verb *to be*, and demonstrative or possessive adjectives suggest an already earned intimacy between speaker, reader, and setting. When H. D. translated a Greek epitaph into the English "epigram," she turned a first-person lament into a third-person description at once emotionally neutral and familiar; "the golden one" is not explained, and past time (the time of banquets, love, chattering) is presented as a flat panorama. The Imagists avoided main verbs because they wanted to create a sense of temporal stasis through a neutral affectless manner. It is up to the reader to determine what the image might mean, and with what pathos or emotion it is freighted. The poem published in *Des Imagistes* in 1914 is also, like Pound's haiku, constructed symmetrically. The four lines are arranged in a chiastic pattern; the first and final lines are situated in the present, chiming on the perfect participle "gone," and the two middle lines use apposition to describe Homonoea's life.

> The golden one is gone from the banquets;
> She, beloved of Atimetus,
> The swallow, the bright Homonoea:
> Gone the dear chatterer.

In his 1972 edition of H. D.'s collected poems, Louis Martz includes the original final line, "Death succeeds Atimetus," which seems to have been removed before book publication.[21] This line breaks the frame of the poem by adding a main verb, and compared to the recalcitrance of the first four lines it feels heavy, too obvious. Steven Yao makes the attractive speculation that this might be the "one that Pound excised when he saw H. D.'s poems in the British Museum tea room."[22] But, in fact, the *Poetry* magazine version included it.

Ellipsis and the Iceberg Principle

Imagism itself was short-lived as a poetic movement; by 1914, Pound had already abandoned the use of the term, merging some of his original concepts with the new language of the "vortex," "the point of maximum energy."[23] This was in part because he wanted to write longer poems, and Imagism seemed capable of producing only the shortest, most fleeting of epiphanies. In his 1914 "Vorticism" essay he mused rather wearily, "I am often asked whether there can be a long Imagiste or vorticist poem."[24] One wonders if the questioner might have been Pound himself.

If modernist form can be summed up as a "cluster of stylistic practices" including simultaneity, juxtaposition, montage, fragmentation, paradox, ambiguity and uncertainty, then what better way to achieve a modernist effect than by following a writing protocol that *inevitably* leads to simul-

taneity and fragmentation?[25] Excision emphasizes the visual or pha-
nopoeic snapshot above discursive argument and conventional narrative
and, through making them shorter, it tends to make texts more difficult.
How does the excising writer know when the process is finished? What
is redundant and what is necessary? There is an obvious danger of over-
shooting the mark: take one word from an economically expressed complete sentence, and you run the risk of ending up with nonsense. If extension makes texts more difficult through comprehensiveness,
proliferation, complexity of diction, and parataxis, excision makes texts
hard by asking its readers to fill in the gaps. The verb that we need to
supply to make sense of separate images is usually, as in the case of
Pound's haiku, *to be.* Consequently, Imagist poems tend toward flat-
ness and stasis and toward presenting historical time as a panorama
rather than a narrative. In this sense they might even be regarded as
antihistorical.

As an example of the extreme frustration that ellipsis can produce, we
might consider the first part of Eliot's epigraph to the poem "Burbank
with a Baedeker: Bleistein with a Cigar," which begins: "Tra-la-la-la-la-
la-laire—nil nisi divinum stabile est; caetera fumus—the gondola stopped,
the old palace was there, how charming its grey and pink—goats and
monkeys, with such hair too!" This is a kind of miniature or microcos-
mic example of a trend pursued in *The Waste Land,* where borrowed
phrases are splintered into shards and then run up against each other.
Each quotation or fragment can be identified and placed—Gautier's
representation of the gondolier's cry; the Latin tag on Mantegna's painting of St. Sebastian; the Venice of the Aspern papers; Othello's jealous
outburst; Browning's "A Toccata of Galuppi's"—at some point, with the
aid of notes, I noted the sources in my edition. But I am not confident
that without some kind of guide or key most readers would pick up anything except perhaps the *Othello* and Henry James references. Each quotation seems shorter than the minimal sampling size required to activate
recognition; like someone listening to a half-forgotten song, we want a
few more bars, or words, as a further aid. The relationship between each
fragment, wrested sharply from its linguistic source, is also hard to
parse. Do they work as a group to give depth to the picturesque historical panorama—the spectral corrupt city through the ages—or do they

act against each other, dissolving the present (the Rialto, Burbank with his tourist guidebook) through self-contradiction? This question is importantly unanswerable, because Eliot has given us no syntactic enjoinder with which we can connect the parts: whether this is a narrative, a grouping of like things, a medley of unlike ones, a schizophrenic babble, or curious curse is impossible to tell. In his 1933 lectures at Harvard, as Ronald Schuchard has noted, Eliot began by comparing his indirect method of approaching Venice to Henry James's, but then added that his epigraph was "perhaps illicit."[26]

Unlike Jamesian rereading, or Joycean addition, excision is a method of both revision and editing. It is pedagogically transmittable and not necessarily very difficult to do. Pound developed the strategy "Cut this out, shorten this line" for dealing with H. D.'s early poetry, but he was soon to apply the same advice to his own work and that of his other contemporaries, in both prose and verse. Amy Lowell remembered that Pound "rewrote" her poems "before her eyes, underscoring *clichés* (Ezra's word) and heaving them out; compressing; making more visible."[27] When Ernest Hemingway gave some of his early stories to Pound, they "came back to him blue-penciled, most of the adjectives gone."[28] He quickly internalized the method and began a program of stylistic self-reduction. And the facsimile documents of *The Waste Land* are a visual testament to the confidence of a master exciser at the top of his game; Pound's clean, bold lines drawn through whole verse paragraphs and sections are sculptural and exacting, and they contrast pointedly with Eliot's anxious substitutions.

When Pound described the effect of excision in a short poem, he used the provocative phrase "super-position." In the 1914 "Vorticism" essay, for example, he describes the effect of a one-image haiku-like poem as "one idea set on top of another" with all the surrounding dross weeded out. In a haiku, superposition can be understood formally. In "A Station of the Metro" or the Japanese lyric that Pound offers as another example, one line provides the mundane actuality, the other the metaphorical leap, so "The footsteps of the cat upon the snow: (are like) plum-blossoms," just as the faces in the crowd are (like) petals, or the sea's waves (like) "pointed pines" in H. D.'s "Oread." One of the struggles in applying the technique to longer works—that is, in producing the elusive Imagist long poem—was working out how to expand dédoublement beyond simple metaphor. The "Homage to Sextus Propertius," a poem that Pound always rated higher than his critics have, was his first attempt at condensation in a longer form. Rather than following the traditional, linear model of translation, Pound selected a series of short scenes from Propertius's text and spliced them together to produce a consciously discontinuous version, which sacrifices fidelity and cohesion for Imagistic vividness and musical cadencing. Moreover, the "Homage" is itself an act of reduction that transforms Propertius's four books of elegies into a formally splintered, much shorter poem that, nonetheless, claims to stand in relation to the *whole* of Propertius's work.

Once again, Pound explained his technique here with the word "super-position": in fact, he told Thomas Hardy that he feared readers would not understand "the super-position; the doubling of me and Propertius, England to-day and Rome under Augustus."[29] At one level, then, the doubling is an act of ventriloquism as a speaker faced with "the infinite and ineffable imbecility of the British Empire" talks through the voice of someone two thousand years earlier confronting "the infinite and ineffable imbecility of the Roman Empire." But it is not an uncritical or perfect act of mimesis. We might say that Pound *does* Propertius in a self-consciously wavering accent, moving between an accurate and lyrical mode of translation and what Donald Davie calls the poem's "translatorese."[30] So a line such as "Out-weariers of Apollo will, as we know, continue their Martian generalities" isn't, or isn't merely, a rendering of Propertius in English; it is also an encouragement to consider the difficulties of doing so. It gestures to the mask's slippage. This slip or tug between tenor and vehicle, Pound and Propertius, English and Latin is, in fact, essential to the method of condensed super-position. The haiku "In a Station of the Metro" makes us simultaneously aware of both the similarity *and* the incongruity between a bough wet with spring rain and an urban crowd. It does this by approaching, but falling short of, a logical statement of identity. The "Homage" also allows for incongruity or dissimilarity between the source text and its English rendering. For example, one of the things that Pound seems to have liked about Propertius was his aesthetic commitment to Callimachean "leptotes" (slenderness), a kind of learned and allusive minimalism. Propertius addresses this quite explicitly in the programmatic elegy that opens book 3, and which Pound takes as the opening of his entire poem ("Shades of Callimachus, Coan ghosts of Philetas"). A few lines later, Propertius announces that he will turn away from epic themes. Instead, he wants a book smoothed carefully with fine pumice *(a valeat, Phoebum quicumque moratur in armis/ exactus tenui pumice versus eat).* Pound translates the third-person subjunctive of the pentameter as "We have kept our erasers in order," a heavy, anachronistic, and sibilant line. It is not a conventionally good translation, being neither accurate nor attractive, but it is an excellent guide to Pound's principles for a lean modernism.[31]

Pound regarded his next poem, "Hugh Selwyn Mauberley," as another exercise in condensation. In fact, he even suggested that it functioned as a translation of a translation, a rendering of the "Homage" into plain style for readers too stupid to understand the act of superposition that the first poem produces.[32] In discussing its effects, he made the additional suggestion—not irrelevant to *The Waste Land*—that excision could effect genre shifts, "it was the definite attempt to get the novel cut down to the size of verse."[33] Elsewhere he described the poem—whose narrative structure has remained puzzling—as "a study in form, an attempt to condense the James novel."[34] On the other hand, "Mauberley" is no more *plotted* than the Imagist haikus Pound had been writing earlier in the decade. Just as those two-line equivalences seem to turn away from the possibility of making a syntactic proposition, so Mauberley is a series of unconnected potential plot points rather than a narrative: novelistic detail without a novelistic motor. It also moves abruptly between different pronouns, so the "he" of section I "out of key with his time," is lost in II in externalized description of what the "age demanded," before mutating in III into a generalizing "we" ("we see το καλόν/ Decreed in the market place") and then, out of nowhere, into a plaintive I ("what god, man, or hero/ Shall I place a tin wreath upon!"). In this respect, it is completely unlike James's careful management of point of view. The effect resembles a James novel with the frames and speech tags removed, so it becomes impossible to determine whether ideas are to be taken seriously or with a degree of irony. What, for example, is the effect of the pincers around "age demanded" when the phrase is used for the second

time in section II? What does it mean to have another, pairing poem titled "'THE AGE DEMANDED'/ VIDE POEM II" in the "Mauberley"
second half? Criticism of the poem has tangled itself up repeatedly in
very basic questions. As John Espey puts it, what is "the relationship
between Ezra Pound himself and Hugh Selwyn Mauberley" and should
the two "be identified wholly or in part or not at all"?[35] Max Saunders
returns at dazzling and ingenious length to the problem of *who is speaking* in his recent study of modernist life writing. I am not so sure that the
problem is solvable. Pound suggested as much when he said "Mauberley
is mere surface"—just like Imagism, which he also described as "a
spreading, or surface art."[36] What he was pointing to, perhaps, is the *essential* ambiguity that the method of doubling produces. Mauberley and
E. P. stand in the same kind of relationship of superposition as Pound
and Propertius or the mundane objects and sharp metaphors in the earlier Imagist poems: they are in relation to each other, but the exact nature of that relation is not, and cannot be, structurally articulated. Indeed, between the first and subsequent publications of "In a Station of
the Metro," Pound revised the punctuation mark connecting the two
lines from a colon to a semicolon as if uncertain whether he was propos-
ing a relationship of identity (metaphor) or contiguity (metonymy). Either way, the closest the haiku gets to a verb is a verbal noun, "the apparition." In the end, superposition is syntactically *evasive*.

The Sun Also Rises

Pound's ideas about using excision to weed out cliché and produce
charged aesthetic effects remain familiar in contemporary writing culture. Often they come packaged in a metaphor that is itself about the relationship between surface and depth: *the iceberg principle*. This was
the formulation that Hemingway—a good Pound student, who "listened
at E. P.'s feet, as to an oracle"—formulated in his posthumously published autobiography *A Moveable Feast*.[37] There he tells us about his
methods for dealing with writer's block. If he felt uninspired, he tells us
that he "would stand and look out over the roofs of Paris," and give himself the following advice: "Do not worry. You have always written before
and you will write now. All you have to do is to write one true sentence.

Write the truest sentence that you know."[38] If, however, this maxim proved hard to follow, Hemingway adds that he also had a method of revision in place: "If I started to write elaborately, or like someone introducing or presenting something, I found that I could cut that scrollwork or ornament out and throw it away and start with the first true simple declarative sentence I had written." The simple is preferred to the ornamental, the declarative sentence to the rhetoric of "someone introducing or presenting something." In a 1958 interview with the *Paris Review,* he had conveyed the same point, this time using the suggestive metaphor of the iceberg: "If it is any use to know it, I always try to write on the principle of the iceberg. There is seven eighths of it under water for every part that shows. Anything you know you can eliminate and it only strengthens your iceberg. It is the part that doesn't show."[39] This is a very seductive idea, but what does it mean in practice? We may not have the long original version of "In a Station of the Metro," but many of Hemingway's manuscripts, typescripts, and galley proofs have been preserved. Comparing the different genetic strata gives an idea of how "anything you know" can in practice be submerged, producing a glittering and elliptical surface.

Like many Imagist poems, *The Sun Also Rises* was written very quickly and then extensively reduced through a drawn-out and painful process of revision. Hemingway claimed to have written the first draft in a burst of romantic inspiration—"one sprint of six weeks"—but was only able to "make it into a novel" by spending a entire winter revising at Schruns.[40] The published 1926 novel is about 15 percent shorter than the manuscript, which ran to just over eighty-three thousand words, on thirty-two loose sheets, and in seven draft notebooks. Frederic Svoboda's detailed study of Hemingway's work at Schruns, which aims to track "the steps he followed in reshaping the form," lists several of the major shifts of emphasis. As he revised, Svoboda claims, Hemingway moved toward "delicacy and restraint" and away from "literal transcription of reality," ruminations on "narrative method and reliability," travelogue; and "overly sentimental dialogue."[41]

In fact, Hemingway had been working excisively from the beginning. The surviving genetic strata show a propensity toward restraint and omission from the manuscript onward. In the manuscript, the text's propensity for condensation is rendered first at the level of character, and Jake (originally "Hem") frequently rebukes himself for verbal excess, poor storytelling, and narrative confusion: "I ~~don't~~ not know why I have put all this down. It may mix up the story." [42] Besides thematized self-critique, we also find that some of the most digressive passages are already substantially reworked in manuscript. So Hemingway crossed out the passage "To understand this situation in Pamplona you have to understand Paris," which ran to two manuscript pages, before beginning again "To understand what happened in Pamplona you must understand the quarter in Paris." [43] Again he was unhappy, and crossed out the next two sentences "This is probably too much to ask of any reader. There has already been so much stuff written about the quarter that it needs defining" before proceeding. In the manuscript, anxieties about verbosity are frequently underpinned by self-reflexive uncertainty about the novel as a form. Before beginning the passage about Paris, the emerging Jake narrator had quarrelled in his head with Gertrude Stein and, implicitly, with the program of Imagist excision. "Stein once told me that novels are not literature. All right, let it go at that. Only this time all the remarks are going in and if it is not literature who claimed it was anyway." When he decided *not* to put all the remarks in, Hemingway was also able to take away Jake's tone of querulous ambivalence.

In the first draft of the novel, Jake spends a lot of time musing on the best way to express things; in the final version he is more mysterious and laconic, as if not only parts of his own past but some of his creator's compositional anxiety had been submerged. At the end of the published book, for example, he replies to Brett's distressed summons ("COULD YOU COME HOME HOTEL MONTANA MADRID AM RATHER IN TROUBLE BRETT") in a terse telegram: taking out his fountain pen, he writes "ARRIVING SUD EXPRESS" and signs off "LOVE JAKE." In the original version the conversational sign-off "LOVE JAKE" had engendered an explicit meditation on his emasculating war wound. So, before being enacted genetically, the desire for repression was acted out through the seesaw of internal monologue:

> There was nothing else to say. ~~I put the~~ What else was there to say?
> I printed LOVE JAKE and handed the concierge the wine. There I

was, doing it again. Why not let it alone. I knew there was not any use trying to let it alone. I felt perfectly bad about it. I had certainly acted like anything but a man . . . ~~I was not a man anyway. Oh stop that stuff. There was not going to be any of that stuff.~~[44]

In the first draft, Jake begins by trying psychologically to shut himself up, "Oh stop that stuff," but on rereading, Hemingway takes his character's advice and simply cuts it out so none of "that stuff" remains. In the final version, hesitant and self-reflective monologue is replaced with inconsistent behavior from which we must draw our own conclusions: "That was it. Send a girl off with one man. Introduce her to another to go off with him. Now go and bring her back. And sign the wire with love. That was it all right. I went in to lunch."

The next paragraph in the published novel moves directly to evening and Jake's nighttime journey to Madrid. "I did not sleep much that night on the Sud Express": a typically laconic Hemingway sentence. In the manuscript, however, three whole cahier pages had separated the self-reproaching "There was not going to be any of that stuff" from the subsequent train journey. Most of the deleted material has little immediate plot purpose and presumably, in this sense, it seemed to Hemingway something that he could cut. It takes the form of an extended meditation on the manners and mores of the English aristocracy, and it is savagely critical of some writers' excessive interest in the topic:

> All the Jews and Americans and Welshmen and ex clerks and ex school teachers all wrote about the aristocracy. The aristocracy when they wrote wrote about the wallabies natives of distant countries or about horses or salmon or other things. Of course the best ones did not either write or read . . . (*TSAR* MS, 6:42–43)

Jake is equally critical of those who fetishize aristocratic behavior, the behavior itself, and his own attempts to ape it. He comments, "In actual life it seems there was a great deal of sleeping about among good people, much more sleeping about than passion and when there was any actual passion nobody believed in it," but he also rebukes himself for caring about his own emasculation, "That was not how the 'good people' acted." This guilty interior monologue is then followed by a panoramic description of the train journey to Madrid:

> But I took the Sud Express and slept well in a compartment by myself and had breakfast in the morning and ^ looked out of the window and ^ saw the Escorial, grand and gray and cold in the sun with ~~and forty~~ the ~~five~~ cheerfulness of the little town below it and forty five minutes later Madrid ~~while~~ a compact ~~scattered~~ white skyline on the top of a ^little^ cliff away across sun hardened country. (MS, 6:43)

In the final version, of course, the whole monologue disappears, along with the description of different aspects of the Spanish landscape passed at speed on the train. The sentence that replaces it, "I did not sleep much that night on the Sud Express," is suggestive of the unhappy insomniac material that has been erased. In fact, we might say that it *stands* metaphorically for the deleted material, just as "petals on a wet, black bough" stands for Pound's initial, perhaps more realistic, attempt to describe the faces in the Paris crowd.

Hemingway finished his first round of revisions alone at Schruns, but the book underwent a further series of deletions after the "completely rewritten and cut manuscript" had been sent to Scribner's for publication and to F. Scott Fitzgerald for approval.[45] Fitzgerald's critique reads like an augmentation of Hemingway's own revisionary principles, advocating further cuts of discursive and argumentative material. By comparing Hemingway's problems to his own, Fitzgerald's letter makes it clear that the desire for brevity ("direct treatment of the thing") is a *shared* literary aesthetic: "I find in you the same tendency to envelope or (and as it usually turns out) to *embalm* in mere wordiness an anecdote or joke that casually appealed to you that I find in myself in trying to preserve a piece of "fine writing."[46] Besides finding the tone "snobbish," Fitzgerald objected to the "feeling of condescending casuallness" (*sic*), to "sneers, superiorities and nose-thumbings-at-nothing," to elements of narrative self-consciousness, to travelogue ("this is in all guide books"), and to things that he found trite, old-fashioned, or already done. He attacked the phrase "beautiful engraved shares" with the comment "Beautifully engraved 1886 irony," a marginal prompt to be modern that we might compare to the "1880" that Pound put in a large round bracket on the 1921 manuscript of *The Waste Land*.[47]

Fitzgerald's main suggestion was that Hemingway discard his (already reworked) opening, cutting wholesale. "From here Or rather from p. 30 I began to like the novel but Ernest I can't tell you the sense of disappointment that beginning with its elephantine facetiousness gave me. Please do what you can about it in proof. Its 7500 words—you could reduce it to 5000. And my advice is not to do it by mere pareing but to take out the worst of the *scenes*." A few days later, Hemingway wrote to his editor, Maxwell Perkins, to authorize the cut. "I believe that, in the proofs, I will start the book at what is now page 16 in the Mss. There is nothing in those first sixteen pages that does not come out, or is explained, or re-stated in the rest of the book—or is unnecessary to state. I think it will move much faster from the start that way. Scott agrees with me."[48] The mild duplicity of "Scott agrees with me" shows Hemingway attempting to regain editorial control, turning editorial criticism *back* into self-directed revision. As if playing a game of one-upmanship, Hemingway also went further than Fitzgerald had suggested, not "pareing" merely, nor "taking out the worst of the scenes," but removing sixteen pages in their entirety. (We might compare the bravura of Eliot's "Perhaps better omit Phlebas also???," which Lawrence Rainey characterizes as "remarkable".)[49] The next fourteen pages he left alone. For William Balassi this is an indication that he was trying "to save face or to retain his sense of editorial control over the text."[50] Destroying textual matter thereby becomes an act of manly control, a way of giving rigor and clarity to a text that threatened to be chatty, formless, and digressive.

After the loss of fourteen pages, the novel began not only in medias res but also, as Balassi argues, "in the middle of the text," with the words "Robert Cohn was once middleweight boxing champion of Princeton." Balassi remains optimistic, nevertheless, about readers' ability to infer what has been removed, "Without the opening scene in Pamplona, readers have to sense the importance of lines that have lost their context, to sense more than they know, which is often possible because the text still resonates with the significance of the opening material even though the

story itself is no longer there."[51] This is a deeply appealing aesthetic possibility, akin to the argument that a partially destroyed or aged painting
"still resonates with the significance" of the lost original, suggesting
outlines and shapes that are no longer clearly discernable. It is also a re-
statement of Hemingway's own "iceberg principle," which assumes that
authorial knowledge ("anything you know") can be translated into readerly affect ("it only strengthens your iceberg"). But how exactly does a
text resonate with the significance of an absence? What type of thing is
that resonance? Is it a fact that can be known ("Jake Barnes is Catholic")
or an imprecise feeling (a sense of "the Quarter state of mind") or is it a
self-producing sense of aesthetic fracture (there is more to be known
than we can know)?

What if some of Hemingway's omissions were not buried under the
surface but merely omitted? Hershel Parker is one of the few literary critics to have considered this possibility, which allows that editing and revision may not always be meliorative. Discussing his own confusion over
whether Jake is or is not a Catholic, he argues, "The loss of the opening,
and the failure to revise thoroughly to *cover* for that loss, caused the confusion."[52] The "iceberg principle" also fails to account for genuine
changes of mind. In the first draft of *The Sun Also Rises,* we were told
that Robert Cohn was "the hero" of the tale, that he had written "a skil-
fully and neatly done" novel, and that he had lived for two years with a
woman "who lived on gossip and so he had lived in an atmosphere of
abortions, doubts . . . dirty rumors, dirtier reports." These descriptions are not only omitted from the final text but are also, more problem-
atically, inconsistent with it: the Cohn of the final version is not the hero,
his novel is not such a success, and his relationship with Frances is presented more conventionally. If texts are corrected as well as revised,
should we assume that final texts only "resonate with the significance"
of certain, correct, parts of the earlier version?

Critics who praise excisive revisers are prone to claiming first that the
original version (figured as baggy, loose, unformed) was *aiming to become* the final version (figured as tight, condensed, perfected), and second that the original version contained or embodied the final version
within it, as if the long, baggy original were pregnant with its condensed
alternative. Whether or not we agree with the value judgment being

rendered in a particular case, it is important to understand that these arguments are logically problematic. To begin with, they both involve attributing agency and intention to an inanimate thing (a written document). This may be a legacy of anti-intentionalism in literary studies: oddly, critics tend to be more comfortable saying, as Wayne Koestenbaum does, that "the manuscript of *The Waste Land* embodied a desire for Pound's curative arrival" than that "T. S. Eliot wanted Ezra Pound's help editing his poem."[53] The first, teleological argument assumes that because a text *is* a certain way, that it was always destined to become that way. The second argument, which is a variant of the first, attaches an organic idea of pregnancy or embodiment to the causational problem. It is true in one sense that the long version of *The Sun Also Rises* contained the laconic, teasing opening line "Robert Cohn was once middleweight boxing champion of Princeton," but it also contained many other alternative openings. Remove more, and the book might have started, "That winter Robert Cohn went over to America with his novel, and it was accepted by a fairly good publisher."

Waste in *The Waste Land*

Since the publication of the facsimile version in 1971, criticism of *The Waste Land* has rehearsed the argument inherent in the iceberg principle: long early versions of texts contain short later versions and, as time passes, they become increasingly eager to produce them. In the second half of this chapter, I want to reconsider the genetic and revisionary history of that poem for, if *Ulysses* is the epitome of additive revision, the 434-line final version of *The Waste Land* is the canonical example of revision by subtraction. Almost every critical debate about the poem—from the question of its intelligibility to the supplementary usefulness of the notes, from psychoanalytic to deconstructive to historicist readings—takes a position on its genesis and, almost always, that genesis is represented as a triumphant Poundian act of salvage, a wresting of the jewel from the mud. Vincent Sherry is one of the few critics to have recognized that the "usual views" are far from adequate. Originating in the period when the drafts of the poem were unknown, rather than supporting, they have stymied critical debate. He argues: "This work [i.e., Pound's] represents an event in the critical history of an ideal modernism rather like the lore of the Great War: it is *supposed* to be significant. The actual work of its archaeology, the excavation of its manuscript record, represents an effort that has been suspended under the benediction of the 'usual views.' Thus Pound's massive excisions, reducing the length of the poem by hundreds of lines, can be taken as the work of imagist concision—on a grand scale."[54] In fact, I will argue, *The Waste Land* was produced by a kind of compositional counterpoint. Eliot began composing in short fragments, which he slowly pieced together; Pound then applied his blue pencil and excised. By doing this, Pound turned a poem that in its first draft had been interested in parallel and contrast, in knitting together different historical moments *sub specie aeternatis,* into something much more fragmented and evasive. He was particularly tough on the novelistic sections of the original draft, and the poem that he produced is, like "Hugh Selwyn Mauberley," full of partial stories, or stories presented without the narrative part preeminent. In "A Game of Chess," for example, the rape of Philomela is rendered only as an image, "Above the antique mantel was displayed," within a frame that is itself static, "The chair she sat in." The storytelling mode of "First we had a couple of feelers down at Tom's place" or "This ended, to the steaming bath she moves" or "Then came the fish at last" disappears between the draft and the published poem.

Why have critics been so confident that the final version of the poem is best? The usual story originated with Eliot himself, beginning with his 1925 dedicatory genuflection to "il miglior fabbro." In 1936 he explained that Pound put the long first draft "through the sieve," thereby turning a "jumble of good and bad passages into a poem,"[55] and a decade later that Pound had tamed a "sprawling, chaotic poem" into one "reduced to about half its size." "I placed before him the manuscript of a sprawling chaotic poem called *The Waste Land* which left his hands reduced to about half its size, in the form in which it appears in print."[56] Pound concurred. In the dedicatory verses "Sage Homme," with which Eliot considered prefacing his poem, Pound imagines himself as a surgeon performing the "caesarean Operation."[57] Wayne Koestenbaum has argued that Pound's representation of the scene of poetic production is strongly gendered, and that Eliot's formless, hysterical, babbling female patient was acted upon and cured by Pound's hard excisive work, just as H. D.'s inchoate early poems were toughened up through deletion into Imagism.[58] The bibliographic framing of Valerie Eliot's facsimile edition of *The Waste Land* affirmed this view: Pound not only received heavy billing on the cover, but his edits were represented on the recto pages in red ink, as if they were more notable, even more *correct*, than the other handwriting on manuscript and typed pages (including Eliot's own manuscript drafting, his manuscript revisions, and Vivien Eliot's manuscript edits).

Geoffrey Hartman once described Wordsworth's *Prelude*, which was subject to an enormous amount of private revision over many decades (but no editing), as a "self-corrupting" poem.[59] *The Waste Land*, which was both revised and edited, has, following Eliot and Pound's lead, been almost unanimously regarded as efficiently self-purging. It is extremely difficult to find a critic who suggests that a single image or line might conceivably have been spared. Cecelia Tichi sums up the consensus concisely: "Eliot's editorial cohort, Ezra Pound, cut the 'waste' from *The Waste Land*."[60] "No one will deny," Richard Ellmann argued, shortly after the facsimile was published, "that it is weaker throughout than the final version. Pound comes off very well indeed."[61] Figuring the first draft as a hysterical female patient, Wayne Koestenbaum has claimed that "the manuscript of *The Waste Land* embodied a desire for Pound's curative arrival."[62] For Marjorie Perloff, "Pound's excisions and revisions made Eliot's central themes and symbols more prominent than they would otherwise have been."[63] This argument about genetic process has sometimes blended into an argument about the poem's thematic preoccupations: as Maud Ellmann reminds us, it is, after all, called *The Waste Land*. Just as the text rids itself of excess so, Ellmann argues, the landscape of the waste land clutters itself with surplus only in order to remove it: "A ceremonial purgation, it inventories all the 'stony rubbish' it strives to exorcise."[64]

Does *The Waste Land* really try to exorcise the material detritus and overheard voices that it enumerates? I have been suggesting that texts often develop in ways that represent their author's thematic preoccupations, and will explore this idea in more detail in the next chapter. But in the case of *The Waste Land*, the "purgation" reading—we might equally well call it the "excisive reading"—rests not so much on what Eliot composed as on what Pound did with it. In fact, both Eliot's early piecemeal drafts and the short remnants of those drafts in the final poem are more hospitable to waste than is often supposed.

Before exploring the contrapuntal tension between Eliot's extrinsic remaindering and Pound's excisions, we should note that, once again, the usual arguments about the poem's genesis make assumptions that are problematic even in principle. In 1931, Herbert Butterfield criticized Whig historians for studying "the past with reference to the present," being "interested in the agency rather than in the process," confusing series of events with lines of causation, and misunderstanding the length and complexity of "the process of mutation which produced the present."[65] The same criticisms can be leveled against a textual meliorism that represents Pound and Eliot's chaotic, hasty, and sometimes confused work on the drafts as predictable and even predestined. How plausible is it that Eliot wrote 434 brilliant lines, lines that epitomize modernism as a project, and that he interspersed and sometimes formally enveloped these in another 400 or so lines of dross, beginning "The Burial of the Dead" with a "vapid prologue," and "The Fire Sermon" with "sequential clichés" stemming from a "deficient grasp of Pope"?[66] The "weaker throughout" assumes an extreme qualitative difference between the portions retained and lost. But, in that case, why couldn't Eliot himself—"the most gifted and most influential critic in English in the twentieth century"—see it?[67] In fact, Eliot appears to have had no foresight into Pound's editorial process, and often not to have entirely understood what was being suggested. As late as January 1922, he was writing, "Cher maître: Criticisms accepted so far as understood," before helplessly asking, "Perhaps better omit Phlebas also???"[68] The extreme equivocation—the "perhaps" and three final question marks—suggest that by this stage Eliot was ready to remove almost anything, and that he saw no difference between the Phlebas lyric (self-translated from "Dans le Restaurant" and, in its English version, highly praised) and the narrative second half of "Death by Water" (much condemned since it was published in 1971). After the editorial process was finished, Pound was highly satisfied with the shape, length, and closure of the final product: "the thing now runs from April . . . to shantih without [a] break." He continued, in a comment that has puzzled critics, "That is 19 pages and let us say the longest poem in the English langwidge. Don't try to bust all records by prolonging it three pages further." Eliot never seemed so sure that, in its final form, the poem was a well-made, formally closed whole. As Richard Baden-hausen has noted, he "repeatedly resisted placing boundaries around the poem" and was willing to "contaminate the structural borders by considering attaching 'Gerontion' as a prelude, printing *The Waste Land* in four separate sections in successive issues of *The Dial*, or even split-ting it into two for the first two numbers of *The Criterion*."[69] Despite success as an editor at Faber, he was also a curiously sloppy proofreader of his own work. In 1923, he explained to Virginia Woolf, his proofread-ing was so "abominable" that the Hogarth edition of *The Waste Land* contained several errors, including "under London Bridge" for "over London Bridge," and "coloured dolphin" for "carven dolphin (sic)." His response was to go into the booksellers, Jones and Evans, and correct the mistakes by hand.[70]

After *The Waste Land* was published, Eliot seems to have been im-mediately dissatisfied with it. Between 1922 and 1965 he made a series of weary, belittling, disowning comments. By November 1922, the poem was already "a thing of the past so far as I am concerned"[71]; later a "per-sonal and wholly insignificant grouse against life," "just a piece of rhyth-mical grumbling,"[72] and followed by notes providing "a remarkable exposition of bogus scholarship."[73] Most importantly, it was "structure-less." In his 1959 *Paris Review* interview, Eliot was asked by Donald Hall "What sort of thing did Pound cut from The Waste Land? Did he cut whole sections?" and "Did the excisions change the intellectual structure of the poem?"[74] He replied: "No. I think it was just as struc-tureless, only in a more futile way, in the longer version."

In fact, the 1921 draft of *The Waste Land* is not structureless. Its struc-ture was simply different from the excised 434-line poem that Pound produced. Eliot's natural tendency was to work accretively, shoring up small fragments and then thinking of how to put them together. By the end of 1921, he had produced a draft of almost one thousand lines, and a poem that worked synthetically, gathering up and opposing different viewpoints, rendering London to us through different speakers and styles, and drawing lines of contrast between present and past. Always anxious that poetic inspiration might desert him, Eliot was a parsimonious, even miserly, composer. His letters to Conrad Aiken from the 1910s are full of bodily metaphors to describe the misery of drying up, so Eliot presents himself as "intellectually constipated" and "writh[ing] in impotence."[75] As a result, he was never quick to classify any of his fragments as waste. He could be playful about this tendency and, as John Haffenden has shown, he republished some of the discarded parts of *The Waste Land* in one of Vivienne's articles in the *Criterion*.[76] He even pressed the printers to make sure that this would appear on April Fool's Day. They wrote back on March 3: "We note that you are very anxious that this should be published on April 1st and we will do everything possible to work towards this date."[77]

The facsimile edition consists of materials written over a period of about seven years, some of which Eliot circulated as individual poems before reconceiving them as parts of a larger whole. Lawrence Rainey's recent investigation of the poem's composition has shown that, by February 1921, Eliot had completed seven short and unconnected pieces of writing, with an average length of 13.7 lines; at this rate, it would have required 48 separate drafts "to make a poem of 433 lines."[78] Rainey concludes: "The trick in writing such a long poem, then, was how to stitch together between 48 and 55 separate drafts. Connectedness, plainly, was a pressing problem." Conrad Aiken recollected that he had got to know parts of the final poem, such as "A woman drew her long black hair out tight," as "poems or part-poems, in themselves," before seeing them "inserted into *The Waste Land* as into a mosaic."[79] Early unpublished poems containing lines that were later to turn up in *The Waste Land* include "The Death of Saint Narcissus" and "The Death of the Duchess,"[80] while the Phlebas lyric is a self-translation of the end of the published poem "Dans le Restaurant." If Pound hadn't objected, "Gerontion" would have been the "prelude in book or pamphlet form" to the rest of the poem.[81]

Eliot maintained this retentive practice of composition throughout his life. He explained that a few lines "that had to be cut out of *Murder in the Cathedral*" became the seedbed for "Burnt Norton," just as some of the poems published as "Minor Poems" functioned as "the preliminary sketches" for major works. "Ash Wednesday" and "The Hollow Men" both "originated out of separate poems," which were only later considered as a potential sequence: "That's one way in which my mind does seem to have worked throughout the years poetically—doing things separately and then seeing the possibility of fusing them together, altering them, and making a kind of whole of them."[82] Both Helen Gardner's study of the manuscripts of *Four Quartets* and E. Martin Browne's description of the genesis of the plays corroborate this: his instinct was toward "What Precisely," and "If and Perhaps and But." In the recalcitrant terza rima passage in "Little Gidding," for example, Eliot made repeated local substitutions of individual words, sometimes in an oscillating pattern. So the M7 typescript contains the line "Communing at the intersection time," where "communing" is struck through and replaced by "accepted." In the next (M8) typescript, we find "Consenting to this intersection time," altered to "Compliant," and then back again to "Consenting."[83] The parts of the *Quartets* composed in freer forms show the same, worried propensity to lexical substitution at all stages in the genetic process. As a playwright, Eliot again lacked confidence in his ability to make structural revisions. E. Martin Browne quotes from letters that he received from the author about revisions to the tricky final scene of *The Cocktail Party:* "I don't want to work on lines until scheme is approved" and "I am certainly not confident about anything."[84] In fact, even in his work as an editor and translator, Eliot showed a preference for modest readjustment rather than textual transformation. Andrew Kappel describes his 1935 edition of Marianne Moore's *Selected Poems* as an "elaborate and brilliant" rearrangement of her earlier work, which revises our sense of Moore's oeuvre as a whole by moving the poems out of chronological order.[85] It remains faithful, however, to the full range of Moore's poetic vision, allowing an evenhanded balance between long, meditative, free-verse poems and short, elaborate syllabics. We might also compare Eliot's very straightforward 1930 translation of St.-John Perse's poem *Anabasis* to Pound's sculptural misprision of Propertius. Insisting on a facing-page format (*"en regard* with the French text"), Eliot translated the French original very literally and, in fact, came back in 1949 to revise his work in the direction of "a greater fidelity to the exact meaning."[86] The small alterations that he did make work at the level of the individual word rather than the structural frame, as when "Levez un peuple de miroirs" in the seventh section becomes the self-alluding "Levy a wilderness of mirrors."[87]

Eliot was a lexical reviser rather than a structural reviser, a substituter rather than an exciser or an adder. Curiously, the greatest of modernist poets did not himself make much use of the transformative practice of revision that this book diagnoses as central to literary modernism. What he did with *The Waste Land* was to turn over his slowly accreted, piecemeal composition to Pound, entrusting the jagged process of excision to someone else. With *Four Quartets,* he found an utterly different kind of editor and correspondent. The result was a set of poems whose shape, equipoise, and generic balance—poised between symbolist lyric and diegetic narrative—resemble *The Waste Land* that Eliot seems to have wanted rather than the one he got. C. K. Stead has suggested the "probability of a major disaster in English literary history" if Eliot had had "to consult, not Pound, but the kind of people he consulted while writing *Four Quartets.*"[88] Richard Badenhausen argues that "trying to locate the better collaborator" misses the point, but it seems to me extremely perceptive. *The Waste Land* may not necessarily be a better poem because of Pound's intervention, but it is certainly a much more *modernist* one.

Despite the weight of scholarship devoted to Pound's transformations of *The Waste Land,* critics have paid curiously little attention to the way that Eliot himself had already begun to transform the poem before handing it over. The format of the facsimile edition itself may be, in this respect, partly to blame. By presenting the materials diplomatically in order of their relationship to the final version, the edition tends to flatten out the historical narrative connecting the different documents. It presents a winner's history rather than the story of Eliot's actual writing. Lawrence Rainey's recent work on the process of composition has been fundamental in supplementing the draft documents with a clear chronological order of composition. But this in itself is not necessarily adequate, because Eliot did not work or imagine in a linear direction. For example, he wrote the lines that now make up the opening of "The Fire Sermon" by hand on the back of the subsequently abandoned but already typed-up couplets about Fresca. Most of the criticism of the facsimile documents assumes that they all possess a similar quality of draftliness, but this isn't really true: the materials that remain represent many different strata of composition. The quickly written cursive lines "The rivers [*sic*] tent is broken" may be chronologically subsequent to the Fresca passage, but they are also genetically (or even ontologically) *prior* to it: they represent something closer to first thoughts. It would be easier in a sense to discuss Pound's work on *The Waste Land* if Eliot had simply handed him a chaotic series of early-stage materials. What in fact we have to analyze is the tension between Pound's deletions and Eliot's two-stage process of production by accretion and substitution. The effect is a bit like watching someone sculpt wet papier-mâché.

One of the most notable things about Eliot's original materials is their fondness for elaborate and imaginative montage. The first four sections of the poem proceed by flatly juxtaposing scenes from different historical time periods. Similar locations, from the shore of the Thames to a fallen woman's bedroom, are reduplicated across historical periods, and in borrowed prosodic and metrical forms that sometimes match and sometimes satirically invert their content. In the Fresca passage, for example, the Popean couplets fit well with the satirical tone and the eighteenth-century bedroom aesthetic, but the elegiac quatrains which Eliot chose for the story of the typist and young man carbuncular are at odds with the insistent modernity of "food in tins," Oxford Street, and the mediating devices of typewriter and gramophone. The juxtaposition of high form and low content is a technique that Eliot had played with extensively in his second volume of poems. We might think of the final stanza of "Sweeney Among the Nightingales," itself slightly revised ("siftings" a replacement for "droppings"):

> And sang within the bloody wood
> When Agamemnon cried aloud,
> And let their liquid siftings fall
> To stain the stiff dishonoured shroud.

Here, a sordid scene in an urban dive is raised by a subtle sound modulation ("sing"/ "sang"), and the half rhyme ("wood"/ "aloud") becomes in turn the absolute closure of "shroud." Yeats approved of this moment of high lyricism as "the great manner."[89] It is not a technique that Pound makes much use of in his own work.

In the 1921 draft, acts of parallel and contrast take place within individual sections, and the structure of each section is reduplicated in the next. "The Burial of the Dead" gives us versions of modern city life: a boozy visit to a prostitute in a city that appears to be Boston, coffee in Munich, Madame Sosostris dealing her wicked pack of cards in postwar London, and the spectral scene of a buried corpse sprouting through the soil of the "Unreal City." "A Game of Chess" or "In the Cage" furnishes scenes of distressed or violated sexuality. The woman sitting in a throne is listening for "footsteps on the stair," and the luxurious furnishings of her room contain a painting of the raped Philomela's metamorphosis. She melts into the "photography" realism of an unhappy middle-class couple playing chess, Lil's abortion, the mad Ophelia's "good night," and the pub-goers "goonight." The original title for this section had pointed to "the framed and wired confinement" of Henry James's telegraphist. Had the title remained, it would have formed another link forward to the passive typist in "The Fire Sermon."[90] The title that Eliot chose instead makes the section's major theme more explicit by referring to the game of chess played in *Women Beware Women* to cover Bianca's seduction, and it refocuses "A Game of Chess" around the issue of sex. Following this, "The Fire Sermon," offers up scenes of waste and purging: Fresca shits and scribbles, the Thames riverbank is emptied of litter, Mrs. Porter and her daughter cleanse themselves, London's "swarming life" is apostrophized, and the typist gives in to the young man carbuncular in her squalid flat. "Death by Water" then shows us three sailors in increasingly precarious positions: a "drunken ruffian" limps ashore, a first person narrator describes a terrifying voyage off the New England shore, which ends with the ship breaking up on an iceberg, and the lyrical coda memorializes the ancient Phlebas, "a fortnight dead."

The Waste Land was conceived in a symmetrical structure and, throughout its composition, Eliot kept insisting that it was "in four parts." Critics have interpreted this statement with difficulty, and rather differently. Lawrence Rainey suggests that when Wyndham Lewis described a poem "in four parts," he had seen it "before it acquired a fifth part or the beginning scene of the drinking binge," *but* that when Eliot spoke in January 1922 of "a poem of about four hundred and fifty lines, in four parts" he was thinking of something close to the final version, minus the "Death by Water" section.[91] This, though, is not an obvious conclusion to draw from the internal evidence of the draft materials, most of which are unnumbered. After typing the initial drafts of what became "The Burial of the Dead" and "A Game of Chess," Eliot added the second titles, "He Do the Police in Different Voices: Part I," and "He Do the Police in Different Voices: Part II." These titles themselves, however, do not obviously attach to the poem as a four- or five-part whole, and the numbers come after the Dickens framing. They are positioned at the very top of the page at a slight slant and are clearly a late addition, produced after feeding the already typed page back into the machine. The only other number in the draft materials is a "Part IV" written above the fair copy manuscript of the long "Death by Water." One possibility might be that "He Do the Police in Different Voices" was intended to be a single internally subdivided first section, with three additional parts to follow. Another is that Eliot spoke of four parts only before he composed "What the Thunder Said," which came more quickly and easily than the other parts.

The constitution of the four parts may be obscure but the important point is quite clear. During the process in which he was thinking about and composing *The Waste Land,* Eliot saw it as having a square, symmetrical, four-part shape quite different from the irregular form it eventually assumed. As Marshall McLuhan noted in the 1970s, a five-act structure tends toward rhetorical or narrative progression, toward a dénouement, whereas a four-part structure promotes balance and juxtaposition.[92] When Pound edited, he undid Eliot's attempt to produce a long poem with the symmetrical structure of classic symphonic form. His five-part structure is unevenly weighted, and the relationship among the sections of the poem is abstruse. Like the reader of "In a Station of the Metro," the reader of the 1922 text must do all the grammatical work, supplying the syntactic relationships between separate contexts and clusters of images. So, where the draft of "Death by Water" had consisted of clusters of materials placed in provocative adjacency, the final version proceeds metaphorically. Phlebas now stands as a symbolic representation of *all* of those who have perished or might perish at sea, just as the unhappy coupling of typist and young man carbuncular stands in for the other kinds of bad sex Eliot had originally imagined.

This is the same selective textual logic that Pound had used in the "Homage to Sextus Propertius."

By cutting the original opening and the long description of a sea voyage, Pound also removed all traces of America from *The Waste Land*, opening Eliot to the charge of having become an un- or anti-American poet. William Carlos Williams remarked bitterly that the poem's publication "struck like a sardonic bullet," and that "Eliot returned us to the classroom just at the moment when I felt that we were on the point of escape to matters much closer to the essence of a new art form itself—rooted in the locality which should give it fruit."[93] Originally, however, Eliot had balanced reference to a European literary tradition with colloquial American dialect, interlayering present and past time, the particular and the general. "April is the cruellest month," was preceded, as the first line of the second part of "The Burial of the Dead," by "First we had a couple of feelers down at old Tom's place" (4:1-2).[94] Phlebas' death followed the description of a shipwreck off the Atlantic coast. The inattentive sailors ignore the signs of a brewing storm, thinking only of "home and dollars and the pleasant violin/ At Marm Brown's joint, and the girls and gin" (64:49-50). After the understated last line of this section, "there is no more noise now," we have to assume that the voyage will only end with the crew's death. In this context, a snatch of dialect "Where's a cocktail shaker, Ben" (68:80), becomes an ironic and macabre joke, as the ice cubes used to blend a drink (a glamorous image in prohibition America) become the limitless "cracked" ice on which the ship has begun to break up.

The scenes set in America suggest that, as in "Burbank," Eliot was still taking the James novel as one of his models: the naïve good-time innocence of the characters drinking at Tom's place and on the sea voyage tragically or proleptically prefaces postwar London as a site of experience and loss. At the same time, contemporary London was to be set against London at other historical moments, producing a panorama of perspectives through space *and* time. Like the Cubist painter, Eliot broke up and reassembled the places of his waste land in abstracted forms. History becomes represented not as a story in time but as a temporally arrested "simultaneous order." Indeed, in the summer of 1921, while Eliot was actively engaged in drafting *The Waste Land*, he had commented that Cubism itself was "not license, but an attempt to establish order."[95] Where Imagism had attempted to reduce experience to a single heightened instant, Eliot produces a surfeit of mysterious temporal markers. In the drafts, we watch the narrative, personal past of "First we had a couple of feelers down at Tom's place" shift into the generalizing present of "April is the cruellest month," and then the allusive, distancing past of "The chair she sat in."

Comparing the drafts and published form of "The Fire Sermon" provides a particularly clear lens on the tensions between Eliot's extrinsic style of composition—a knitting together of fragments, followed by fastidious acts of substitution—and Pound's bold, excisive editing.[96] The typescript (which also contains some manuscript drafting) flickers between London present and past, with a particular focus on the eighteenth century. Eliot began with a series of heroic couplets about "white-armed" Fresca performing her morning toilet, and he put this carefully wrought, Popean passage in dialogue with other scenes set in London, and flavored with an eighteenth-century feel. Set in a woman's dressing room and grimly focused on the interplay between nature and artifice, French perfume, and "the good old hearty female stench" (22:41), the Fresca passage is also reminiscent of Swift, in particular of poems such as "A Beautiful Young Nymph Going to Bed" and "The Lady's Dressing Room," which, as Tita Chico has argued, satirize the female body as a "site and producer of excrement" to manage anxieties about female sexuality and women's potential for independence.[97]

One of the most important things about this passage is its historical simultaneity: Fresca is a character suspended between the eighteenth-century form in which she is narrated and a modern, even modernist twentieth-century setting. Eliot bolstered this slightly as he revised. Originally, he described his heroine in her bedroom reading two eighteenth-century authors, Richardson and Gibbon, both of whom fit well with the stylized eighteenth-century aesthetic and details like "a polished tray/ Of soothing chocolate, or stimulating tea." But in a typescript revision, he scratched out "a page of Gibbon" and altered it to "the Daily Mirror." Why? The newspaper is more disjunctive, certainly, and it fits better with some of Fresca's up-to-date and perhaps pretentious art tastes. (She reads "a clever book by Giraudoux" in much the same way that the woman in "Portrait of a Lady" talks of Chopin, or the women in "Prufrock" of Michelangelo.) It may also point to her protofeminism and erotic self-confidence. The *Daily Mirror* had been founded in 1903 by Alfred Harmsworth, later Lord Northcliffe, as a tabloid for women providing "a mirror of feminine life as well on its grave as on its lighter sides." Thirdly, and most subtly, it may be an indirect nod—in a pleasingly eighteenth-century manner—to Eliot's own patron and financial backer. In 1914, Alfred Harmsworth sold the paper to his brother, Viscount Rothermere. His wife, Lady Rothermere, was Eliot's patroness and the founder of *The Criterion*—the site of *The Waste Land*'s first English outing.

As the passage proceeds, it pans out from Fresca's bedroom to consider her as a Tiresias-like figure capable of occupying other times and places, "Fresca! in other time or place had been/ A meek and lowly weeping Magdalene." On the back of the neat typescript page containing the first forty lines and headed "The Fire Sermon," Eliot drafted in manuscript the passage that opens the 1922 poem. On the back of the second typescript page, he worked rather harder over some other manuscript lines that have not survived. These in fact are the most heavily revised manuscript lines that survive in the entire facsimile, and they are a tribute to two things: first, Eliot's relentless attempt to compress historical moments and, second (not unrelated), his propensity for substitution, swapping out. The first few lines, representing Fresca as the young Aphrodite rising from the sea, are cleanly written:

> From which, a Venus Anadyomene
> She stept ashore to a more varied scene,
> Propelled by Lady Katzegg's guiding hand
> She knew the wealth and fashion of the land . . . (28: 1–4)

But then the page starts to get messier. Eliot begins with another metaphor that works in temporal reverse, where the eighteenth-/twentieth-century Fresca can be imagined as "Minerva in a crowd of boxing peers." Then he switches direction and tries to compare Aeneas recognizing his mother, the goddess Venus, to the kind of celebrity worship that takes place in a modern cinema. Of course, this is a much weirder and riskier metaphoric gambit. The lines caused him great difficulty. The bottom layer of writing runs:

> She reigns no less distinguished spheres,
> Minerva in a crowd of boxing peers.
> Aeneas' mother, with an altered face,
> Appeared once in an unexpected place:
> He recognized the goddess by her supernatural grace
> So the close millions
> The sweating rabble in the cinema
> Can recognise a goddess or a star.
> And hushed silence silence worships from afar. (28: 7–15)

The second "silence" in line 15 seems to be a pure *currente calamo* revision; Eliot writes the word, cancels it, and then immediately reinstates it. How long it took him to make the other acts of substitution in this passage is not so clear. As he reworked, Eliot altered "reigns" firstly to "dominates," and then to "governs." He then drew a bubble around the couplet and wrote "But F. rules" in the small amount of remaining space in the left-hand margin. He also played around with the modifier "no less," changing it to the almost equivalent "even more." Here we have five substitutions in a single couplet. In the subsequent lines, he scratched out the second half of the word "appeared" and wrote the semantically similar "approached" in superscript; he changed "unexpected" to "unfamiliar," "goddess" to "divinity," "supernatural grace" to "smooth celestial pace," "close" to "pact," "rabble" to "thousands" and "millions" (it is not clear in which order he did this), "recognize" to "identify" and "know," and "hushed" to "reverent."

This is revision working by the principle of the thesaurus. Words are replaced by words that mean similar things, have similar prosodic shapes, and often similar etymologies. It is a very fine-grained iterative process, and it was always Eliot's preferred mode of revision. We see similar versions of it throughout the poem, including the swap from one Platonic character to another—"Ademantus" to "Glaucon"—in the very next passage (the cancelled apostrophe to London). Of course, neither the Fresca couplets (in manuscript) nor the address to London (in type-script) made it into the 1922 poem. In this sense the revisions have a ghostly status: they mark the genetic process of a poem that merely *could have been.* Pound did not spend very much time on either passage because, presumably, he saw no possibility of keeping them. Nonetheless, the visual counterpoint on page 30 of the facsimile document is striking. Eliot has carefully crossed out his typed "O Ademantus" and written "Glaucon" in small neat writing above it. Pound, on the other hand, has drawn a thick black vertical line through the entire passage. In the right-hand margin, he has also added various Poundian comments, including "dam per'opsey" next to Mr. Eugenides's initially cautious proposition, "And perhaps a weekend at the Metropole." Below, next to "London, the swarming life you kill and breed," he writes simply "B——ll——S."

Exactly the same process happens in the parts of the draft that did survive. In "The Burial of the Dead," Eliot's typescripts show him changing "Terrible city" (8:114) into "Unreal city," and oscillating from "expired" to the more exhausted "exhaled," then back to "expired," and then forward again to the final "exhaled" (8:118). Pound marked this revision "J. J.," perhaps thinking of the sinister, metamorphic moment in "Circe" where a beagle reveals himself to Bloom as Dignam who has "gnawed all. He exhales a putrid carcasefed breath." At the very end of "The Burial of the Dead," substitutive revision works in the opposite direction—away rather than toward the allusion—as Webster's "foe to men" is transformed into the more paradoxical "friend to men" (8:128). Later in the poem, other important but local substitutions include "demotic" for "his vile" for the original "abominable" in the description of Mr. Eugenides's French (30:98), and "Inexplicable" for "their joyful" and "inviolable" in the manuscript description that was to become "Inexplicable splendour of Ionian white and gold" (36:6). Here, Eliot also toyed with the substitution of "music" for "splendour" before reverting to the original reading and, between the manuscript and final version, without leaving any record, he changed "Corinthian" to the less architecturally decorative "Ionian." On most of these sheets, Pound has either drawn arrows and lines suggesting structural transformation or, on

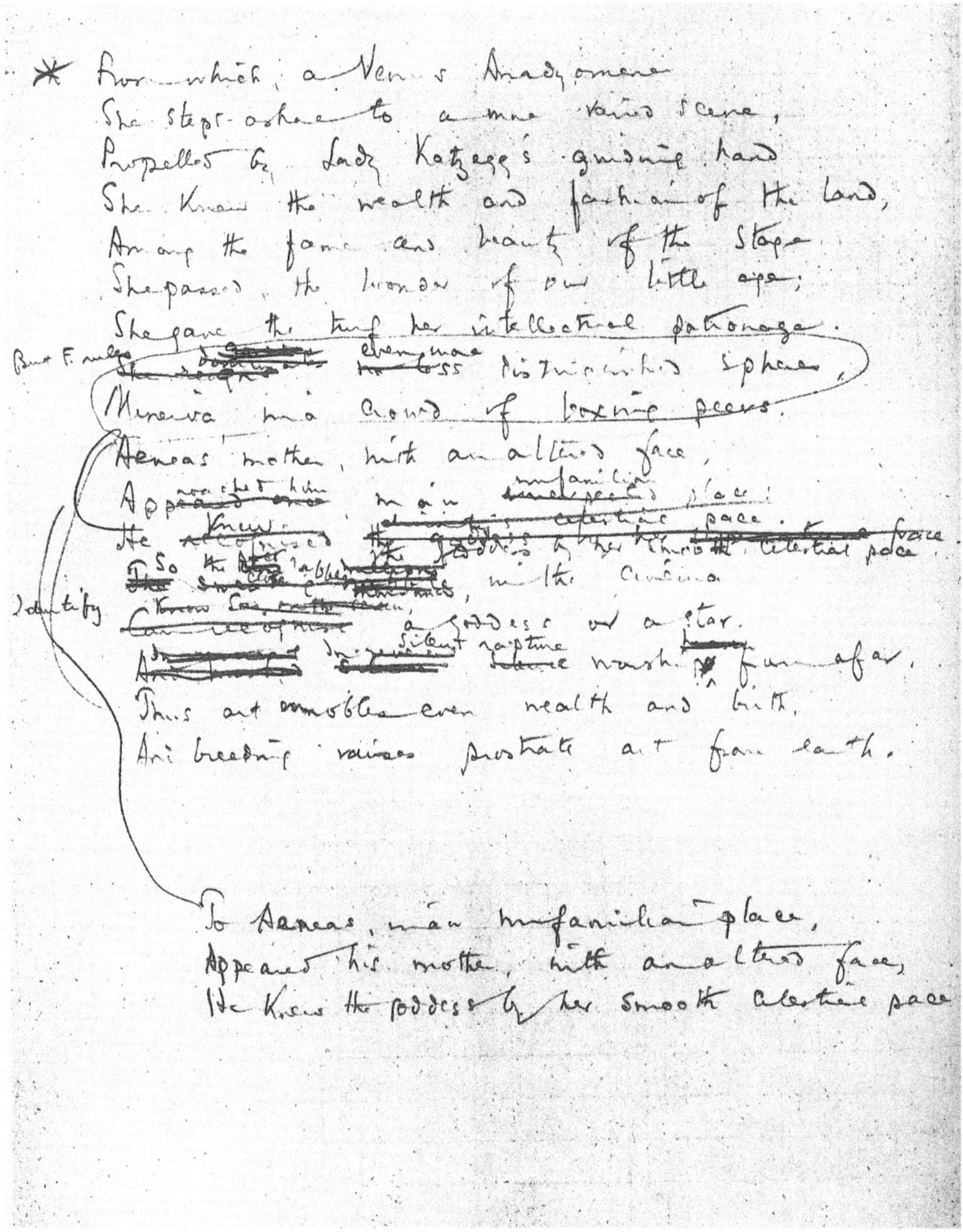

From which, a Venus Anadyomene
She stept ashore to a more varied scene,
Propelled by Lady Katzegg's guiding hand
She knew the wealth and fashion of the land,
Among the fame and beauty of the stage
She passed, the wonder of our little age;
She gave the turf her intellectual patronage.

Minerva in a crowd of boxing peers.
Aeneas mother, with an altered face,

a goddess or a star.

Thus art ennobles even wealth and birth,
And breeding raises prostrate art from earth.

To Aeneas, in an unfamiliar place,
Appeared his mother, with an altered face,
He knew the goddess by her smooth celestial pace

Figure 4a: Eliot's own revisions on a page of manuscript of *The Waste Land*.
Extract taken from *The Waste Land: A Facsimile and Transcript* © Estate of
T. S. Eliot and reprinted by permission of Faber and Faber Ltd.

```
Twit twit twit twit twit twit twit
Tereu tereu
So rudely forc'd.
Ter

Unreal City, I have seen and see
Under the brown fog of your winter noon
Mr.Eugenides, the Smyrna merchant,
Unshaven, with a pocket full of currants
(C.i,f. London: documents at sight),
Who asked me, in abominable French,
To luncheon at the Cannon Street Hotel,
And perhaps a weekend at the Metropole.

Twit twit twit
Jug jug jug jug jug jug
Tereu
O swallow swallow
Ter

London, the swarming life you kill and breed,
Huddled between the concrete and the sky,
Responsive to the momentary need,
Vibrates unconscious to its formal destiny,

Knowing neither how to think, nor how to feel.
But lives in the awareness of the observing eye.
Phantasmal gnomes, burrowing in brick and stone and steel!
Some minds, aberrant from the normal equipoise
(London, your people is bound upon the wheel!)
Record the motions of these pavement toys
And trace the cryptogram that may be curled
Within these faint perceptions of the noise,
Of the movement, and the lights!

Not here, O Glaucon, but in another world.

At the violet hour, the hour when eyes and back and hand
Turn upward from the desk, the human engine waits -
Like a taxi throbbing waiting at a stand -
To spring to pleasure through the horn or ivory gates,

I Tiresias, though blind, throbbing between two lives,
Old man with wrinkled female breasts, can see
At the violet hour, the evening hour that strives
Homeward, and brings the sailor home from sea,
```

Figure 4b: Pound's excisions and changes on a page of typescript of *The Waste Land*. Extract taken from *The Waste Land: A Facsimile and Transcript* © Estate of T. S. Eliot and reprinted by permission of Faber and Faber Ltd.

the sections he most approved of, he has simply made witty, elliptical comments, "Marianne," "photography."

Pound did not approve of Fresca and put a series of nine diagonal lines through the passage, explaining that "if you mean this as a burlesque, you had better suppress it, for you cannot parody Pope unless you can write better verse than Pope—and you can't."[98] One of the gashes through the lines runs so deep that the ink has bled onto the other side of the paper. This has usually been read formally, as a criticism of Eliot's versification, but the word "burlesque" is also important. Pound was objecting to the basic principle of Eliot's upside-down style, his mixing of high and low elements, and his fusing of eighteenth- and twentieth-century content. Most importantly, I think, he misunderstood Eliot's attempt at producing an aesthetic of simultaneous time where different historical periods would appear as aspects or modes of thought rather than as a causally connected sequence.

When he came to the final section of "The Fire Sermon," he dissolved Eliot's Augustan frame more subtly. Here Eliot had originally been working in an unusual stanza form. Hugh Kenner was the first to comment on Eliot's fondness for this "uncommon stanza, recognizable to most modern ears because Gray used it in his *Elegy*," noting that Dryden was also fascinated by its "leisurely authority."[99] In particular, it is the form of "Annus Mirabilis"—a poem which is deeply relevant to *The Waste Land*, not only because it "elaborate[s] a sustained analogy between modern London and ancient Rome," but because of its sustained thematic preoccupation with rubbish and refuse, with London as a modern "waste land."

Take this stanza, for example:

> He, the young man carbucular, will stare
> Boldly about, in "London's one café,"
> And he will tell her, with a casual air,
> Grandly, "I have been with Nevinson today." (32:153–156)

If the delayed adjective, "weightily felicitous Latinism," repeated adverb structure, and satirical antithesis ("casual"/ "grandly") recall Restoration verse, the mention of the artist Nevinson—a futurist who became a celebrity in 1916 after exhibiting a one-man show of war paintings—locates the action in contemporary London. When Pound edited, he emphasized the "now" of narrative time by deleting the eighteenth-century manner. In the published poem, this stanza is collapsed with the next, and eight lines become four lines of Arnold Bennett–like realism:

> He, the young man carbuncular, arrives,
> A small house agent's clerk, with one bold stare,
> One of the low on whom assurance sits
> As a silk hat on a Bradford millionaire.

Elsewhere, Pound urged the deletion of individual lines and pairs of lines, destroying the quatrain structure, and minimizing the antithesis between inherited form and up-to-date content. The suddenness of this couplet, for example, results from the excision of the second *b* rhyme:

> I Tiresias, old man with wrinkled dugs,
> Perceived the scene, and foretold the rest—
> I too awaited the expected guest.

On the second copy of the typescript, against the third line of the quatrain, Pound wrote, "Too easy." Originally it had run

> I Tiresias, old man with wrinkled dugs,
> Perceived the scene, and foretold the rest,
> Knowing the manner of these crawling bugs,
> I too awaited the expected guest. (44:141–144)

The comparison below gives an illustration of Pound's excisive editing in practice. Like a collapsing concertina, the green lines showing textual difference map inward as the large amount of text shaded in the left window is deleted.

At the violet hour, when the eyes and back and hand
Turn upward from the desk, the human engine waits—
Like a taxi throbbing waiting at a stand—
To spring to pleasure through the horn or ivory gates.
I Tiresias, though blind, throbbing between two lives,
Old man with wrinkled female breasts, can see
At the violet hour, the evening hour that strives
Homeward, and brings the sailor home from sea,
The typist home at teatime, who begins
To clear away her broken breakfast, lights
Her stove, and lays out squalid food in tins,
Prepares the room and sets the room to rights.
Out of the window perilously spread
Her drying combinations meet the sun's last rays,
And on the divan piled, (at night her bed),
Are stockings, dirty camisoles, and stays.
A bright kimono wraps her as she sprawls
In nerveless torpor on the window seat;
A touch of art is given by the false
Japanese print, purchased in Oxford Street.
I Tiresias, old man with wrinkled dugs,
Perceived the scene, and foretold the rest,
Knowing the manner of these crawling bugs,
I too awaited the expected guest.

At the violet hour, when the eyes and back
Turn upward from the desk, where the human engine waits
Like a taxi throbbing waiting,
I Tiresias, though blind, throbbing between two lives,
Old man with wrinkled female breasts, can see
At the violet hour, the evening hour that strives
Homeward, and brings the sailor home from sea,
The typist home at teatime, clears her breakfast, lights
Her stove, and lays out food in tins.
Out of the window perilously spread
Her drying combinations touched by the sun's last rays,
On the divan are piled (at night her bed)
Stockings, slippers, camisoles, and strays.
I Tiresias, old man with wrinkled dugs
Perceived the scene, and foretold the rest—
I too awaited the expected guest.

Figure 5: Comparison of the longer typescript and shorter 1922 version of the "At the violet hour" passage.

Compositional Counterpoint: Eliot vs. Pound

Paradoxically, Eliot's *revisions* to *The Waste Land* look more like edits than Pound's editorial alterations. Pound reimagined the poem structurally, making bold deletions of whole passages and frames, but Eliot was often content to work within individual parts of speech. Many of his changes are devoted to subtle improvement of the poem's aural and musical qualities, like the replacement of the curt "expired" for the more drawn-out and mimetic "exhaled." Pound, on the other hand, was happy to dissolve formal patterns entirely. This is apparent on a larger level in the reduced Dryden quatrains, but it also takes place within individual lines. Earlier in "The Fire Sermon," for example, Pound introduces disorder into the completely regular iambic pentameter "Unreal City, I have seen and see" by bracketing off all but the fragment phrase "Unreal City."

Pound cut the waste out of *The Waste Land*: this is the party line. I would add that, if he did so, he was not so much intuiting as ignoring the formal and aesthetic principles of Eliot's drafts. He applied a method of editing designed to promote extreme verbal efficiency to a poem that was, in its original form, hospitable to mess and proliferation. Suzanne Raitt and Tim Armstrong have recently argued that Pound's early poetics of Imagism, with its focus on hardness, precision and "direct treatment of the 'thing,'" can be understood in the context of a culture "in which efficiency, economy, and the elimination of waste were increasingly heralded as industrial and social ideals."[100] But, unlike the agricultural land of Northern France, which seemed in the immediate aftermath of the 1914–1918 war to have been made "a desert and worse than a desert," Eliot's waste land was never a purely ruined landscape.[101] In fact, at the beginning of "The Fire Sermon," in the manuscript passage originally drafted on the back of the Fresca couplets, the speaker mourns the *absence* not the *presence* of litter:

> The river bears no empty bottles, sandwich papers,
> Silk handkerchiefs, cardboard boxes, cigarette ends,
> Or other testimony of summer nights. The nymphs are departed.

Here, material objects are not simply reminders of a single occasion in the past ("testimony of summer nights"), but pointers to both past and future time, considered simultaneously. Elsewhere, and not only in the allusions to Ovid, *The Waste Land* shows great fondness for acts of metamorphosis and transformation. Madame Sosostris plucks a drowned sailor from her "wicked pack of cards," but the dead man's eyes have been replaced by shining pearls (48). A murder is potentially a source of vegetable life: "That corpse you planted last year in your garden,/ Has it begun to sprout? Will it bloom this year?" (71–72). Philomel is "rudely forced" (100) by Tereus but, transformed into a nightingale, is able to fill the desert land with "inviolable voice." Animated by a melancholic attachment to the past and the dead, the poem also conjures up multiple spectral supplements, "the third who walks always beside you," "the wind under the door" that sounds like a human voice. "What the Thunder Said" extends the strategy of using a linguistic turn or pun to figure a physical metamorphosis. As "forced" became "inviolable," so "He who was living is now dead/ We who were living are now dying" (328–329). To oppose the purgation reading of the poem, we might say that waste is never the problem in *The Waste Land*. The poem's fear is not excess but emptiness, drought, and rigidity. Its most chilling image is not any description of vegetal metamorphosis, but the description of "seals broken by the lean solicitor/ In our empty rooms" (408–409).

Despite my sympathy for its implicit value judgment, I find Marjorie Perloff's claim that "Pound's excisions and revisions made Eliot's central themes and symbols more prominent than they would otherwise have been" completely erroneous. This is the seductive claim of meliorism—a kind of winner's history—but it is not a clear description of the relationship between the materials that Eliot drafted and revised and the final 1922 poem. Pound produced an elliptical, superposed version of *The Waste Land* from the many possibilities latent in the drafts, and he did so at an important junction in his relationship with Eliot—at the moment that the two poets' sensibilities were beginning dramatically to diverge. This created a *maximal version* of aesthetic counterpoint in the 1922 poem. Five years later, Eliot would have given his drafts to someone else—an Arnold Bennett or a John Hayward.

Sometimes we think of patterns of revision—like patterns of style in general—as "merely" formal, as if they represent technique blandly devoid of content. In fact, Pound's fondness for excision and his tolerance for the difficult, elliptical, gaping structures that it produced was itself an aesthetic preference—not only a technical one. His principles of Imagism and then excision in general were developed in the service of a future-oriented modernism, a modernism that intended to sharpen literature, and "break the surface of convention." His instincts were to preserve the lyrical rather than the narrative or even novelistic parts of the poem, and he preferred passages set definitively in a particular place and time to those, like the abandoned Fresca section, that wove together past and present on a line-by-line basis. When he compared writing to digging through the mud for a diamond, he was assuming that diamonds were present but obscured by the dirt. But Eliot seems to have realized that—at least in his own case—the dirt was actually producing the pearl. This is the import of one of the couplets that Pound crossed out most energetically. His perfectly neat zigzag line cancels out Eliot's whimsical—and wonderfully messy—question, as if to stop us from even entertaining a dangerous idea.[102]

> From ~~For~~ such chaotic misch-masch potpourri
> What are we to expect but poetry? (40:60–61)

This couplet comes toward the end of the Fresca section and after a historically discontinuous description of Fresca's own literary tastes and reading matter. Pound's heavy zigzag scribbles might be read formally (as objections to Eliot's "deficient" grasp of Pope), but they are also objections to the moral sentiment that binds together "poetry" ("something made," from the Greek) and "potpourri" ("a dish of mixed meats," from the French *pourrir*, to rot).[103] He is objecting to Eliot's messiness, his lack of commitment to efficiency.

Eliot's attitudes to waste and to history—the two primary subjects of *The Waste Land*—were different from and more complicated than his editor's mania for direct focus on "the thing." In his doctoral dissertation on Bradley, he had already been arguing for a notational, antirealist view of history: "Ideas of the past are true, not by correspondence with a real past, but by their coherence with each other and ultimately with the present moment."[104] "Tradition and the Individual Talent" extends this argument into the province of literature, positing past, present, and future time as a permanently available set of ideas: "The existing order is complete before the new work arrives; for order to persist after the supervention of novelty, the *whole* existing order must be, if ever so slightly, altered; and so the relations, proportions, values of each work of art toward the whole are readjusted; and this is conformity between the old and the new."[105] The poem that he began writing—a kind of flat panorama of different ages, a Cubist rendition of London through sharply different perspectives—was just such an attempt to find conformity between old and new and parallels between contemporaneity and antiquity. Pound's fondness for excision, which began as a method for capturing the single instant, was at odds with this view, with Eliot's original method of making dissimilar fragments cohere through elaborate parallels, and with the thematic logic of the poem.

Had Eliot produced the *The Waste Land* that he wanted, some of the difficult questions about continuity in his career might seem less puzzling. Terry Eagleton asks why, "despite his extreme political conservatism," Eliot was "an avant-garde poet who selected certain 'progressive' experimental techniques from the history of literary forms available to him"?[106] Kenneth Asher wonders how to fit together the early lyric poet with "the plus orthodoxe que les orthodoxes champion of cultural institutions."[107] But, in fact, Eliot was not a "progressive" poet or ever very interested in "making it new." These questions are wrongly formulated because they take their own arguments for premises. His instincts were not melioristic: he believed it was "obvious" that "art never improves," and he was a historical antirealist. Like Michael Oakeshott, who argues in his Bradleyan book *Experience and Its Modes* that "the historical past is always present, and yet historical experience is always in the form of the past," Eliot saw history as a method of epistemic organization rather than a line connecting the past to the present.[108] His style of composition and revision fits with this fundamentally conservative disposition. As he produced new drafts, he gathered together different kinds of material (self-authored and stolen) into synthetic arrangements, and he preferred "shoring up" to the radical, future-oriented length alterations of Pound and Joyce. In both these acts of accretion and in his fiddly substitutive revisions, we see the attempt to produce a poem that surveys past and present with the cool, classical perspective of *sub specie praeteritorum*, giving us Fresca as Minerva, Venus as a movie star.

Since the 1960s, critics have sometimes suggested that *The Waste Land* is a Cubist poem. Jacob Korg found that just as "in the Cubist painting, the laws of space are suppressed" so the laws of time are suppressed in *The Waste Land;*[109] Frank Kermode argues that the poem "had something in common with Cubism . . . it permitted a view of history without perspective";[110] and David Tomlinson wonders if Eliot's visit to the Picasso exhibition at the Leicester Galleries in 1921 helped to produce "A Game of Chess" by analogy to *La femme assise dans un fauteuil* (1914).[111] Eliot himself had described Cubism as "an attempt to establish order" and the analogy seems particularly pertinent to the balanced, spatial form of the original drafts. The poem that Pound returned in early 1922 is much more jagged. In every respect it is more *dis*-ordered and entropic. Before Eliot turned over his materials, he had, like the synthetic Cubists, been working quite literally through the technique of "papier collé": self-translating, incorporating earlier poems, pasting, stitching together. What Pound did was to cut through this process, like a sculptor chiseling away unevenly at a composite set of materials and producing surprising lines of fracture.

In his famous essay on authorial intention, Thomas Tanselle once used Eliot and Pound as a model of collaborative work: "Eliot's intention merged with Pound's intention."[112] I would prefer to invert the formulation. *The Waste Land* isn't a model of collaborative work because Eliot's drafts sought or intuited Pound's attention, or because Pound continued a process already in motion. The enigmatic success of the poem in its final form derives instead from the aesthetically pleasing counterpoint between excision and accretion, economy and synthesis.[113] It is less unevenly elliptical and superficial than "Hugh Selwyn Mauberley," but it is also more charged and surprising than the repeating, classical structures Eliot devised on his own for *Four Quartets*. It may not be simple to work out who is speaking in each section of *The Waste Land*—there is nothing as straightforward as the sincerity of "So here I am, in the middle way"—but, on the other hand, the voicing is not intrinsically or finally indeterminate. Unlike "Hugh Selwyn Mauberley," *The Waste Land* allows us to establish a point of view about its different voices; it contains enough framing for us to be able to establish, and enjoy, the banality of a line such as "One must be so careful these days." In this sense, the excised and reduced poem, poised between elliptical license and a classical attempt "to establish order," is *just difficult enough*—Pound's greatest poem.

CHAPTER 4

Joyce and the Illogic of Addition

Henry James's struggle "to keep compression rich" was the first of many. Modernist texts often threaten to be too long, uncontainable within conventional or practical bibliographic forms. They generate excesses of words and paper, as Joyce recognized when he proudly told Myron Nutting in 1923 that his "unused" notes for *Ulysses* weighed twelve kilograms.[1] So, too, Frank Budgen remembered that Joyce's Zürich flat was full of envelopes stuffed with fragments produced at lightning speed, "a multitude of criss-cross notes in pencil."[2] In fact, he was able to force many of these elliptical phrases ("golden syrup," "in the shape of solid food") *back* into the typescripts, placard, and page proofs of *Ulysses* during the long period of time in which the novel was being revised.[3] In this chapter, I explore the strategy and effects of revision by extension. How does it differ from revision by excision, and why might a writer prefer one kind over the other? In an essay on Marianne Moore, Andrew Kappel makes the brief and tantalizing general claim that excision is the choice of poets, extension of novelists: "Anyone who has glanced at corrected proofs of *À la recherche du temps perdu* or *Ulysses* knows to what extent modern writers could be given to expansion and elaboration when revising. Where Proust and Joyce add and add, Moore cuts and cuts. Of course, perhaps we are here seeing a difference of temperament between novelists and poets, or between the modernism of the novelists and the modernism of the poets, for the modernism of the poets was characterized by a commitment to concision."[4] This is a good starting point, but the true state of affairs has to be more complicated: Hemingway and Gertrude Stein both wrote elliptical, highly crafted prose by cutting, and as early as 1917, Pound had begun to abandon the protocols of deletion for accretion and accumulation. He told John Quinn that his *Cantos* were to be "really LONG, endless, leviathanic."[5]

Might extension and excision be tied not to "the modernism of the novelists and the modernism of the poets" but to two different aesthetic or representational strands within modernism? Where excision produces ellipsis and asks the reader to fill in missing syntax, extension can lead to overdescription and the flat "and and and" of parataxis. Where excision tends to suggest metaphor, so "petals on a wet black bough" *are* "these faces in the crowd," and Phlebas *stands* for all the other drowned sailors that Pound's blue pencil removed, addition tends toward metonymy and relationships of adjacency. The intrinsic association between metaphor and hypotaxis, metonymy and parataxis, has been clearly described by N. Katherine Hayles in her work on postmodernism. She describes the two poles as follows: "Metaphor is simultaneous pattern; metonymy successive sequence. Metaphor operates through substitution, metonymy through deletion. Metaphor draws on the past and on traditions; metonymy points toward the future and innovations. Metaphor foregrounds thought and depth and leads to relations of hypotaxis; metonymy emphasizes sensation and surface and leads to parataxis."[6] Of course, many critics have also suggested that prose (particularly nineteenth-century fiction) works through contiguity and tends toward the metonymyic pole, while poetry proceeds through formal rules of similarity (sound patterning, repeated rhythms) and tend towards metaphor.[7] Regrounding rather than dismissing Kappel's speculation, we can say that excision is associated with the metaphoric pole, and poetry; addition with metonymy, and prose.

We have already seen that excisive revision has a propensity to make texts more difficult, by removing explanatory frames and syntactic connections. In some ways, *The Waste Land* was less enigmatic before Pound removed Eliot's elaborate acts of balance and montage, and the typist (who remains) would have been explained more clearly if the "In the Cage" frame from James and the untidy boudoir where Fresca scribbles had also survived. Does this mean that the opposite form of revision makes texts easier, more expansive, more self-explanatory? In fact revision of a complete, syntactically sensible first draft through repeated addition can also tend, like excision, to produce sentences that are *less* rather than *more* grammatically clear and comprehensible. It promotes difficulty and gives the reader more work to do. But the kinds of difficulty it introduces have a different flavor. Take, for example, this sentence from "Eumaeus," which began in the first set of proofs:

> Bloom was the first to rise from his seat having first and foremost taken the wise precaution to motion to mine host a scarcely perceptible sign . . . [8]

After *five* sendings of proof, Joyce interleaved it with qualifiers and clichés producing a series of adjacent, qualifying clauses, so that it read,

> To cut a long story short Bloom, grasping the situation, was the first to rise from his seat so as not to outstay their welcome having first and foremost, being as good as his word, that he would foot the bill for the occasion, taken the wise precaution to unobtrusively motion to mine host as a parting shot a scarcely perceptible sign . . . (16.1691–1695)

The phrase "to cut a long story short" is peculiarly apt or inept in the circumstances, given that what Joyce is doing is in fact the opposite—he is extending a short story long. We might even say that this genetic fact comments on the false thinking in the cliché: the kind of people who talk of "cutting a long story short" are often, like the speaker of "Eumaeus," prone to being unnecessarily verbose. The other clichés, including the phrase "so as not to outstay their welcome," are also grammatically disruptive. "Their welcome" introduces a subject shift between singular and plural, Bloom and they, and the syntactically straightforward participle clause "having first and foremost taken the wise precaution" is so confused by the interleaving of two additional clauses that its meaning seems to melt away.

Roman Jakobson's famous 1956 identification of metaphor and metonymy as two poles in normal language develops from a discussion of two kinds of aphasic disturbances.[9] By suggesting that aphasia can be understood either as a problem of selection or combination, Jakobson was overturning a more traditional distinction between emissive and receptive speech problems. David Lodge has argued, in turn, that "this evidence from the clinical study of aphasia is not merely fascinating in its own right and persuasive support for Jakobson's general theory of language" but "of direct relevance to modern literature and its notorious 'obscurity'"; in fact, he suggests that modernist writing "aspires to the condition of aphasia."[10] At one end of the spectrum, patients with a similarity disorder (selection deficiency) exhibit some of the following problems: difficulty with metaphor, difficulty initiating sentences that are not directly reactive to other sentences or a simple external situation ("it is raining"), a tendency to substitute general nouns ("chose," "Ding," "thing") for specific ones; a tendency to spare words with direct relevance to an immediate context (pronouns, connectives, auxiliaries) while losing the capacity to make general propositions (121–122). Like this sentence from "Eumaeus" they seem to have too much grammatical framework for their minimal content. Jakobson gives an example of a patient presented with the word *knife* who "never uttered the word *knife* alone but, according to its use and surroundings, alternatively called the knife *pencil-sharpener, apple-parer, bread-knife, knife-and-fork;* so the word *knife* was changed from a free form, capable of occurring alone, into a bound form." Joyce's revisions by addition very often have this quality: often, in fact, they turn single adjectives into bound, compounded forms. Others increase specificity by positing literal relationships of adjacency. At the beginning of "Ithaca," for instance, Joyce originally had Bloom and Stephen deliberating on "the growth of trees," then "the growth of adjoining trees," and then in the proofs, "adjoining paraheliotropic trees" (Gabler III.1454; *U* 17.14) while Molly's "my new white shoes all ruined with the saltwater" extended to "my new white shoes all ruined with the saltwater and the hat I had with that feather all blowy and tossed on me" (III.1690; 18.971).[11] By contrast, Jakobson's second kind of aphasia, the contiguity disorder (combination deficiency) "diminishes the extent and variety of sentences" (126) and leads in its most extreme case toward "agrammatism": a pile of verbal rubble. In more moderate cases, or at the beginning of the disorder, he argues that "words endowed with purely grammatical functions, like conjunctions, prepositions, pronouns, and articles, disappear first, giving rise to the so-called 'telegraphic style'." Jakobson continues to distinguish the two disorders by explaining that words that kernel subject words—those that do not depend strongly on the grammatical context—fall out quickly in similarity disorders and remain stubbornly persistent in contiguity disorders. We might think about the heaped fragments at the end of *The Waste Land,* or the epigraph to "Burbank" as examples: these are jeweled phrases without a grammar. And "telegraphic" is a good description, in the more moderate case, of Hemingway's prose style.

In other words, if modernist literature aspires to the condition of aphasia, we might say that it achieves this state not from the first draft, but through two separate, disordering processes of revision. Excision bears down heavily on context-dependent words and those with purely grammatical functions to leave behind charged fragments. Many Imagist poems are, quite literally, "infantile one-sentence utterances." Extension or addition, on the other hand, produces grammatically complicated, long-winded, and literal paratactic sentences. Cognitive scientists have suggested that some writers known to suffer from Alzheimer's disease develop a similarity disorder as their disease progresses; Iris Murdoch's late prose, for example, has been described as less rich in vocabulary than her earlier writing, more repetitive, richer in filler words and vague words, and richer in verbs than in nouns.[12] This is an example of genuine aphasia. Modernist writers, who we can think of as would-be aphasics, doers of different abnormal voices, had more control.

Two Kinds of Addition

It is important to distinguish between two basic kinds of addition. If the work as a whole has a fixed plan and end point, addition can take place interlinearly, so that each section becomes longer, encrusted with more detail, but without altering the balance of the work as a whole. Wordsworth's *Prelude,* expanded from two parts in 1798–1799 to five and then thirteen books in 1805, is one example of a text of this kind; Jonathan Arac finds Wordsworth "spinning out more and more material to stand between parts that were originally compacted together." He provides the useful term "interlinear glossing" to describe this process, and compares it to Coleridge's marginal revision of "The Rime of the Ancient Mariner."[13] *Ulysses,* which Joyce added to in proof, after completing and sometimes publishing the individual episodes, is another exemplary case: between the Rosenbach manuscript and the published novel, we see the text grow inside-out. The third volume of Clive Driver's facsimile edition, which prints the first edition as a base text and then circles every word, phrase, or sentence added for the *Little Review* or after looks, at first glance, like a page attacked at random with a highlighter pen. Very few pages contain less than 10 percent of additions, and some, particularly in the "Cyclops" and "Ithaca" episodes are closer to 100 percent of postmanuscript addition.[14] But because the episodes are stylistically and formally discrete units, the revisions also take place within certain fixed boundaries; in fact, Joyce developed subtly different methods of addition to match his different prose styles. "Joyce's unit of composition," as Michael Groden explains, "was the episode, not the entire book."[15] Molly's monologue gets longer principally through the addition of short single-breath phrases inserted between other ones; in "Ithaca," the catechistic structure allows for the addition of complete new question-and-answer units to be inserted; while the revisions to the verbose, cliché-laden narrative of "Eumaeus" tend to be longer, syntactically complex sentences or sentence parts.

Other writers found that their works developed serially, in a kind of multiplicative structure. Pound carried on adding more *Cantos* until his death, despite reaching a series of possible numerical and formal stopping points: the structure he designed was one of infinite extensibility. He explained that the principle had to be one of maximum inclusivity: "it had to be a form that wouldn't exclude something merely because it didn't fit."[16] He sometimes spoke of stopping at "100 or 120," but soon realized "Cantos won't be finished until my demise" or, rather, that there would never be a satisfactory formal end. Before beginning work on this lifelong project Pound was the most relentless and versatile of excisers—

always in pursuit of economy of expression—but in the *Cantos* his method began to switch, from hypotactic condensation into additive, encyclopedic structures that knit together different sources. This is noticeable at the level of syntax and form from the very beginning, in the subjectless list "And then went down to the ship. . . . And / so winds from sternward," which Pound retrieved from what was originally Canto III to become the opening of the whole poem; in doing so, he also freed a paratactic structure from the dramatic frame in which it was embedded ("Here's but rough meaning:. . .").[17] Canto II ends with a soft ellipsis "And . . ." that produces an effect of fading and multiplying, as if the list of heard things could be extended forever. Canto III then opens with an apparently determinate lyric structure, "I sat on the Dogana's steps," that immediately replicates itself, into another list of "ands": "And there were not 'those girls' . . . / And the Buccentoro . . . / And the lit crossbeams . . . / And peacocks . . ." It seems that Pound's migration from excision to serial and unfolding expansion happened alongside a shift in his poetic style from the hypotactic to the paratactic pole. Did his renunciation of a commitment to condensation act as an unconscious driver toward a new poetic style, or did he stop writing long and excising because he had a different end product in mind? The question of cause and effect, product and process, is probably unanswerable.

Early readers of the later volumes of Proust's *À la recherche* criticized the text's development or outgrowth from the three volumes planned in 1914 to the sixteen (including posthumous work) published by 1927 as a gross perversion of normal form. Albert Feuillerat's 1934 study, with the pleasingly straightforward title *Comment Marcel Proust a composé son roman*, put forward the suggestion that there were two different Prousts, who had composed two different works and called them one: the first had begun writing before the war "in the freshness of an almost childlike soul"; the second, dispirited and aged by the war, was "infinitely older than his age."[18] A preference for the earlier of these writers led Feuillerat to depict the text as subject to a process of monstrous late development. Using the same language as de Selincourt, in his 1926 edition of Wordsworth's 1805 *Prelude,* he portrayed the additions as "deux énormes excroissances." A few years later, Robert Vigneron made a similar argument: although the 1913 version of the novel had been guided by a unified and carefully thought-out plan ("organique et complexe"), the text then proceeded to break its own boundaries: "With these additions of every kind, the end of the work took on, in the space of a few years, exaggerated proportions: the two volumes announced in 1913 for 1914 became five by 1918 and would eventually become thirteen. Unfortunately, this growth of the work was not a natural and harmonious growth. It bore almost exclusively upon certain sections, which swelled up into monstrous tumours."

As Christine Cano has shown, this kind of accretion frustrates the romantic principle of organic form. Instead of coming in natural and just quantities, like leaves to a tree, words threaten to multiply exponentially, producing a final product riddled with outgrowths.[19] "The result," Vigneron concluded, "is unimaginable chaos." At the same time, despite extending the work *across* volumes, Proust was not necessarily or even usually an additive reviser at the more local level. Indeed, the most vexed editorial debate in recent Proust scholarship centers on the 1987 Grasset edition of *Albertine disparue,* which omits 250 typescript pages apparently cancelled by Proust in a last-minute gesture of excision.[20] This final injunction—cross out everything—has been interpreted as putting an end to the process of accretion that was leading the narrative to become glutted ("l'interminable travail du deuil et de la jalousie dans lequel s'engluait l'action").[21]

Woolf also left a late recantation from addition, in the unbearably poignant form of an ill-written suicide note, "Will you destroy all my papers."[22] In the next chapter, I read Woolf's series of autobiographical writings as an extensive series of this kind: each adds, returns to, and complicates a history whose basic outline is fixed. Despite the strong aspectual claims to closure made in *To The Lighthouse* ("it is finished," "it was done," "I have had my vision") and in Woolf's subsequent statements about the novel's cathartic function, "A Sketch" shows that the process was incomplete. By choosing to structure "A Sketch" in the open form of diary, Woolf seems to acknowledge this, ending her "lifelong intractable struggle with the infantile" in a form that reverts from the past perfect of completion and opens out into a structure that could, in principle, always accommodate one more thing.[23]

Irregular Growth and Archival Excess

Ulysses grew slowly and irregularly from notebooks to manuscript, from typescript to *The Little Review,* and most famously received a final burst of additions in the placard and page proofs produced by Darantiere. Joyce continued composing new episodes as he revised the work he had already completed and in some cases published, and so rather than the sharp division and temporal distance between composition and revision that we find in the case of James's work on the New York Edition, revision became an intrinsic, embedded part of the writing process. Joyce described the blurring of traditionally distinct activities in a letter from 1921 as "trying to revise and improve and connect and continue and create all at the one time."[24] The paratactic unfolding of this sentence shows that these various activities are simultaneous; in fact, the order in which they are listed is the opposite of a normal compositional process: revision usually comes last, not first. Curiously, this sentence itself resembles many of the long, additive "and . . . and . . ." sentences that the process it describes allowed Joyce to produce. In the end, he finished the novel in the fairly arbitrary sense of "stopping" rather than the Jamesian sense of "perfecting"; he had determined that it should be published on his fortieth birthday, February 2, 1922.

Hans Walter Gabler's synoptic edition of *Ulysses* is the first and primary resource for anyone interested in the compositional history of the novel. His afterword to the third volume outlines its extreme complexity. Even Joyce's notebooks—the most preliminary stage of all—are baffling. Phillip Herring's edition of *Joyce's Ulysses Notesheets in the British Museum* prints more than five hundred pages of the elliptical phrases that Joyce captured, and then crossed out, in his notebooks, noting the particular colored pencil used in each case to mark the evacuation but also that "no one has yet produced a rationale for Joyce's color scheme in the manuscripts" (8). (Phrases are only crossed out if they were successfully plugged into the final text.) After that, we have the Rosenbach Manuscript, but this is neither a unified compositional document nor a fair copy, and then multiple typescripts, often confused and interleaved by Joyce during the revision process. For some episodes, there seems to be "a direct line of descent from the Rosenbach Manuscript to the lost or extant typescripts," but for others (6–9, 11, 13–14), the fair-copy manuscript and typescript stand in a collateral relationship.[25] Some episodes were then published in *The Little Review*, leading to further levels of revision and censorship, and all of the episodes were then set in multiple series of proofs, which Joyce revised (not always consistently) in turn. Not all the documentary layers survive, and those that do are dispersed widely across institutions and libraries.

The advantage of Gabler's edition is that it presents the entire history of Joyce's additions in condensed form; the synoptic notation on the left-hand pages, combined with detailed descriptions of the composition of each episode in the textual notes, allows the reader to piece back together the story of the revision process. It is a formalization of a complex material process. At the same time, the edition can tell us only *when* a revision was made: it is silent about *how*, about the manner and style of Joyce's marginalia. It is also relatively unintuitive to use. Unlike the facsimile of *The Waste Land*, it would be difficult to use in the classroom, and the hermeneutic *meaning* of the revisions has to be carefully extracted. For example, the passage from "Nausicaa" represented in the first of my textual comparisons beginning "Gerty was dressed simply") is marked in Gabler's synoptic text with the half-brackets $^{\ulcorner_2}2^{2\urcorner}$ around "of a votary of Dame Fashion," $^{\ulcorner_1}1^{1\urcorner}$ around "little love of a hat of wide-leaved," and $^{\ulcorner_3}3^{3\urcorner}$ around "contrast trimmed"—these marks indicate "levels of revision at successive proof stages"—as well as several $^{\ulcorner(B)}B^{(B)\urcorner}$ and $^{\ulcorner(D)}D^{(D)\urcorner}$ marks to indicate "stages of revision belonging to the typescripts extant or lost," and superscript circles to indicate a "single-word emendation note or footnote." The notational marks also have different meanings in each episode, because each episode was written and revised in different ways, so a "6" in the synoptic text of "Nestor" and "Proteus" refers to the first edition but, in "Calypso," to the sixth stage of proofs (the fourth page proofs). This may be a general problem with formalized, critical editions. The experienced editor Donald Reiman reflected in an essay on "Versioning" that when faced with a textual crux, he has tended to find "difficulty in reconstructing the primary textual authorities from the notes and collations in even the most accurate critical editions."[26] More specifically, as D. F. McKenzie argued in his Panizzi lectures, Gabler's edition disguises the ways in which Joyce deliberately toyed with the form of the material object he was producing. For example, the 1922 first edition contains 366 leaves, the numbers of days in the year 1904 (a leap year); on page 88, Joyce added a sentence of eight words in proof; and the passage in which Bloom reflects on an object falling to earth at "thirty-two feet per second" was heavily reworked to make it the thirty-second sentence in the paragraph. In some cases, then, Joyce's revision process was stimulated, rather than constrained, by the fixed shape of a particular material book.[27]

Gabler did not put his edition together entirely from original documents. He also made heavy use of the sixty-three-volume facsimile *James Joyce Archive,* which he called a "publisher's gift to Joyce studies."[28] This gives the synoptic edition a kind of doubly derivative quality; it is a synchronic representation of a diachronic process that had already been flattened out into adjacent facsimile volumes. Michael Groden describes the history of this project (which he supervised) very clearly in *Ulysses in Focus,* noting that only 250 copies were produced and that the price was a "staggering five thousand dollars (1977 dollars)."[29] This means that very few university libraries have a complete set.[30] Groden also notes that in the first few years after publication—really, until the moment in the 1990s when French genetic methods began to influence English-language scholarship—"people dipped into the books occasionally," but few critics used them systematically. The 1971 facsimiles of *The Waste Land* could be absorbed immediately into a literary criticism relatively *naïve* about textual matters. The quickly established meliorist dogma (Pound improved the poem in every respect), and the general tendency to refer to disparate documents as a continuous manuscript are evidence of this. But the much messier *Ulysses* archive, published in 1978 and 1979, seems to have been a project ahead of its time. Moreover, like *The Waste Land* facsimile, it is now potentially incomplete. John Haffenden has argued that the early Fresca couplets he found among Vivienne Eliot's papers "need to be instated alongside the bulk of the Berg drafts in any future edition of the *Facsimile.*"[31] In 2002, the National Library of Ireland announced that it had acquired a large new collection of Joyce manuscripts for a sum of $11.7 million. Michael Groden was the first to analyze the contents of these manuscripts in his 2001 report, and has subsequently produced a useful table showing where they fit in the existing archive of materials: we have new very early drafts of "Proteus" and "Sirens," of "Scylla and Charybdis," of "Ithaca" and "Penelope," and intermediate drafts of "Circe" and parts of "Oxen of the Sun."[32] Because most of these draft materials represent a stage prior to that of the "fair copy" Rosenbach Manuscript, Groden concludes that "the new *Ulysses* materials will likely have only a minimal impact on the text of *Ulysses*" but that they will be will be "of great interest to genetic critics" (16).[33] Nonetheless, for those with access, the facsimiles provide a very important supplement to Gabler's edition: they show paralipomena, as well as something of the spirit of the genetic process. For example, is Joyce confidently overwriting a base layer of text, cancelling in light pen, or worrying after a word in the margins?

Bloom's Expanding Mind

Like Henry James, Joyce began revising more, and at more points in the growth of the text, when unshackled from the conventional requirements of print publishing. The episodes up to and including "Nausicaa," which were serialized in *The Little Review*, are shorter, and were more quickly completed, than the episodes that follow. They also received more external editing, sometimes of a censoring, excisive kind. In *The Little Review* version, the famous description of Bloom reading *Titbits* on the jakes is strongly toned down. "He felt heavy, full: then a gentle loosening. He stood up. The cat mewed to him" was edited back from this more happily scatological description in the manuscript: "He felt full and heavy: then a gentle loosening of his bowels. He stood up, undoing the waistband of his trousers. The cat mewed to him."[34] Later in the passage, the serial publication omitted the six sentences from "He kicked open the crazy door of the jakes," the description of Bloom "asquat on the cuckstool" turning the pages over on bared knees, and his worries about constipation and piles ("he allowed his bowels to easy themselves quietly as he read"). These descriptions were removed in 1918 by none other than Ezra Pound, acting as the foreign editor of *The Little Review*, and, as Paul Vanderham has argued, his primary motive appears to have been anxiety about the reaction of the government authorities in the

United States.[35] This very early attempt to alter Joyce's prose might also be understood aesthetically as a tentative attempt to apply the principles of excision to the evolving text of *Ulysses*. This, of course, was not destined for success: Pound might have boasted to Quinn that he had "deleted about twenty lines from the typescript of "Calypso,"" but *Ulysses'* natural propensity to expand outward could not be arrested for long.[36] Jean-Michel Rabaté finds the right word when he says that Joyce "consistently repulsed" Pound's attempt "to play an active editorial role with Joyce during the serial publication of *Ulysses*."[37]

When Joyce reread the already published part of his novel in placard proofs, he both restored omissions that had been made, and added new material. In "Calypso," for example, he developed the range and flow of Bloom's morning thoughts, adding more speculation about other consciousnesses. The cat, originally described only in terms of its understanding, became "Vindictive too. Wonder what I look like to her. Height of a tower? No, she can jump me" (4.29), and Bloom's thoughts about his marital bed extend to encompass Molly's linguistic knowledge, "Forgotten any little Spanish she knew" (4.33). Overall, the tendency is to a more penetrating, curious kind of internal monologue, that "wonders" more frequently about others, and ranges further outside the immediate present into future and past time. We might say that the precise, distinctive quality of Bloom's thinking style is added in revision; for instance, Hugh Kenner gives the lines about Bloom's vindictive cat as examples of the "in and out, in and out" balance that distinguishes him from Stephen (all inside) and Mulligan (all outside).[38] Other examples of these kinds of additions, all made after serial publication, would include: "Boland's breadvan delivering with trays our daily but she prefers yesterday's loaves turnovers crisp crowns hot" (4.82); "Woods his name is. Wonder what he does. Wife is oldish" (4.149); "Must get that Capel library book renewed or they'll write to Kearney, my guarantor" (4.360–361); and "Anemic a little. Was given milk too long" (4.433–434). In each of these sentences, it is as if a small spotlight—pointed most directly on Bloom making breakfast at 9 am—expands concentrically, to include some of the more typical preoccupations of the realist novel: Molly's preferences, iterative commercial activity, the possibility of drawing inferential conclusions from limited evidence ("wife is oldish"), anxieties about the future, memories of the past. Simple observations tend, in revision, to lead to other kinds of speech acts—directives, commissives, declarations. For example, in the typescript of "Hades," created after the episode's publication in *The Little Review*, Joyce developed Bloom's noticing Ned Lambert's soft tweed suit (dyed) by adding the reflexive self-injunction at the bottom of the page, "Must get that grey suit of mine turned by Messias."[39]

As Joyce revised *Ulysses*, Bloom became at once a more scattered and more curious thinker; in other episodes focalized through his consciousness, we see the same tendency to add more thoughts, which feels like an increased propensity to digression, and the insertion of material that ranges outside the immediate moment and physical sensation. In the serialized version of "Lestrygonians," Bloom leaves the Burton after being disgusted by the dirty, bestial eating habits of its customers: "Perched [squatted in MS] on high stools by the bar, hats shoved back, at the tables calling for more bread at no charge, swilling wolfing [chewing crossed out in MS] gobfuls of sloppy food, their eyes bulging, wiping wetted moustaches."[40] He notices the smells, the men "ramming" food down their throats, the "illgirt" servers, and splashing beer, and leaves with a shudder of distaste to get something light at Byrne's. In the published version of the novel, Bloom's sharp sensory recoil is amplified with a more wandering, self-reflexive set of questions, that allows for the possibility of some similarity between himself and the man with "sad booser's eyes" and no teeth to chew the gristle of his meat. This passage is all new: "Bitten off more than he can chew. Am I like that? See ourselves as others see us. Hungry man is an angry man. Working tooth and jaw. Don't! O! A bone! That last pagan king of Ireland Cormac in the schoolpoem choked himself at Sletty southward of the Boyne. Wonder what he was eating. Something galoptious. Saint Patrick converted him to Christianity. Couldn't swallow it all however" (8.661–667).[41]

The faint double entendre in "bitten off more than he can chew"—as if the eater is more chewed than chewing—modulates into a question, the indefinite verb "see," which could be either an indicative ("we do in fact see ourselves as others see us") or an imperative ("we should do"), and then the sonically similar adjective pair "hungry" and "angry." The effect of these added phrases is to trouble the relationship between self and world, between a disdainful Bloom and the "dirty eaters" he reviles. By referring to the muddled legend of King Cormac—supposedly punished by druids after his conversion to Christianity by choking on a salmon—Bloom also widens the historical frame, moving from a stream of bodily impressions and responses to a more abstract awareness of the relationship between greed and punishment. There is a similar additive movement in the second half of the "Nausicaa" episode. Repelled by Gerty's limp ("She's lame! Oh!"), Bloom had originally thought only this:

> Thought something was wrong by the cut of her jib. Jilted beauty. Glad I didn't know it when she was on show. Hot little devil all the same. Near her monthlies, I expect, makes them feel ticklish.

Across two sets of placard proofs, the thought is expanded:

> Thought something was wrong by the cut of her jib. Jilted beauty. A defect is ten times worse in a woman. But makes them polite. Glad I didn't know it when she was on show. Hot little devil all the same. I wouldn't mind. Curiosity like a nun or a negress or a girl with glasses. That squinty one is delicate. Near her monthlies, I expect, makes them feel ticklish. (13.772–377)[42]

If the final version is less than generous, it is still more sympathetic because more general; Gerty is transposed and seen in the company of other kinds of women with "a defect" who still feel and act upon sexual desire.[43]

The additions to Bloom's monologues tend to produce a wider-ranging character and one who is "wittier" in Eliot's sense of the term, in that his immediate felt experience is balanced by a recognition of "other kinds of experience that are possible."[44] When Joyce expanded sections of the novel focalized by or narrated through other characters, it was often with the opposite effect: Gerty becomes more poignantly and inhumanly trapped in the language of commodity culture; the cliché-ridden narrator of "Eumaeus" becomes more pompously long-winded and self-qualifying; the obscurity of the scientific jargon offered in answer to

"Ithaca's" simple questions is more extreme; and Molly's monologue becomes, simply through the nature of interleaved additional phrases, more absurdly digressive and rambling.

We have seen that James's revisions sometimes seem to nudge toward self-parody, as when this description of Newman in the first edition, "His eye was of a clear, cold gray, and save for a rather abundant mustache he was clean-shaved" is transformed into the long-winded and Latinate phrasing of the New York Edition, "His eye was of a clear, cold grey, and save for the abundant droop of his moustache he spoke, as to cheek and chin, of the joy of the matutinal steel." It was precisely this tendency to overload and overgird that the excisive revisers were trying to avoid, and James's sentence would never have passed Pound's rule "to use absolutely no word that does not contribute to the presentation." When Joyce adds more in the early Bloom chapters, this is not the effect; the premise of Bloom's rambling interior monologue is that it can include anything and, by thickening it and adding thoughts outside the immediate moment, Joyce's contiguities become Bloom's and seem realistic. Later in the novel, the principle of addition remains the same but the amount added increases. In addition, because the focalization is less clear—because we often are not entirely sure who is speaking—the effects are often ironic or parodic diminutions of realism. Toward the beginning of the "Eumaeus" episode, for example, Joyce revised the sentence "Mr Bloom actuated by moments of delicacy moved off but nevertheless remained on the *qui vive* with just a shade of anxiety" into "Mr Bloom actuated by moments of inherent delicacy inasmuch as he always believed in minding his own business moved off but nevertheless remained on the *qui vive* with just a shade of anxiety though not funkyish in the least" (16.116–119). For Daniel Schwarz, who does not comment on the textual history, the word "inherent" is important in pointing to Bloom's heroism—which "survives the clichés."[45] He assumes, in other words, that Joyce is interleaving Bloom's own idiolect amid the clichés, so "inherent" functions as a flat, sincere descriptor: he *is* inherently delicate. But the genetic history seems to trouble this reading. Is delicacy really restricted to the clause also added in revision, defined by "inasmuch as he believed in minding his own business"? And, despite referring to something felt inside, isn't "inherent" a word more likely to appear in an externalized, third-person description than privately focalized one? So Miss Wade, at the end of her embedded narrative in *Little Dorrit,* tells us not that she is inherently opposed to "swollen patronage and selfishness," but that she has heard these characteristics "described as inherent in my nature."[46]

The effect of this addition is different and, I think, more complicated than the enriched stream-of-consciousness we find in the earlier Bloom episodes where we are more secure of auditing his own thoughts. One of the troubling things about revision in lyric poetry—say, Auden's change to "we must love one another or die"—is that overt rethinking destabilizes a contractual and modal commitment to sincerity. Here, the problem is almost the opposite: in those episodes of *Ulysses* that begin with more complex, layered, or ironized speech acts, the effects of addition magnify the reader's confusion: the problem is not a known speaker's change of mind, but mounting confusion about who is speaking in the first place. Mark Osteen describes the second half of *Ulysses* as prone to excess, and he sees Joyce's "proliferating narrators, long catalogues, absurdly inflated diction, incongruous descriptions of banal activities" as an invitation to the reader to "engage in extravagant exchange with the text."[47] Franco Moretti argues that *Ulysses* should not "be read as a *criticism* of ideologies, even less of ideology in the abstract, as the specific form of consciousness of capitalist alienation. In *Ulysses,* Joyce presents styles and ideologies as purely formal entities, products of an experiment lacking any motivation and purpose."[48] With the latter part of this statement I entirely agree. At the same time, the artificial and external nature of the final episodes of *Ulysses,* whose narrators and thinkers are rigorously idiosyncratic, inevitably produces the possibility of an ironic reading. When Joyce extravagantly extended the speech tics of his constructed narrators—Gerty's women's magazine talk, the Eumaeus everyman-bore, the Ithaca pedant—he extended the possibility of our complicit laughter.

The Comedy of One Word More

"Nausicaa," the last of the episodes to be serially published, points the way to the instability of speech act—and the irony that this produces—dominating the second half of *Ulysses*. When Joyce told Arthur Power that the whole episode "took place in Bloom's imagination," he begged the question himself: how far is Gerty a real speaker, given a stream of thoughts of her own?[49] This description of Gerty's attempt at modish fashion is one of the most familiar passages from the "Nausicaa" section, and critics have argued over whether it renders a flat self, "merely a site of commodity spectacle," or a more active attempt at self-fashioning.[50] The image shown is a comparison of the shorter version in the Rosenbach Manuscript and the final published text of the novel, an increase of almost 50 percent.[51] The rather formal, even antiquarian, phrase "votary of Dame Fashion" (13.148–9) adds a layer of irony to the original description: to be a votary of "Dame Fashion" is presumably to worship a false god, and we begin to imagine Gerty's "simple" dress as more artful than honest.[52] In his expansions to the rest of the passage, Joyce zooms in and out of a voice that is Gerty's, or one that she has assumed: "spoiling the sit," "contrast trimmed," and "little love of a hat" are tossed about proudly, as the technical diction of expertise. (One might compare the fashion-expert of today who talks about "a boot," "a trouser" in the assertive singular.) At the same time, the laborious parenthetical addition "because it was expected in the Lady's Pictorial that electric blue would be worn" makes it clear that this language is borrowed and derivative. "Electric blue" seems vivid the first time it is introduced but then, through immediate repetition, becomes monotonous, while the agentless "because it was expected" leaves the question of who forms these bizarrely specific expectations unanswered.

The other revisions made to "Nausicaa," most of which were effected on the placard and page proofs after *The Little Review* publication, also trend toward a more passive, spectatorial description of Gerty, and a playful amplification of the "namby-pamby jammy marmalady drawsery (alto là)" style. In other words, it was by adding and inserting that Joyce was able to achieve the "new" and patentable style that he described as his "specially new fizzing style (Patent No 7728 S.P.E.P.B.P.L.P)."[53] Many are adjectives or adjectival modifying phrases—"wealth of ^wonderful^ hair," (13.116) "^awfully pretty stitchery^" (13.174), "her ^rosebud^ mouth" (13.88)—and the adjectives themselves are often clichéd or new-fangled, "fine ^selfraising^ flower" (13.227), "ruched" teacosy swapped

Gerty was dressed simply but with instinctive taste for she felt that there was just a might that he might be out. A neat blouse of electric blue selftinted by dolly dyes with a smart vee opening and kerchief pocket (in which she kept always a piece of cotton wool scented with heliotrope) and a navy three quarter skirt cut to the stride showed off her slim graceful figure to perfection. She wore a coquettish wideleaved hat of nigger straw with an underbrim of eggblue chenille and at the side a butterfly bow of silk to tone.

Gerty was dressed simply but with the instinctive taste of a votary of Dame Fashion for she felt that there was just a might that he might be out. A neat blouse of electric blue, selftinted by dolly dyes (because it was expected in the *Lady's Pictorial* that electric blue would be worn), with a smart vee opening down to the division and kerchief pocket (in which she always kept a piece of cottonwool scented with her favourite perfume because the handkerchief spoiled the sit) and a navy threequarter skirt cut to the stride showed off her slim graceful figure to perfection. She wore a coquettish little love of a hat of wideleaved nigger straw contrast trimmed with an underbrim of eggblue chenille and at the side a butterfly bow to tone.

Figure 6: Description of Gerty's clothes in the Rosenbach Manuscript and the 1922 novel.

in for "embroidered" (13.460), "Cissy saying ^an unladylike^ thing like that" (13.265). Joyce had captured some of these "massproduct" phrases in his initial notebooks, and then found a place for them in longer sentence structures either during initial composition or revision, so "tense suppressed meaning" entered the manuscript as an additional description of Gerty's face: "Mayhap it was this, the love that might have been, that lent to her softlyfeatured face at whiles a look, tense with suppressed meaning" (13.105). This revision tendency is, or becomes, reflective of Gerty's own thinking processes and her preference for adjectival embellishment. To begin with, Joyce had her thinking only of one possibility for Bloom's nose, "she could not see whether he had an aquiline nose from where he was sitting," but in the second layer of proofs the hypothetical is doubled, "or a slightly retroussé" (13.420). Gerty's fantasies about her future "dreamhusband," itself an added, manufactured word, received particular attention during the process of revision. He begins merely "tall" but becomes in the 1921 typescript "tall ^with broad shoulders^" and his own fond, imagined speech is incorporated into the text so that he doesn't merely give "her a good hearty hug" as he leaves for work but "his dear little wifey a good hearty hug" (13.241–242). At the same time, much of Gerty's fantasy of married life focuses on her own wifely behavior rather than her husband. In the manuscript, she had received praise only for her "teacakes and queen Ann's pudding," but by the final version she plans to care for the dreamhusband with "griddlecakes done to a goldenbrown hue and queen Ann's pudding of delightful creaminess" (13.224–225). "Goldenbrown hue" and "delightful creaminess" are, of course, the kinds of advertising words used in recipe books rather than the natural language we use to describe food. Joyce also expanded the description of her ideal home, making the drawing room "beautifully appointed," and decorated not only with "pictures" but "engravings and the photograph of grandpapa Giltrap's lovely dog Garryowen that almost talked it was so human." These slightly cloying details are doubly poignant: in a less disastrous marriage market, Gerty's modest ambitions ought to be easily realized; and the modest, unrealizable ambitions are all the more poignant for being so hackneyed. Garry Leonard has argued that Gerty purchases and consumes "in order to feel like a woman," noting that in turn-of-the-century Ireland, she would have faced "diminishing prospects for marriage."[54]

The "Eumaeus" and "Ithaca" chapters show a similar propensity to accrete worn language across the typescript and stages of proof. In "Eumaeus," the additions tend to be slightly longer than in "Nausicaa" and often have a more complex syntactic structure. Many are relative clauses or other clauses of qualification, which add layers of nice, pedantic discrimination like a legal document. The addition of these clauses beyond the common rules of "good style" produces the humor that Derek Attridge finds in the episode's overpedantic adherence to convention and nervous "hypercorrectness."[55] At one point in the dialogue, for example, Bloom asks after Stephen's father. Meeting with an indifferent response, he continues, "A gifted man, Mr Bloom said of Mr Dedalus senior, in more respects than one," adding "and a born *raconteur* if ever there was one" in the page proofs (16.260–261). The original sentence already contained the indefinite "in more respects than one" and the concessive clause "if ever there was one" adds a further layer of slightly ungrammatical, hence class-marked, doubt. In the passage that follows, Joyce qualified "a versatile allround man" with "^by no means confined to medicine only^" (16.288); "an exceedingly plucky deed" with "^which he could not too highly praise^" (16.294–295), and the description of Italians arguing with "in heated altercation" (16.310) and "^there being some little differences between the parties^." As he reread his own draft, Joyce hedged its already hedged bets with relative pronouns, hanging present participle phrases ("he dwelt ^being a bit of an artist in his spare time,^ on the female form"), extra adverbs ("so that ^frankly^ he was utterly at a loss"), and further concessives ("^inasmuch as he always believed in minding his own business^"). The result, as with some of James's revisions, is that an already idiosyncratic style hardens into a more extreme version of itself. Did Joyce chuckle as he reread and intensified the virtuosity of his *un*virtuoso style? If excision can be represented as a painful process of loss, and substitution as a nervous attempt to get it right by "pricking lights," accretion often seems light-hearted pleasure, linguistic freewheeling without limits.

"Ithaca" was the last chapter of *Ulysses* to be finished, Joyce's favorite and, perhaps unsurprisingly, among the most heavily rewritten.[56] Richard

Madtes calculated in his 1964 study of "The Building of 'Ithaca'" that forty-two percent of the episode (9,380 words out of 22,421) was composed after the first fair copy.[57] Its catechistic structure allows not only for the insertion of additional adjectives, or short modifying clauses, but the introduction of entirely new question-and-answer pairs, and the expansion of already paratactic answers (often in the form of lists) to extreme limits. The general tendency is for the episode to become more insistently particular, specific, and deictic as it develops. Many of the shorter revisions add scientific or specialized jargon, so a gasflame is qualified as "of 14 CP" (17.110), a parachute as "aeronautic," a corkscrew as "spiral" (17.566), and "arithmetical values of 3, 1, 4, and 100" is interleaved with the language of mathematical proof, "as ordinal and cardinal numbers, videlicet" (17.739–740). The answer to the question "What in water did Bloom, waterlover, drawer of water, watercarrier, returning to the range, admire?" (17.183–184), and itself expanded with the three mock-Homeric epithets about water, is one of the most virtuoso passages of growth, a kind of list-encomium that draws more and more words into its flow. On the various typescripts, among other things: "its ^democratic^ equality," "homeothetic islands, peninsulas, and" (17.200), "Artesian wells, eruptions, torrents" (17.205–206), "its variety of forms in loughs and bays" (17.217–218), and then in successive layers of proof, "its climactic and commercial signficance" (17.192–193), "currents, gulfstream, north and south equatorial courses" (17.204–205), "its infallibility as paradigm and paragon" (17.216), and so on. Like the patient suffering from a similarity disorder, unable to construct hierarchical relationships through substitution, this passage slides zanily from "water" to more and more specialist or particular words related to water, building up paratactic lists with no real order or logic. At other points Joyce develops and adds to lists of proper names, or lists derived from numerical calculations (e.g., "in 1936 when Bloom would be 70" [17.449]). The vertical budget for June 16, 1904, with its long list of debits ("pork kidney," "copy *Freeman's Journal*," "Loan (Stephen Dedalus) refunded" [17.1455–1478]) outweighing its meager three credits, was added in the typescript, and then rebalanced on both page and placard proofs.[58]

One of the messiest pages in the "Ithaca" page proofs is the list of books offered in answer to the question "What final visual impression was communicated to him by the mirror?" Like an obsessive bibliographer, Joyce added both more books to Leopold Bloom's shelves and more details about the books he had already listed: so "Hardiman's <u>History of the Russo-Turkish War</u> (brown cloth, with gummed label on Garrison Library, Governor's Parade, Gibraltar, on verso of cover" was added on the placard proof (Gabler III.1562), before being changed to "Hozier's" in the page proof (17.1385).[59] *Soll und Haben* was, at this point, given an author and specified to be in "Gothic characters." In a French note to Darantiere at the bottom of the page, Joyce begged for a particular stylistic format for the *Short but yet Plain Elements of Geometry,* "si possible employer pour ce lettre 's' ancienne en forme de 'ʃ.'" As many critics have pointed out, "the accuracy that Darantiere managed to achieve is amazing," and this request was duly noted: in the published text, the eighteenth-century edition is translated "into Engliʃh," and explained to have been initially the property of a "Michael Gallagher, carpenter, Duʃery Gate, Enniʃcorthy."[60]

If Joyce could specify an additional detail, or know a further fact about his fictional universe, he did: in "Ithaca," in particular, no one ever "sits" or "looks" or "drinks" or "goes" without an adverbial modifier, and no object is simply "a book" or "water." The question "Was the guest conscious of and did he acknowledge these marks of hospitality?" originally received the answer:

> His attention was directed to them by his host jocosely and he accepted them seriously as they drank in silence.

But became, in the page proof:

> His attention was directed to them by his host jocosely and he accepted them seriously as they drank in jocoserious silence Epp's massproduct, the creature cocoa. (17.368)[61]

The addition of "Epp's massproduct, the creature cocoa" obeys the principle that no verb can go without a direct object when it can hold one: here it gets two, in apposition. "Massproduct" itself, of course, is one of the compound nouns that Joyce liked to add as he revised: in its compression, it suggests the efficiency and speed of mass industrial

The^c Child's Guide[⊃] (blue cloth).°

The^c Beauties of Killarney[⊃] (wrappers).°

When^c We Were Boys[⊃] by William O'Brien M. P. (green cloth, slightly ⌜ᴮ[faded)] faded, envelope bookmark at p. 217).°ᴮ⌝

5 *Thoughts^c from Spinoza[⊃]* (maroon leather).°

⌜ᴮ*The^c Story of the Heavens[⊃]* by Sir Robert Ball (blue cloth).°

Ellis's *Three^c Trips to Madagascar[⊃]* (brown cloth, title obliterated).°

The^c Stark-Munro Letters[⊃] by A. Conan Doyle, property of ⌜the⌝ City of Dublin Public Library, 106 Capel street,° lent 21 May (Whitsun Eve)

10 1904, due 4 June 1904, 13 days overdue° (black cloth binding, bearing white letternumber° ticket).

Voyages^c in China[⊃] by "Viator" (recovered with brown paper, red ink title).°ᴮ⌝

Philosophy^c of the Talmud[⊃] (sewn pamphlet).°

15 Lockhart's° *Life^c of Napoleon[⊃]* (cover wanting, marginal annotations⟨⟩), minimising victories, aggrandising defeats of the protagonist).°

Soll^c und Haben[⊃] ⌜ᴮby Gustav Freytag⌝ (black ⌜ᴮ[boards)] boards, ⌝Gothic characters,⌝ cigarette coupon bookmark at p. 24).°ᴮ⌝

⌜⌝[Hardiman's] Hozier's⌝ *History of the Russo-Turkish War* (brown cloth,

20 ⌜2 volumes,⌝ with gummed label,° Garrison Library, Governor's Parade, Gibraltar, on ^⟨reverse⟩ verso^ of cover).°

Laurence Bloomfield in Ireland by William Allingham (second edition, green cloth, gilt trefoil design, previous owner's name on recto of flyleaf erased).°⌝

25 *A^c Handbook of Astronomy[⊃]* (cover, brown leather, detached, ⟨f⟩ 5 plates⟨⟩), antique letterpress long primer, author's footnotes ⌜[pica,] nonpareil,⌝ marginal clues ⌜[brevier).°] brevier, captions small pica).°⌝

The^c Hidden Life of Christ[⊃] (black boards).°

In^c the Track of the Sun[⊃] (yellow cloth, titlepage ⌜[missing).°] missing,°

30 recurrent title intestation).°⌝

---

1 *The--Guide*] sD; *NU* aR   1 cloth).] sD; cloth) aR   2 *The--Killarney*] e; *NU* aR; *TD: ABSENT* tC   2 (wrappers).] e; (wrappers) aR; *TD: ABSENT* tC   3 *When--Boys*] sD; *NU* aR 4 p. 217).] sD; p. 217) aB   5 *Thoughts--Spinoza*] sD; *NU* aR   5 leather).] 1; leather) aR 6 *The--Heavens*] sD; *NU* aB   6 cloth).] 2; cloth) aB,a1   7 *Three--Madagascar*] sD; *NU* aB 7 obliterated).] sD; obliterated) aB   8 *The--Letters*] sD; *NU* aB   9 street,] e; Street, aB 10 overdue] tC; overdue, aB   11 letternumber] a2; letter-number aB   12 *Voyages--China*] sD; *NU* aB   13 title).] 1; title) aB   14 *Philosophy--Talmud*] sD; *NU* aR   14 pamphlet).] 1;

Figure 7a: Synoptic text of "Ithaca" in Gabler's edition of *Ulysses*.

1. *Hardiman's History of the Russo-Turkish War* (brown cloth, with gummed label on Garrison Library Governor's Parade, Gibraltar, on preverss of cover) *verso*

Laurence Bloomfield in Ireland by William Allingham (second edition, green cloth, gilt trefoil design, previous owner's name on recto of flyleaf erased

The Stark-Munro Letters by A. Conan Doyle, property of the City of Dublin Public Library, 106 Capel Street, lent 21 May (Whitsun Eve) 1904, due 4 June 1904, 13 days overdue (black cloth binding, bearing white letter/number ticket).

Voyages in China by « Viator » (recovered with brown paper, red ink title).

Philosophy of the Talmud (sewn pamphlet).

Lockart's Life of Napoleon (cover wanting, marginal annotations, minimising victories, aggrandising defeats of the protagonist),

Soll und Haben (black boards, cigarette coupon bookmark at p. 24).

A Handbook of Astronomy (cover, brown leather, detached, 5 plates, antique letterpress long primer, author's footnotes, nonpareil marginal clues brevier, captions small pica).

The Hidden Life of Christ (black boards).

In the Track of the Sun (yellow cloth, titlepage missing).

Physical Strength and How to Obtain It by Eugen Sandow (red cloth).

Short but yet Plain Elements of Geometry written in French by F. Ignat. Pardies and rendered into English by John Harris D. D. London, printed for R. Knaplock at the Bishop's Head MDCCXI, with dedicatory epistle to his worthy friend Charles Cox, esquire, Member of Parliament for the burgh of Southwark and having ink calligraphed statement on the flyleaf certifying that the book was the property of Michael Gallagher, dated this 10th day of May 1822 and requesting the person who should find it, if the book should be lost or go astray, to restore it to Michael Gallagher, carpenter, Dufery Gate, Enniscorthy, county Wicklow, the finest place in the world.

What reflections occupied his mind during the process of reversion of the inverted volumes?

The necessity of order, a place for everything and everything in its place: the deficient appreciation of literature possessed by females: the incongruity of an apple incuneated in a tumbler and of an umbrella inclined in a closestool: the insecurity of hiding any secret document behind, beneath or between the pages of a book.

Why, firstly and secondly, did he not consult the work in question?

Firstly, in order to exercise mnemotechnic: secondly, because after an interval of amnesia, when seated at the central table, about to consult the work

which volume was the largest in bulk? Hardiman's History of the Russo-Turkish War.

Figure 7b: Bloom's books: the heavily revised placard proof.

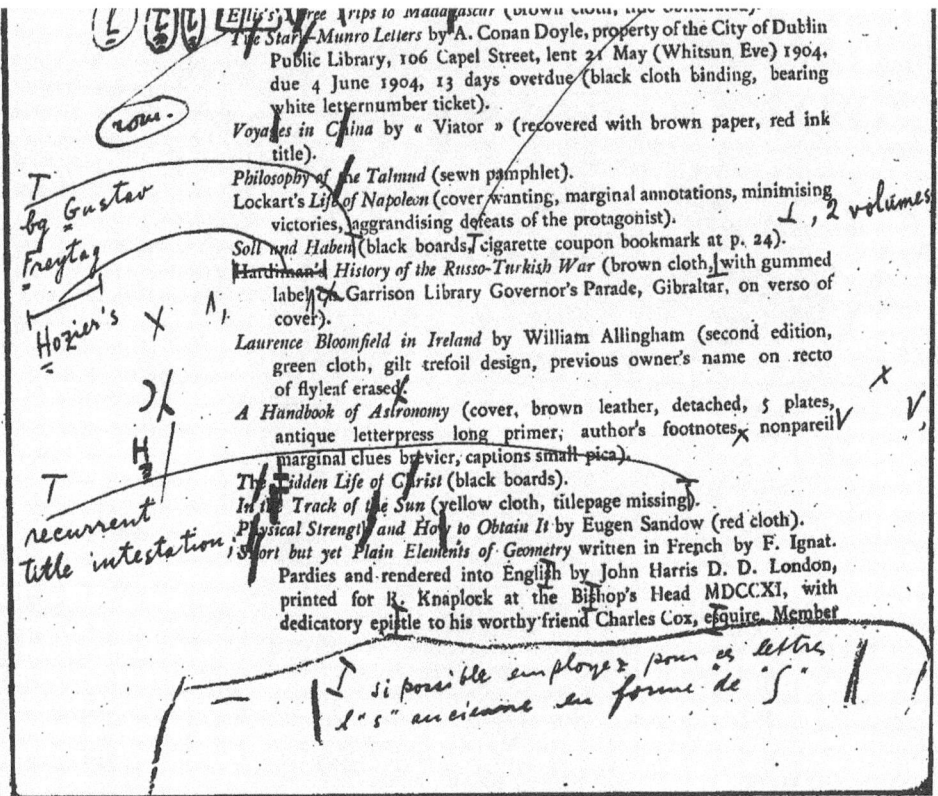

Figure 7c: Bloom's books: the heavily revised page proof.

production, just as Gerty's "dreamhusband" points to her naïve conflation of male sexuality with an (industrial) fantasy of domestic bliss.[62]
"Jocoserious" is a compound word of a slightly different kind, blending
Bloom's initially "jocose" action and Stephen's "serious" one. As Richard Madtes has noted, some of the changes Joyce made in the "Ithaca"
episode seem designed to emphasize the symbolic link between Bloom
and Stephen, presenting them "in a relationship of unity, equality, or
even consubstantiality." Five pages later on the page proof, Joyce wrote
the portmanteau words "Stoom" and "Blephen" in the right-hand margins. Before correction, the page proofs had read:

If Stephen had been Bloom he would have passed successively
through a dame's school and the high school; if Bloom had been

Stephen he would have passed successively through the preparatory, junior, middle and senior grades of the intermediate and
through the matriculation, first arts, second arts, and degree courses
of the royal university.

After revision, the printed text of the novel read:

Substituting Stephen for Bloom Stoom would have passed successively through a dame's school and the high school. Substituting
Bloom for Stephen Blephen would have passed successively through
the preparatory, junior, middle and senior grades of the intermediate and through the matriculation, first arts, second arts and arts
degree courses of the royal university. (17.549–554)

Earlier on the same page, Joyce had had added the words "reciprocal"
and the paralleling addition "and about Stephen's thoughts about
Bloom's thoughts about Stephen," producing an echo chamber effect of
reverberation, where words are repeated to the point of becoming nonsense. The antepenultimate question in "Ithaca," a simple "With?"
takes this form of linguistic game to its endpoint, providing the answers:
"Sinbad the Sailor and Tinbad the Tailor and Jinbad the Jailor and
Whinbad the Whaler and Ninbad the Nailer and Finbad the Failer and
Binbad the Bailer . . . and Vinbad the Quailer and Linbad the Yailer
and Xinbad the Phthailer" (17.2322–2326). Beginning with the familiar
character of Sinbad, whose name and profession are "real words," Joyce
begins inventing proper names according to an alliterative rule (the name
must end "-inbad" and take its first letter from the profession that follows), before breaking his own rules with a flourish of some of the weird-
est, least-used initial consonants in English, "V," "Q," "Y," "X," "Phth."
Robert Martin Adams describes it as a "piece of inspired stupidity . . .
containing layer after layer of meaninglessness—an unfathomable depth
of mental void."[63] Fritz Senn sees it as "a last, climactic effort of compulsive cataloguing" that shows the "prevailing method" of the chapter has
been "paradigmatic automatism."[64] Given that the "Ithaca" episode was
the last Joyce composed, this string of self-generating sounds without
meaning is in some sense the true genetic end of the novel, mimetic of

the way that language drifts into aphasia as Bloom falls asleep. It is also the most extreme version of the wider tendency, typical of the similarity disorder, to turn contiguous free forms (Stephen and Bloom, mass and product, jocose and serious) into bound forms.

What Molly Never Had

One of the features of the nineteenth-century realist novel is that it learned to contain an overwhelming amount of material detail. Indeed, one of Woolf's criticisms in 1924 of her Edwardian predecessors was that "they spend immense skill and immense industry making the trivial and the transitory appear the true and the enduring." In "Mr. Bennett and Mrs. Brown," written after her own attempt to dispense with external particulars in *Jacob's Room,* she criticized the "thinginess" of Edwardian prose, its tendency to reduce characters to their surroundings, and its obsessions with the material and economic. Describing the way in which Arnold Bennett might figure Mrs. Brown, she tells us:

> He, indeed, would observe every detail with immense care. He would notice the advertisements; the pictures of Swanage and Portsmouth; the way in which the cushion bulged between the buttons; how Mrs. Brown wore a brooch which had cost three-and-ten-three at Whitworth's bazaar; and had mended both gloves—indeed the thumb of the left-hand glove had been replaced. And he would observe, at length, how this was the non-stop train from Windsor which calls at Richmond for the convenience of middle-class residents, who can afford to go to the theatre but have not reached the social rank which can afford motor-cars, though it is true, there are occasions (he would tell us what), when they hire them from a company (he would tell us which).[65]

How is this different from Joyce's obsessive noting of Gerty's clothes and dress, the brand of cocoa Stephen and Bloom drink, or the particularity with which he revises the address "South Anne Street" to "46, 47, 48, 49 South King Street" in page proofs? If Bloom's list of books functions, as Mark Osteen argues, as a "fragmentary autobiography," where each volume "substantiates an element of his character or history," isn't Joyce performing the same trick as Arnold Bennett, describing Bloom's character at one remove by noting the objects and possessions that surround him?[66] In that case, why was Joyce iterating toward the kind of excess mimesis—a world represented in too much detail, from too many angles— that, to begin with, the Edwardian and Victorian novelists found easy enough to do, and whose facile clutter Woolf then depreciates?

Although some of the revisions in "Ithaca" seem to point up or emphasize a particular facet of the relationship between Stephen and Bloom, the vast majority of changes are there, as Richard Madtes concludes, because Joyce "wanted *more*," and "was primarily concerned with the need for expansion. Indeed, such addition in Ithaca becomes its own justification, for an almost stupefying accumulation of factual detail is, in itself, one of the episode's major purposes."[67] Before *Ulysses*, after all, Joyce hadn't been a particularly additive reviser. The part of *Stephen Hero* that survives shows that Joyce was originally planning to make the Stephen-Bildungsroman novel long—he completed a thousand pages before giving it up and yet stated that these twenty-five chapters represented only half of the book.[68] *Portrait*, which can be regarded as a revision of *Stephen Hero* in only the second, extrinsic sense, is much more condensed; its lyrical cadencing, temporal spottiness, and focus on a selected number of epiphanic moments also move further away from the nineteenth-century realist tradition. Derek Attridge suggests we might even read it, "especially in the light cast backwards by *Ulysses*" as a kind of anti-Bildungsroman, a self-conscious "undermining of readerly expectations of progress from innocence and naïvety to self-knowledge and success."[69] On the whole, the textual history of *Portrait* and of *Dubliners*, with its style of "scrupulous meanness," shows that additive revision and a pushing of styles and genres to their limit was not so much Joyce's "natural" or organic style of writing (as "piecing together" seems to have been for Eliot), as a deliberate choice made for *Ulysses*. It was also a learned choice: Joyce added least to the earliest episodes, and most to the later ones, and it was the final year of the novel's composition that witnessed its most extravagant extension.

In that case, what aesthetic goal did "wanting more" serve, and what stylistic or representational effects does the "moreness" produce? These additions do not seem to be attempting to perform the trick that Woolf dislikes—that of "hypnotising" the reader into constructing character from things. The books on Bloom's shelf do a very poor job of telling us more about him or his tastes: in fact, they raise more questions than they answer. The printed matter that we see Bloom read in the novel is low-brow, and his purposes as a reader are utilitarian: the mass-market magazine *Tit-bits* is an effective laxative; in the newspaper entry about Dignam's funeral that he reads aloud to Stephen, his name is misspelled Boom; newspaper adverts flog products ("What is home without/ Plumtree's potted meat"); the smutty novel *Sweets of Sin* proves variously arousing; and he looks for messages in private correspondence and letters. Critics have labored hard to find links between the rather abstruse, and sometimes antiquarian, volumes on Bloom's shelves and the plot of the novel, but it remains unclear why or when he would have purchased an early-eighteenth-century book about geometry, translated from French, or an anti-Semitic nineteenth-century German novel, or a semiautobiographical novel in letters by Arthur Conan-Doyle. The facts that we are given about these books—and what detailed facts they are—are grossly in excess of their symbolic value.

Joyce's additive revisions in "Ithaca" do not attempt to "hypnotise" the reader into constructing character from things: the lists are for their own sake. This is not to say that they are, as some critics have suggested, "hyperreal," a gesture to a purely linguistic set of simulacra with no grounding in any point of origin, or anti-real in the strong philosophical sense of denying the objective reality of their constituent parts.[70] I will come back to this question at the end of the chapter and think we might more accurately term the effect excessively real or over-realist. The detail is simply not there to stand in for something else. It has become the foreground rather than the background, the end rather than the means. Woolf criticized the Edwardian materialists for trying to make an accumulation of detail about things stand in or substitute for the essence of human beings, but she essentially agreed with Arnold Bennett that "the foundation of good fiction is character-creating."[71] By the later episodes of *Ulysses,* the possibility of the "fabric of things" standing in a symbolic relationship to character has been lost. When Joyce decides to add an additional title to the list, or insists on *s* being printed with a long-*s*, he is improving the mimetic register of the novel without improving our knowledge of its inhabitants. As the city itself is depicted from more angles, in ever-finer grain, it becomes the foreground. In the earlier episodes, the revisions seem to expand Bloom's consciousness and to redraw him as a character; this is because Bloom's register and the novel's register are the same. But by "Ithaca" it seems unlikely that the increasingly precise catalog of books represents either what Bloom sees (he is looking in the mirror and they are "improperly arranged") or what he remembers about his own possessions. Cordell Yee notes that the headings in "Aeolus," also added at a late stage of composition, "do not perform the normal function of headlines or captions in that they are often unreliable guides to the content of the passages they introduce."[72] They are irrelevant.

Instead of standing in a metaphoric or symbolic relationship to character, detail has become metonymic: these books are near to Bloom, and in his line of sight, without being an explanation of his particular vision. When Arnold Bennett told us about the kind of house that Hilda Lessways lived in, the result seemed absurd and unsuccessful to Virginia Woolf, but the aim is clear enough: by describing the things that Hilda sees from her window, and delineating her socioeconomic world as finely as possible, we are supposed to understand what kind of person she is. Woolf's choice of quotation is designed to show the method at its worst, so here is the relevant passage (with Woolf's chosen selection italicized).

> Hilda held Mr. Skellorn in disdain, as she held the row of cottages in disdain. It seemed to her that Mr. Skellorn and the cottages mysteriously resembled each other in their primness, their smugness, their detestable self-complacency. Yet those cottages, perhaps thirty in all, had stood for a great deal until Hilda, glancing at them, shattered them with her scorn. *The row was called Freehold Villas: a consciously proud name in a district where much of the land was copyhold and could only change owners subject to the payment of 'fines,' and to the feudal consent of a 'court' presided over by the agent of a lord of the manor. Most of the dwellings were owned by their occupiers, who, each an absolute monarch of the soil, niggled in his sooty garden of an evening amid the flutter of drying shirts and towels.*

> *Freehold Villas symbolized the final triumph of Victorian economics, the apotheosis of the prudent and industrious artisan. It corresponded with a Building Society Secretary's dream of paradise. And indeed it was a very real achievement. Nevertheless Hilda's irrational contempt would not admit this.* (102)

Bennett's method is not so brutally unsophisticated as Woolf claims; through her choice of quotation she omits to register the doubling on which the passage turns. In Bennett's hands, we are given first what the cottages "had stood for," a legacy of home ownership, domestic pride, and the cultivation of rural soil to fit modern industrial purposes, and only then Hilda's "scorn" and "irrational contempt," which renders the cottages' (or rather, the cottagers') pride as "their primness, smugness, and their detestable self-complacency." The cottages stand in metonymically for their cottagers, but the alternative readings we are offered of the occupiers, as smug or "absolute monarchs," are metaphoric or symbolic interpretations. "The flutter of drying shirts and towels" might be understood as the "apotheosis of the prudent and industrious artisan" (mapping the cottager to a monarch, the fluttering shirts to a royal standard). But Hilda refuses this metaphoric interpretation and prefers a more clichéd one: long narrow gardens mean mental narrowness to her, uniform houses mental uniformity (mapping physical space to mental space).

By the standards of this kind of fiction, Joyce adds not only "more" but "too much." The ending of "Penelope"—the literal ending of the novel—is a good example. Critics have debated whether Molly's final thoughts of Gibraltar as she drifts off to sleep show "a reaffirmation of her relationship with Bloom in the present of 1904" or pure escapism, a reaffirmation of her desires for men other than her husband. In his 2009 guide, *Ulysses and Us,* Declan Kiberd has even suggested that this passage might be read as an implied monologue, as Bloom's projections of Molly's thinking: "What better climax to a male fantasy than to imagine a wife planning how to woo and win her husband all over again?"[73]

The problem is that the novel ends indeterminately, with a strange expansion of its geographic range—a new set of facts about Molly's mother and childhood in Gibraltar—and with "innumerable details which supplement, modify, sometimes contradict what we have come to suppose."[74]

As Jonathan Quick points out in an article on "Molly Bloom's Mother," the final revisions for the novel concentrate on "Molly Bloom's girlhood Gibraltar and her mysterious mother 'Lunita Laredo'" but the "results of this revision are so inconclusive that they appear to evade rather than answer the questions of background that Joyce usually addresses directly and in detail when a principal character's immediate origins are at issue."[75] The very final words that Joyce dictated for the book, over the telephone to Darantiere, treat this vacuum directly as Molly thinks of "what I never had." In its closing lines, which were as heavily revised and expanded as anything in the novel, Molly thinks again about "what is not" or, more precisely, about what Bloom "didnt know" in the past (Gabler III.1725–1726; 18.1582–1609).

The temporal structure of this passage is strange and in a sense misleading. Molly is remembering first "the day I got him to propose to me" in 1890, and then facts about her own girlhood that occurred before that, and which Bloom didn't know on the day he proposed to her. The uncertainty arises in knowing whether to translate the emotions felt in and about past time to the present. Is Molly implicitly renewing her marriage vows and saying "yes I will Yes" to the Bloom of 1904? Does he now know some or all of the things that were hidden in the past?[76] Even though Molly tells us that she engineered the proposal, her reply was not immediate: before "yes I said yes I will Yes," she thought of a series of romantic images drawn from an eastern past—the exotic Spanish girls, handsome Moors, the "wineshops half open at night," the "glorious sunsets and the figtrees." Not only is the privacy of this detail part of the original proposal, but it is an important part of the memory of the proposal: now Molly makes her list in words, but sixteen years ago she had only given her husband-to-be "the seedcake out of my mouth," and said "yes."

Almost all of these "swarming" details were added in revision, as the comparison below shows.[77] On the left side is the 110-word passage in the Rosenbach manuscript; on the right is the 393-word passage in the final novel: an increase of some 250 percent. Some of the changes are made in the typescript, but the most significant change occurs on the placard proofs. Four sets were needed. On the first, Joyce added the passage from "^and the sailors . . . all in white like kings^" (18.1583–1593; *JJA* 21, 366). The second set is surrounded with insertions, marked by heavy black lines radiating from the center of the passage to the end: the marginal notes include the long passage about "all the little queer streets," the recovered memory "^first I gave him the bit of seedcake out of my mouth^," the description of "^the fowl market all clucking^" (Gabler misses this), and "^asking you to sit down in their bit of shop^," and one additional "yes" (368). The third version is much neater, and was corrected twice. On the first sheet, Joyce qualified the "foul market all clucking" with the enigmatic "^outside Larby Sharons^," substituted "I shall wear a white rose" for "I shall wear a red," and added four "yeses," as well as capitalizing the final end-point "Yes" (*JJA* 21, 370). These changes were not all marked on the duplicate sheet (372), where he added only the long phrase "^for her lover to kiss the iron and the night we stayed the watchman going about serene with his lamp^," as well as the qualifying genitive "^of the posadas^." The fourth set includes the changes added on both of these separate sheets, but Joyce was still unsatisfied; on the last set of placards (375–376), he added the description of "^the old castle thousands of years old^," the "geraniums" and two more rhythmical "yeses" ("I shall wear a red ^yes^" and "I asked him with my eyes to ask again ^yes^"). Compared to "Ithaca," where a significant (and costly) amount of further addition took place on the page proofs, "Penelope" achieved something close to its final form in placards. Still, even after these four corrections of printed copy, the page proofs received a little final tinkering with the addition of "^and the wineshops half open at night and the castanets^," and "^missed the boat at Algeciras^." Figure 8 emphasizes the two points of maximal textual difference, and shows the addition of one long nostalgic passage, and then a few shorter phrases and words (mostly affirmations). In a nonbinary depiction, we would see that this long passage was itself built up palimpsestically from a series of smaller additions.

In the manuscript, Molly's thoughts of things "he didn't know" were limited to five people, "Mulvey and Mr Stanhope and Hester and father and old captain Groves," and then two exotic places, "the Alameda gardens and Gibraltar as a girl where I was a flower of the mountain." As he lengthened this list, Joyce crowded Molly's monologue with picturesque detail in rhythmical phrases. In general, revision in "Penelope" means the addition of phrases of varying lengths (from a simple "ah") to multiple

I was thinking of so many things he didn't know of Mulvey and Mr Stanhope and Hester and father and old captain Groves and the Alameda gardens and Gibraltar as a girl where I was a flower of the mountain and how he kissed me under the Moorish wall and I thought well as well him as another and then I asked him with my eyes to ask again and then he asked me would I to say yes my mountain flower and first I put my arms around him and drew him down to me so he could feel my breasts all perfume and I said I will yes.

I was thinking of so many things he didnt know of Mulvey and Mr Stanhope and Hester and father and old captain Groves and the sailors playing all birds fly and I say stoop and washing up dishes they called it on the pier and the sentry in front of the governors house with the thing round his white helmet poor devil half roasted and the Spanish girls laughing in their shawls and their tall combs and the auctions in the morning the Greeks and the jews and the Arabs and the devil knows who else from all ends of Europe and Duke street and the fowl market all clucking outside Larby Sharons and the poor donkeys slipping half asleep and the vague fellows in the cloaks asleep in the shade on the steps and the big wheels of the carts of the bulls and the old castle thousands of years old yes and those handsome Moors all in white and turbans like kings asking you to sit down in their little bit of a shop and Ronda with the old windows of the posadas glancing eyes a lattice hid for her lover to kiss the iron and the wineshops half open at night and the castanets and the night we missed the boat at Algeciras the watchman going about serene with his lamp and O that awful deepdown torrent O and the sea the sea crimson sometimes like fire and the glorious sunsets and the figtrees in the Alameda gardens yes and all the queer little streets and pink and blue and yellow houses and the rosegardens and the jessamine and ger aniums and cactuses and Gibraltar as a girl where I was a Flower of the mountain yes when I put the rose in my hair like the Andalusian girls used or shall I wear a red yes and how he kissed me under the Moorish wall and I thought well as well him as another and then I asked him with my eyes to ask again yes and then he asked me would I yes to say yes my mountain flower and first I put my arms around him yes and drew him down to me so he could feel my breasts all perfume yes and his heart was going like mad and yes I said yes I will Yes.

Figure 8: Comparison of the short first draft and longer 1922 version of the end of *Ulysses*.

lines ("still its a lovely hour so silent I used to love coming home after dances the air of the night they have friends they can talk to weve none either he wants what he wont get or its some woman ready to stick her knife in you I hate that in women no wonder they treat us the way they do we are a dreadful lot of bitches I suppose its all the troubles we have makes us so snappy Im not like that"). Derek Attridge has shown that "Molly's sentences, syntactically defined, are, on the whole, fairly short," and the effect of the revision is not so much simple parataxis as the effect he calls "frequent postponed resolutions."[78] The interpolated phrases express thoughts that can be either less or rather more complex than a normal English sentence, and the longer phrases are sometimes added to again, producing layer on layer of disconnected, breathy asides. In the manuscript, Molly's thoughts were already disjointed and sometimes self-contradictory, leaping from an emotion to an image, or past time to present, and the interstitial addition of more thoughts only emphasizes this tendency. On the whole, the revisions are slightly more likely than the base text to move outside the immediate moment and two particular aspects of Molly's thought process are expanded in revision—loose sexual fantasy and speculation, and nostalgic thinking about past time. Molly's sexual thoughts expand both by enriching her own desires and speculatively, in her thinking about what Bloom, Boylan, and various other characters want. So in typescript Joyce adds to the description "I wish some man or other would take me sometime" the excited and self-revealing "there's nothing like a kiss long and hot down to your soul almost paralyses you" (18:105–106), and Bloom's fondness for drawers is enhanced by a specific memory of him "always skeezing at those brazen-faced things on the bicycles with their skirts blowing up to their navels even when Milly and I were out with him at the open air fete that one in the cream muslin standing right against the sun so he could see every atom she had on" (18.289–293). A few lines later this irritable memory from the past is transformed into another more pleasant recollection of Bloom trying "to put his hand ~near~ ^anear^ me drawers drawers ~all~ the ^whole blessed^ time" (18.304–305). Up until the third set of proofs, Molly recollected only that she then "so I touched his trousers outside the way I used to Gardner" but, at that point, she starts to think of her own pleasure and complicity, "so I ^lifted them a bit and^ touched his trousers" *(JJA* 21, 185) In the fourth set of proofs, we find out *how* she touches him, "with my ring hand," and *why,* "I was dying to find out was he circumcised" (202). Many of the additions not specifically to do with sex also take a nostalgic relationship to the past, and they seem more likely to be memories than present-tense sensations: among other things, Molly comes to remember "^our 1st death too it was we were never the same since^" (18.450), and what it felt like "^when I used to be in the longing way^." In the first version, her desires for clothes were future-oriented only "I'd have to get a nice pair of slippers like those Turks with the fez used to sell or yellow and a nice semitransparent morning gown that I badly want" (18.1494–1496). In the fourth set of proofs, Joyce added a third item to the list, "or a peachblossom dressing jacket," and then, in the fifth set, he made this item not hypothetical but something that Molly has already seen, wanted, and observed the price of—so her desire turns retrospective and wistful and she thinks of a jacket "like the one long ago in Walpoles ^only^ 8/6 or 18/6."

In the final passage of *Ulysses,* Joyce uses a closural trick familiar from the end of *Dubliners,* creating a lilting, lyrical movement by choosing and ordering words in specific rhythmical patterns. In a sense, the subject matter is also an inverted replaying of the ending of "The Dead" for, where Gabriel Conroy imagines his wife's past lovers while observing the present pallor of snow faintly falling over Ireland, Molly remembers her own sexual past, hidden from her husband, with a series of oriental and exotic images.[79] In both the short story and *Ulysses,* the effect is a poetic coda, a movement away from present-day Dublin. The prose in both cases is highly metrical. "The Dead" verges on iambic pentameter, while Molly begins to add more in downward-falling trochees, "sailors playing all birds fly and I say stoop" (18.1583–1584) before moving into the giddier running rhythms of dactyls, "governors house with the thing round his white helmet poor devil half roasted and the Spanish girls laughing in their shawls and their tall combs and the auctions in the morning the Greeks and the jews and the Arabs . . ." This quick, downward falling pattern is arrested only by the novel's very last word—the "yes" on which Joyce had long planned to end *Ulysses.* And "yes" is itself made rhythmically conspicuous or supplementary by being tacked on to a line that is almost a Homeric hexameter: instead of the expected spondee, Joyce gives us another dactyl, "yes I will," and a single stressed "yes."[80] This rhythmic movement heightens the effect of nostalgic orientalism: late night in colorful, scented Gibraltar, with its wineshops, castanets, and Moors dressed in white seems squarely the opposite of nighttime in Dublin. Even the sea is "crimson sometimes like fire" rather than the unpleasant "snotgreen" with which the novel began.

The effect is moving, affirmative. How could it be otherwise with all of those many added "yeses"? And yet the lyricism also threatens to be excessive, out of key with the situation it describes. To begin with, all of the objects lovingly remembered are grammatically the objects of a negative verb; the speech act is not Molly thinking anew in the present about her girlhood, but her memory of keeping key details private in the past. Moreover, the proposal itself seems sadly inauspicious: Molly is remembering not the day Bloom proposed but the day she cleverly "got him to propose to me," then a private emotional landscape to which he has no access, and finally her first beau, Mulvey. Critics sometimes read "as well him as another" as referring to Bloom; so Pericles Lewis concludes, "He asked her to marry him but she was overcome with thoughts of other men. Nonetheless, she decided to marry Bloom, here typically, the everyman ('as well him as another')."[81] But the setting of the kiss makes it clear that Bloom was the second—or subsequent—man to whom Molly applied this indifferent logic; the first "as well him" is Mulvey, whom Bloom remembers being told about in the detumescent part of "Nausicaa." "First kiss does the trick. The propitious moment. Something inside them goes pop. Mushy like, tell by their eye, on the sly. First thoughts are best. Remember that till their dying day. Molly, lieutenant Mulvey that kissed her under the Moorish wall beside the gardens. Fifteen she told me. But her breasts were developed" (13.886–890). When in revision Joyce added "^and his heart was going like mad yes^ I said ^yes^ I will Yes," he increased the possibility of a dual reading; the beating heart can be both Mulvey's in Gibraltar and Bloom's on Howth Heath. In the National Library pre-fair-copy draft, we can see that the more definite "will" had been originally the hypothetical "and I said I would yes," but he changed this immediately in a *currente calamo* revision.[82]

The lyricism and opening range of this passage have encouraged many to read it as pure affirmation: "and so the novel ends, with existential celebration, regretting nothing"; "Molly says 'yes' to Leopold and herself becomes a Bloom"; "in no uncertain terms, it seems, Bloom's quest has ended."[83] And yet the added details and confusing parataxis, where one lover either blurs into or is added to another, make it hard to be entirely sure. Joyce's own second thoughts, added in five stages to the manuscript text, bolster the sense Bloom had earlier in the day that "first kiss does the trick." Ironically, they suggest that "first thoughts are best."

The Afterlife of the Elongated Sentence: Updike, Ellis, Hysterical Realism

The kind of sentence that Joyce developed by revising *Ulysses,* and which is most in evidence in the baroque but precise lists of "Ithaca" and Molly's breathy contradictions, has had a long afterlife. If the legacy of modernist excision is the spare, often elegiac, landscapes of Beckett or Carver, the metonymic long sentence leads us toward maximalism. I have already distinguished between the effects of Joyce's additions in the earlier chapters of *Ulysses,* which enrich Bloom's focalizing consciousness, and those made in the "Ithaca" and "Penelope" chapters, which work at a higher degree of ironic distance. Both kinds of excess have had a subsequent history. The first kind of long sentence, which renders someone else's thoughts in extreme detail, has been used by postwar writers to suggest richer, more luxurious internal realities than characters are themselves able to voice. The second, more external, narratorial kind of excess leads toward kinds of hyper self-conscious postmodernism, and what James Wood has described as "hysterical realism," the pursuit of "vitality" above all else.[84] This is not to say that contemporary writers who write long, and who stuff in everything including the kitchen sink, necessarily do so as a result of additive revision. Joyce had to learn how to describe the motion of water as "seaquakes, waterspouts, artesian wells, eruptions, torrents, eddies, freshets, spates, groundswells, watersheds, waterpartings, geysers, cataracts, whirlpools, maelstroms, inundations, deluges, cloudbursts" but more recent writers seem able to achieve excess from the first draft.

Take these two sentences, drawn more or less at random, as examples. The first is John Updike's description of Rabbit's thoughts about his abandoned wife, as he falls asleep in his car. "But there were good things: Janice so shy about showing her body even in the first weeks of wedding yet one night coming into the bathroom expecting nothing he found the mirror clouded with steam and Janice just out of the shower standing there doped and pleased with a little blue towel lazily and unashamed her bottom bright pink with hot water the way a woman was of two halves bending over and turning and laughing at his expression whatever it was and putting her arms up to kiss him, a blush of steam on her body and the back of her soft neck slippery."[85] The Joycean lineage here is obvious enough: "bottom" is one of Bloom's favorite words, and has a faint Anglo-Irish awkwardness in Rabbit's mouth, while the indefinite phrases "the way a woman was" and "whatever it was" recall the way in which many of *Ulysses'* characters amplify or generalize their thoughts. Most importantly, Updike uses excess—the three participles, the interleaved "expecting nothing," the adjectives "soft" *and* "slippery," "doped" *and* "pleased"—to voice a memory that we might expect Rabbit to have difficulty articulating. The five short words before the colon introduce the laconic premise that we can imagine Rabbit actually saying: "There were good things." The words that follow, full of important and poignant detail at the level of the phrase (the Eliotic "expecting nothing," the slight zeugma of "lazily and unashamed") expand his consciousness: they make it, in John Neary's phrase, "luxurious."[86] In fact, Neary compares Updike's technique quite explicitly to Joyce, "He does this, as Joyce does, by making the contents of his character's mind quite unexceptional—they are simply tidbits of American culture—while nevertheless conveying them with a linguistic vividness that makes the character's perception of them seem downright epiphanic." The Shakespearean idea that a woman is "of two halves" is something we would not expect Rabbit to reach for directly, but Updike presents it in straightforward free indirect speech, giving ownership of the words clearly to his character, "[Rabbit thought about how] a woman was of two halves." Amid the whole sentence's prodigality, it fits.

This kind of long sentence opens itself up to restitutive and democratic ends: it levels out differences in articulacy by allowing characters to voice unconsciously or internally something that they would have difficulty saying aloud. It disguises the weirdness of Bloom noticing and thinking like Joyce, or Rabbit activating an allusion to *King Lear* ("Down from the waist they are Centaurs,/ Though women all above"), or even Rabbit thinking like Molly Bloom. By wrapping ordinary words or observations around extraordinary ones, it conceals their artifice. It has something in common with the "lower-middle-class modernism" that Mark McGurl identifies as a problem for Joyce Carol Oates. In an early review, Alfred Kazin criticized Oates for giving us "an impenetrably voluminous history of emotions, emotions, emotions."[87] McGurl may not share this opinion of Oates' work, but he shows how her excessive prodigality, combined with experiments in genre fiction, and characters drawn from the ordinary middle classes has lowered her stock among "serious" critics.

The other kind of long sentence, the "list for its own sake" that Joyce began producing for the later episodes of *Ulysses*, also tends to convey social or political critique. This is from Bret Easton Ellis's novel *Glamorama*.

> How it got to be eleven so suddenly is confusing to us all, not that it really means anything, and conversation revolves around how Mark Vanderloo "accidentally" ate an onion-and-felt sandwich the other night while viewing the Rob Lowe sex tapes, which Mark found "disappointing"; the best clubs in New Zealand; the injuries sustained at a Metallica concert in Pismo Beach; how Hurley Thompson disappeared from a movie set in Phoenix (I have to bite my tongue); what sumo wrestlers actually *do*; a gruesome movie Jonathan just finished shooting, based on a starfish one of the producers found behind a fence in Nepal; a threesome someone fell into with Paul Shrader and Bruce Wagner; spinning lettuce; the proper pronunciation of "ooh la la."[88]

The forward propulsion of the sentence, in terms of plot, is almost nothing: Ellis is describing a late night conversation and the participants' "confusion" about the rapid passage of time. But individual speakers are not picked out, conversation only "revolves around" certain topics, and these topics themselves seem randomly chosen and disconnected. The weird precision of the single inverted commas around "accidentally" appears to draw attention to the non-causal logic that governs action in this world, but also manages to suggest that accidental events are sinister or off-key: if "Mark Vanderloo 'accidentally' ate an onion-and-felt sandwich," we have to assume that he did so, for some unknown reason, on purpose. The rest of the sentence associates a range of different commercial media (music, film, sex tapes, commercial sport) with geographically dispersed locations (New Zealand, Pismo Beach, Phoenix, Nepal), and both the narrator and other characters take a vague but inarticulate ("I had to bite my tongue") stance of disappointment toward them.

It is tempting to read the aimlessness of this list as a satirical mimesis of commoditized art, the lives of the jet-setting rich, celebrity, or even cultural hybridity. "Ooh la la" is itself an Anglicized, dramatic rendition of a French phrase: why worry about its pronunciation? But behind the inverted commas around "disappointing," or the italicized *"do"* lies a more genuine anxiety about the purpose of labor. If sumo wrestlers do nothing, why watch them? What good is a movie based on the random discovery of a starfish? Like Patrick Bateman's obsessive detailing of his own and others' clothes in *American Psycho*—a monotonous, self-conscious set of catalogues that stands in a genealogical relationship to Gerty's "neat blouse of electric blue, self-tinted by dolly dyes"—this paratactic list incorporates fragments derived from the language of commodity culture. Unlike the plot- or character-driven sentences of realist novels, it is also infinitely extendable: the list could always easily accommodate another contiguous item.[89]

Parataxis has been described by Bob Perelman as "the dominant mode of postindustrial experience."[90] As examples, he cites panels presented at the MLA, where "Yeats and Real Estate" illogically follows "Androgyny in Chaucer," and, with more perplexity, the contemporary poetry scene which always requires an et cetera—"language writing, Chicana poetry, academic poetry, cowboy poetry, workshop poetry, *et cetera*."[91] He suggests that "the new sentence," a term coined by Ron Silliman, achieves its novelty not by being a new *kind* of sentence but by being a new way of *organizing* sentences: grammatical units that have tangential relevance are placed together, arranged neither at random nor in a wholly clear subordination to a larger narrative frame. He is

particularly interested in the possibility of using parataxis opposition-
ally, as a way of criticizing some of the features that Fredric Jameson
has associated with postmodernity: depthlessness, schizophrenia, the
loss of personal identity, "a rubble of distinct and unrelated signifi-
ers."[92] His readings of Silliman's *What* focuses on the ways in which it
fights "reified parataxis—commodification" with a "more committed,
critical parataxis" but he also admits that the two can balance on a knife
edge. A heavy-handed parody of the language of women's magazines or
soap adverts is easy enough to detect, but subtle, "critical" parody leaves
fewer traces. The first half of "Nausicaa" comes packaged in frames that
allow us to pick out its irony, its playfulness with confidence: it is by
Joyce (who doesn't usually write like this); it succeeds other episodes in
Ulysses that experiment with different styles; it is strongly focalized
through Gerty; and its tumescent longings are rudely, even comically
shattered, as the "O!" of orgasm becomes "She's lame! O!" (13.771). The
additions to "Penelope," which has a less clear speech-act structure, and
which gains indeterminacy from its very position at the novel's end, are
harder to read. Some critics have relied heavily on Joyce's own closing
signature, "Trieste-Zurich-Paris 1914–1921" as an indication that Molly's
breathless last words fall short of the traditional comic ending—
reconciliation, romance.

   If excision tends to produce logical puzzle pieces, texts that revolve on
a mystery or difficulty that the acute reader can hope to discern, extension leads to more substantial uncertainty about who is speaking, and
tonal vagueness. Is this the author or the character's observation? Beyond a certain point, the inherited conventions of focalization begin to
break down. Or, in the second case, the naturally satiric possibilities of
too many words clash with the obvious pleasure that catalogues of ver-
biage seem to be affording their writers. Why name so many streets,
products, dates, or mediocre eighties songs if not to critique their vapid-
ity or lack of symbolic value? Clustering more and more things together
produces the effect that Walter Benjamin associated first with film: a
"withering of the aura" that occurs proportionately to ease of consumption.[93] At the same time, the sheer zaniness of these lists—the part of "hysterical realism" that is "hysterical"—often seems like self-congratulation.

To *know* and name so many things is itself a fine consumerist cleverness; like the élite Yelp reviewer or fashion blogger, the list-maker inspires grudging awe.

In the end, the question about the effects of paratactically arranged material—is it "critical" or "reified," a catalogue of celebration or contempt?—is wrongly formulated. When we read texts that have been dramatically cut at a late stage of the genetic process, it is helpful to have a certain tolerance for or acceptance of puzzles: is Jake Barnes Catholic? What kind of war wound did he receive? Readers of *The Waste Land* have to balance the intellectual desire for a key, a missing fact that will unify the different unreal cities into one, explain the relationship between "currants" and "currents," or give an account of the transitions between voices, with a tolerance for its loose ends. Through ellipsis the poem both solicits and refuses systematization. After magazine publication in *The Dial* and *The Criterion,* Eliot added his famously baffling notes to the first book edition: at a practical level, he was using the paratextual surround of the poem to compensate for its now too-short text. He was also beginning a process that has continued to the present, where a series of fragments already shored against ruin has gathered more and more other explanatory fragments to itself, and where attempts to "shore up," finding protective common ground, often lead to a deepening of the puzzle. Even the word "shore" itself is puzzling, meaning to prop but also to threaten, to bring in safely to shore, but also to run aground.[94]

Texts that have been extended inside-out produce a different kind of *essential* indeterminacy. Instead of looking for the missing fact, the extra piece that will solve the puzzle, we may need to deal with facts that contradict each other, detail whose purpose seems divorced from immediate points of plot, and speech-act structures that are hard to discern. If we are uncertain about who is speaking, then how can we decide on a passage's rhetorical effect? To read something as ironic, satirical, eulogistic, or elegiac depends on determining the illocutionary context.

One helpful way of understanding the indeterminacy of the long, additive sentence is through a concept in modern philosophy and information science known as the "Inverse Relationship Principle." This states that there is an inverse relationship between the probability of p and the amount of information that it carries, so that tautologies carry no information at all (having a probability of 1) and statements that verge dangerously close to being contradictions carry a very high amount of information. You can increase the amount of information that a sentence carries but it will become less and less likely; in the end, it will simply "implode."[95] The linguists Bar-Hillel and Carnap stated this paradox clearly in 1953 and since its formulation it has been regarded as an unfortunate but necessary consequence of a quantitative theory of semantic information. "It may perhaps, at first, seem strange that a self-contradictory sentence, hence one which no ideal receiver would accept, is regarded as carrying with it the most inclusive information . . . A false sentence which happens to say much is thereby highly informative in our sense. Whether the information it carries is true or false, scientifically valuable or not, and so forth, does not concern us. A self-contradictory sentence asserts too much; it is too informative to be true."[96] In the case of the Joycean long sentence, achieved through revision, and its descendents and imitators, whose all-inclusiveness may emerge from the first draft, the threat of self-contradiction is always present, as realism tips into a kind of excess and therefore into over-realism. Take as a final example Molly's musing on the silliness of names. When Joyce received the first set of placard proofs, his text had read: "I never thought that would be my name Bloom when I used to write it in print to see how it looked on a visiting card or practising for the butcher and oblige M Bloom youre looking blooming Josie used to say after I married him well its better than Breen or those awful names with bottom in them Mrs Ramsbottom or some other kind of a bottom Mulvey I wouldn't go mad about either" (*JJA* 21, 282–283).

As in the closing of "Ithaca," the toying with proper names produces a vertiginous effect; Molly's marriage to "Bloom" produces a "bloom" in her, denying the normally arbitrary nature of the sign. But Joyce did not leave it here. First, in the placard proofs, he added an "or" clause, to allow Molly's consideration of her named identity to range exhaustively from first love to recent love, "^or suppose I divorced him Mrs Boylan^" (18.846). The quickness of this thought is unsettling and unexplained; neither Molly nor Bloom thinks elsewhere in the novel directly of divorce. In the page proofs, Joyce added another layer of uncertainty by having Molly muse, indefinitely, on her mother, "whoever she was," and

on the nicer name that she herself might have received (*JJA* 27, 252). He
also displayed some *currente calamo* uncertainty about the identity of
Molly's mother: in neat writing at the bottom of the page he added, "my
mother whoever she was might have given me a nicer name the Lord
knows after the lovely one she had ~~Luna~~ Lunita Laredo."

After her earlier thoughts about the descriptive value of proper names,
there is a powerful awkwardness in Molly's disjunction of "whoever she
was" and the exotic, deliberate name. If Molly Bloom blooms, what does
Lunita Laredo do? And why might this name conceivably be a better
one for Molly herself? Critics have had a field day of speculation with
this short passage, wondering if it implies that Molly's mother was Jewish, and therefore that she is?[97] Is it a real name, or an alias? Is it a
"pseudo-Iberian transmogrification of Lily Langtry" and, if so does it
imply that she was "evidently a demimondaine"?[98] Given that the name
Tweedy is not mentioned, might we perhaps assume that Lunita and
Molly's father were unmarried? Could someone else be her father? The
temptation to try to answer these questions is powerful, but there is also
something absurd about posing them. In the first version of the sentence, "either" is comfortably an intensifying adverb, but by being
placed next to "or" it bleeds into the next thought. The phrase "Mulvey
I wouldnt go mad about either," followed by a fresh train of thought,
implies that Molly is reconciled to her situation with Bloom ("as well
him as another"), but the proximity of "or," Boylan, and the possibility
of her mother's infidelity, shakes open a set of ramifying further possibilities, a new chain of "either or and either and." From a logical perspective, adding more is very often adding too much. Hugh Kenner
puzzled many years ago that "*Ulysses* commences in tacit adherence to
the canons of naturalism, of Objectivity, and then disorients readers by
deserting them, for reasons that have never been satisfactorily explained."[99] The self-begetting compositional process, which developed
a rather strange and unpredictable logic of its own, is one answer. The
additions that Joyce interleaved into typescript and proof might have
begun as an attempt to leave nothing out, rendering the Dublin of 1904
in the most fine-grained mimetic detail possible, but at some point the
accretions began to produce a different kind of aesthetic pattern: a realism that is too informed, too fulsome, to seem any longer quite true.

CHAPTER 5

"I Am Dead": Autobiography Revisited

O NE OF THE QUESTIONS that "The Middle Years" leaves open is whether Dencombe's marginal alterations—we are never told what they *are*—improve the fabric of his work. In the James chapter, I focused primarily on revision's capacity to disrupt writer-reader relations, and argued that Dencombe's deferral of a "form final for himself" was a way of retaining hermeneutic control over his text until the end. The post-positive position of the adjective—the phrase is a delicate inversion of the more common "final form"—hints at his fundamental anxiety that completing the book may finish off its author, too. Like Henry James, whose practice of revision has been described, variously, as "reckless," unnecessary, onanistic, and self-absorbed, Dencombe's revisions may be an attempt to render a fictional, but somehow "real," world from the most accurate angle. In his preface to *The Golden Bowl,* James described this process as meeting his former self "halfway, passive, receptive, ap-preciative, often even grateful; unconscious, quite blissfully of any bar to intercourse, any disparity of sense between us."[1]

Another possibility is that Dencombe's single-volume novel is, like James's *The Middle Years,* more autobiographical than fictional, and that by returning to its text he is compulsively replaying the events it de-scribes. He claims that he needs an "extension" because his literary skill has been slow to develop: "he had followed literature from the first, but he had taken a lifetime to get alongside of her. . . . He had ripened too late and was so clumsily constituted that he had to teach himself by mistakes." A skeptical Freudian might ask if this stylistic explanation is the whole story. When Dencombe tells Doctor Hugh, "I've outlived. I've lost by the way," the young—Germanic—doctor probes deeper, "Whom have you lost?" Dencombe's reply indicates that his own middle years were marked by tragedy. "I once had a wife—I once had a son. My wife died when my child was born, and my boy, at school, was carried off by typhoid." Might his need to continue rewriting *The Middle Years* in old age represent a—perhaps futile—attempt to relive and, by reliving, master these two traumas?

In his 1920 essay *Beyond the Pleasure Principle*, Freud asked why some patients obsessively, and apparently pointlessly, found themselves repeating past trauma. Why, for example, did "dreams occurring in traumatic neuroses have the characteristic of repeatedly bringing the patient back into the situation of his accident" rather than recalling pleasant memories from the "healthy past"?[2] As if they had become "stuck" on the moment of trauma, some of his patients seemed "obliged to *repeat* the repressed material as a contemporary experience instead of . . . *remembering* it as something belonging to the past." For Freud, this repetition compulsion was puzzling primarily because it seemed to contradict the pleasure principle. Excessive revision—repeatedly *going over* an already achieved text—begs the same question. Why do writers continue to revise after revision ceases to be pleasurable and, arguably, after they have ceased to make substantial improvements? As James's example illustrates, revision is never the *mere* repetition of a fort/da game—it produces new words, a new text—but it may also be the only way of "reliving" or "re-dreaming" the original experience of writing.

Freud began his exploration of repetition in 1914, in the essay "Remembering, Repeating, and Working Through," but his understanding of traumatic repetition underwent significant changes after analyzing soldiers returning from the war. Cathy Caruth argues that Freud's examples—"the patient repeating painful events in analysis, the woman condemned repeatedly to marry men who die, the soldier Tancred in Tasso's poem wounding his beloved again" are all instances where "the outside has gone inside without any mediation."[3] The trauma becomes twofold, consisting not only in the original and shocking event, but in the equally shocking fact of *"having survived, precisely, without knowing it."* In a clinical setting, Freud found repetition compulsions hard to cure, and other doctors dealing in the late 1910s with war neuroses and shell shock had the same experience. The literature of the Great War is also full of examples of linguistic perseveration: we might think of the thrice-repeated "Cat!" in Robert Graves's "A Child's Nightmare," or Nancy Rufford's monotonous "shuttlecocks" in *The Good Soldier*, or even Eliot's "HURRY UP PLEASE IT'S TIME."[4] In fact, Eliot was to diagnose Hamlet as seeking relief through repeating: "the levity of Hamlet, his repetition of phrase, his puns, are not part of a deliberate plan of dissimulation, but a form of emotional relief."[5]

In this chapter I focus on revision in autobiographical writing. The aspectual structure of retrospective life writing—its twin focus on the present moment of writing and the past remembered—has a structural similarity with revision as the process of *going over* and remaking for the present a text already accomplished in the past. Martin Löschnigg explains that this is the case in principle; in this chapter, I will show that it is often also genetic fact: "As opposed to biography, where the author renders someone else's life story, autobiography is necessarily incomplete and (theoretically) open to constant rewriting."[6] In particular, I argue that traumatic events are particularly prone to reworking: either through direct revision of earlier drafts, or through repetition across a textual series. In a sense my argument is transhistorical: in every period, autobiographies—from Rousseau's *Confessions* to Wordsworth's *Prelude* to Proust's *À la recherche*—seem more liable to revision than other literary forms. At the same time, the early twentieth century saw an efflorescence of autobiographical and "autobiografictional" writing, as well as the development of psychoanalysis as a discursive practice. As Max Saunders has recently argued, however sternly modernist writers urged "impersonality" as a virtue, their own writing tended to revisit real events—Hemingway's early months in Paris; Stein's relationship with Alice B. Toklas; Pound's anxiety about being banished from "the world of letters"; the death of Joyce's mother.[7] This is true across genres and becomes almost normative in the modernist novel. For Avrom Fleishman, "during the years in which *A Portrait* was taking shape, other major novelists were charting the direction of their careers in autobiographical novels we scarcely think of as personal stories because they have become paradigmatic of modern fiction and its attendant forms of self-consciousness."[8]

To the Lighthouse, Virginia Woolf's most autobiographical novel, provides a good starting point; its structure is so delicately balanced between openness ("The Window") and resolution ("The Lighthouse"). Although the book opens in a conditional mood, premising its journey forward—the movement to the lighthouse—on tomorrow's weather, the final pages are bent on aspectual closure, on rendering the plot as finished and done. To begin with, "Yes, of course," requires qualification, "if it's fine tomorrow," and even Mrs. Ramsay's knitted sock remains hypothetical, "If she finished it tonight, if they did go to the Lighthouse after all, it was to be given to the Lighthouse keeper for his little boy."[9] Woolf's strategy at the novel's end is to transform openness and uncertainty into the indicative mood and the perfective aspect. Mr. Carmichael observes that Mr. Ramsay and James "will have landed," and this echoes Lily's unvoiced thoughts, "he has landed," "it is finished." Finally, we have the first person triumph of artistic completion: "She looked at the steps; they were empty; she looked at her canvas; it was blurred. With a sudden intensity, as if she saw it clear for a second, she drew a line there, in the centre. It was done; it was finished. Yes, she thought, laying down her brush in extreme fatigue, I have had my vision" (211).

In "The Window" section, Mr. Ramsay had imagined knowledge stacked before him like the letters of the alphabet, "the last of which is scarcely visible to mortal eyes, but glimmers red in the distance" (37), and he perceived his own progress as a slow and incremental progress from one to the next. His fear is "that R was beyond him. He would never reach R." By the novel's end, this serial metaphor—a movement akin to James's belief that history itself is "gradual betterment"—is refigured into a single bold action, a sudden leap into empty "space." For a moment, the isolated intellectual becomes a leader, "and they both rose to follow him as he sprang, lightly like a young man, holding his parcel, on to the rock."

Mr. Ramsay Reaching R: Allegories of Finishing

If Dencombe's desperate desire for an extension attempts to keep finishing at bay, replacing a definitive ending with a series of revisionary stages, we can read Lily Briscoe's last brush stroke as an allegory of *not revising*. The painting she has had so much difficulty producing remains unsatisfyingly "blurred" until a few words from the novel's end. It is only with a final, inspired act—the drawing of a single line "in the centre"—that the painting can be completed. Unlike Matisse, who repainted over the surfaces of his already achieved canvases many times—he made numerous changes to both the colors and sculptural forms of "Bathers by a River"—Woolf leaves no possibility that Lily will add anything more. Just as Mr. Ramsay's unreachable "R" is transformed into a literally concluded journey when he leaps into space, so for Lily a mere second of mental clarity seems to be enough. Her "vision" is definitive and final, not a Prufrockian matter of "visions and revisions." It brings back Mrs. Ramsay in the form of art and it also dispenses with the need to continue thinking of her.

This preference for closure and completion at the end of *To the Lighthouse* can be read as a projection of Woolf's own desire to be rid of the troubling, traumatic material of her childhood. It is wish fulfillment. Like Lily, she wants to "be done," dispensing with the traumatic family history that the book narrates. In her final work, "A Sketch of the Past," written during an extensive reading of Freud, she herself insisted that the earlier novel had functioned as a successful exorcism.[10] Here, she renders her work as an autobiographer as swift, unhesitating, and psychologically conclusive. "Then one day walking round Tavistock Square I made up, as I sometimes make up my books, *To the Lighthouse*; in a great, apparently involuntary, rush. One thing burst into another . . . I wrote the book very quickly; and when it was written, I ceased to be obsessed by my mother. I no longer hear her voice; I do not see her. I suppose that I did for myself what psycho-analysts do for their patients. I expressed some very long felt and deeply felt emotion. And in expressing it I explained it and then laid it to rest" (81).[11] Most critics have read this self-diagnosis as accurate, but Woolf's claim is muted by the specific context in which it was made and also by our knowledge of her compositional labor on *To the Lighthouse*.[12] If the novel had successfully laid to rest an "obsession" with her mother, why did she find herself renarrating Julia's death a decade later? Maud Ellmann compares Woolf to Freud's Wolf Man as someone haunted by early parental death, suffering from a grief "incurable and virtually professional," and ambivalent about the contradictory desire to preserve and overcome the dead.[13] Here, the ebb and flow of the text itself makes clear this basic irresolution. After poignantly stating that her vision of and feeling for her mother has become "so much dimmer and weaker" over time (81), she begins the next paragraph with a masterful act of resurrection. The short, jumpy prose rhythms open out into a more confident, periodic movement and Woolf effectively repeats the phrase "there she was" to produce a calm sense of complete presence. "Certainly, there she was, in the very centre of that great Cathedral space which was childhood; there she was from the very first." This, of course, is very like the affirmative ending of *Mrs. Dalloway*, "For there she was."

Moreover, despite the confident claim that *To the Lighthouse* was written "very quickly," its most autobiographical parts were in fact heavily revised. In 1927, she admitted in a letter that the epitaphic "Time Passes" section had caused her "more trouble than all of the rest of the book put together," and the manuscripts bear this out.[14] In 1983, James Haule edited and republished a typescript of this section, which Woolf sent to the French magazine *Commerce* for translation. He notes that both the original holograph and this intermediate stage lack "the presence, both direct and indirect, of the characters so carefully developed in 'The Window' and in 'The Lighthouse,'" and Woolf did not add her remarkable, factual parentheses until the final version.[15] Even "A Sketch," which Woolf left unfinished at her death and which consistently pretends to being a quickly written, casual project, was revised in several stages. Again, Woolf's revisions to her manuscript and typescript cluster most heavily around the work's traumatic center. Before she made the formal announcement of Stella's death with which the A.5a typescript ends, "and so, after three months of intermittent illness, she died—at 24 Hyde Park Gate, on July 27th, 1897," Woolf had produced, and then reworked, two separate manuscript versions.

Autobiography, Diary, Aspect

Ceasing and restarting, laying to rest and bringing back to life: these are the poles within which autobiographical writing oscillates, and they engender revision. In her 2003 essay, "The Name and the Scar," Maud Ellmann recognizes that this dialectic of completion and incompletion has puzzling genetic consequences. Comparing Joyce's difficulty finishing the autobiographical novel *A Portrait of the Artist as a Young Man* to Wordsworth's revisions of the *Prelude,* she asks, "what is it about self-portraiture, for Joyce as for Wordsworth, which makes them so reluctant to conclude?"[16] In his work on "auto-genesis," Philippe Lejeune asks a version of the same question when he wonders whether "generic specificities" govern the process of composition.[17] Most suggestively, he raises that possibility that autobiography has "a different relationship to its avant-textes than do texts of fiction, poetry or thought." This provocative idea begs further questions. Is autobiography accordingly the most *revisable* of genres or modes? If a text is only partially, or in a disguised way, autobiographical, is it also likely to produce revisionary second thoughts? And how far is the relationship between autobiography and genetic complexity a historical problem?

My argument is this chapter has three parts. First, I claim that autobiography is a genre or mode particularly prone to revision; second, that this "revisability" is sharpened when writers find themselves describing traumatic material. In the final part of the chapter, I provide detailed genetic readings of three texts written between 1895 and 1940 where trauma acts first as a compositional stumbling block, and then as a spur to revision. These are Leslie Stephen's *Mausoleum Book,* which he left unpublished at his death, James Joyce's "autobiografiction" *A Portrait of the Artist,* which was remaindered from the abandoned *Stephen Hero,* and Virginia Woolf's final, unfinished "A Sketch of the Past." All of these texts begin retrospectively but, puzzlingly, all turn into evolving, prospective diaries. What is the benefit of moving from the closed form of autobiography—a form that, like the ending of *To the Lighthouse,* depends on aspectual completion—to the unfolding, permanent present of the diary form? One possibility is that it removes the constraint of needing to make the life–writing *perfect:* that is, it removes the hope and then the threat latent in a Jamesian practice of revision.

In suggesting that autobiography is hard to finish, I am developing and critiquing an argument made by Philippe Lejeune. In fact, he has repeatedly argued that diaries are more difficult to end than autobiographies. If diary is "virtually unfinishable from the beginning" because the form is open, prospective, and tilted toward the future, he thinks autobiography is easily finished because it is aspectually closed, a record of past time: "It is as diary that autobiography is unfinishable. Likewise, it is as autobiography that the diary can be 'finished.' All autobiography is finishable. The proof is that 'how to' handbooks devote entire chapters to the rituals of closure."[18] He cites, among other examples, André Gide's extreme reluctance to write the final entry in his notebook. "No! I cannot admit that with the end of this notebook, everything will be over; that it will be done. Maybe I will want to still add something more. Add I don't know what. Just add. Maybe. At the last minute, add still something more . . ." (189). According to Lejeune's reading, we see here "in the first paragraph the refusal to finish, the desire to write, to write anything at all, in order to go on living; in the second, a theatrical 'final word,' doubtless premeditated." His study of Anne Frank's diary has shown that this reluctance to come to an end can coexist with substantial revision of the achieved first draft. Frank in fact produced two "heterogenous" and "incomplete" documents, from which her father created the published text. Lejeune focuses in great detail on the textual history of this tragic and peculiar work but, in fact, Anne Frank's situation is not an anomalous one. Because the majority of diarists do not seek publication during their lifetime, and because many diaries are ended only at the writer's death, the price of a diary's publication is, all too often, posthumous intervention by an editor.[19] Max Brod turned Kafka's thirteen quarto notebooks into "a text as complete as it was possible to make it"; Woolf's enormous mass of diary material was first condensed by her husband, Leonard, in 1954 and then reedited in a five-volume edition by Anne Olivier Bell; John Middleton Murray published *The Journal of Katherine Mansfield* in a heavily expurgated form four years after her death.[20]

Lejeune makes an eloquent point about the difficulty of finishing a diary, but his use of the term "finish" requires some modification. There is, after all, more than one way of "finishing" something. In the first sense, finishing is "to come to the end of," and "to provide with an ending"—that is to reach a narrative or diegetic close—but it also means "to perfect finally or in detail," and "to put the final and completing touches to a thing"—that is, to complete genetically.[21] In the first, narratological sense, it may indeed be easier to complete an autobiography than a diary—the writer can always select an epiphany or stopping point through which to stage a close—but in the second, genetic sense autobiography is harder to end. The diary form aims not to see life steadily and see it whole but, as Felicity Nussbaum puts it, "to imitate human chronology without overt rearrangement, evaluation, or closure."[22] On the other hand, because autobiography is always already retrospective—its power comes from the present self's analysis of past time, not the spontaneous recording of an immediate present—rereading, and then revising, an autobiography does not transgress the form. For Georges Gusdorf, the genre's "deepest intentions" are not to replay the past but to justify the past to the present, offering the writer a "final chance to win back what has been lost" and a "kind of apologetics or theodicy of the individual being."[23]

We might say, then, that *perfective aspect* is the autobiographer's master-illusion. If diarists are forced to maintain what Liz Stanley and Helen Dampier have termed the simulacrum of "presentness," concealing the possibility that entries are not written within the immediate moment, autobiographers maintain a simulacrum of finishedness.[24] Because the very subject matter of autobiography is the writer's own life story, the events narrated continue to matter—and may appear to form part of a different narrative—as the writer continues living. In her final memoir, written in her nineties, Sybille Bedford commented on the necessity of rewriting events that her earlier memoir and autobiographical novels had already covered. "Yet the alembic of memory does not stand still. Perspectives shift."[25] Graham Greene began his own autobiography, which he titled *A Sort of Life*, by admitting that its conclusion must, by necessity, be premature: "If one cannot close a book of memories on the deathbed, any conclusion must be arbitrary, and I have preferred to finish this essay with the years of failure which followed my first novel. Failure too is a kind of death."[26] If posthumous editing is the supplementary act required to finish a diary whose author could never write "this is the final entry," the textual process that shadows and supplements autobiography is retrospective authorial revision.

Diaries pretend to "presentness," realist novels to mimesis, the lyric poem to sincerity, autobiography to completion. These are structural—we might even say contractual—aspects of different literary genres, and they stem from the speech act postulated between writer and reader. When a writer publishes her own autobiography, she is implicitly forcing the alembic to stand still. The life narrative is to be considered formed and finished before every final piece of evidence can be taken into account. As Derrida observes in his essay "The Deaths of Roland Barthes," finishing means pronouncing, albeit implicitly, a sentence that is "legitimately impossible as a performative utterance": "I am dead."[27] Paul de Man was pointing to the same paradox when he argued that "the dominant figure of the epitaphic or autobiographical discourse is, as we saw, the prosopopoeia, the fiction of the-voice-from-beyond-the-grave."[28] For de Man, the interest of autobiography is that it functions as a kind of limit case for all writing, revealing "the impossibility of closure and of totalization." Indeed, the paradoxical relationship between autobiography's will to finish and its fear of finishing was much mined in the 1980s by deconstructive critics. Laura Marcus lists some of the ways in which the "thanatographic" impulses of deconstruction fitted with the autobiographic mode: the romantic link between self-consciousness and self-murder; the link between autobiography and allegory; "a focus on mourning, melancholia and memory, particularly in Derrida's work"; a noncommunicative theory of writing, where writing is not "a supplement to the self but a substitution for the autobiographical subject, so that the self 'dies' to the letter."[29]

Posthumous Nineteenth-Century Autobiographies

Understanding that autobiography is *structurally* prone to revision helps to explain why literary history is full of revised autobiographies. It should not be surprising that, for example, Benjamin Franklin "kept revising and adding" to his "during war, peacemaking, and old age,"[30] or that Nabokov needed the subtitle "An Autobiography Revisited" for the

1966 second edition of *Speak, Memory.*[31] In the nineteenth century, we might think of Wordsworth's *Prelude;* De Quincey's *Confessions,* whose "autobiographical passages were much expanded in [the] 1856 revision";[32] J. S. Mill's *Autobiography,* written in separate chunks between 1853 and 1868; Whitman's *Leaves of Grass,* published in at least six editions over thirty-seven years;[33] and Samuel Butler's *The Way of All Flesh,* composed with difficulty over a twelve-year period. These texts are all experiments at autobiography in different modes, and they presented their writers with substantial compositional difficulties. A second curious fact is that very few of the major Victorian autobiographies were published in their authors' lifetimes. Their first readers were, quite literally, hearing a voice speaking from beyond the grave.

Why were Victorian autobiographers unable to bring their own autobiographical writings into print? The traditional explanation has emphasized that they were uneasy about the "wisdom, propriety, or usefulness of autobiography": accordingly, they shrank from self-revelation, feared the charge of self-promotion, and viewed their autobiographical writings as intimate, familial documents, not worth the sustained attention of a published text.[34] Certainly, the pervasive and stylized modesty of many of these texts suggests that their authors could barely bother with them. After stating that his avowed aim was to write "as if I were a dead man in another world looking back at my own life," Charles Darwin added that, "I have taken no pains about my style of writing."[35] Like Leslie Stephen in his *Mausoleum Book,* he also claimed that his desired audience stretched no further than his immediate descendants. "I have thought the attempt would amuse me, and might interest my children or their children." For his son, who brought the text into print, it was immediately obvious that the real audience the text would find was far larger. Like Percy Lubbock, who marked corrections on James's memoir "silently," Francis Darwin omitted various passages: "I have not thought it necessary to indicate where such omissions are made."[36] Even Anthony Trollope, who explains in his own *Autobiography* that his immensely prolific output as a novelist depended on writing by certain "self-imposed laws" and by proceeding only ever forwards by an average of forty pages a day, did not leave that text quite as finished as the others.[37] He left the pages behind for his son, with a letter instructing,

204 THE WORK OF REVISION

"My intention is that they shall be published after my death, and be edited by you."

A different explanation for these texts' posthumous status might be that their authors were unable—or simply couldn't bear—to shape their life into forms final for themselves. Recognizing that their work fell short of the standards of closure that they demanded, they consequently shied away from publication. J. S. Mill's work on his own autobiography was strongly associated with intimations of mortality. He began it in 1853, under the belief he had only a few months to live. By 1855, he was rereading it, "I find it wants revision which I shall give it," and noticing things "said very crudely" as well as significant omissions.[38] He returned to it in a more substantial way in 1861 after the death of his wife, and again in 1868. On both occasions, he added more by continuing writing up to the present time, but he also revised the original document substantially, "making such stylistic changes as might contribute to greater clarity and uniformity of the document as a whole."[39] The uneven genetic process can be explained by his shifting and uncertain views about the amount of time remaining: when he was in poor health, Mill added more; when he felt more relaxed about the possibility of "outliving," he reread what he had written and made substitutive corrections to it. In this regard, his process of writing autobiography differed substantially from the compositional method he adopted for his other works, and which he in fact described in the pages of his autobiography as a "double rédaction." Given that this method was reliant on first putting everything into an ideal order ("the only thing which I am careful, in the first draft, to make as perfect as I am able, is the arrangement") and subsequently considering stylistic polish, it was profoundly ill-suited to a genre in which the true series of events is revealed only *after the fact*.

Wordsworth's *Prelude* is only a partial autobiography; its narrative aim is to trace the formation of the poet's vocation, not his whole life. Its long revisionary history is, accordingly, a sharp illustration of the difference between finishing a text by extension (writing up to the final day, as Gide tried to do) and by genetic completion (perfecting a narrative with a fixed end point). Wordsworth had completed a first draft before the nineteenth century had even begun, but he continued rewriting the poem for another *fifty* years. Stephen Gill explains this as a matter of fidelity to the present self, a "compulsion to reuse his earlier poetry and to remould it in such a way that it becomes congruent with his current perception of himself."[40] A more pathological account is given by Eugene Stelzig, who argues that one could see the intermittent and drawn-out revisions as "a neurotic attempt at self-correction which diminishes the vitality of the 1805 version."[41] As Jonathan Arac relates, Wordsworth had looked forward to the "most happy" day on which it would be finished, but soon found that "it was not a happy one": "when I looked back on the performance it seemed to have a dead weight about it, the reality so far short of the expectation."[42] After 1805, Wordsworth continued to work on his poem until his death. He made additions and alterations to mimetic detail about the outside world, as in this description of Newton's statue in Trinity College, Cambridge. In the 1805 *Prelude,* the speaker notices only: "The Antechapel, where the Statue stood/ Of Newton with his Prism and silent Face." At some point in the 1830s, perhaps under the influence of new scientific ideas of time, distance, and journeying, he added, "The marble index of a mind for ever/ Voyaging through strange seas of Thought alone."[43] A higher proportion of the revisions are substitutive and personal; that is, they rewrite the *attitude* of the self to the outside world, giving past events a different symbolic weight. In her reading of the drowned-man episode, which was significantly transformed between the 1799 two-book and 1805 twelve-book *Prelude,* and then again between 1805 and 1850, Susan Wolfson shows that the "tragic and disturbing contents of the event" are gradually made more artificial and spectacular, "a literary staging, a composed 'scene.'"[44]

Comparing the 1805 and 1850 texts, which readers have been able to do since the middle of the modernist period, raises a series of important questions about the development and integrity of the individual self over time. In his inaugural facing-page edition, Ernest de Selincourt raised many of the questions that continue to haunt *Prelude* criticism. Why did a poet apparently committed to "the spontaneous overflow of powerful feelings" find himself bestowing on revision an effort "at least equal to that of first composition"? He ended up suggesting that the ideal text of the poem would be an editorial conflation of the two versions that "would retain from the earliest version such familiar details as have any autobiographical significance," accept changes "designed to remove crudities of expression, or to develop or clarify his original meaning," but reject "later excrescences of a manner less pure, at times even meretricious, which are out of key with the spirit in which the poem was first conceived and executed."[45]

The scope that de Selincourt allows for revision is a very limited one, and his argument fails to address the psychological compulsion that kept Wordsworth at his work of rereading and altering. By representing "good" revision as a matter of correction and cosmetic improvement, and "bad" revision as an overlay of a later style on an earlier one, de Selincourt was also writing within a distinctive tradition. When nineteenth-century autobiographers address their own rewriting projects, they tend to figure revision as the search for representational accuracy. Within the modernist period, as autobiography changed in status and kind, it too shifted from a genre reluctant to "tamper with precise fact" to a genre that openly acknowledged its own "revisedness." Twentieth-century writers were, arguably, not only more comfortable revealing personal facts about their lives, but they were more satisfied with the provisional shapes that life narratives necessarily take. This may be part of a wider aesthetic appreciation for what Barbara Herrnstein Smith, discussing poems by Eliot and Yeats that end with important questions, terms "the expressive qualities of weak closure": that is, "a sense of open-endedness, a refusal to speak the unspeakable, solve the unsolvable, resolve the un-resolvable."[46] Both Joyce's *A Portrait* and Woolf's "A Sketch" have hesitant and indefinite titles, as if various other portraits or sketches of the same subjects could have been produced in their stead. In the second part of this chapter, I compare the hesitant, self-interrupting way in which Stephen's *Mausoleum Book* admits its autobiographical preoccupations to Woolf's confident assertion in "A Sketch" that all life writing is provisional, "What I write today I should not write in a year's time" (275). Where the *Mausoleum Book* dissolves only gradually and apologetically into a diary, Woolf announces her discovery of "a possible form for these notes" with excitement, repeatedly making recollection of the past dependent on her specific present.

Leslie Stephen's *Mausoleum Book*

Leslie Stephen's memoir acquired its gloomy title only in retrospect; his descendants, whom the memoir directly addresses, had a sharp eye for the melancholy excesses of Victorian grief. We know that he began writing it in May 1895, a few weeks after his second wife's death, but do not have the first draft. The surviving document—it is really a nested cluster of related documents—consists of a large green album and some loose papers lodged at the British Library as MSS. 57920–57922. In 1977, the year *after* Virginia Woolf's own unpublished autobiographical writing had been brought into print, it was edited and published with minor excerptions by Alan Bell.[47]

Stephen was troubled from the beginning by the problem I diagnose as germane to autobiographical writing—the problem of *finishing.* He had difficulty getting to the diegetic end of the memoir, and then he had difficulty remaining satisfied with what he had already written. By the time he came to write his own memoir, Stephen was an expert in the contemporary genres of life writing, and yet he was also uneasy about what *kind* of document this was to be. From 1885 to 1891, he had served as the first editor of the *Dictionary of National Biography* and written many of the entries within it; in 1895 he had published a biography of his brother, Sir Fitzjames Stephen; and in the 1893–1894 essay "Biography," he had argued strongly against the proposition that history is merely the biographies of great men: "every life . . . has its interest." In his essay on "Autobiography," he began sharply, "No one ever wrote a dull autobiography. If one may make such a bull, the very dullness would be interesting."[48] And yet, when presented with the possibility of writing his own autobiography, Stephen became overwhelmingly anxious that the document would be otiose or boring. As Virginia Hyman argued in one of the first discussions of the memoir, "Stephen's memorial seems to run at cross purposes with itself," and despite "explicitly reject[ing] the confessional mode, through its pattern of assertion and negation, the book reveals many of Stephen's deepest fears."[49]

The first entry in the book is dated May 21, 1895, but that entry is itself preceded by a framing note dated two months later, "July 1895." Written in a fluent, cursive hand with very few corrections, this opens: "I am about to copy here a paper which I wrote last May. You will find the original in a manuscript book, which I have placed in the box containing my correspondence with Julia. I shall probably make a few alterations, some of them in consequence of remarks that have occurred to me upon again looking through our letters. But unless any special reason occurs, I shall not think it worth while to mark any changes" (3).[50] By copying out a memoir that he had already *written,* Stephen tries to frame the memoir's contents as already complete and perfect. His original manuscript does not survive, but by also explaining that he will be making "a few alterations," he immediately enters into the revisionary regress that had troubled Dencombe. "Final forms" tend to recede in proportion to the strenuousness with which they are sought.

In a strict sense, the memoir itself is neither biography nor autobiography nor diary—it is a letter, addressed by a grieving husband to Julia's children.[51] A careful semicolon distinguishes the three children from her first marriage from the Stephens: "George Herbert, Stella, and Gerald de l'Etang Duckworth; and Vanessa, Julian Thoby, Adeline Virginia and Adrian Leslie Stephen." The relative formality of the epistle form harkens back to eighteenth-century models, such as Chesterfield's tutelary *Letters to His Son,* and feels at times impersonal; it was, however, to be adopted by Virginia Woolf in the first of her own autobiographical writings, and can be regarded as a family mode. One of its effects as form is to minimize the role of the autobiographical subject, oscillating between second person invocation ("I am writing to you personally") and third person descriptions of Julia's own life. The governing figure of speech is *praeteritio:* "I could give a history of some struggles through which I have had to pass—successfully or otherwise" we are told on the second page, "but I have a certain sense of satisfaction in knowing that I shall take that knowledge with me to the grave. There was nothing unusual or remarkable about my inner life." The reluctance to address personal concerns is typical of Victorian anxieties about the "wisdom, propriety, or usefulness of autobiography" and creates generic instability from the beginning—is this biography or autobiography? Is it about Leslie or Julia? There is also great literary self-consciousness about the act of writing; Stephen's anxiety has been provoked in part "by reading Horatio Brown's life of Symonds, virtually an autobiography, and reflecting how little of the same kind of internal history could be told of me" (4).

A brief coda at the end symmetrically balances the prefatory note, linking the activities of remembering, rereading, and rewriting. After the rhetorical flourish of the letter's ending, "We will cling to each other,"

Leslie Stephen signs off. The coda that follows is dated one week after the prefatory note, and explains: "I finish copying this on 11 July 1895. I have made a good many alterations, as I proceeded . . . These were suggested by re-reading the letters of the time and copying many passages from them in the volume of 'Extracts.' I have altered a good many later passages, partly correcting slovenly phrases and repetitions, partly from a few letters, etc., which have since turned up, and partly adding a few thoughts which occurred to me as I read my manuscript over again" (97). Like many revisers, Stephen begins by suggesting that the work of revision is merely factual correction, moves from there to stylistic burnishing, and finally admits to a genuine desire to add new thoughts. From the three dates given, we can deduce that it took Leslie Stephen about a week to "copy out" his original letter and, consequently, that about a sixth of the time devoted to the project was spent on copying rather than first draft composition. By this point, the memoir has been finished twice. It begins at the beginning and ends with Julia's death, "the last terrible time," when Leslie Stephen saw his "beloved angel sinking quietly into the arms of death" (96–97): it is, apparently, complete. What remains to be said?

In fact, Stephen continued making additional entries in his *Mausoleum Book* for the next eight years, until his own death in 1903. Having begun by revising an already complete first draft during the process of copying, he then retroactively revised it in two further ways: intrinsically, by continuing to improve and correct the original version (e.g., some of these entries provide additional information about places and dates), and extrinsically, by extending the boundaries of the document as a whole. Rather than copying out the memoir a second, third, or fourth time, he wrote the first kind of revisions neatly on the notebook's blank verso pages. In 1895, for example, he had noted in the main body of the text, "I wish chiefly to say that I have no cause of regret for any of my pecuniary relations to Anny." Three years later, the *apologia* is added: "In regard to the opposite statement, I have now (July 1898) a statement to make." Anny is preparing an edition of her father's work (her father was William Makepeace Thackeray) for publication and has offered Leslie Stephen a share of the proceeds, which he has accepted. "I don't know whether this was right: but—I did it." The other revisionary additions have the same shyly assertive tone, "10 April 1897. An odd little incident has just happened . . ." (16), "I shall just say that" (23), "I must just give the reason" (30).

The underlying belief—that it is theoretically possible to give the definitive, legalistic "statement" of events—can be understood historically, as an extreme version of Victorian positivism. The habit of verso correction should also serve, however, as an illustration of a more general truth, that it can be difficult or impossible to elide the present "I" from accounts of past time. All of the revisions made to the original manuscript concern Leslie Stephen's own actions and thoughts—not new facts about Julia's biography. Memoir has often been distinguished from autobiography by virtue of its greater concern with the exterior world, so the entry in the *Encyclopedia of Life Writing* tells us, "as a general rule, traditional autobiography makes the individual life central, while memoir tends to focus on the times in which the life is lived and the significant others of the memoirist's world."[52] By revising the memoir, and by subtly interpolating the present self into an account of past time, Leslie Stephen weakened its generic claim to *be* a memoir. As it proceeds, *The Mausoleum Book* becomes ever more autobiographical.

As well as making changes to the body of the memoir, Stephen also continued to add new materials to the end of the coda. Having reached the present date of writing, July 1895, in his final note, he then reverted to the beginning of his life to list "some of the dates to which I have referred in the preceding—partly because I like to fix them in my own mind, partly because, if you look at the letters, you may find them convenient" (97). The text's gradual tilt toward subjectivity is evident in the selection of events, which gives a good deal of weight to relatively trivial incidents in Leslie's own life.[53] Alan Bell omits the four folio pages of dates from his edition on the grounds that "scarcely any . . . supplement the narrative except in closer datings," but this is not quite the whole story. In the list, which begins with Stephen's own birth, we see the major elements of the traditional late Victorian Bildungsroman: birth, education, maturity, and the renunciation of faith. "I was born 28 November 1832: to school at Brighton end of 1840; to Eton at Easter 1842 . . . I went to Trinity Hall, Cambridge, in October 1850; B.A. January 1854; became fellow soon afterwards & tutor in 1855; resigned my tutorship in

1862 and left Cambridge at the end of 1864." Having reached the now of writing time by the end of the memoir, we return to 1832, and work our way back to the present. The notes end, in fact, with an entry that returns to Julia's death and the genesis of the book. This second set of last words could stand synecdochally for the book as a whole: "5 May—alas!"

After writing up to the present moment *twice,* Stephen was still far from finished with the large green album. Had he ended his own life story on May 5, 1895, he would have been entombing himself (like the original manuscript) with his dead wife. This was the melancholy choice made by Rossetti, who buried his manuscript poems with his dead wife, Lizzie, in 1862 only to find that he wanted to disinter them to continue revising in 1869. By this point, the papers were in a "disappointing state" with a "great hole right through all the leaves of *Jenny.*"[54] Stephen chose instead to return sporadically to his text, and he did so as both autobiographer and diarist. By making verso corrections to the original memoir he made it congruent with his current feelings, and by adding a series of new dated entries in the present he migrated from retrospective memoir-writing to diary. He made the first of these journal entries in November 1895, with a familiar gesture of contrition: "I propose to make a few notes in this book of anything likely to interest you hereafter" (98). Many of the subsequent entries note mundane events and activities in the life of the Stephen family, including Thoby's successes at school, holidays in England and abroad, and various illnesses. Others remain close to the book's original purpose as an extended eulogy and obituary by cataloging the deaths of various people whom Leslie Stephen had known; at times, as Alan Bell has it, this section approaches "a mixture of a necrology with obituary notes."[55]

The *Mausoleum Book* is a generically confused document: a mixture of past-focused memoir, autobiography, and factual catalog, and then an unfolding present-tense diary. Stephen seems to have reread all of his pages, many times over, and at least on one occasion he made a significant revision to the apparently spontaneous diary. The entry for June 26, 1897, begins in the usual laconic style with the death of Margaret Oliphant. "Mrs. Oliphant died. I first met her at Grindelwald when we were staying there in the summer of 1875 . . ." It continues by noting that "Stella . . . is still laid up. She has had two relapses," but insists that the danger is not serious, "The doctors, however, give good accounts of her now." A little more information about this mysterious illness had been given in the previous entry, dated April 10, as Stephen described his "selfish pangs" at his step-daughter's marriage, the honeymoon abroad, and subsequent return: "Stella returned on Sunday 25 April from her wedding-trip. She was apparently quite well that day and on Monday. She was taken ill on Tuesday. The attack soon appeared to be peritonitis. On Thursday things looked very serious. That night, however, she improved: on Sunday the doctors admitted that she was really out of danger—and a terrible fear has been removed" (103). The peculiarity of the diary as a narrative form is its propensity to self-contradiction and sudden irony. As Adam Parkes observes in relation to Ishiguro's diary fictions, "The cumulative effect of several different entries is that they relativize each other; each one has the potential to cast the others in an ironic light."[56] The infrequency of Stephen's entries only exacerbates this. Directly underneath the hopeful calm of "good accounts," on a new line but not in a new entry, he added the final words, "My darling Stella died early on the morning of 19 July 1897."

Stephen did not write again in the book until late September, when he mentions in his breezily informative style that the family has come back from a holiday. The sole link to the emotional abyss opened in the previous entry comes, ironically, in the place name, for they have been in "Painswick." Stella's death is mentioned only at second hand, as Leslie notes that her new husband, Jack Hills, has "offered, and I felt it right to accept his offer, to contribute to my expenses out of the income which he receives as Stella's heir" (104). Several discomfiting questions immediately present themselves. Why did Leslie Stephen not give the announcement of Stella's death—which occurred three weeks after June 26—a new entry and heading date of its own? Is it because the item seems poignantly to cling to the previous discussion of her health? Is it because a one-line entry would be too melodramatic? Why, moreover, in a book heavy with the gloom of the mausoleum, is Stella's death recorded so briefly? The page on which her death is recorded in one sentence contains eleven sentences about the demise of the seventy-six-year-old Frederick Waymouth Gibbs, who lodged with the Stephens while Leslie was a child, and became "one of the few people whom I could trust absolutely." One answer would be that Leslie Stephen was not particularly affected by the death of a step-daughter from his wife's first marriage. This, in fact, is the explanation that Quentin Bell offered in his 1972 biography of Virginia Woolf, where Leslie was described as coming "very near the end of the funeral procession. He was of course afflicted, but his tread was elastic, his eyes were dry."[57]

The other answer is that Stella's death was recalcitrant to being written, a stumbling block. In part, this may be because it contravenes one of the narrative assumptions of the text—that the great tragedy of the Stephen family has *already happened* and so can be stably examined either within the retrospection of memoir, or within a cautiously evolving diary frame. Stephen presents the diary itself, introduced with "I propose to make a few notes in this book of anything likely to interest you hereafter," as a simple supplement, and "hereafter" as minimally interesting compared to the past. Because the event cannot be adequately digested within the "few notes" format, it produces a genetic overspill: that is, it requires revision. Three years later Leslie Stephen added the following note on the verso page. "I had not the heart to say more when I wrote the words above. I read this in 1900 and will just add that the most striking thing was the singular revelation of Stella's beautiful character, when after her mother's death she had to take care of me and again when she became engaged to Jack. It did not seem as if she really changed but as if she showed her true self more clearly and brightly. Everyone near to her noticed it. Alas!" (104).

This facing-page note (rendered as a footnote in Bell's edition) has the effect of putting the first statement, "My darling Stella died early on the morning of 19 July 1897," into quotation marks. It also breaks the frame of the diary, interpolating the year 1900 between July and September 1897. In this respect, the addition seems to transgress an essential feature of the form—its linear ordering, and its emotional spontaneity. What does it mean to update a form whose entire affect derives from the immediate evocation of a (now vanished) "now"? Even rereading a diary has a certain awkwardness; this is the source of humor in Gwendolen Fairfax's quip: "I never travel without my diary. One should always have something sensational to read in the train."[58] In this case, by evoking the figure of *aporia*, Stephen does not so much veil over the initially inadequate response as draw attention to it. Like all supplements, "I will just add that" draws attention to the original lack. Elsewhere, *The Mausoleum Book* is fluent and sometimes prolix in its obituary notices. But Stella's death exceeds its epitaphic conventions by being more shocking, more sudden, and perhaps more tragic than the death that the original *retrospective* memoir had been constructed to record.

Although *The Mausoleum Book* presents itself on the first page as already finished, the closed memoir mutates later in the volume into an open and evolving diary, and the memoir is repeatedly supplemented, "I will just add that." Like many other nineteenth-century autobiographies, it was not published by its author, and contains a variety of ambivalent instructions and warnings about its own future use value. At times, Stephen seems to hope that the document will provide raw material for his future biographer; at other points, he boasts about having prevented an "adequate history" from ever being written, concluding that "the world will lose little by that." The album is composed of a series of attempts—a memoir, a series of dates, a diary—to reach the present time and be finished, but Stephen in the end delayed so long that he was unable to make the final entry in the book. When he was dying of stomach cancer in 1904 he nominated his youngest daughter Virginia as his amanuensis, and she wrote the final words in the book: "It comforts me to think that you are all so fond of each other that when I am gone you will be the better able to do without me" (112).

In the manuscript, there is a visually arresting shift in handwriting from Leslie's taut scrawl to his daughter's larger, more flowing—and much more familiar—script. The last words of the father's writing life therefore become, in a curiously graphic instance of writerly inheritance, the first words of the daughter's. After reading Woolf's own descriptions of her ambivalence about her father, we may also find something ironic in her material transcription of these last words. Taken literally, Leslie's words seem to beg the mawkish response, "Oh no, we'll be much worse off without you." In fact, Virginia's own various autobiographical writings frequently returned to the sense of liberation that she and her siblings felt after their father's death. In 1928, she noted in her diary: "Father's birthday. He would have been 96, 96, yes, today; & could have been 96, like other people one has known; but mercifully was not. His life would have entirely ended mine. What would have happened? No writing, no books;—inconceivable."[59]

Stephen Hero to *A Portrait of the Artist as a Young Man*

A few months after Virginia transcribed these last words, the young James Joyce—he happened to be eight days younger than Stephen's youngest daughter—began writing a semiautobiographical account of his own family and upbringing.[60] By March 13, 1906, he had essentially stopped working on it, although it was to take another decade before the project could be considered, in a genetic sense, entirely finished. He wrote to Grant Richards, "You suggest that I should write a novel in some sense autobiographical. I have already written a thousand pages of such a novel, as I think I told you, 914 pages to be exact. I calculate that these twenty-five chapters, about half the book, run into 150 thousand words."[61]

The usual explanation for Joyce's abandonment of the incomplete *Stephen Hero* and his transformation of its material into *A Portrait of the Artist as a Young Man* (1916) is stylistic: it is part of a story about learning how to be modernist.[62] So Joyce Carol Oates has argued that it was only *because* of the failure of *Stephen Hero* that Joyce "was freed to invent works of a kind never before attempted in literature," in particular the "telegraphic, lyric, contemplative" style of *Portrait,* which she sees evolving naturally into the early episodes of *Ulysses.*[63] From the first publication of the surviving manuscript in 1944, critics have argued that the earlier novel is more editorializing than the final version, in which "there is not a single comment or generalization; every thought, every feeling is particularly Stephen's";[64] shows less control of narrative perspective; provides more incidental detail about Stephen's social world; and reduces Emma Clery's character to "the initials E.C., a wraithlike fantasy of Stephen's desire."[65] For Theodore Spencer, who wrote the introduction to the New Directions edition, the relationship between the two texts was like that between the first and final version of an Imagist poem. *A Portrait* "has more intensity and concentration, a more controlled focus, than the earlier version."[66] This suggests that the process of revision was one of *excision* and that, like the texts I discuss in chapter 3, the final condensed version was winnowed out of a diffuse and baggy first draft. If this is correct, then the genetic histories of *Portrait* and *Ulysses* provide a curious example of a writer working in diametrically opposite ways. "Dublin 1904/Trieste 1914" would describe a process of taking away; "Trieste–Zurich–Paris 1914–1921," as I discussed in the previous chapter, a process of accretion and adding more.

At the same time, where we can compare individual episodes or snatches of speech between *Stephen Hero* and *Portrait,* it is not always obvious that Joyce was selectively pruning his material. Many of the set pieces in *Portrait* are in fact expansions of the earlier narrative. In *Stephen Hero,* for example, we are told only that "a trivial incident set him composing some ardent verses which he entitled a 'Villanelle of the Temptress'" (211). In *Portrait,* Joyce zooms in and sounds out the word "ardent" four times in the printed text of the villanelle, a poem that he had himself composed in 1900 (196–197). Stephen's conversation with the dean, where he points out that the word "detain" has a different meaning "according to the literary tradition or according to the tradition of the marketplace" (*P* 164) is also substantially expanded in the later novel. In *Stephen Hero,* "Yes, yes, Mr Daedalus, I see . . . I quite see your point . . . detain . . ." (28) leads straight to a one-paragraph description of the dean's attempt to light a fire. In *Portrait,* "Yes, yes: I see, said the dean quickly, I quite catch the point: detain" segues into a much longer discussion of the difference between a "tundish" and a "funnel," and to Stephen's internal reflections on his linguistic disenfranchisement, "The language in which we are speaking is his before it is mine" (166). Although the fifth section of *Portrait,* which maps to the entire surviving portion of *Stephen Hero,* is much shorter than its ur-version, Joyce was not necessarily condensing at the level of the individual episode. In *Ulysses,* by contrast, each chapter seems to grow from inside-out, picking up small details at every level of typescript and proof.

Joyce's process of transforming *Stephen Hero* into *Portrait* is much more explicable when we consider the book not only as fiction but *also* as autobiography. Susan Stanford Friedman has carefully drawn attention to the traumatic autobiographical material—the death of Joyce's mother and his brother—that the series of life writings struggles to absorb. In addition, I would suggest that Joyce was troubled by the problem that confronts all autobiographers—the problem of knowing where to end. *Portrait* feels unfinished not because it is a failure, or because Joyce was struggling with the weakness of the late Bildungsroman as a form, as Franco Moretti argues, but because it is not exactly or not only a Bildungsroman.[67]

For Susan Stanford Friedman, *Stephen Hero* can be read "as the textual and political unconscious of the 'final' text, *Portrait of the Artist*," and "may contain elements that are repressed and transformed by the linguistic mechanisms analogous to the dream-work as the author revises the text."[68] The examples she provides include the movement of Stephen's aesthetic theory from the middle of the *Stephen Hero* manuscript to the very end of the novel, as Stephen walks with his boorish friend Lynch; the removal of the "a" from Stephen's name ("the Greek name Daedalus is both there and not there"); and an intensifying of lyric and rhythmic sound patterning ("linguistic processes that Freud associates with the dream-work"). She suggests that over an entire autobiographical series— beginning with the short poem "Tilly" (which Joyce wrote right after his mother's death), "The Sisters," published on the first anniversary, and moving on through *Stephen Hero* and *Portrait* to *Ulysses*—Joyce was learning to write about his mother's death, but did not do so overtly until *Ulysses*. On the other hand, if we look only at *Stephen Hero* and *Portrait*, it seems that some traumatic autobiographical material is more fully worked out in the *earlier* version. There, the grim description of Isabel's death begins with Stephen's mother calling:

> What ought I to do? There's some matter coming away from the hole in Isabel's . . . stomach . . . Did you ever hear of that happening? (*SH* 168)

This is itself a rewriting of one of the early epiphanies, where Joyce's mother bursts into the room to announce that his dying brother Georgie is hemorrhaging.

> Do you know anything about the body? . . . What ought I to do? . . . There's some matter coming away from the hole in Georgie's stomach. Did you ever hear of that happening?[69]

Isabel's death can be read as both a *displacement* of Joyce's brother's death and perhaps as a condensation of the two family deaths—mother and sister—into a single event. By the time that he wrote the fifth section of *Portrait,* however, Joyce decided not to represent Isabel's death or Stephen's meditation on "the futility of his sister's life."

Leslie Stephen's rereading and revision of his memoir might be described as intensive perseveration. Instead of finishing his memoir, he copied out a fair draft, extended it past its natural end, and added more on the verso pages by way of footnoting and correction. Joyce's writing process was marked instead by repeated attempts to transform, condense, and displace material and, instead of producing a single palimpsest, he abandoned texts and restarted new ones. This is the kind of serial revision that I have been terming extrinsic. He had almost equally substantive problems, however, with completing first drafts and finding narrative closure. Despite its length, the *Stephen Hero* manuscript appears never to have reached a diegetic end; in the final few pages, Stephen hangs about on the shores of Dublin, waiting for his journey to Paris to begin. *Portrait* has an ending, but what a strange, flyaway, *un*-ending it is!

After a decade writing autobiographical fiction in the third person and the past tense, Joyce decided to end his project by switching to a first-person, present-tense diary form. When Edward Garnett decided to reject *Portrait* for publication by Duckworth, he cited the unsatisfactory close as a major reason: "At the end of the book there is a complete falling to bits; the pieces of writing and the thoughts are all in pieces and they fall like damp, ineffective rockets."[70] More recently, Michael Levenson has noted that Stephen's diary "has had the rare distinction of being a virtually unannotated specimen within the Joycean oeuvre," creating a strange effect of un-ending, where "a novel on the point of reaching its end suddenly alters to a form that only uneasily accommodates an end."[71] Stephen may be threatening to leave Ireland, but he doesn't in fact manage to; for Levenson, the periodic form of the diary means that "that intention, restated from day to day, acquires a past of its own. His romantic revolt threatens to become a tradition."

If the serial logic of diary makes a determined ending impossible, then I wonder if Joyce turned to the form precisely because he wanted to defer or delay providing the end of Stephen's—and, by implication, his own—narrative of exile? In other words, we can read this formal choice not as a refusal to end but a struggle, in a difficult situation, to meet the minimum requirements for closure.

At a genetic level, there is a second kind of ironic unending in the diary. Not only does it present Stephen still in Ireland, still thinking of his father and mother, but it does so by recycling or ventriloquizing some of Joyce's own earliest writings. If the novel itself produces a chiastic shape, where Stephen's final thoughts—first his mother, then his father—invert his first—his father, then his mother—so too the writing process ended by reverting to its beginning.[72] Three of the most lyrical passages in the diary turn out to be straight reprints from Joyce's notebook of epiphanies. These include the entry for March 25, morning, which narrates a dream, "A long curving gallery. From the floors ascend pillars of dark vapours"; April 10, "Faintly, under the heavy night, through the silence of the city which has turned from dreams to dreamless sleep," and April 16, "The spell of arms and voices: the white arms of roads, their promise of close embraces and the black arms of tall ships that stand against the moon, their tale of distant nations."[73] This last epiphany follows on from Stephen's desperate, slightly hollow cry "Away! Away!" The irony, according to Levenson's reading, would be in the contrast between Stephen's dream of "soaring away into the future" and the fact that he is physically constrained in Dublin, in his parents' house, as his mother puts his "new secondhand clothes" in order. Stephen's villanelle—a poem that enacts a return to origins in its ending, and which was written a decade before *Portrait*—seems also to have been added at the very end of the compositional process, at some point in 1914.

Stephen's diary delays or prevents closure by switching from the teleological past of the Bildungsroman to an eternal present. So, too, reusing early genetic strata late in the process of composition provided Joyce with another, more private, way to keep *repeating* his own writing project. Levenson argues that the novel "relies heavily on a formal principle that challenges finality with repetition and that encourages a view of Stephen as bound within a perpetually unfolding series—as the sort of character, that is, who having done a thing once, would as soon do it a million times." And, although he notes the repetition of "the spell of arms and voices" epiphany from *Stephen Hero,* he treats *Portrait* primarily as a novel, and Stephen as a fictional, ironized, even "spurned" character. If, on the other hand, we slant toward an autobiographical reading—Gérard Genette has suggested the figure of the "whirligig" to describe the difficulty of reading in both ways at once—we can extend the same argument to Joyce. Returning to the earliest materials acknowledges that the process of autobiographical writing is not, or not always, a successful, teleological process of self-analysis. Like Leslie Stephen, who let his own unfolding diary be completed by his daughter, and like Woolf herself, who returned at the very end of her life to write about material that she had already written about many times, Joyce's autobiographical revisions look more like *mere* repetition than unidirectional repression or expression.

Stella's Death and the Impossibility of Writing

Virginia's own final memoir has important similarities with *The Mausoleum Book:* it was left unfinished among her papers at her death; it covers much of the same life material, "those two great unnecessary blunders," sometimes borrowing Leslie's language to do so; and it repeatedly interrogates the relationship between the present moment of writing and the traumatic past, "the years 1897–1904, those seven unhappy years." And, like both *The Mausoleum Book* and *A Portrait of the Artist as a Young Man*—a book that Woolf does not seem particularly to have liked—it mutated during the writing process from memoir to diary.[74] The published text begins, casually enough, in the past tense: "Nessa said that if I did not start writing my memoirs I should soon be too old"; and it is several pages before Woolf introduces the habit of beginning an entry with a present-tense header.[75]

"A Sketch" has almost nothing to say about the middle period of Woolf's life, about her marriage, or her work as a novelist: instead it steadily alternates between the present moment—the beginning of the Second World War—and her childhood. This meant that Woolf was coming back to material that she had already written about many times and in many forms. Before I begin to describe intrinsic revision within "A Sketch," which was itself revised in typescript and manuscript in ways that contradict its apparently casual style, I will consider this final memoir as an extrinsic revision, the final piece in the "Stella's death stemma."

In 1897, the first year in which she had kept an adult diary, Woolf recorded the event with a brevity that resembled her father's: "At 3 this morning, Georgie & Nessa came to me, & told me that Stella was dead—That is all we have thought of since; & it is impossible to write of."[76] Given that translating thought into writing is the purpose of the diary form, the semicolon between "thought of since" and "& it is impossible" is powerfully disjunctive. The diary seems to have let its writer down. This impression is strengthened by the gap left against the next day's entry—the first day in 1897 that Virginia did not record. The blankness enacts the trope of incapacity visually, as a gap on the page.[77] Ten years later, in the first of her retrospective memoirs, the "impossible" death has become "incredible": "But once more she fell ill; again, almost in a moment, there was danger, and this time it did not pass away, but pressed on and on, till suddenly we knew that the worst had actually come to pass. Even now it seems incredible."[78] As in the previous diary entry, the disordered syntax and punctuation, combined with multiple temporal references ("once more," "again," "in a moment," "this time," "till suddenly"), formally enact the frightening nonsequentiality of events. Earlier, Woolf had called the tragedy "impossible" to describe, while suggesting that it remained perfectly possible—even necessary—to consider it. "Incredible" implies that the event continues to beg belief, but also that it might be possible to find some formal analogue for it.

In the mid-1920s, when she came to revise the "Time Passes" section of *To the Lighthouse,* Woolf discovered a more formally innovative way of representing an old impasse, and turned present-tense confusion into the sealed past of the gravestone. Erasing both the autobiographical content and the "I" mourner, she described Prue's marriage and sudden death from a radically impersonal perspective. Nonetheless, the manuscript of the novel, available in Susan Dick's facsimile edition, bears witness to Woolf's own intuition that the "Time Passes" section was "the most difficult abstract piece of writing," giving her "more trouble than all of the rest of the book put together."[79]

In the original draft of the "Time Passes" section, the only mention of the absent Ramsay family comes filtered through the distracted consciousness of Mrs. McNab, who thinks about the possibility that the house might be sold, and the war, and then adds:

> So Mrs. Ramsay was dead; & ~~your~~ Mr. Andrew killed they said & Miss Prudence, who had married, she had died too, with her first ~~bady~~ baby they said, but Everyone ~~w~~ had lost someone, in these years. Prices had gone up shamefully: they didn't come down either.[80]

When Woolf revised this in 1926 for translation before independent publication in the French journal *Commerce,* the structure remained the same. In fact, by turning "either" into the ungrammatical "neither," Woolf focalizes this thought more obviously through Mrs. McNab. The typescript runs:

> So she was dead; and Mr. Andrew the tall young gentleman killed; and Miss Prue with the fair hair, masses of it twisted round her head, dead too they said, with her first baby; but everyone had lost someone these years. Prices had gone up shamefully, and they didn't come down again neither.[81]

The use of parentheses to separate off this information, drawing attention to the way in which personal and public tragedies are ironically juxtaposed, was one of the last revisions made to the finished novel. Only in the final version, moreover, is the ironic sequence of events fully felt: Prue's marriage is now narrated *just before* her death, rather than as an additional piece of information to be added after it. The "main" body of the narrative tells the story of Mrs. McNab working to clean the disused house, and of the house's decay across different seasons. The life of the Ramsay family is presented tersely within square brackets, inverted and obscure like the white spaces on a photographic negative.

> [Prue Ramsay, leaning on her father's arm, was given in marriage. What, people said, could have been more fitting? And, they added, how beautiful she looked!][82]

After a short interlude about summer weather, the ironic turn is utterly unexpected. As readers, we are inevitably as foolish and complacent as the unnamed "people" who believed that "everything had promised so well."

> [Prue Ramsay died that summer in some illness connected with childbirth, which was indeed a tragedy, people said, everything, they said, had promised so well.] (136)

The troublesome use of parenthesis is reminiscent of both Leslie and Virginia's 1897 diary entries. Important information is marginalized and sealed off, while mundane accounts of domestic life proliferate around it. The use of a series of indefinite pronouns here—"they," "some illness"— also creates epistemological instability, reminiscent of the uncertainty built into diary writing. The narrator of "Time Passes" seems to know as little about the illness "connected with childbirth" as Virginia Stephen had done in 1897. In this best-known piece of the long genetic "Stella's death" stemma, we see the accidental irony of the diary form hardened into the permanent, formal irony of art. For Alan Friedman, this is typical of the modernist novel's treatment of death: "as Forster's characters usually 'die in relative clauses,' so Woolf's deaths, if not averted through sleep or trance, are consigned to parentheses, to another country, or to a scapegoat double."[83]

"A Sketch of the Past"

To the Lighthouse is Woolf's most austere and formally inventive way to deal with the "impossible" and "incredible" suddenness of Stella's death. In the late 1930s, and despite her protestations that the novel had laid her traumatic childhood to rest, she also found that it was not completely adequate: or, rather, that she needed to write her family history one more time. In her last, self-consciously unfinished and "sketchy" reworking of the past, she returned from the tight inversion provided by the brackets, to the looser, more open form of diary. The manuscripts and typescripts of "A Sketch," preserved at Sussex and the British Library, bear witness to the extreme difficulty she had in doing so. On the surface, "A Sketch" is a Freudian text. Like Stanford Friedman's argument about Joyce, it puts great faith in the idea of writing as a cure, "I expressed some very long felt and deeply felt emotion. And in expressing it I explained it and then laid it to rest" (81). And yet its own complicated genesis and preoccupation with the very problems it claims as solved is unsettling. If the impersonal method of *To the Lighthouse* had been fully adequate, why did Woolf rip open and rework that novel's traumatic center?

The description of Stella's death comes at the very end of the first of the two typescripts that Woolf produced, cataloged at the University of Sussex as A.5a. The diagram sets out the relationship between the surviving documents, which were used by Jeanne Schulkind to set the two, different, published editions. Although Woolf tried to represent the project's development as always a matter of horizontal, extrinsic revision—returning after a period of time to add one more entry—she also made multiple vertical revisions and corrections on earlier texts. The fact that the typescript breaks off with a rather formal announcement suggests that Woolf recognized it as a closural relief; in fact, in the manuscript draft, it had not been a breaking point: "One fortnight was the length of their honeymoon. And directly she came back she was taken ill. It was appendicitis; she was going to have a baby. And that was mismanaged too; and so, after three months of intermittent illness, she died—at 24 Hyde Park Gate, on July 27th, 1897."[84]

In "Reminiscences," written more than thirty years earlier, Woolf had also made this unnaratable event a place of narrative breakage in her text; the description ending "even now it seems incredible" closes chapter 3, and chapter 4 picks up by describing Vanessa's assumption of Stella's "central position."[85] But whereas the earlier version had insisted, once again, on the death's "incredible" quality, the 1939 description moves from "she died," via a long dash, to a simple statement of fact. Unlike the fictional version, this bald statement does not attempt to introduce a point of view—either that of Virginia herself, or the trivial chatter of "they" observing an irony of situation.

In fact, "A Sketch" consistently turns away from providing a stable perspective on past time. Rather than suggesting that history leads to, or

Genetic layer 1

	A.5b	A.5c	A.5d	A.5d
Date of entry	June 20th	19th July 1939	^June^-May 8th 1940/ June 8th 1914	22nd September 1940
	I was thinking as I crossed the channel last night, of Stella: thinking in a jerky disconnected way...	I was forced to break off again & rather suspect that these breaks will be the end of my memoir writing.	I have just found this sheaf of notes & in part [reading uncertain] in my wastepaper basket	I continue (,22nd September 1940:) on this wet day & we think of the weather now as it affects invasion, as it affects raids on London —not as weather that we like or dislike privately...
		Oh I remember the rapture of that love.... It was lyrical... (12)	so intense, so exciting, so rapturous... so lyrical, so musical...	

Genetic layer 2

A.5a ts	A.5a ts	A.5a ts	A.5a ts	BL 61973	BL 61973
Two days ago— Sunday 16th April 1939 to be precise, Nessa said that if I did not start writing my memoirs I should soon be too old.	"June 20th, 1939. I was thinking as I crossed the channel last night of Stella; in a very jerky disconnected way."	19th July 1939. I was forced to break off again, and rather suspect that these breaks will be the end of this memoir.	June 8th 1940. I have just found this sheaf of notes, thrown away into my waste-paper basket.	*June 19th 1940 As we sat down to lunch two days ago....*	I continue (22nd September 1940) on this wet day—we think of weather now as it affects invasions, as it affects raids, not as weather we like or dislike privately

Text in italics is typescript with no ms. antecedent

Chronological writing process

Genetic development

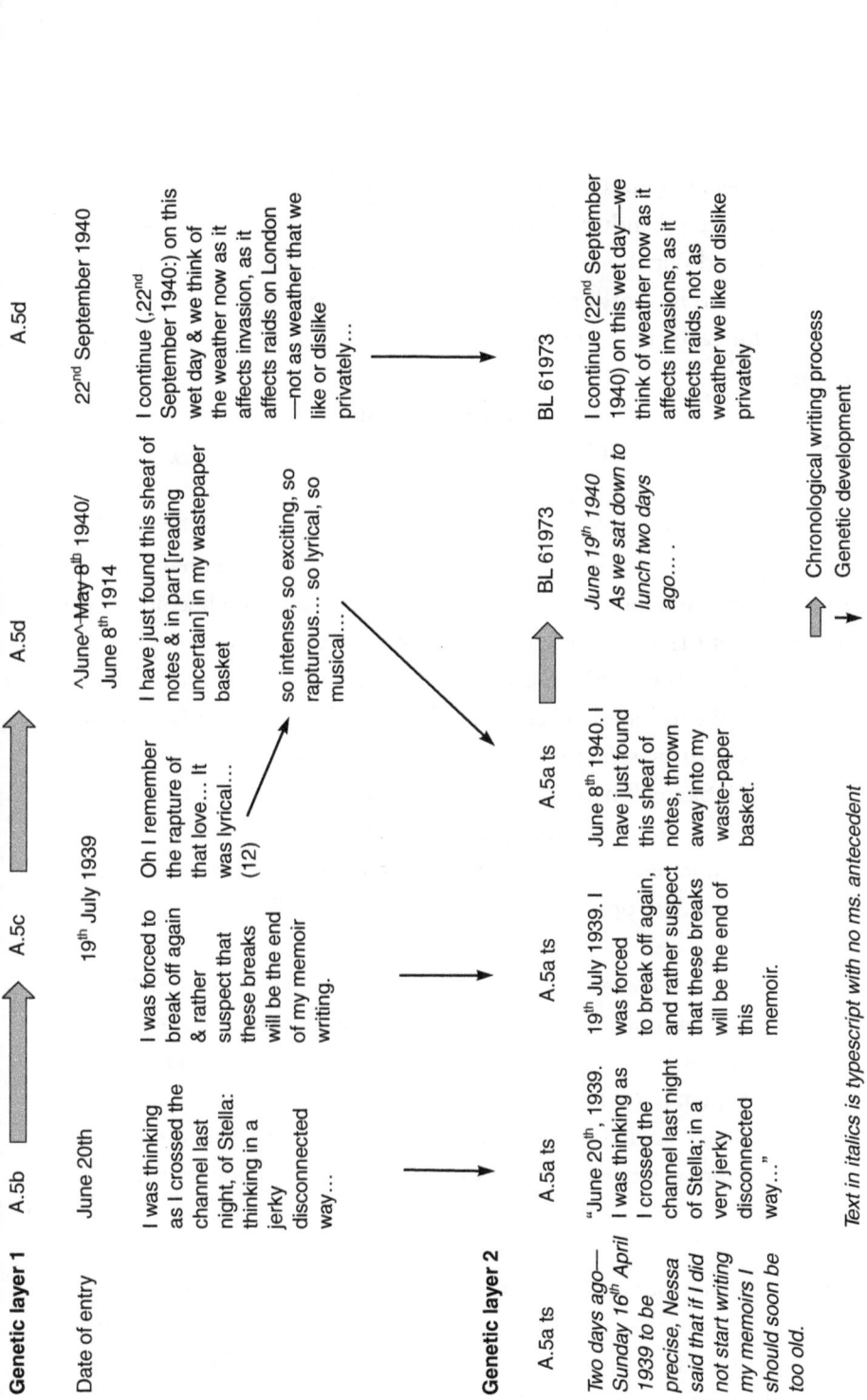

Figure 9: Image of genetic layers in "A Sketch of the Past."

even has meaning in, the present moment, Woolf repeatedly sets up arbitrary or chancy conduits between present and past. One of her main methods for doing this is to structure the memoir in the form of a diary, so that apparently ordinary dates in the present—which provide the headers for each entry—make a portal to more significant periods in the 1890s.

On first reading, one might assume that the present tense dates—"16th April, 1939"; "2nd May"; "May 15th 1939"; "May 28th 1939"; "June 20th 1939"; "19th July 1939"; "June 8th 1940"; "June 19th 1940"; "18th August 1940"; "22nd September 1940"; "October 11th 1940"; "15th November 1940"—are a literal record of Woolf's compositional process. And yet, even without looking at the manuscripts, it soon becomes clear that many of these entries are too long to have been written on a single day; and that others fail to accord with the account of her actual diary, which Woolf continued to keep until the end of her life.[86] In fact, she announced the diary structure as a formal discovery a few pages after beginning. "A Sketch" had opened as a project of "writing my memoirs," but Woolf subsequently changed the generic classification to "notes," and the method of observation from retrospective concern with the past ("livre refermé") to open-ended diary ("livre ouvert").

> 2nd May . . . I write the date because I think I have discovered a possible form for these notes. That is to make them include the present—at least enough of the present to serve as a platform to stand upon. It would be interesting to make the two people, I now, I then, come out in contrast. And further, this past is much affected by the present moment. What I write today I should not write in a year's time. (75)

This extremely subjective position, which assumes that the past is at least partially a construction of the present and, consequently, that no autobiographical writing can be final, sits curiously with Woolf's frequent descriptions of her other concurrent project—a real biography of Roger Fry. She appears to present this process of "conveying Roger from one end of his life to the other" as serious, meticulous work, and "A Sketch" as a worthless *epsrit,* found in the wastepaper basket, written at haste, and beneficial only as a "holiday from Roger." Even fact checking is eschewed: "I could settle the date by seeing when I wrote *To the Lighthouse,* but am too casual here to bother to do it" (80). And yet her insistence on the tenuous and subjective nature of life writing, and the fragility of memory, is so convincing and often so poetic that it becomes impossible for the reader of "A Sketch" to continue believing in "straight" biographical writing. The trick Woolf plays here is not unlike her dismantling of Edwardian "materialist" novels by showing how absurd their relentless metonymic naming and listing becomes. When, for example, she asks if her memory of her mother "will weaken still further" in the coming years, she questions the very principle of turning life material into a "final form." If the memory of events starts to fade before the literary skill needed to represent them can develop, then how would one know when, if ever, to write an autobiography? The difference between staid, serious biography—already starting to look a bit suspect as a form—and this light self-representation is brought up again in the June 8, 1940, entry. Now Woolf is almost finished, engaged on the "antlike meticulous labour" of correcting the page proofs. By contrast, she tells us that "A Sketch" has been serendipitously rediscovered, quite by chance: "I have just found this sheaf of notes, thrown away into my waste-paper basket. I had been tidying up; and had cast all my life of Roger into that large basket, and with it, these sheets too" (100).

In fact, it was not true that Woolf began writing this entry—not coincidentally, the entry that ends with Stella's death—afresh in 1940, after ignoring the memoir for almost a year. Much of its material had already been drafted in 1939 in note form. When she began the document now known as the A.5d manuscript, Woolf was actually revising an earlier manuscript rather than simply continuing in a linear direction. Moreover, the manuscript itself did not begin with exactly these words. The published text, set from the A.5a typescript, is itself a revision of the A.5d manuscript, which had begun, "I have just found this sheaf of notes [illegible] in my wastepaper basket. For I have thrown away the MS of Roger; and am indeed correcting the final page proofs." So, by the time that she came to type up the description of casually finding "this sheaf of notes, thrown away," Woolf was really revising the *already revised* manuscript beside her.

The date-frame in the manuscript version is also different. At the top of the page, in the margin, Woolf had first written "May 8th 1940" and then crossed out "May" and written over "June." Directly above the entry, rather more mysteriously, is another date in the past, "June 8th 1914." In her account of the published text, Anna Snaith has noticed how anxieties about the present war function as "invasions of the text," and that steady focus on the past requires an almost physical "turning away from something."[87] In the manuscript Woolf acknowledges the irony and perhaps the futility of this project by mapping the present against the summer of 1914, a moment in British history that has come to stand for "anything innocently but irrecoverably lost."[88] Three moments of imminent tragedy are accordingly pulled together: the happiness of Stella's marriage (which resulted immediately in her death), the summer of 1914 (before the First World War), and the uncertainty of the present moment. Before settling down to the past, Woolf linked the tentativeness of her chosen form to extreme doubt about future time. "Shall I ever finish these notes—let alone make a book out of them? The battle is at its crisis; every night the Germans fly over England; it comes closer to this house daily." In the typescript, this attempt at three-way dating was abandoned.

Why had Woolf been unable to complete the A.5c manuscript? The way in which that document peters out, degenerating into a confusing and badly written list of notes, suggests that she did not so much casually lay it aside as give up on being able to complete it. In the 1939 A.5c manuscript, Woolf found herself petering out after describing:

> Anecdotes of old Buzzy.
> One—when Susan Lushington was at Corby.
> ~~Oh yes. I feel I was with~~
> Your friend—husband . . .
> I feel I am sitting on a tripod and foretelling the future.
> Here Mrs H. grinned.
> Jack looked glum.
> Russian toffee
> & his Sh-ean sonnet.

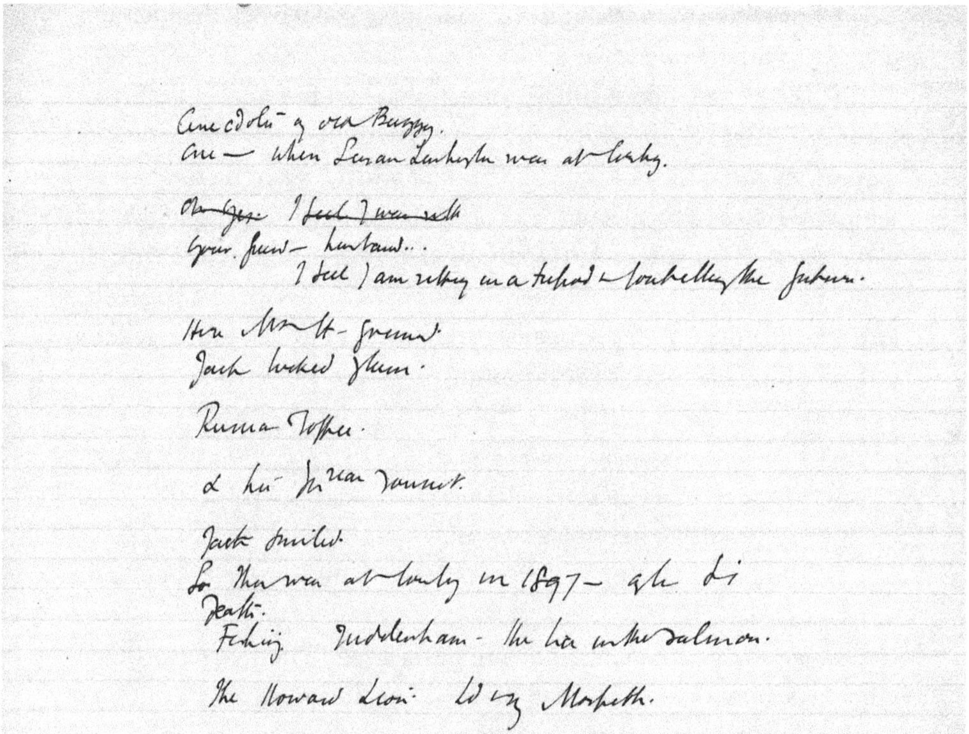

Figure 10: Image of a manuscript page of "A Sketch of the Past." Courtesy of the Woolf Estate.

The following year, in the first entry for 1940, she tells us that Jack's father, known as Buzzy, gave the Stephen children "Russian toffee up at Corby. Buzzy had once written a sonnet that had been taken for Shakespeare's." After beginning fluently enough with the beautiful meditation on present and past time, "for the present when backed by the past is a thousand times deeper than the present that is only the present," Woolf had started to get stuck. As if willfully delaying the inevitable end, she wrote in a diffuse way about Stella's suitor Jack Hills for five pages, before petering out into lists of names and places. The acknowledged aim is that of filling in Stella's background:

> These jottings must now converge.
> They fill in S's background. Here she hands like a pale rose
> against that queer still brick wall.
> Brot to return then to 1896 . . .

Other parts of this manuscript were never used. There is more of Virginia herself in this version than the final one, including a description of her first mental breakdown in 1896, which was associated with a total loss of interest in writing. "The desire left me: which I have had all my life, with that two years break. Never wrote a story or essay; never wished to. Perhaps the excitement was too great—the distraction of that racing pulse." There are also more reflections on the hazards of autobiographical writing, including the problem of "point of view," and the question of how to reconcile the experiences of body and mind. ("So I lived the 2 years between my mother's death and Stella's in a state of physical distress exclusion[?] How again separate the body and the mind?") As it continues, the text becomes more and more badly written, with words cascading down the center of the page and multiple crossings out and underlinings. Nothing is said about the process of Virginia's recovery from her first breakdown, and the manuscript ends with a marked shift toward the impersonal, considering the relationship of her mother's family to history ("They could not foretell 1917, let alone Hitler") and ending with witty descriptions of various distant relatives under the subheadings, "The Crofts" and "The Vaughns."

In an appropriately odd correspondence between past and present, it was only the following year, when she returned to the manuscript, that Woolf was able to proceed past the aphasia of 1896 and to continue writing about 1897. Only in the A.5d manuscript does she finally get to Stella's death, and only in the A.5a typescript does she decide to make the formal announcement a place to end. The second typescript, which was only discovered *after* the first edition of *Moments of Being* had been published, begins "Yesterday (18th August 1940) five German raiders passed so close over Monks House that they brushed the tree at the gate. But being alive today, and having a waste hour on my hands—for I am writing fiction; and cannot write after twelve—I will go on with this loose story."[89] When we compare this to the manuscript, on which the first edition of *Moments of Being* was based, it becomes obvious that Woolf is manipulating and aestheticizing her writing process. Like her father, who *wrote up* his memoir after finishing it, Woolf is *typing up* this loose story rather than "going on" with it. This is also true for some of the other diary dates. Just as Joyce framed his early epiphanies within Stephen's dated diary, Woolf only gradually decided how to place her moments of being with respect to the present. Georgia Johnston comments on the studied nature of the "diary approach": "This 'diary approach' would raise few questions if in fact the frame reflected actual writing moments. Because it was deliberately added in revision, however, the frame not only raises questions of content, but also draws attention to issues of aesthetics, and accounts in particular for the many references to the *Roger Fry* biography-in-progress."[90]

Earlier in her career, Woolf had assumed that her diary—which she kept with astonishing care for over forty years, producing thirty separate notebooks—was *pre-writing,* a kind of unfolding avant-texte that might eventually be mined for a serious, retrospective autobiography. In February 1926, she wrote in her diary, "But undoubtedly this diary is established, & I sometimes look at it & wonder what on earth will be the fate of it. It is to serve the purpose of my memoirs. At 60 I am to sit down & write my life . . ."[91] She had expressed the same sentiment seven years earlier, consoling herself that the formless "rapid haphazard gallop" of the 1919 diary would serve her well in the end. In 1919, the moment of final, retroactive memoir writing had been dated a decade earlier, and Woolf gave her older self license to burn the rough notebooks from which a final form might be achieved. The shapeless quality of the diary is justified by the possibility of being transmuted into something permanent. "If Virginia Woolf at the age of 50, when she sits down to build her memoirs out of these books is unable to make a phrase as it should be made, I can only condole with her & remind her of the existence of the fireplace, where she has my leave to burn these pages to so many black films with red eyes in them. But how I envy her the task I am preparing for her! There is none I should like better. Already my 37th birthday next Saturday is robbed of some of its terrors by the thought." By 1939, she was less clear "what my intention is in writing these continual diaries. Not publication. Revision? a memoir of my own life? Perhaps."[92] Later in the same year, the "dear old red–covered book" seemed hopeless as a way to "reach the depths," and "what the point of making these notes is I don't know." Unlike Miss La Trobe in *Between the Acts,* who believes Platonically that "another play always lay behind the play she had just written," Woolf gave up in her own final work on the idea of a finished, ideal text lying behind or beyond the tentative surface she had achieved.[93]

"A Sketch" may not explicitly mine the content of the earlier diaries, but its form does make use of Woolf's forty years as a diarist: in particular, it benefits from her experience of writing in an eternal present. At some points it even seems to supplement or substitute for the traumatic diary entries that Woolf could not write in the past moment; the present-tense frames lead so directly into past time that it appears almost as if Woolf is rewriting, rather than reusing, her old diaries. "May 28th 1939," for example, leads straight to "Led by George with towels wrapped round us and given each a drop of brandy in warm milk to drink" (91). At others, the excursions into the past become a way to escape the dispiriting present: London battered by bombers, the privations of war. But even if "A Sketch" resembles or imitates a diary, it is important to remember that it did not grow like one. Rather than writing the memoir in a bound notebook, which forces a writer to keep on going forward, Woolf pulled out a new sheet of notepaper or typewriter paper when she wanted to add a new entry. This means that horizontal, extrinsic development can coexist with vertical, intensive revision. Woolf tries to get at

Stella's death and her portrait of Thoby in successive entries, but she
also revised the individual descriptions after achieving them. The result
of these revisions is to produce a text that feels curiously static. "Why do
I shirk the task, not so very hard to a professional—have I not conveyed
Roger from one end of life to the other?—like myself, of wafting this boy
from the boat to my bed sitting room at Hyde Park Gate?" (136)[94]

"A Sketch" is rarely read as one of Woolf's most serious works, but I
would suggest that in it she found a solution to the problem that had
dogged the composition of *The Years.* Woolf began that work, too, by
oscillating between two genres: a first-person lecturing voice, and third-
person extracts from a supposedly complete historical novel. The first
discursive essay, in *The Pargiters,* argues that "we cannot understand
the present if we isolate it from the past," and the fictional "excerpt" that
follows, set on November 16, 1880, retreats into the diegetic past of novelistic realism, "She looked tired. She had been collecting rents for a
philanthropic society in <among the poor of> Lissom (sic) Grove."[95] By
the time Woolf had finished with "that interminable book" *The Years*—
earlier it had been *The Pargiters* and *Here and Now*—she had also given
up on the dyadic novel-essay structure. Mitchell Leaska suggests that
her enormous revisionary labor on that book might itself be read as an
act of "pargeting" or sealing over the cracks between the two forms.
"How was she to 'cement and smooth over' those deep cracks which
normally separate historic fact from immediate feeling?" (xv).[96] In the
end, Woolf sutured the two parts of the book, producing the polemical
Three Guineas and the "more conventional novel" *The Years.*[97]

"A Sketch" is more successful at maintaining the oscillation between
here and there, now and then, and this is due in large part to the fragile,
apparently casual nature of the framing. Woolf's embrace of provisionality as an aesthetic may be studied; as Phyllis McCord argues, "careful
study of the drafts . . . shows that its tentative form, its quasi-journal
appearance and pretense of being only notes or raw material for art, is
actually deliberate and permanent."[98] It is also an extremely elegant solution to the problem of finish that, I have been suggesting, all autobiographers eventually face.

In his study *Late Modernism,* Tyrus Miller has suggested that "two extreme tendencies" in modern fiction often thought to exist simultaneously

are in fact part of a historical trajectory.[99] The first is "marked by purity, formal mastery, and orientation toward unique interiorized experience; the second, by heterogeneity of materials, montage techniques, and orientation toward everyday life and speech" (15). In later modernism, Miller finds "a reaction to a certain type of modernist fiction dominated by an aesthetic of formal mastery" which was "centred on the novel" (18); and he even notes that this reaction occurred to some of the high modernists themselves. According to Samuel Beckett, Joyce was eventually to worry that he "may have oversystematized *Ulysses*."[100] So, too, we can read Woolf's movement from the autobiographical novel *To the Lighthouse* to the open-ended, generically mixed "Sketch" as a move away from systematization. The novel is freighted with heavily symbolic ways to mark time and distance, from "the hoary Lighthouse, distant, austere" to Mr. Ramsay's alphabetic arrangement of knowledge and Lily's abstract purple shape representing "things in themselves." The clear, vertical perception of the novel becomes something vaguer and more chaotic in "A Sketch": now reality is the recurrent sound of waves, the "semi-transparent yellow" film of seeing *out of* a grape, the "globular; semi-transparent" and "curved" shape of flowers, the "cotton wool" that may cover a pattern and, perhaps ominously, repeated images of puddles and still water, which are associated with nonbeing. "There was the moment of the puddle in the path; when for no reason I could discover, everything suddenly became unreal; I was suspended; I could not step across the puddle; I tried to touch something . . . the whole world became unreal." (78).

In particular, the two works take very different approaches to mourning. *To the Lighthouse* aims at the fixed, "perfected" form of the gravestone, but "A Sketch" gives up on the epitaphic for a looser kind of recommuning with the dead. One reason for this may be the relationship between Woolf's own private tragedies in the late 1890s and the public tragedies with which she symbolically associated them. From the vantage point of the mid-1920s, Woolf chose to have Mrs. Ramsay and Prue die during the Great War; she was writing, of course, at the period that turned out in retrospect not to be *post*war but *inter*war. As T. S. Eliot recorded in "East Coker," these were "twenty years largely wasted, the years of *l'entre deux guerres*." "A Sketch," which was begun in 1939, quickly becomes not only a memoir about the late nineteenth century but a present-tense record of a new European conflict. In writing it, Woolf's own approach to mourning reverses the narrative that Jay Winter describes in *Sites of Memory, Sites of Mourning*.[101] Reverting from the impersonal closure of the memorial or epitaph, she produced a text in which the "I" narrator is a kind of medium, conducting an endless séance.

By premising autobiography on the serial, unfolding present of the diary, Woolf produced a structure that is, at least in principle, always extensible. And by allowing that the relationship between present and past moment is arbitrary—"jerky" thoughts of Stella are produced by a jerky journey over the Channel; "men calling strawberries in the Square" leads to Leslie Stephen; being unable to write fiction "after twelve" means "I will go on with this loose story"—there is no possibility that the past can ever be described completely, or exhausted. "I want to go on thinking about Thoby" is the memoir's true method.

Earlier in the modernist period, writers had worried over the difficulty of closure in autobiographical writing. Sometimes, as we saw in the case of Joyce, a partial turn to diary seemed the only solution. Even John Dowell, that preeminently unreliable narrator and unobservant participant, wishes at the end of *The Good Soldier* that he could relieve his narrative distress by shifting genre: "It is so difficult to keep all these people going . . . I wish I could put it down in diary form."[102] Woolf manages, at least in part, to resolve the problem of finish by laying it openly on the surface of the text; at one point, she even suggests that "composing this" would be an activity beyond or exceeding a conventionally defined, bounded, autonomous work of art. "I have no energy at the moment to spend upon the horrid labour that it needs to make an orderly and expressed work of art; where one thing follows another and all are swept into a whole. Perhaps one day, relieved from making works of art, I will try to compose this" (75). In making so studied a turn to an open form, one that could unfold indefinitely, Woolf made a choice that resembles other late modernist experiments. Pound's *Cantos*, which have been called his "intellectual diary," and which Ron Bush sees as vacillating "between the openness of a diary and the shapeliness of a distinct thematic organization," provide another structure of great revisionary sophistication.[103]

Not only did Pound continue to add more cantos, exceeding all of his previously declared numerical stopping points, but he could return to those that had already been published to revise them, and also make extrinsic revisions, where later cantos playfully rework earlier ones. He used the word *Draft* for different editions throughout the project even though, as Jerome McGann has shown, he "arranged and carefully over-saw the production" of his work in finished books.[104] These books them-selves were strategically and carefully designed, with titles that point to medieval calligraphy, ornamental letters, and headpieces. One might say they were designed to resemble books in the period before a final, me-chanically reproducible *text* was conceivable. Even the final installment was subtitled *Drafts and Fragments.* So too, we might compare Beck-ett's mid-career play *Krapp's Last Tape,* which ends neither with Krapp recording his last tape, nor with the tape running out, but with the re-playing of an earlier tape that both predicts and fails to enact an end: "Perhaps my best years are gone. When there was a chance of happiness. But I wouldn't want them back. Not with the fire in me now. No, I wouldn't want them back."[105] In high modernism, revisionary labor tends to be pushed under the surface or away from the final frame of the text, so that daring experimental styles seem as if they had always been present. In later modernism, writers became more interested in making the traces of revision—a process that might be considered a failure—visible *in* the text. The next chapter explores this shift.

CHAPTER 6

Revision, Late Modernism, and Digital Texts

WRITERS DID NOT STOP revising after the end of high modernism, or late modernism, or after any of the dates (1939, 1945, 1950, 1960 . . .) that we use to divide the first and second parts of the twentieth century. If anything, writers in the postwar period have displayed a more complete devotion to the idea of revision than their prewar forebears.

Modernist polemic might have been responsible for undoing the romantic preference for first thoughts, compositional spontaneity, and a retroactive teleology that located the ideal text always in the past, but the opposite, pro-revisionary position only became fully entrenched in the second half of the twentieth century. As the examples of Eliot, Woolf, and particularly James have shown, many early twentieth-century writers were disconcerted or even ashamed by the amount of reworking they did. James refused to categorize a belated practice of rewriting as anything *more than* mere rereading, while Eliot, even in an essay attacking Shelly and Coleridge as "repellent" and "unsound," still showed himself susceptible to romantic images of creativity. With a certain amount of calculating obfuscation, he praises Shelley in a modernist guise, noting "the magnificent image which Joyce quotes somewhere in *Ulysses* ('the mind in creation is as a fading coal, which some invisible influence, like an inconstant wind, awakens to transitory brightness')."[1] In the high modernist period, writers' general tendency was still to downplay, rather than exaggerate the work of revision.

In the second half of the twentieth century, as modernism was institutionalized and writers became college professors, passionate correction began to seem not abnormal or excessive, but a *necessary* precondition of good writing. This was the period in which modernist style and difficulty were fetishized. Writing protocols, such as Hemingway's iceberg principle, became classroom staples, and a series of big, influential biographies—Ellmann's *James Joyce,* Kenner's *The Pound Era*—drew repeated attention to their subject's compositional struggles. Paradoxically, however, this commitment to the work of revision does not mean that postwar writers necessarily revised *more*. In this chapter, I explore some of the ways in which they drew attention to their work's "revisedness" while actually revising less—that is, without making radical changes to drafts, wastefully discarding work, or obsessively annotating proofs. In particular, postwar writers seem to have returned to substitution—improvement of the individual word or phrase—as the primary tool of revision.

Thomas McFarland's distinction between cultural forms and shapes is useful for understanding the phenomenon whereby something once radical is tamed and domesticated.[2] He describes shapes as cultural objects that "masquerade under the prestige attached to forms of culture," as "what is left when form breaks down," and as centripetally organized. To borrow loosely from these terms, we might say that revision became a cultural shape—a shibboleth, even—only after the moment when it was most urgently practiced. Part of this story has to do with changing technologies of writing, and I return at the end of the chapter to some of the differences between modernist textuality, strung out between hand and machine, manuscript and typescript, and texts composed "straight onto" the typewriter or the computer. Equally important, however, is the reverberation of Pound's cry, "make it new," long after modernism's first battles had been won. Philip Roth's novel *The Ghost Writer,* which is as much about reading James's short story "The Middle Years" as writing anything, is one example of the anxiety—or desire, nostalgia, or jealousy—that a waning modernism has cast in its wake. The second chapter of the novel, titled "Nathan Dedalus," shows us Nathan Zuckerman reading Lonoff's copy of "The Middle Years" in considerable detail, paying attention to the meaning of the marginalia inscribed by the older writer in the book, before standing on the volume to eavesdrop—and avoid an Icarian fall.[3]

The literary value of new writing has been closely correlated since the 1920s with its perceived difficulty or shock value. The sociologist Daniel Bell has even argued that, given the "lack of a single unifying principle" at the level of form, "original difficulty" might be the best criterion of a work's modernism.[4] He continues: "It is willfully opaque, works with unfamiliar forms, is self-consciously experimental, and seeks deliberately to disturb the audience—to shock it, shake it up, even to transform it as if in a religious conversion."

For authors such as Marianne Moore and W. H. Auden, who began their careers in the modernist period but then outlived it, postpublication revision could be a way to defamiliarize circulating work and to make it new for the second time. Moore's radical reduction of "Poetry" for her ironically titled *Complete Poems* (1967) is one such example. She didn't merely reduce the poem to these three lines from its original thirty-five, as if finding the perfect final form:

> I, too, dislike it.
> Reading it, however, with a perfect contempt for it, one discovers in
> it, after all, a place for the genuine.

She also carefully gestured to its earlier textual history, as if reminding new readers that this "famous complaint against her own medium" had once been other (in fact, it had taken eleven different forms).[5] In the notes, she printed the 1951 twenty-nine-line version as the "Original Version" and also used her epigraph to point out something about the construction of this late volume, "Omissions are not accidents." The bibliographic, even scholarly self-consciousness of this gesture is different from the casual, wasteful textual attitudes of writers in the 1920s. Earlier in the century, writers had genuinely jettisoned their excised parts, often figuring them as "waste," but in 1967 Moore chose to make "explicit in a consistent way the fact that omissions have been made."[6] How strange would it seem now if Eliot had placed some of the abjected lines of *The Waste Land* in his notes, amid references to Ovid and Dante? By laying out her poem's genetic status openly, Moore was making a gesture more akin to Woolf's aesthetic of "draftliness" in "A Sketch."

As "revisedness" became a symptom of literary value, so a younger generation of authors began *ab ovo* to flag up or advertise their own practice of postcompositional change. For those who received formal education in "creative writing," this was part of what they were taught to do: Mark McGurl has shown that MFA programs emphasize "the value of craft as represented by the practice of multiple revision," and sees this as part of the "long shadow thrown by Hemingway across the Program Era."[7] McGurl's study focuses only on fiction, but an equally compelling argument could be made about poetry. In fact, given the difficulty of making a living as a poet, a higher proportion of poets than novelists teach creative writing as a day job. Robert Lowell—himself a self-diagnosed "endless" reviser—picked out Elizabeth Bishop as the only poet of his generation who didn't teach, and then wondered, "the revision, the consciousness that tinkers with the poem—that has something to do with teaching and criticism."[8]

Indeed, in creative writing classrooms and handbooks, the pro-revision stance can sometimes approach hysteria. This is Wendy Bishop's 1997 account of how she teaches creative and nonfiction writing. The word "revision" tolls out like a bell, both as noun and adjective: it is the passage's idée fixe.

> I teach revision by offering a course schedule that *demands* revision, by offering revision instruction and opportunities; by requiring an experimental, radical revision assignment; by orchestrating community-response sessions that encourage revision; by nurturing a class attitude that revision is worthwhile; and by insisting on class publishing that illuminates the benefits of revision.[9]

Joyce Carol Oates, who might seem not to revise very much—how could she, given her sheer rapidity of production?—offered a corrective in her 1978 *Paris Review* interview: "My reputation for writing quickly and effortlessly notwithstanding, I am strongly in favor of intelligent, even fastidious revision, which is, or certainly should be, an art in itself."[10] She even imagines that, like James, she will become increasingly "infatuated" with revision as an art in itself as she gets older.

For today's writers, revision no longer means literal alteration but, by metaphoric extension, a whole host of other literary practices, from painstaking attention to detail to self-critical acuity. Even novels about writers—a popular metafictional subgenre in the late twentieth century— are full of drafts, from Grady Tripp's endless, digressive novel in *Wonder Boys* (he speaks, at one point, of "the whole exploded clockwork of draft chapters and character sketches") to John Shade's series of drafts in *Pale Fire*.[11] His troubled editor and commentator, Kinbote, keeps finding passages that are "different in the draft" or lines "crossed out lightly . . . in the draft" that have been excised from the final text. In fact, "Pale Fire" seems to have been produced through a kind of radical excision and addition familiar from high modernism. At one point, the corrected draft of Canto Four—itself a Poundian title—is described as resembling the texts that Pound edited: it is "extremely rough in appearance, teeming with devastating erasures and cataclysmic insertions" (14). It is also incomplete at a purely formal level, being "a poem in heroic couplets, of nine hundred ninety-nine lines." In the program era, revision—a double figure of rereading and rewriting—acts as a kind of master trope, modeling the awkward balance between creator and critic, artist and professor, that writers within universities need to find.

"Oh God, what rubbish": W. H. Auden's Repudiations

Before asking how digital culture has changed contemporary writers' practice of revision, I would like to dwell in a little more detail on two poets who might be regarded, like Kinbote, as late modernists, and whose careers are illuminated by understanding the rising value of "revisedness."

W. H. Auden began his publishing life in the high modernist period— like Moore, as a distinct protégé of Eliot—but continued to wrestle with organizing and revising his canon until the end of his life. Auden's revisions have traditionally, following the work of Edward Mendelson, been taken very "seriously," as a determined attempt to manage the meaning—even the propositional truth value—of his work to accord always with present feeling. For a long time, Allen Ginsberg was thought not to have revised at all, but to have composed "spontaneously" in accordance with Jack Kerouac's edicts. Kerouac is one of the very few writers in the last two centuries to advocate a strong position of anti-revisionism: in fact, he spoke of revision as an act of deceit. In his interview with the *Paris Review*, Ginsberg remembered,

> Kerouac told me that in the future literature would consist of what people actually wrote rather than what they tried to deceive other people into thinking they wrote, when they revised it later on. And I saw opening up this whole universe where people wouldn't be able to lie anymore! They wouldn't be able to correct themselves any longer. They wouldn't be able to hide what they said.[12]

In the 1980s, however, Ginsberg helped to issue a facsimile edition of "Howl," collating the final version against a series of manuscript and typescript drafts. Both of these actions—Auden's careful pruning of his canon, and his overt self-criticism of ejected poems; Ginsberg's scholarly reframing of his poem à la *The Waste Land*—can be understood by thinking about what happened after modernism. They are highly self-conscious, but not particularly transformative or stylistically torquing, acts of revision.

Edward Mendelson has written more than anyone else about Auden's revisions, and he does so from a position of peculiar intimacy and involvement. In his work as Auden's executor and editor, he has repeatedly defended the poet's final intentions—the end product of his revisions—and in the 1996 essay "Revision and Power," he argues that Auden used revision not to strengthen but to eschew his rhetorical power over readers. Philip Larkin might have thought that the later Auden was "too verbose to be memorable and too intellectual to be moving," "unserious" in attitude, with an uncomfortable "lisping archness" of manner,[13] but Mendelson comes out strongly in favor of the later poet. In his editorial preface to the *Collected Poems*, he justifies his own decision to omit "the poems Auden published in his earlier years but finally discarded" first by reference to the traditional doctrine of authorial final intention, and then on grounds of taste:

> This edition includes all the poems that W. H. Auden wished to preserve, in a text that represents his final revisions . . . Fortunately, obligation and judgement are agreed in requiring that this first post-humous collected edition conform to its author's wishes to the extent that they can be determined.[14]

The adverb "fortunately" makes the argument in passing. From a legal or even ethical perspective, there are substantial reasons for preferring an author's own final intention: this is the belief behind the Anglo-American "ideal of an author's fair copy of his work in its final state."[15] But Mendelson suggests, in addition, that Auden's final arrangement of his poems is better than any earlier form.[16] More particularly, he has argued that the dialectic between "empty sonorities" (something Auden found in Yeats) and plainspoken truthfulness was at the heart of his behavior as a reviser. "Auden understood that revision was an act of power over his own text, and he therefore revised his texts in ways that renounced the kind of power he employed in revising."[17] The only way to prevent the reader "whoring after lies" was to strip the text bare of its most basic visual and musical pleasures: "when he revised his early drafts into publishable form, and, later, when he revised his published works for new editions, he repeatedly rejected his most *compelling* metaphors, and called attention to his own artifice."[18]

This elegant argument—Prospero using a rod to break his rod—has become almost an orthodoxy, but it leaves questions unanswered. The logical problem it creates is one of regression, for is the compelling rejection of "compelling metaphors" not, in itself, a form of compulsion? It is important to be clear about this, because critics who write about other poets who revise heavily have taken Mendelson's view of Auden for granted. So Stephen James argues that "Lowell, like Auden, came to distrust mere rhetorical effectiveness as a means to an end, and the progress of both poets' careers may be judged as a means of accepting an increasing burden of guilt for their past words and deeds."[19] Zachary

Leader refers to Auden in his study of romantic revision as a comparison point for Wordsworth, and as a poet "who cared passionately about consistency."[20] "The poems that Auden altered or rejected," he continues, "were ones that misrepresented original meanings and intentions."

I read Auden's behavior as a reviser less "seriously" than Mendelson does. He might have liked to draw attention to his own changes, particularly in the postwar period, but when his practice of revision is understood comparatively—particularly when compared to Pound, Eliot, or Yeats—it looks minimal. Between manuscript and first book publication, he devoted most of his energies to selecting the best poems, working out the best order of poems, and to making small verbal substitutions (swapping out an adjective or noun); in addition, he sometimes deleted stanzas whole. After first publication, he continued to revise in much the same way: reordering his poems for collected and selected editions, making small substitutions, and, notoriously, sometimes deleting poems or parts of poems entirely. The Yeats elegy, for example, lost the three stanzas beginning "Time that is intolerant" after several book publications.[21] Between typescript and first magazine publication in the *New Republic*, "September 1, 1939," also lost two stanzas.[22] Auden seems, in other words, not to have regarded publication itself as a particularly important breach in the creative process. Unlike Eliot or Joyce he didn't furtively and privately labor over drafts but nor did he dismiss published work as "as thing of the past so far as I am concerned." He rarely changed more than a single line (most of the revisions are to a word or phrase), and despite half a dozen or more reprintings of his poems, he hardly ever had third or fourth thoughts. In other words, once made, a revision tends to stay. Auden did not torment himself with the regress that Dencombe feared, or wallow addictively in an iterative, multistage process.

As a reviser, Auden is best known for the retraction of his political poems. And yet, curiously, he did not manage to fully erase them. By repeating so firmly that "this is a lie," he might even—through a form of negative advertising—have kept them in people's minds. The Swarthmore library has a copy of the first edition of *On This Island* (1937), which Auden apparently used when he was rereading for the first of his collected editions. Against poem XIV, which begins with urgent fellow-feeling ("Brothers who when the sirens roar"), he made the pencil comment "Oh God, what rubbish." On the other side of the page comes the editorial or authorial command: "Omit. (WHA)."[23] He made a similar comment on Cyril Connolly's edition of *Another Time,* crossing out the last two lines of "Spain, 1937" and writing "this is a lie" in the margin.[24] Mendelson would see this as a straightforward act of purgation, and John Haffenden describes it as an "apperception of his own insincerity," but I think it is also performative and responsive. Connolly had criticized "Spain" when it was first published ("the Marxian theory of history does not go very happily into verse").[25] In doing so, he was less forthright than George Orwell, who thought Auden's espousal of the Republican cause ignorant and complacent, premised on his own "soft-boiled emancipated middle class" liberalism. Orwell showed particular distaste for the phrase "conscious acceptance of guilt in the necessary murder": it could only have been written, he said, "by a person to whom murder was at most a word . . . Mr. Auden's brand of amoralism is only possible if you are the kind of person who is always somewhere else when the trigger is pulled."[26] So too, Auden's excision of his openly communist poems from the canon was perhaps less as an earnest renunciation of a sincerely held position than a politic retraction of an idea with which he had enthusiastically flirted. In fact, with the logic of *praeteritio,* he drew attention to the existence and importance of these poems even as he repudiated their value. Certainly, as both Nicholas Jenkins and Stephen Burt have discussed, "September 1, 1939" was available enough to be "endlessly quoted and reprinted" after September 11, despite not being in Auden's *Collected Poems.* It seemed "weirdly prescient" to some commentators and to others offered the comfort of "something akin to religious ritual."[27]

The preface to the final volume of poems published in Auden's lifetime is a good example of his revisionary equivocations. It is not a description of "acts of revision performed in secret by the poet," as Mendelson puts it; nor is it a Dencombian narrative of furtive compulsion. At one point, Auden scolds literary critics who "are apt to find revisions ideologically consistent. One, even, made a great to-do about what was in fact a typographical error." But, confusingly, this follows a defense of his own revisions as primarily ideological; the closing lines of "Spain, 1937," for example, are quoted, and then criticized. "To say this is to equate goodness with success. It would have been bad enough if I had ever held this wicked doctrine, but that I should have stated it simply because it sounded to me rhetorically effective is quite inexcusable."[28] Elsewhere, "some poems which I wrote and, unfortunately, published, I have thrown out because they were dishonest, or bad-mannered, or boring."[29] Only a few lines later, however, this content-based argument gives way to an almost flippant formal explanation: "The definite article is always a headache to any poet writing in English, but my addiction to German usages became a disease . . . I also find that my ear will no longer tolerate rhyming a voiced S with an unvoiced."[30] These two principles—revising toward truthfulness, and revising to remove "slovenly verbal habits"—are not commensurable. Certainly, Mendelson's ethical position struggles with the latter, and he disapproves of this change:

> Abandoned by his general and his lice,
> Under a padded quilt he closed his eyes. (1938)
> /Under a padded quilt he turned to ice. (1966)

He comments, "the new version corrected the rhyme but sacrificed the plain truth that Auden always demanded when he wrote about the art of poetry."[31]

In fact, the majority of Auden's local revisions look like this. Although he was an exciser at the level of the poem—he did not publish all of the poems in his notebooks, and he slowly winnowed down his published work for the *Collected* and *Selected* volumes—he was primarily a substituter within individual poems. This, according to the argument that this book has been developing, shows a *reversion* from the practice of high modernism.

In these substitutions, we once again see a relatively high preference for sonically driven, metaphoric changes—even the substitution of homophones—rather than logical, metonymic corrections. Where editors (and scribes) prefer the "lectio facilior," we find that authors often prefer vertical, sense-transforming changes to horizontal adjustments. Take, for example, the 1933 Christmas poem "Earth has turned over; our side feels the cold," titled "Through the Looking Glass" for the 1945 *Collected Poetry*. Auden broods on the difficulty of returning to his parents' home, and the impossibility of embracing the poem's object—"you"—in "the great bed at midnight." In the first published version of the poem, he complains that he no longer securely possesses the home he had once had:

> As I, their author, stand between these dreams,
> Son of a nurse and doctor, loaned a room[32]

By the 1945 *Collected Poetry*, "home" has taken on a metaphoric, or metapoetic, meaning:

> As I, their author, stand between these dreams
> Unable to choose either for a home[33]

This is one of the few poems that Auden actually revised more than once; in the intervening *Selected Poems* (1938), he had supplied a word which sounds like "room" but begins moving to a more abstract dimension, "Son of a nurse and doctor, loaned a dream." The final two stanzas of the poem work up an elaborate, almost Spenserian, voyaging metaphor to describe the speaker's own situation. In revision, Auden glides from "Islands of self through which I sailed all day; Planting a pirate's flag, a generous bay" to a strange self-descriptor, as if once again the speaker has taken on the characteristics of his physical situation, "Planting a pirate's flag, a generous boy." In "Spain, 1937," we find a similar kind of change, as "They clung like birds to the long expresses that lurch" became "They clung like burrs."[34] It would be hard to say with complete confidence that these are either corrections (e.g., of a compositor's mistake) or revisions. In these two cases, the latter reading seems perhaps more expected or logical, and the first reading was printed once only. In other cases, though, Auden let the initial reading stand through several editions before making a change, and this suggests retroactive revision rather than the discovery of a mistake. In "Paysage Moralisé," for example, the reading "And all the year trees blossomed on the mountains" was changed to the syntactically different but sonically similar "And all the green trees blossomed on the mountains" only in its eighth printing.[35]

The list below gives examples of some of the revisions that Auden made between early and late editions: many are changes to a single word, and more than a few have an uncanny sonic resemblance. Sometimes, of course, this was necessary to save or improve the rhyme.

"the mourning's injured"	"the morning's injured"[36]
"Coldest love will warm to action"	"Dark and dull is your distraction"[37]
"subtle useless faces"	"sad and useless faces"[38]
"We cannot postulate a General Will"	"Each has his comic role in life to fill"[39]
"Disturbs the stray"	"Distracts the stray"[40]
"The leading classic of his generation"	"The Latin Scholar of his generation"[41]
"Songs came no more"	"Lines came to him no more"[42]
"The peaks" "Far Peaks"	"Tall Peaks"[43]
"Where men can only recollect and stare"	"Gigantic terraces, imposing stairs"[44]
"The careful child with charm"	"The child with careful charm"[45]
"When words of"	"When worlds of"[46]
"rivers screaming"	"rivers howling"[47]

This list could be extended for many more pages.[48]

The final way in which Auden used revision to reshape his canon was by reordering and retitling poems. For the first of his collected volumes (*Collected Poetry*, 1945), he arranged the poems by alphabetical sequencing of first lines, as if pointing to the necessary randomness of arrangement in a lyric collection.[49] This arrangement is also profoundly ahistorical: it throws the poems out of the chronological order in which they were written or first published, and avoids providing a developmental story. Admirers of Auden's earlier work would also have found the book confusing and tricky to navigate. Take as an example the very first poem in the current edition of *The Collected Poems*, which is titled "The Letter" and begins "From the very first coming down/ Into a new valley with a frown." It is tempting to read this poem programmatically; its primacy seems appropriate because it is inscribed. Here are all the essential elements of early Auden: a northern English landscape filled with sheep-pens but also a "solitary truck"; suspicion and disenchantment about the prospect of romantic love, combined with an intense desire for it ("love's worn circuit re-begun"); a sense of alienation ("different love"), possibly linked to homosexuality; and anxiety about the performative function of speech, or the relationship between saying and meaning ("Always afraid to say more than it meant"); grandstanding mastery of a difficult form. James Fenton calls it "the earliest of Auden's published lyrics," but, in fact, it was only in 1966, at the end of his writing life, that Auden decided he would like to begin his oeuvre here.[50] In his first book, *Poems* (1928), it was the eleventh poem and in *Poems* (1930) it was fifth. In the 1927–1929 notebook it came even later, on the nineteenth (recto) page, and after thirteen other poems.[51] If you look at the facsimile notebook, which itself represents a secondary state of composition, you will see that it was also revised lexically and substitutively in manuscript, so preliminary "giggle" became "shiver" and "solitary waggon" the more modern "truck."

His earlier volumes had presented their contents in numbered order, but without titles. In the 1945 *Collected Poetry,* instead of providing a list of first lines, the table of contents is arranged by title—and yet these titles had been created only *for* the collected edition. So the sonnet, "Just as his dream foretold," describing a surreal dream sequence, now appears under the arch mantle, "Nobody Understands Me," while "This lunar beauty/ Has no history" is now, and obscurely, titled "Pur."[52] In later editions, these titles were to change again; the *Collected Shorter Poems* (1950) substitutes "more serious titles for some of those in the 1945 collection which had been especially flippant."[53] This purpose of this reordering, which never produces stable strings of poems, is quite hard to understand. Is it a kind of decorative flower arranging? Or is there a more concerted effort to "épater le lecteur," to continue making the work new? Rather than being a method of revision that we can read directionally, this is an oscillating story that does not easily offer up the "revision narrative" that critics tend to seek.

Allen Ginsberg and the "Howl" Facsimile

Auden retold the story of his own poetic development, reshaped his canon, and repeatedly gestured to its political significance through public acts of repudiation and reordering. Another strategy for keeping work in the public eye and for gesturing to its genetic complexity is to give readers a peak behind the scenes—to release the original draft materials. This was Allen Ginsberg's solution when in 1986, thirty years after the first appearance of "Howl," he published *Howl: Original Draft Facsimile, Transcript, and Variant Versions.*[54] He explained that it was meant to be "an emotional time bomb that would continue exploding," a kind of slow-release avant-gardism.[55] And yet, the facsimile looks utterly different from the punchy small format black-and-white volume released (and still printed) by City Lights bookstore: it is the product of Ginsberg grown up and turned professor. The poet taught at Brooklyn College from 1986 until his death in 1997, a career choice that Bill Morgan interprets as part of "an increasing interest in consolidating and passing on his legacy."[56] More particularly, as several critics have noticed, the edition is tightly and self-consciously modeled on Valerie Eliot's *The Waste Land: A Facsimile and Transcript of the Original Drafts Including the Annotations of Ezra Pound.* Ginsberg's volume is the same size, uses the same typefaces, and similar scholarly sounding title, and follows the same method of arrangement: original manuscript or typescript is presented in facsimile on the verso; a clean version on the recto; with revision marked in black and red ink.[57] The resemblance is in fact so exact, and Ginsberg's choice of title so long and scholarly, that one might even interpret the volume as a spoof of academic convention. Its full title was *Howl: Original Draft Facsimile, Transcript, and Variant Versions, Fully Annotated by the Author with Contemporaneous Correspondence, Account of First Public Reading, Legal Skirmishes, Precursor Texts, and Bibliography.*

At the beginning of his career, Ginsberg had presented himself as an anti-revisionist following Jack Kerouac's neoromantic mode of spontaneous composition: "Never afterthink to 'improve' or defray impressions, as, the best writing is always the most painful personal wrung-out tossed from cradle warm protective mind—tap from yourself the song of yourself."[58] In a 1974 interview, for example, he claimed that the poem "Sunflower Sutra" was "completely untouched from the original" and that "it took me a long time to get on to Kerouac's idea of writing without revision."[59] He was also to argue that Kerouac's eventual decision to admit alterations into the draft—going against his stated principles—substantially worsened *On the Road,* so "the original mad version is greater than the published version," which "was hacked and punctuated and broken—the rhythms and swing of it broken—by presumptuous literary critics in publishing houses."[60] This was written in 1958, at a moment when the young Ginsberg was setting the new poetics of himself and his friends *against* the tedious academic or publishing industry convention of reworking. When the 1951 scroll manuscript of Kerouac's novel was published in 2007, most critics found this judgment to be only partially true. Although Kerouac did make some changes to his original manuscript to fit the needs of the market, he also continued between 1951 and 1957 to revise it in more traditional ways and produced three subsequent, conventionally formatted drafts.[61]

At some point toward the end of his life, Ginsberg suffered a change of heart, realizing perhaps that the revisionists had won the day, or perhaps simply impressed by the cultural interest that the facsimile of *The Waste Land* engendered. From the beginning, he had been fascinated by Eliot's reputation, owning in a 1958 poem that he had dreamed of visiting the older poet to pay homage: "I dream of my kindness to T. S. Eliot / wanting to be a historical poet / and share in his finance of Imagery- / overambitious dream of eccentric boy."[62]

Despite the hard-won physical similarity, Ginsberg's volume is surprisingly different from Valerie Eliot's: this difference, of course, is one marker of the gap between high modernist revision and the textual culture of the postwar period. To begin with, Ginsberg's text was never quite as "fixed" as Eliot's had been in October 1922. The poem was introduced to its original audience through powerful performances, and in these oral renditions Ginsberg treated his printed text flexibly, ad-libbing from the script, and adding phrases or markers to fit his specific environment.[63] So, although he had pronounced "mother finally fucked" aloud at the 1956 Reed College recording, he was subsequently to treat the printed asterisks as the poem's literal words, reading "mother finally asterisked." In the 1970s, he even considered rewriting the poem to reflect the euphoria of the hippie movement with a "positive redemptive catalogue" beginning "I saw the best minds of my generation turned on by music."[64]

Even more importantly, the "Howl" facsimile is a self-authorized book rather than a posthumously constructed one. Eliot dismissed the original manuscript of *The Waste Land*—displaying so little interest, in fact, that he never learned it had been recovered—but Ginsberg patiently preserved and then sutured together his original drafts. He also commented on them. The exhaustive practice of self-annotation begins with a note to the first line of the poem, which was revised from "I saw the best minds of my generation destroyed by madness, starving mystical naked," to "starving hysterical naked." He explains: "Crucial revision: 'Mystical' is replaced by 'hysterical,' a key to the tone of the poem. Tho [*sic*] the initial idealistic impulse of the line went one way, afterthought noticed bathos, and common sense dictated 'hysteria.' One can entertain both notions without 'any irritable reaching after fact and reason,' as Keats proposed with his definition of 'Negative Capability.' The word 'hysterical' is judicious" (124). This may be self-justifying but it is also deliberately academic in its style, pressing the New Critical phrase of appreciation "a key to the tone" against a textual critical formulation of reasonable empiricism: "common sense dictates." The Keats reference points to a strong command of literary and lyric tradition and, counterintuitively, locates "Howl" within it. To Marjorie Perloff, this self-promoting and even intrusive act of authorial return seemed at first unnerving. She admits that she at first found Ginsberg's annotations "somewhat irritating: isn't it pretentious of the poet to inform us that the replacement of a single word is 'crucial' and 'judicious'?" but, laying aside this prejudice, that she has now come to see the note as "just."[65] Ginsberg did make a crucial change, because all three terms in the final list designate bodies, and consequently "a mental hunger so intense as to seem literally physical."

Like Auden, Ginsberg was mostly a substitutive reviser. One might assume from the paratactic, endlessly unfolding, additive structure of "Howl" that it was written, like *Ulysses,* by addition, but Ginsberg's typescript drafts do not indicate this. In fact, in the "Guide to Original Manuscripts" (the surviving documents are really typescripts with manuscript alteration), he described the genetic process as follows: "Successive drafts rearrange and rehook the verses into their appropriate groups; some further refine rhythm, syntax or diction to create an even and elastic flow verse to verse" (11). Comparing the published version of "Howl" to the strophe drafts suggests that "rehooking" was indeed the major work of revision. The free-flowing excess was present from the first draft, dated August 1955, and the process of substitutive revision was relatively brief: the notorious first performance took place at the Six Gallery two months later. Between the August and October versions, we see word inversions ("thru the angry streets at dawn looking for a negro fix" becoming "through the negro streets at dawn looking for an angry fix"); strophe inversions ("who passed through universities" moving from the seventh to the third "who"); and changes to individual words. At some points, the verse becomes thicker or more clotted between a syntactically simpler earlier version and a more difficult later version. These lines, for example, were corrected by hand on the August typescript.

> ^screaming &^ vomiting ~~out~~ their facts and anecdotes
> —memories and eyeball kicks and shocks
> of hospitals and jails and wars (12)

In all of the other typescripts the reading is close to the final, published version:

> yackatayaking screaming vomiting whispering facts and memories
> and anecdotes and eyeball kicks and shocks of hospitals and jails
> and wars (26)

The Moloch section, which is represented in eighteen surviving drafts, shows slightly more genetic complexity, but it still startling to see how close Ginsberg was from the very beginning. The first draft is written by hand on the bottom of a discarded piece of typescript and opens, "Moloch! Moloch! Whose hand ripped out their brains and scattered their minds on the wheels of subways?" (58). By the second typescript, it has morphed into almost the final form: "What sphinx of cement and aluminum bashed in their skulls and ate up their brains and imagination?" (62).

Despite Ginsberg's meticulous, even mock-scholarly work on presenting and annotating these drafts, and despite his consistent attempts to draw attention to the process of revision, "Howl" was actually an easily achieved poem. It was begun on August 24, 1955, and the first section was read aloud in final form on October 7. The format of the facsimile and even some of Ginsberg's own terminology, like the Eliotic "flashing phrases" or Poundian emphasis on elimination, try to win the poem a place within a long twentieth-century history of avant-gardism, and to present it as the postwar *Waste Land*. And yet, the more we learn about the two poems' genetic histories, the less they seem to resemble each other: from the beginning, Ginsberg knew how this poem ought to sound and he worked on it with surprising authorial control; Eliot produced a series of false starts, was talked out of some passages, composed others in response to Pound's deletions, and essentially surrendered or abandoned the work by the beginning of 1922.

Track Changes: Revising on the Computer

The difference between Eliot's revision process and Ginsberg's cannot be attributed simply to technological apparatus. Writers in the immediate postwar period used essentially the same method of composition as the high modernists: manuscript drafting, some typescript drafting, making fair copies by typescript, marking up of proofs, marking up of printed editions. In fact, medial diversity is one of the distinctive features of twentieth-century literary culture from the beginning until the 1990s. It would have looked puzzling to nineteenth-century writers who composed only in longhand, and it begins to look puzzling to those of us today who write only "straight onto" the laptop. Before arriving in a twentieth-century writer's archive, for example, it is very difficult to say what *kind* of documents it will contain and how textual changes will be marked on manuscripts or typescripts. Who, for example, would guess that Joyce Carol Oates's earlier novels are typescripts and the later ones in manuscript?

A more subtle, and significant point is the shift around midcentury from using the typewriter primarily as a device of remediation—for typing up—and using it as a primary compositional tool. None of the high modernist writers that I study wrote directly on to the machine; Eliot, for example, said in his *Paris Review* interview that he wrote "partly on the typewriter" but, by this, he meant that even in 1959 he was typing up material drafted by hand. Other early- and midcentury writers spoke of a soft migration from hand to machine, where the most important and creative kinds of writing remained handwritten longest. Conrad Aiken said that he began writing on the typewriter for some kinds of work in the 1920s: "I began by doing book reviews on the typewriter and then went over to short stories on the machine, meanwhile sticking to pencil for poetry," and as late as 1981, Elizabeth Bishop said, "I can write prose on a typewriter. Not poetry."[66]

By the late age of the typewriter, the choice of medium and instrument became associated with aesthetic, even political strategies. On the one side, a lingering, nostalgic commitment to the pen; on the other a future-oriented enthusiasm for the speed of the machine. The conservative position, by midcentury, is suspicion of writers who have completely ceased *writing;* this is the touched nerve in Capote's criticism of *On the Road,* "it isn't writing at all, it's typing."[67] Randall Jarrell made the same point in a famous one-sentence review of a forgettable book of poetry (by Oscar Williams), it "gave the impression of having been written on a typewriter by a typewriter."[68] Here, the criticism hardens around a common early-twentieth-century metonymy. As Friedrich Kittler and others have discussed, not only the machine but the machinist (who was almost always a woman) was called a "typewriter," and so Jarrell implies that the poems have been mechanically or quickly produced, and perhaps also that they are effeminate. In the 1950s and 1960s, drafting by hand and then typing up was artisanal, slow, deliberate, and often retrospective; working straight on to the machine was fluid, spontaneous, future-oriented, and not necessarily selective. To identify these poles as conservative and progressive is simplistic, given the diverse and formally experimental writing that handwriters have continued to produce, but some younger writers in this period did focus on typewriting as a way of achieving new stylistic effects. For Kerouac, who emphasized "Not 'selectivity' of expression but following free deviation (association) of mind into limitless blow-on-subject seas of thought," writing straight on to the machine was a way to achieve a lighter, quicker kind of style. Frank O'Hara made the same point when he spoke of "playing" the typewriter as lovingly as a musical instrument, as if it had ceased to be a prosthesis or tool and become instead a kind of accompanist, producing the Coleridgean effect of "rhythm in all thought, and joyance everywhere."[69] Perversely, typing quickly, straight on to the machine became associated with a reinvigorated romantic commitment to spontaneity. In O'Hara's case, typing allowed him to produce the casually thrown together, processive aesthetic of the lunch poems, which Helen Vendler describes as having "the perfect freedom" of diary.

The shift from typing up to typing "onto"—a shift completed with the advent of the personal computer—may have made complex, belated, laborious revision less likely. The multistage iterative process of writing and then typing up seems to have encouraged writers to rethink and to see their work anew. In this way, the typewriter when used as a remediating tool, rather than a writing machine, functioned rather like the piece of glassine that John Berryman described as a tool for slowing down his writing process, and for encouraging revision. Instead of studying and annotating typescript drafts, Berryman inspected his work in manuscript, alienating himself from a recently written stanza by rendering it literally untouchable, and only typing up at the very end, when the text had fixed itself in a final form.

> I got one of those things that have a piece of glassine over a piece of paper, and you can put something in between and see it but not touch it. I would draft my stanza and put it in there. Then I would sit and study it. I would make notes, but I wouldn't touch the manuscript until I thought I was in business—usually not for hours. Then I'd take it out, make the corrections, put it back in, and study it some more. When I was finally satisfied, I'd take it out and type it.[70]

The last thirty years have seen very significant changes in most writers' methods of composition and the typewriter—now a metonym for modernist textuality—has become a curio rather than a common writing machine. Today writers can upload their own Word documents directly to Amazon and distribute a Kindle "book" within seconds. And whenever they want to, they can return to and revise these books simply by submitting a new file. The cost of revision has fallen almost to zero. For a writer as bent on alteration as Joyce or James, it seems as if this would have been an extremely dangerous possibility.[71] What happens in fact? Are contemporary novelists—trained in environments where revision is pedagogically advocated, working in software that makes alteration very easy, and publishing in environments that make it free—continually re-submitting their work? At the end of chapter 1, I ventured the claim that digital culture will make revision not more likely, because it is practically easier, but less necessary, because no text is ever really fixed. How would we prove or disprove this hypothesis?

To do so would require patient comparison of born-digital with pre-digital archives. Indeed, genetic critics have recently been arguing that digital forensics is the only direction in which their work can go, "The choice is simple: either redefine diplomatic studies to include the digital world, or abandon any attempt to study the textual genesis of modern works."[72] One would want to know how writers working directly on a computer manage the drafting process, and then whether they save drafts or simply "write over" them: in the latter case, we might ask in ad-dition if the original file has been automatically saved, and whether we can still access it.

To the technological optimist, it looks as if digital genetic criticism might be just around the corner. In the last five years, writers have begun to leave the first digital archives to university archives. As well as papers and books, John Updike bequeathed to the Houghton Library at Har-vard "50 three-and-a-half and five-and-a-quarter-inch floppy disks—artifacts from late in the author's career when he, like many of his peers, began using a word processor";[73] Emory University has salvaged four of Salman Rushdie's computers and eighteen gigabytes of data; and Stan-ford archivists have been using forensic software to try to open up the (often-corrupted) files of Robert Creeley. So far, however, these archives remain mostly closed to scholars, and the question of future access is unresolved; in Matthew Kirschenbaum's words, "the question of schol-arly access to born-digital collections remains an uncharted wilder-ness."[74] A pessimist might wonder if the difficulties of assessing, cata-loging, and then preserving this work are almost insurmountable. Even *reading* files produced in software on old and rapidly decaying media—floppy disks, CDs, partially defunct hard drives—poses substantial dif-ficulties. As Patricia Cohen puts it in a *New York Times* article about

Salman Rushdie's archive, "Imagine having a record but no record player."[75] And then there are difficult additional questions about representation. How far should digital archivists attempt to replicate a writer's original (dated) technological environment? Should the archives be placed online? In the case of limited human or technical resources, which parts of the archive should be opened up first? Critics interested in textual process might want to investigate early and draft versions of major poems or novels, but other researchers will naturally be more interested in other parts of the archive. How important is the poem that was slightly different in an early Word file next to completely unknown finished work, or juicy biographical information? So far at Stanford, archivists have worked primarily on deciphering the text of Robert Creeley's e-mails—not his poems.[76]

Furthermore, even in the best-case scenario, it is far from clear that these materials will prove as rewarding to study—or to write over—as the interlined manuscripts, typescripts, and proofs of twentieth-century writers. Outside large corporations, where documents are produced collaboratively, most people do not use meticulous "version control" when composing on a computer. Many of the changes we make simply disappear as a new version is saved over the last. In this regard, Microsoft Word is more like Freud's chalk slate than a mystic writing pad. At least, this is true at first sight and for ordinary users' experience. Michael Hancher makes the more subtle point that electronic documents are really neither impermanent nor insecure, but this cannot be known experientially and can be proved only by a digital expert.[77]

Microsoft introduced the Track Changes function for Word 97 to preserve an archaeology of textual process—a depth structure—within a surface medium, but writers can easily turn this feature off and "permanently hide revision marks." In fact, in corporate environments, these traces are eventually designed to vanish: "at some point in the editing cycle, the entire history of changes is meant to be accepted or rejected, removing them from the textual strata of the finished document."[78] Even documents that do contain a complete set of tracked changes may seem less compelling than the paper trails of a previous era. The graphic fossils of thinking in action—Pound's hasty strikeouts, James's unfurling additive bubbles, or Eliot's scrawl, "The river's leaf is broken" on the back of the Fresca couplets—contain information above and beyond the change itself. They also tell us something about *why* the revision was made, and about the shudder of distaste or bold new idea that motivated it. As Dirk Van Hulle points out, a word or phrase that appears in an early manuscript, is removed and replaced by something else, and then chosen again for the printed text, is also subtly other than a phrase that was never called into question.[79] An example of this oscillating pattern occurs in the manuscript of Beckett's *Stirrings Still,* where the Dantean phrase "per lungo silenzio fioco" is translated first as "faint" then as "hoarse from long silence" and then once again as "faint." These kinds of paraliopmena—Van Hulle suggests we need an "unelegant neologism like the 'manuscriptographical code' "—are an inevitable part of the genetic process on paper.

In digital culture, the computer often autosaves drafts without the writer even realizing it, producing a series of versions that is unconscious rather than selected. As Matthew Kirschenbaum observes, Track Changes has no intelligence: "it lacks the ability to determine '*this* is a major revision, those are just some minor tweaks.' "[80] Doug Reside, the digital curator at the New York Public Library, discovered just this in his recent work on Jonathan Larson's Word files from 1986 to 1996. First, he found that early versions of Microsoft Word used "fast save" to append revisions to the end of a file rather than completely overwriting the existing text.[81] Then he found this revision data. To the literary critic it presents a distinctly unappetizing object of study; by itself it has no semantic or symbolic meaning. Throughout this book, we have seen that writers are often driven to revise when they see their work in new formats, and particularly when those formats contain space for overwriting—like the wide margins on James's revision copies of his earlier novels. This screenshot *shows* revision, but it would never motivate it. The evidence is no longer the means.

Second, digital archives do not always preserve the identity of the person who made changes. Individual autographs or even, as Lawrence Rainey has shown, unique typewriter ribbons and paper leave evidence about *when, where,* and *by whom* changes were executed. Archivists responsible for buying and curating digital archives are equally concerned to make sure the files they receive are "genuine," but they work under

```
00028b60   09 09 09 2a 2a 2a 31 2f   31 36 2f 39 36 4f 55 52   |...***1/16/96OUR|
00028b70   20 57 45 44 44 49 47 47   4f 4e 20 54 48 45 20 53   | WEDDINGON THE S|
00028b80   4f 46 41 53 4f 46 41 54   48 45 20 56 49 52 55 53   |OFASOFATHE VIRUS|
00028b90   20 54 41 4b 45 53 20 48   4f 4c 44 4d 45 45 54 20   | TAKES HOLDMEET |
00028ba0   59 4f 55 20 41 54 20 54   48 45 20 53 48 4f 57 49   |YOU AT THE SHOWI|
00028bb0   27 4c 4c 20 54 52 59 20   41 4e 44 20 43 4f 4e 56   |'LL TRY AND CONV|
00028bc0   49 4e 43 45 20 52 4f 47   45 52 20 54 4f 20 47 4f   |INCE ROGER TO GO|
00028bd0   43 4c 4f 53 45 20 4f 4e   43 41 4e 20 49 20 48 45   |CLOSE ONCAN I HE|
00028be0   4c 50 4d 69 73 73 20 50   6f 72 74 65 72 27 73 46   |LPMiss Porter'sF|
00028bf0   4f 52 47 45 54 20 49 54   50 41 55 4c 2a 2a 2a 2a   |ORGET ITPAUL****|
```

Figure 11: Image of Jonathan Larson's revision data. Courtesy of the New York Public Library digital archives.

the threat of posthumous alteration; family members often want to clean up a few things—financial data, health records—before they give up the data. So interpolation or contamination is common and hard to trace.

The Pale King and Digital Archives

As an example, we might think of Michael Pietsch's recent work editing David Foster Wallace's incomplete and now posthumously published novel *The Pale King.* Wallace left only a disk with the phrase "For LB advance?" on it, and "hundreds and hundreds of pages" of the novel in progress scattered around his study in a wealth of different media, "hard drives, file folders, three-ring binders, spiral-bound notebooks, and floppy disks."[82] Percy Lubbock edited James's typescripts before he published them posthumously, but the Houghton documents preserve the evidence of those changes quite clearly. Pietsch carted Wallace's jumble of boxes, printouts, and disks home with him in 2008 "in a duffel and two Trader Joe's bags," and only then began the process of reconstructing the novel. Whether or not he made changes to the files during the process of editing may be difficult to determine. In the worst-case scenario, we would know that the files had been "last modified" after the date of Wallace's death, but without being able to reconstruct how this had happened. "Modify," of course, does not imply any egregious interventionism: one inserted and then deleted space is enough to produce a new version.

By a strange piece of luck, we can go a little further into the genetic story of the reconstituted digital novel *The Pale King.* On March 7, 2011, *The New Yorker* published the thirty-sixth section of the novel (pages 281–290) as a freestanding piece called "Backbone." It is listed only as fiction, and there is no mention in the magazine version of its place in the longer novel. But it does work as an individual unit, albeit one with weak closure: Wallace is telling the story of a young boy whose one, unexplained, goal is "to be able to press his lips to every square inch of his own body," who becomes injured and receives treatment from his father's chiropractor, and who then begins stretching incrementally to achieve increasing feats of contortion. The genetic tale becomes more interesting when we discover that the posthumously edited "Backbone" is similar, but not identical, to something that David Foster Wallace read aloud in December 2000 at the Lannan Foundation as part of "Three Fragments of a Longer Thing." Wallace's text of that story has not come to light—it is perhaps among the papers and disks carted off by Pietsch in the Trader Joe's bags—but a recording of the reading does survive, and even before the publication of "Backbone," it had been transcribed as text.[83] The excerpt published in the *New Yorker* is, in addition, slightly different from the version published in the novel itself the following month.

After the publication of the *New Yorker* story, someone had the smart idea of using the "compare documents" option under the Track Changes function in Microsoft Word to produce a variorum comparison of the two texts. This very readable document shows deletions in red and insertions in blue and provides some measure of genetic change between the 2000 reading and Wallace's death in 2008. At the same time, it is not a mirror image—a digital facsimile—of Wallace's own computer files, as some readers have assumed. One blogger thought he was seeing "what *The Pale King* might have looked like, if its editors had chosen to leave it in the disarrayed state it was discovered in"—but this document is completely artificial. It was produced after the fact by someone typing the published *New Yorker* story over the Lannan transcript, and neither of these textual states are necessarily ones that Wallace would have seen into print. We don't know if the version he read aloud was identical to the script he carried with him to the reading, and Pietsch's version is certainly, as he himself admits, the product of some creative editing.

This document was circulated widely during the spring of 2011; Lorin Stein in the *Paris Review* described it as a "curiosity."[84] What does it tell us about Wallace's method of composition? The document is heavily striated with red and blue, suggesting at first sight a very complex and thoroughgoing revision process. On closer inspection, however, it becomes clear that the changes are, once again, mostly simple substitutions—small nudges toward stylistic felicity. They resemble the kind of edits that a sensitive reader or teacher would prompt. However, given that Pietsch had been reading and commenting on the project from the beginning, even the first draft may contain editorial, other-inspired changes of this kind. Some of the differences between the *New Yorker* version and *The Pale King* version, like the breaking off of the long sentence about leaning to the side at "a bull's-eye of soluble ink," also seem like gentle editing, though the reason for the difference between these versions—published weeks apart—is not clear.

Besides substitutions within sentences, the most notable difference between the two versions is the addition of three passages between the reading and "Backbone." Does this suggest that Wallace—a writer as intrigued by the piling up of trivial detail as Joyce—worked additively? The three added passages describe first, Dr. Kathy's work with the boy; second, his exclusion at school; and the third (this is by far the longest) is a meditation on pain and asceticism. The first part of this passage, which describes "the Bavarian mystic Therese Neumann's stigmata" and a single bowel movement, a Bengali holy man whose eyes could exit his head in meditation, and a series of "common fallacies about pain," does resemble the kinds of lists that, in "Ithaca," Joyce could never stop himself from increasing, "Artesian wells, eruptions, torrents, eddies, freshets, spates, groundswells, watersheds . . ." The second part of this passage, like the other two, serves a more obvious diegetic function—it tells us about the boy's father. Like the "depressed person" in Wallace's story of the same name, he suffers constant mental pain of a kind that, in any possible description, threatens to seem melodramatic and consequently almost trivial. His suffering can be expressed only in the pat language of psychotherapy: "much of this secret torture—whose causes he perceived as impossibly complex and protean and involving both normal male sexual drives and highly abnormal personal weakness and lack of backbone—was actually quite simple to diagnose."

It makes intuitive sense that Wallace might have expanded the referential world of the boy's life as he moved from a short fragment form to a novel. But it is also quite possible that he had written these passages before the 2000 reading but simply skipped them out as he read. Excerpting for a performed "reading" is very common—it allows the writer to showcase a wider range of work within a manageable time frame. The disks and files that Pietsch carted off might one day be able to give us this answer. In the meantime, we can observe the following: in this passage, Wallace a) never makes a bold excision, and b) never adds substantial material within a sentence or even within a paragraph. That is, he never performs the Joycean trick of turning "Jilted beauty. Glad I didn't know it when she was on show" into "Jilted beauty. A defect is ten times worse in a woman. But makes them polite. Glad I didn't know it when she was on show." The additions work *outside* the individual phrase or even sentence, at a higher structural level.

Take the following passage, for example, which is among the more heavily gone-over. This is how it looks in the circulating Track Changes document:

> **The**—*the* boy had no conscious wish to **'transcend'** *"transcend"* anything. If someone had asked him, the boy would have said only that he'd decided he wanted to press his lips to every last **square micrometer***micrometre* of his own individual body. He would not have been able to say more than this. **Conceits***Insights into* or **conception***conceptions* of his own physical **"**inaccessibility**"** to himself (as we are all of us *self*-inaccessible **to ourselves** and can, for example, **press our lips to***touch* parts of one another **which** *in ways that* we **cannot begin***could not* even **to approach, lip wise, on ourselves***dream of touching our own bodies*) or of **the boy's** *his* complete determination, apparently, to pierce that veil of inaccessibility—to be, in some **idiosyncratic***childish* way, self-contained and -sufficient, **fully available to himself**—these were beyond **the range of** his **consciousness.***conscious awareness.* He was **only,** *after all, just* a **child.**

If we instead represented the 2000 and 2008 versions as facing-page texts, the difference between them looks much less substantial.[85] In fact, like Wordsworth's *Prelude* and unlike *Ulysses* or *The Sun Also Rises* or *The Years,* they keep pace with each other:

The boy had no conscious wish
   to 'transcend' anything. If
someone had asked him, the boy
   would have said only that
he'd decided he wanted to press
   his lips to every last square
micrometer of his own individual
   body. He would not have
been able to say more than this.
   Conceits or conception of his
own physical inaccessibility to
   himself (as we are all of us
inaccessible to ourselves and
   can, for example, press our lips
to parts of one another which we
   cannot begin even to
approach, lip wise, on ourselves)
   or of the boy's complete
determination apparently to
   pierce that veil of
   inaccessibility—
to be in some idiosyncratic way
   self-contained and -sufficient,
fully available to himself—these
   were beyond the range of his
   consciousness. He was only
   a child.

. . . the boy had no conscious wish
   to "transcend" anything. If
someone had asked him, the boy
   would have said only that
he'd decided he wanted to press
   his lips to every last
micrometre of his own individual
   body. He would not have been
   able to say more than this.
   Insights into or conceptions of
his own physical "inaccessibility"
   to himself (as we are all of
us self-inaccessible and can, for
   example, touch parts of one
another in ways that we could not
   even dream of touching our
own bodies) or of his complete
   determination, apparently, to
pierce that veil of
   inaccessibility—to be,
   in some childish way,
self-contained and -sufficient—
   these were beyond his
conscious awareness. He was,
   after all, just a little boy.

Here we have only substitutions. Like the early and late versions of James's novels, these passages could be translations of the same source passage by two competent translators. The second prefers "insights" over "conceits," "touch" over "press our lips," "childish" to "idiosyncratic," "conscious awareness" to "consciousness." Elsewhere in the story we see the substitution of "symptoms" for "discomfort," "disciplined" for "determined," and, phonically, "sheet" for "sheath." In the first two pages, there are thirty-seven changes of this kind; seventeen small additions (e.g., of the word "that" to connect to clauses); ten one-word deletions; and one added passage. In the posthumously published, edited novel, the text is subtly different again. The house style of the *New Yorker* accounts for the double quotation mark around "transcend" and "micrometre" for "micrometer" (kept in *The Pale King*), but why does the magazine version read "in ways that we could not even dream of touching our own bodies" while the final version is "dream of with our own bodies"?

Perhaps it is not a very important question. We may assume that most of the differences between 2000 and 2008 are due to Wallace's own reshaping of his material, and the differences between the two posthumous versions the result of editing. But, either way, there is no great hermeneutic difference between any of the versions because Wallace's revision process *already* resembles editing: he does nothing as surprising as James's homophone leap from "lived" to "dive" in "The Middle Years," and nothing remotely as inventive or laborious as Joyce's additions to "Ithaca." The boy in the story may have no understanding of why he practices his peculiar art, but the author's iteration toward stylistic felicity makes perfect sense. In fact, of all the revision documents that I have discussed in this book, these are the easiest and the most expected.

Coda

We began with James's increasingly strange torquing of his already published work for the New York Edition: this was the process that turned the 1877 "His eye was of a clear, cold gray, and save for a rather abundant mustache he was clean-shaved" into the long-winded and Latinate "His eye was of a clear, cold grey, and save for the abundant droop of his moustache he spoke, as to cheek and chin, of the joy of the matutinal steel." In his work after the New York Edition, and as the constraints of conventional publishing began to relax, James gave free rein to this sinuous long-winded style, producing (after revision) such involuted sentences as "These were considerations of which I recall the pressure, at the same time that I fear I have no account of them to give after they have fairly faced the full, demonstrous demonstration that Tennyson was not Tennysonian."

Early in his career, Joyce scrapped the whole *Stephen Hero* manuscript—this would have been a wasteful decision for a commercially motivated artist. In composing *Ulysses*, he turned out to be an incredible hoarder and preserver of any remotely relevant material. During the agonizing revision process, he fed phrases from his many notebooks back into the text, thickened styles of free indirect discourse, parodically extended lists, and drove certain passages toward the limits of comprehensibility. T. S. Eliot presents in revision, as in many things, a curious opposite to Joyce. Instead of trying to retain meticulous and obsessive control of *The Waste Land,* he abandoned the unfinished poem to Ezra Pound and, as if placing no value on it, he proved willing to omit almost anything that he had produced. "Perhaps better omit Phlebas also???"[86] A creed of textual efficiency through minimalism proved attractive to many other modernist writers: it can be felt in the "laconic speech" of the Imagist poem, and in Hemingway's iceberg principle—itself an instruction to revise. Joyce's particular brand of "wanting more" for *Ulysses* is perhaps unique, but other writers devoted themselves to different kinds of textual excess. Proust found that *À la recherche* spilled over from three planned volumes to sixteen; Pound realized his accreting *Cantos* "won't be finished until my demise"; Woolf found several of her novels "interminable" and hoped at the end of her life to be freed from the "orderly and expressed work of art; where one thing follows another and all are swept into a whole."

All of these acts of revision—these *modernist revisions*—are unpredictable and even unnecessary. They are wasteful of time and labor and serve no commercial purposes; in fact, they tended to prevent commercial success. For some writers, extreme acts of excision and addition seemed to develop an addictive, self-producing logic of their own—for example, Joyce revised the later chapter of *Ulysses* much more than the earlier chapters. Excision may begin as a way of tightening up a draft, and addition of providing one extra piece of detail but, pursued to their end point, both kinds of length-altering revision make texts less, not more, comprehensible; that is, they lead to a willfully disordered language or what, in *Godot*, Lucky calls "divine aphasia."[87] No responsible or even sane writing teacher or editor would have suggested these actions, although they might approve of the results. In this sense, there is an aleatory, chancy aspect to modernist revision: "it" was not always made new through an act of conscious control, and writers did not always give clear accounts of what they were doing.

In the second half of the twentieth century, writers have spoken forcefully and openly about their pleasure in revision, often subtly boosting the value of their work by referring to its genetic complexity. Despite his earlier hostility to second thoughts, this was Ginsberg's strategy for canonizing "Howl" alongside *The Waste Land.* In his interview with the *Paris Review,* Raymond Carver boasted, "I've done as many as twenty or thirty drafts of a story. Never less than ten or twelve drafts" and then referred to Tolstoy, "I'm thinking of the photographs of galleys belonging to Tolstoy, to name one writer who loved to revise. I mean, I don't know if he loved it or not, but he did a great deal of it. He was always revising, right down to the time of page proofs." In one sense this might be simple self-aggrandizement ("I am as good as Tolstoy"), but it is worth noting that Carver, like Ginsberg, refers invidiously to the published facsimile proofs of an earlier writer. He is revising not only to make his own work better, but because revising a lot turns out to be something that famous writers do. *The Waste Land* might have suggested that new poetry had to be difficult to become canonical, but Eliot could equally have quipped: "Poets, in our civilization, as it exists at present, must revise." This, at any rate, was the lesson that later writers drew.

Even though we have moved a long way from the print culture that sustained the modernist practice of multiple reseeing and endless revision, this axiom seems still to have power: it is rare to find writers or writing teachers (increasingly these are the same person) who advocate the power of not revising. And yet revision is a feature of print culture, of the modern printed book. A large number of discrete textual stages fosters rereading and reworking. Those happily old-fashioned writers who continue to work in analogue forms in a digital age may have recognized this: Jorie Graham, who described herself spending "ninety percent of my time in revision. It's a craziness," continues, importantly, to write by hand, "in ink," and uses a computer only "like a fancy typewriter." Those who migrate to a digital world where, in Mark Poster's memorable formulation, "cultural objects have no more fixity than liquid," may find that textual revision ceases to have meaning.[88]

If it is more difficult to instantiate revision in digital media, it is also more difficult to revise. By "writing over" yesterday's words with to-day's, we are destroying yesterday's version; when we write in Microsoft Word, we write in a continual textual present. As a result, the possibility of true "relecture tardive"—the kind of forgetful, self-critical rereading that Valéry saw as underpinning revision—becomes much less likely.[89] It is harder to become estranged from a text that looks as if it could have been written today than one in a younger self's handwriting or on fusty old paper. And, if texts morph easily and freely from one textual stage to the next, some of the urgency of making changes is lost. Sylvia Beach and James's writer-hero Dencombe both spoke of revision as resting on sacrifice. Beach spent inordinate amounts of time and money to allow Joyce to keep revising, while Dencombe speaks of giving up the achieved first edition of his book for a hypothetical second. "His ideal would have been to publish secretly, and then, on the published text, treat himself to the terrified revise, sacrificing always a first edition and beginning for posterity and even for the collectors, poor dears, with a second." In a world where revision becomes effectively free, and where it makes less sense to speak of discrete textual versions than a continual, smooth tex-tual flow, the inadequate final form loses much of its terror. In print cul-ture, revision pointed to the simultaneous fluidity and stability of texts. The very possibility of subsequent editions suggests that texts are muta-ble over time, but the infrequent spacing of these editions and their physi-cal durability as books means that any single version is, for a time, fixed. The text that Dencombe is beginning to alter could endure in its previous form in the libraries of retentive collectors, and that is part of his fear.

In the future, the tools that promise to allow us to "track changes" in digital documents might seem little more than a strange anachronism. Early printed books retained unnecessary but conventional features from manuscript culture—a hierarchy of scripts; red and blue colored letters to aid reading; strokes marking the beginning and end of sen-tences.[90] We may also be clinging to outmoded notions of what text *is*. Specifically, we are carrying forward from print the idea that texts pres-ent themselves in discrete versions. The polarity between the draft and the "final form," the idiosyncratic authorial manuscript and the homog-enous book, came into existence fairly rapidly after the invention of printing. By the beginning of the sixteenth century, authors were filing complaints against printers for making mistakes. In 1529, Thomas More compiled a list of "the fawtes escaped in the pryntynge" in the first edition of his *Dyalogue*.[91] The following year he took the opportunity not only to correct these apparent mistakes but to add a certain amount of new material; the second edition of 1530, "newly oversene by said syr Thomas More," is one of the first examples of an authorially revised book.

The modernist practice of revision began in the service of avant-garde action, but it was perhaps also an exploration of the limit point of print culture, the final flowering of composition through documented paper stages. Describing the excess of authorial evidence that survives from the last two centuries, David Greetham has suggested that "the pre-book manuscript riches of recent times may turn out to have been a brief anomaly in the history of textual evidence" and he asks if the electronic age might end up resembling the classical and medieval periods "in terms of its access to the finished product alone rather than the process of composition."[92] In the modernist period, the age of the typewriter, the manuscript draft stood at several remediations from the printed book and the distinction between final form and malleable process was particularly robust. Those writers who were willing to work without much commercial gain, through multiple drafts and sendings of proofs, revised their work as it passed through each medium and stage, leaving us with an enormous amount of fossilized paper evidence. By comparison, an oral poet can change a name or word in each performance, to fit the context, but never needs to iterate toward a definitive single version, and a writer producing born-digital poetry or fiction can censor or alter an already active work without leaving any traces of the action. From this perspective, a perfectionist and teleological attitude toward revision begins to look more like material conservatism than a means of making work new. "Constant" or "endless" or "passionate" revision shares something in common with the current fetish for refitted manual typewriters.[93] It is an exercise in nostalgia—an attempt to keep hold of the solidity of print.

Notes

Introduction

1. The Princeton Writing Program distributes a guide to college students that begins by arguing against romantic spontaneity: "There is a myth that great writers just sit down at the typewriter, or hunch over a café table, and write brilliantly just by recording what comes to mind. . . . In truth, good writing always involves revision." http://web.princeton.edu/sites/writing/Writing_Center/handouts/html/Revision .htm.

2. Tim Tomlinson emphasizes "deep revision" in *The Portable MFA in Creative Writing,* published by the New York Writers Workshop (Cincinnati: Writers' Digest Books, 2006), 10; Tom Kealey advises applicants to discuss their work with revision in *The Creative Writing MFA Handbook: A Guide for Prospective Graduate Students* (New York: Continuum, 2007), 65, 68. Illustrating the extreme value placed on the term, the Spalding MFA program claims on its home page that "In the Spalding MFA Program, the word revision applies not only to writing but to the Program itself," http://spalding.edu/academics/mfa-in-writing/questions-to-ask-when-seeking -an-mfa-program/.

3. In an interview with Robert Birnbaum, "Birnbaum v. Joyce Carol Oates," *The Morning News,* February 3, 2005, http://www.themorningnews.org/archives/personalities /birnbaum_v_joyce_carol_oates.php.

4. In "At Work," an interview with Thessaly La Force for the *Paris Review,* October 14, 2010, http://www.theparisreview.org/blog/2010/10/14/michael-cunningham/.

5. In Charles Simic, "The Art of Poetry no. 90," interview with Mark Ford for the *Paris Review,* Spring 2005, http://www.theparisreview.org/interviews/5507/the-art -of-poetry-no-90-charles-simic.

6. Elena Moya, "Brick Lane's Monica Ali Aims to Finish New Book by Summer," Reuters, February 13, 2008, http://in.reuters.com/article/2008/02/13/idININdia -31929320080213.

7. Alastair Fowler, *How to Write* (Oxford: Oxford University Press, 2006), 136.

8. In the initial holograph draft from May 1926, Woolf had simply used the associative metonymic technique that she criticized in "Modern Fiction" to reveal Mrs. Ramsay's death, writing of "the brush & comb left on the dressing table, for all the world as if she expected to come back tomorrow" (175). The holograph draft and October/November 1926 typescript (produced for Charles Mauron to be translated into French), are available at woolfonline.com. In the typescript, the passage begins "There were boots and shoes there, and a brush and comb left on the dressing table for all the world as if she expected to come back to-morrow. (She had died very sudden at the end, they said.)" (16). http://www.woolfonline.com/?q=typescript/transcription/page16.

9. Fanny Kemble, who also disliked Tennyson's revisions, admitted in later life, "In justice to Tennyson, I must add that the present generation of his readers swear by *their* version of his poems as we did by ours, for the same reason,—they knew it first." These contemporary responses are considered among others by Thomas R. Lounsbury, *The Life and Times of Tennyson* (New Haven: Yale University Press, 1915), 397–400.

10. Philip Horne details the whole array of James's hopes and disappointments with this collected edition, *Henry James and Revision: The New York Edition* (Oxford: Clarendon, 1990), 2–3.

11. In the 1930s, for example, she remembered working at "that interminable Night and Day" as an "exercise in the conventional style" necessary to produce experimental work. Quentin Bell, *Virginia Woolf: A Biography* (Orlando: Harvest, 1972), 42. Hermione Lee comments that Woolf referred to *The Years*, "only half-jokingly, as 'interminable.'" *Virginia Woolf* (New York: Vintage, 1999), 639.

12. Warwick Gould gives a rich account of Yeats's revisions, noting how he responded to bibliographic opportunity, and describing his process of rereading. "Writing the Life of the Text: The Case of W. B. Yeats," *Miscellanea: A Journal of English and American Studies* 30 (2004): 9–34, 9. Yeats commented that the poet is "never the bundle of accident and incoherence that sits down to breakfast; he has been reborn as an idea; something intended, complete."

13. Henry James, "The Middle Years," *Scribner's Magazine,* May 1893, and published with revisions in *Terminations* (London: Heinemann, 1895) and again, with further revisions, in volume 16 of the New York Edition, *The Author of Beltraffio, The Middle Years, Greville Fane, and Other Tales* (New York: Scribner's, 1909). Unless stated otherwise, I give page references to the first book edition, here 172. See the detailed discussion of the variant texts of "The Middle Years" in chapter 2.

14. Christopher Ricks, *Allusion to the Poets* (Oxford: Oxford University Press, 2002), 9.

15. Jed Rasula comments "Pound's—or Tching Tang's—adage has populated countless accounts of modernism, and it may be the most frequently repeated quip of the early twentieth century." He also notes that it is vaguely anachronistic—not formulated until the 1934 Make It New. See J. Rasula, *Make It New, Modernism/modernity* 17.4 (2010): 713–733, 713.

16. "Tching prayed on the mountain and/ wrote MAKE IT NEW/ on his bath tub/ Day by day make it new/ cut underbrush,/ pile the logs/ keep it growing." Ezra Pound, *Canto* 53, *The Cantos of Ezra Pound* (New York: New Directions, 1970), 264–265.

17. Kurt Heinzelman, *Make It New: The Rise of Modernism* (Austin: Harry Ransom Research Center, 2003), 132.

18. Vincent Sherry, *The Great War and the Language of Modernism* (Oxford: Oxford University Press, 2003), 213.

19. Pierre Bourdieu, *The Rules of Art: Genesis and Structure of the Literary Field,* trans. Susan Emanuel (Stanford: Stanford University Press, 1996), 8–9.

20. For Georg Lukács, *Ulysses* is the prime example of antihistorical thinking in modernism ("reflecting a belief in the basically static character of events"), "The Ideology of Modernism," in *Realism in Our Time: Literature and the Class Struggle* (New York: Harper and Row, 1962), 17–46, 18; for Fredric Jameson, "the archetypal emblem of the process of episodization in modernism," "The Existence of Italy," *Signatures of the Visible* (New York: Routledge, 1992), 155–230, 207; for T. S. Eliot, most famously, it was "the book to which we are all indebted, and from which none of us can escape," "Ulysses, Order, and Myth," in Frank Kermode, ed., *Selected Prose of T. S. Eliot* (New York: Harcourt, 1975), 175–178, 175. The essay was first published in *The Dial* 75.5 (November 1923).

21. "A critical edition of *The Cantos* is not very likely for the present or the immediate future, and for some time beyond as well," Lawrence S. Rainey, introduction, *A Poem Containing History: Textual Studies in The Cantos* (Ann Arbor: University of Michigan Press, 1996), 8.

22. John Bryant's study of textual fluidity, his insistence on "reading the differences between the versions" (57), and his acknowledgment that "versions are revisions" (89) have been significant contributions to Anglo-American textual scholarship. *The Fluid Text: A Theory of Revision and Editing for Book and Screen* (Ann Arbor: University of Michigan Press, 2002).

23. I discuss Christine Froula's 1977 dissertation and subsequent book *To Write Paradise: Style and Error in Pound's Cantos* (New Haven: Yale University Press, 1984) in the next chapter. In 2005, writing on Hugh Kenner's *The Pound Era,* she described the process of discovering the peculiarity of Pound's attitude toward error, "As I pondered the gaps between Pound's and his editors' stances toward error in his 'poem including history'—a history inseparable from error as from epic wandering *(errare)*—I came to see that error, chance, fallibility, divagation are inwoven in Pound's epic 'record of struggle' in ways that illuminate the historical conditions of modern art and thought.' " "Reading Modernism, After Hugh Kenner (1923–2003): Hugh Kenner's Modernism and Ours," *Modernism/modernity* 12.3 (2005): 471–475, 473.

24. Stephen Crook, "Auden on the Record," *The W. H. Auden Society Newsletter* 6 (1990), http://www.audensociety.org/06newsletter.html.

25. James asks what the artistic meaning of "large, loose baggy monsters" might be in the preface to *The Tragic Muse* (New York: Scribner's, 1908). Eliot inveighs in his "Vers Libre" essay against sloppy tendencies in post-Imagist ("Amygist") verse and implicitly promoting the "hard" Gautier-influenced quatrains that he had begun to write.

26. Vladimir Nabokov makes this claim in the (revised) autobiography *Speak, Memory: An Autobiography Revisited* (New York: Random House, 1966); the Capote quotation is quoted in Lawrence Grobel's *Conversations with Capote* (New York: Da Capo, 2000), 205; John Irving is quoted in a 2005 National Book Award interview. See Richard Nordquist, "Writers on Rewriting," http://grammar.about.com/od/advicefromthepros/a/rewritequotes.htm, February, 2012.

27. Mark McGurl, *The Program Era* (Cambridge: Harvard University Press, 2009), 244.

28. This is Propertius 3.1.8. See Timothy Wiseman's discussion of the use of the pumice-stone as a familiar metaphor for literary craftsmanship; he also claims that *tenuis* is the usual translation of the Callimachean *leptos* (slender) in Propertius's generation. *Clio's Cosmetics: Three Studies in Greco-Roman Literature* (Bristol: Phoenix Press, 2003), 169–170.

29. Sigmund Freud, "A Note upon the 'Mystic Writing Pad'" (1925), in *The Penguin Freud Library,* vol. 2, *On Metapsychology: The Theory of Psychoanalysis* (London: Penguin, 1984), 428–434.

30. Jacques Derrida, "The Word Processor," *Paper Machine* (Stanford: Stanford University Press, 2005), 19–32, 23.

31. Cecelia Tichi, *Shifting Gears: Technology, Literature, Culture in Modernist America* (Chapel Hill: University of North Carolina Press, 1987), 71. Tichi also suggests that "The poem itself offers no alternative world and no possibility of redemption, not even implicitly"; I argue for the opposite claim.

32. The first quotation is from Henry James, preface to "The Altar of the Dead," in the New York Edition, reprinted in *The Art of the Novel* (Boston: Northeastern University Press, 1984), 257. The second is from Ezra Pound, "The Serious Artist, IV," *New Freewoman* 1.11 (November 15, 1913): 213–214.

33. I do not write about *Dubliners* in detail. See Derek Attridge for the claim that the use of free indirect discourse in "Eveline" ("words and phrases more appropriate to her limited mental world") is attributable to revision. "Reading Joyce," in Attridge, ed., *The Cambridge Companion to James Joyce* (Cambridge: Cambridge University Press, 2004), 1–27, 26.

34. Lejeune's essay "Autogenesis: Genetic Studies of Autobiographical Texts," in Deppman, Ferrer, Groden, eds., *Genetic Criticism: Texts and Avant-Textes,* 193–217, 195, and republished in Philippe Lejeune, *On Diary,* ed. Jeremy D. Popkin and Julie Rak (Honolulu: University of Hawaii Press, 2009), 213–236, 214.

1. Textual Criticism, the History of Revision, and Genetic Reading

1. David Greetham, *Textual Scholarship: An Introduction* (New York and London: Garland, 1992), 297.

2. Jerome McGann, *A Critique of Modern Textual Criticism* (Chicago and London: University of Chicago Press, 1983), 57.

3. Roland Barthes's formulation, quoted by Dennis Dutton, who shows how easy the shift was—on this issue at least—from New Criticism to high theory, *The Art Instinct: Pleasure, Beauty, and Human Evolution* (New York: Bloomsbury, 2009), 168–169.

4. Natania Rosenfeld is discussing the description of Rachel's journey upriver in *The Voyage Out, Outsiders Together: Virginia and Leonard Woolf* (Princeton: Princeton University Press, 2000), 32.

5. See, for example, Alison Booth, who compares Woolf and George Eliot as producers of a "feminist revision of history," *Greatness Engendered: George Eliot and Virginia Woolf* (Ithaca: Cornell University Press, 1992), 4.

6. Karyn Z. Sproles is comparing Leslie Stephen's and Woolf's account of Charlotte Brontë, *Desiring Women: The Partnership of Virginia Woolf and Vita Sackville-West* (Toronto University of Toronto Press, 2006), 124.

7. Gabrielle McIntire comments on Woolf's "revision of conventional biographic modes," *Modernism, Memory, and Desire: T. S. Eliot and Virginia Woolf* (Cambridge: Cambridge University Press, 2007), 138.

8. Susan Stanford Friedman argues that this revision can be understood through James Clifford's opposition between dwelling and travel, *Mappings: Feminism and the Cultural Geographies of Encounter* (Princeton: Princeton University Press, 1998), 121.

9. Zachary Leader opposes this to "metaphorical revisions, or revision in the Bloomian or intertextual sense," *Revision and Romantic Authorship* (Oxford: Clarendon, 1996), 16.

10. David Crystal's definition of "repair," which can be both a noun and a verb in *A Dictionary of Language and Phonetics,* 6th ed. (Oxford: Blackwell, 2008), 413.

11. These were the second of six total sets of proofs: see Hans Walter Gabler's textual note on "Calypso," *Ulysses: A Critical and Synoptic Edition,* ed. Hans Walter Gabler with Wolfhard Steppe and Claus Melchior (New York: Garland, 1984), vol. 3, 1731, and for the reading, the synoptic text in vol. 1, 108. The first version of the text was published in *The Little Review* in June 1918, 39–52, 39.

12. Compare Henry James's revision of his well-received earlier work. One anonymous reviewer of *The American* praised the novel precisely for its success *as* a novel: "James has made a very near approach to a thoroughly successful novel, the nearest approach by any American for a very long time." Anonymous reviewer, "Our Boston Literary Letter," *Republican,* May 31, 1877, 3, reprinted in *Henry James: A Reference Guide,* ed. Linda J. Taylor (Boston: G. K. Hall, 1982), 15.

13. Mimi Schwartz, "Revision Profiles: Patterns and Implications," *College English* 45.6 (1983): 549–558, 551, 552, 553.

14. Ernest de Selincourt, ed., *The Prelude or Growth of a Poet's Mind,* 48–49.

15. The story is reported by Grace Schulman, "Conversation with Marianne Moore," *Quarterly Review of Literature,* 16.1–2 (1969): 154–171, 160–161.

16. G. Thomas Tanselle, "The Editorial Problem of Final Authorial Intention," *Studies in Bibliography* 29 (1976): 167–211, 193.

17. Wayne Booth also comments on the shift in narrative perspective and the possibility that the epiphanies in the satirical *Stephen Hero* are supposed to be read ironically, *The Rhetoric of Fiction* (Chicago: University of Chicago Press, 1983), 332.

18. See, for example, the account given by Gregory Nagy in *Homer's Text and Language* (Champaign: University of Illinois Press, 2004), 60–66. Committed to the orality of

Homer's text, Nagy describes Aristarchus's work as illustrating the essential "multi-formity" of Homer's text.

19. Housman's talk given in 1921 was published in the *Proceedings of the Classical Association,* accessible online at http://www.umass.edu/wsp/methodology/philology/housman/complete.pdf, 1–8, 1.

20. Jerome McGann, *A Critique of Modern Textual Criticism,* 56–57.

21. Prefaces reprinted in Samuel Johnson, ed., *The Plays of William Shakespeare.* Vol. 1 (London, 1765), xci and cxii.

22. Christine Froula's 1984 book is divided into two halves; the first attends to the genetic process before publication, and the second to editorial issues, 140. The book is based on her 1977 dissertation, *Groundwork for an Edition of* The Cantos *of Ezra Pound,* University of Chicago.

23. When he was asked for permission to include "September 1, 1939" and "Spain, 1937" in a 1964 anthology, *Poetry of the Thirties,* he agreed, but only on one condition: the editor must make it clear that "Mr. W. H. Auden considers [these poems] to be trash which he is ashamed to have written," Robin Skelton, *Poetry of the Thirties* (Harmondsworth: Penguin, 1964). Skelton describes this act as "monumentally generous" in his introduction.

24. Kathryn Sutherland is writing with specific reference to Walter Scott, but this situation persisted throughout the nineteenth century—one reason why we have so few manuscripts of James's novels, "Made in Scotland: The Edinburgh Edition of the Waverly Novels," *Text* 14 (2002): 305–323, 315.

25. See William Beatty Warner, *Licensing Entertainment: The Elevation of Novel Reading in Britain, 1684–1750* (Berkeley and Los Angeles: University of California Press, 1994), 208–210.

26. "Both classical and modern editors work toward their ideal texts by a process of recension that aims to approximate the Ideal as closely as possible. Both are termini ad quem which, though not strictly reachable, enable the critic to isolate and remove accumulated error." Jerome McGann, *A Critique of Modern Textual Criticism,* 56–57.

27. Zachary Lesser suggests that the new revisionists' desire to attribute all textual variation to authorial revision might, in part, be understood as "a conservative reaction against the death of the author," in *Renaissance Drama and the Politics of Publication: Readings in the English Book Trade* (Cambridge: Cambridge University Press, 2004), 14.

28. René Weis comments in a footnote to his facing-page edition that "F's version, with its more subjective emphasis (initially) on *age* death, and unburdening, stresses the firmness of Lear's intention. F reserves the political import of Lear's division of the kingdom till the end of the speech," *King Lear: A Parallel Text Edition,* 2nd ed. (Longman: Harlow, 2010), 83.

29. See W. L. Lorimer, "Lecto Difficilior." *Classical Review* 48 5(1934): 171–173.

30. I discuss this example in more detail in my discussion of "The Middle Years" in chapter 2.

31. See Paola Pugliatti's account in "Textual Perspectives in Italy: From Pasquali's Historicism to the Challenge of 'Variantistica' (and Beyond)," *Text* 11 (1998): 155–188.

32. Peter Shillingsburg suggests that Anglo-American textual criticism has tended to give less attention to revision than German editorial theory because it derives from work with Shakespeare's texts rather than Goethe's. "About Shakespeare's methods of composition and revision we know nothing; about Goethe's we know a great deal," *From Gutenberg to Google* (Cambridge: Cambridge University Press, 2006), 176.

33. Fredson Bowers, *On Editing Shakespeare* (Philadelphia: University of Pennsylvania Library, 1955), 57.

34. Jonathan Bate quotes the passage and argues that "according to Jonson's Horatian poetics, this absence of 'blots' was a deficiency, not a strength," *The Genius of Shakespeare* (London: Picador, 1997), 27.

35. Boswell tells this story in a footnote after describing Johnson's fearful response to the ghost in *Hamlet*. James Boswell, *Boswell's Life of Johnson* (London: H. Baldwin, 1799), 81. Until the early twentieth century, texts issued posthumously, or in subsequent editions, frequently advertised themselves as "revised by" rather than "edited." Samuel Singer advertised his 1856 edition of Shakespeare's plays as "The Dramatic Works of William Shakespeare/ The Text Completely Revised, With Notes, and Variant Readings," Preface, *The Dramatic Works of William Shakespeare* (London: Bell and Daldy, 1856).

36. Samuel Johnson gives two meanings for the noun *revise*, of which the second relates clearly to print culture. 1) "review, reexamination," 2) "Among printers a second proof of the sheet corrected," *A Dictionary of the English Language,* 3rd ed. (described as carefully revised) (Dublin: W. G. Jones, 1768).

37. "revise, n." *The Oxford English Dictionary,* 2nd ed., 1989. *OED Online,* Oxford University Press, May 7, 2008, http://dictionary.oed.com.ezp2.harvard.edu/cgi/entry/50205483.

38. In *Lives of the Poets,* quoted by Marcus Walsh, *Shakespeare, Milton, & Eighteenth-Century Literary Editing: The Beginnings of Interpretive Scholarship* (Cambridge: Cambridge University Press, 1997), 66.

39. Bentley's 1732 preface to *Milton's Paradise Lost,* online at http://andromeda.rutgers.edu/~jlynch/Texts/Bentley/preface.html.

40. Edmond Malone, preface, *The Plays and Poems of Shakespeare in Ten Volumes* (London: H. Baldwin, 1790), xiii.

41. See the introduction to Samuel Taylor Coleridge and William Wordsworth, *Lyrical Ballads 1798 and 1800,* ed. Michael Gamer and Dahlia Porter (Peterborough: Broadview Press, 2008), 15–37.

42. William St. Clair, "Publishing, Authorship, and Reading," in *The Cambridge Companion to Fiction of the Romantic Period,* ed. Richard Maxwell and Katie Trumpener (Cambridge: Cambridge University Press, 2008), 22–46, 26.

43. Randy Robertson discusses the link between censorship, publication rate, and copyright in this period, *Censorship and Conflict in Seventeenth Century England: The Subtle Art of Division* (University Park: Pennsylvania State University Press, 2009), 202–204.

44. Dirk van Hulle makes this point in his discussion of editing, nation-building, and authors' manuscript habits. He argues that European editors around the period of the French Revolution were becoming preoccupied with a desire to "fix" old texts as

part of a project of nationalism, writers themselves were paying renewed attention to process rather than product, "A Darwinian Change in European Editorial Thinking," *European Studies* 26 (2008): 31–43.

45. "The personal trace of an individual creation" is quoted from de Biasi. Laurent Jenny and Richard Watts, "Genetic Criticism and Its Myths," *Yale French Studies* 89 (1996): 9–25, 16.

46. Percy Bysshe Shelley, "A Defence of Poetry," *Essays, Letters from Abroad, Translations and Fragments,* ed. Mary Shelley (Philadelphia: Lea and Blanchard, 1840), 56.

47. Coleridge's account of the origin is quoted in *Selected Poems by Samuel Taylor Coleridge,* ed. William Empson and David Pirie (New York: Routledge, 2002), 248.

48. David Perkins's rephrasing of something that Elizabeth Schneider remarks, "The Imaginative Vision of *Kubla Khan:* On Coleridge's Introductory Note," in Harold Bloom, ed., *Samuel Taylor Coleridge* (New York: Infobase, 2010), 39–50, 39.

49. See Zachary Leader, who notes that this wasn't simply an affect; Byron did revise very little, *Revision and Romantic Authorship,* 78–84. Denise Gigante makes a further link between Byron's interest in unstudied writing and organic form, *Life: Organic Form and Romanticism* (Yale: Yale University Press, 2009), 4–5.

50. Letter to John Murray, September 18, 1820, quoted in *Byron's Letters and Journals,* vol. 7, ed. Leslie A. Marchand (Cambridge: Harvard University Press, 1978), 229.

51. See the chapter on "Manufacturing" in William St Clair, *The Reading Nation in the Romantic Period* (Cambridge: Cambridge University Press, 2004), 181–182.

52. Jack Stillinger, *Coleridge and Textual Instability: The Multiple Versions of the Major Poems* (Oxford: Oxford University Press, 1994), 107.

53. William Wordsworth, Preface, *The Excursion, Being a Portion of "The Recluse," A Poem* (London: Longman, Hurst, Rees, Orme, and Brown, 1814), vi–xiv, viii.

54. Thomas R. Lounsbury, *The Life and Times of Tennyson,* 397–400.

55. "The Malady of Revision," *The Atlantic Monthly* 85.507 (January 1900): 140–141.

56. This is a misquotation. Describing Byron's poetry approvingly, Landor wrote "Tho' hemp and flax and cotton are the stronger for being twisted, verses and intellects certainly are not." In this letter, he actually praises Byron for being "very assiduous in correcting his verses," suggesting that it was this carefulness that produces an effect of spontaneity ("he seems negligent in many places"). Letter to Mrs. Paynter, August 3, 1845, in Stephen Wheeler, ed., *Letters of Walter Savage Landor* (London: Duckworth, 1899), 145.

57. William St. Clair gives a clear account of both the material process and its economic consequences, *The Reading Nation in the Romantic Period,* 182–185.

58. Edmund Wilson, *Axel's Castle: A Study in Imaginative Literature of 1870–1930,* (New York and London: Charles Scribner's Sons, 1931), 1–2.

59. Edward Mendelson lays out this useful dichotomy in "Revision and Power: The Example of W. H. Auden," *Yale French Studies* 89 (1996): 103–112.

60. Letter to William Carlos Williams, May 21, 1909, in D. D. Paige, ed., *The Selected Letters of Ezra Pound, 1907–1941* (New York: New Directions, 1950), 8.

61. The full verse is quoted in *The Selected Letters of Ezra Pound,* 170.

62. Henry James, Preface, *The Golden Bowl,* xiii–xiv.

63. Although this description introduces *The Golden Bowl,* James also tells us that his more recent novels have required relatively little alteration. It is his earlier work that presents a more "frequent lapse of harmony between my present mode of motion and that to which the existing footprints were due."

64. Julie Rivkin, "Doctoring the Text," *Henry James's New York Edition: The Construction of Authorship,* ed. David McWhirter (Stanford: Stanford University Press, 1995), 142–163, 146.

65. From Ezra Pound's *Selected Prose,* 1911, quoted by Daniel Albright, *Quantum Poetics: Yeats, Pound, Eliot, and the Science of Modernism* (Cambridge and New York: Cambridge University Press, 1997), 134–135.

66. Fredric Jameson, *Postmodernism, or, The Cultural Logic of Late Capitalism* (Durham: Duke University Press, 1991), 12.

67. Nicola Trott comments that "the experience of seeing the manuscripts of Milton's early works is couched as a textual "fall" after the paradigm of *Paradise Lost.*" "Milton and the Romantics," in *A Companion to Romanticism,* ed. Duncan Wu (Oxford: Blackwell, 1998), 520–534, 532.

68. Susan Gubar, introduction to Virginia Woolf, *A Room of One's Own* (New York: Harvest, 2005), xliv.

69. This may not have been entirely because in his own case (as opposed to Milton's) he imagined the original version sacrosanct but because of his social and collaborative view of authorship, formed during his work with Coleridge in the 1790s. Here he sees altering each other's work as a friendly, although power-based, form of interchange. "If I offer alterations of my own to your poetry, & admit not yours in mine, it is upon the principle of a present to a rich man being graciously accepted, & the same present to a poor man being consider'd as in insult," quoted by Alison Hickey, "Charles Lamb's Romantic Collaborations," *ELH* 63.6 (Fall 1996): 735–771, 740–741. As the inferior member of the partnership, Lamb proposes neither to revise his own work nor to receive suggestions (punning on his own name, he begs "spare my ewe-lambs!") but to act as Coleridge's editor.

70. Andrew Kappel, "Complete with Omissions: The Text of Marianne Moore's *Complete Poems,*" in George Bornstein's interesting collection of essays *Representing Modernist Texts* (Ann Arbor: University of Michigan Press, 1991), 125–156, 144.

71. See Christine Froula's discussion of the relationship between Pound's errors, his understanding of historical process, and his sense of the history of his own text, *Style and Error in Pound's Cantos,* 147–160. She cites the 1937 letter, printed in *Selected Letters,* 293. Jerome McGann discusses the *Cantos* as a "poem including bibliography," in *The Textual Condition* (Princeton: Princeton University Press, 1991), 129–152.

72. Simon Eliot, "The Business of Victorian Publishing," in *The Cambridge Companion to the Victorian Novel,* ed. Deirdre David (Cambridge: Cambridge University Press, 2001), 37–60, 58.

73. See Peter Shillingsburg, *From Gutenberg to Google,* 37–38.

74. Algernon Charles Swinburne, *The Swinburne Letters,* ed. Cecil Y. Lang (New Haven: Yale University Press, 1959), vol. 2, 1869–1875, 374.

75. "Printers Flatter Typewriters," *Typewriter Topics: The Office Equipment Magazine* 7.4 (December 1907): 266.

76. See Jospeh Leo Blotner, *Faulkner: A Biography* (Jackson: University Press of Mississippi, 2005), 268.

77. Ernest Hemingway, "The Art of Fiction No. 21," interview with George Plimpton, *Paris Review* 5 (1958): 60–89.

78. An anonymous article "Typewriter or Pen?" published in *The Author* in 1891 begins by explaining "Quite a lot of excitement has been caused of late in the literary and journalistic worlds by the decree sent forth from one of the largest receivers of manuscripts in the metropolis, to the effect that only typewritten copy would be read, all other to be returned without inspection." The rest of the article is devoted to contrasting the views of different editors, most of whom prefer the "plainness" of typewritten copy, finding it "easier to edit." See "Typewriter or Pen," *The Author: A Monthly Magazine for Literary Workers* 3 (1891): 65–66.

79. A clear description of the conventional process is provided by Dora Knowlton Ranous, *Good English in Good Form* (New York: Sturgis and Walton, 1916). See especially 230–232.

80. Cook and Wedderburn note that Ruskin's simple style is more studied than it seems, aided by "what publishers are apt to consider the greatest of literary vices, and what authors consider the costliest of indulgences—namely, a habit of rewriting in proof," Introduction to *The Complete Works of John Ruskin*, vol. 15, ed. E. T. Cook and Alexander Wedderburn (London: George Allen, 1904), xix.

81. Paul Valéry, "Note et digression" to the 1919 second edition of his *Introduction à la méthode de Léonard de Vinci* (Paris: Gallimard, 1992), 73.

82. W. H. Auden, *The Dyer's Hand and Other Essays* (New York: Vintage, 1968), 17.

83. Harry Parker Ward, "Author's Changes," *The College Annual Guide: A Book of Information and Suggestions Intended for Use by the Business Manager and Editor-in-Chief* (Columbus: Champlin, 1914), 85–86.

84. Jack London fell afoul of this rule with *The Sea-Wolf*. A first edition by Macmillan based on his original manuscript was followed by magazine publication and then a third version published as a regular book edition with "so many changes from my manuscript-version that I had to pay the cost of making the changes in the plate-proofs." Letter, quoted by John Sutherland in his "Note on the Text," Jack London, *The Sea-Wolf* (Oxford: Oxford University Press, 2000), xxxiii

85. Andreas Huyssen, *After the Great Divide* (Bloomington: Indiana University Press, 1986), vii.

86. See, for example, Kevin J. H. Dettmar and Stephen Watt, eds., *Marketing Modernisms: Self-Promotion, Canonization, and Rereading* (Ann Arbor: University of Michigan Press, 1996), which includes Timothy Materer's brilliant essay on Pound's marketing of Imagism, "Make It Sell! Ezra Pound Advertises Modernism," and Jennifer Wicke's discussion of the relationship between Woolf and Keynes, Bloomsbury and consumption in "Coterie Consumption: Bloomsbury, Keynes, and Modernism as Marketing." Mark Morrisson's study of modernist little magazines, *The Public Face of Modernism: Little Magazines, Audience, and Reception, 1905–1920*, argues against the idea that avant-garde writers sought coterie, elitist publication

and finds them instead engaging actively with modern techniques of advertising and distribution. One interesting suggestion is that Pound revised the early Cantos "into leaner, more focused works" after the experience of performing them at the Poetry Bookshop (77). The question of revision consequent on performance is worth additional study.

87. Lawrence Rainey, *Institutions of Modernism: Literary Elites and Public Culture,* 3.
88. "The last novel in three-volume format was probably published in 1897 . . . and with it came the end of the circulating library." Simon Gatrell, *Hardy the Creator: A Textual Biography* (Oxford: Clarendon, 1988), 5.
89. Rachel Ihara analyzes James's habits of serialization over his career, " 'Rather Rude Jolts': Henry James, Serial Novels, and the Art of Fiction," *Henry James Review* 31.2 (2010): 188–206.
90. See Philip Horne, *Henry James and Revision,* 1.
91. See the discussion of "two economic logics," Pierre Bourdieu, *The Rules of Art,* 142–146.
92. Sylvia Beach, *Shakespeare and Company* (reprinted University of Nebraska Press, 1991), 58–60.
93. Hans Walter Gabler has restored the name in his edition. Michael Groden tells the story of "trop tard" in his important and groundbreaking study *Ulysses in Progress* (Princeton: Princeton University Press, 1977), 165.
94. Paul Delany, "Who Paid for Modernism?" in *The New Economic Criticism,* ed. Martha Woodmansee and Mark Osten (London: Routledge, 1999), 286–299, 291.
95. Derek Attridge's whole piece, "Joyce's Pen," which begins by thinking about Daniel Ferrer's practical interview with Derrida, is of interest in understanding Joyce's assembling, sorting, and addition to his heterogeneous original notes, in *Joyce, Penelope and the Body,* ed. Richard Brown (Amsterdam: Rodolphi, 2006), 47–62, 54.
96. Virginia Woolf, *Three Guineas,* 1938 (New York: Harcourt, 2006), 116.
97. Jerome McGann, *Black Riders: The Visible Language of Modernism,* 17.
98. There is more work to be done on the institutions of *late* modernism, and particularly on the collapse of the twin institutions of patronage and little magazine/coterie publishing during the 1930s and afterward.
99. Sam Slote and Luca Crispi make this estimate in their introduction to *How Joyce Wrote Finnegans Wake: A-Chapter-by-Chapter Genetic Guide* (Madison: University of Wisconsin Press, 2007), 31.
100. Virginia Woolf, "A Sketch of the Past," in *Moments of Being,* ed. Jeanne Schulkind, 2nd ed. (London: Hogarth, 1985), 111.
101. See Hermione Lee, *Virginia Woolf,* 754.
102. Lawrence Rainey and Louis Menand, Introduction, *The Cambridge History of Literary Criticism VII: Modernism and the New Criticism* (Cambridge: Cambridge University Press, 2000), 1–16, 3.
103. The source of this often repeated quip is Richard Ellmann's biography, *James Joyce,* first published in 1959 and revised in 1982 (New York: Oxford University Press, 1983), 521.
104. David Greetham describes it as a "schism," *Theories of the Text* (Oxford: Oxford University Press, 1999), 3.

105. W. K. Wimsatt and Monroe C. Beardsley, "The Intentional Fallacy," in *The Verbal Icon: Studies in the Meaning of Poetry* (Lexington: University of Kentucky Press, 1954), 3–18, 3.

106. An anecdote recorded by Stephen Spender, "Remembering Eliot," in *T. S. Eliot: The Man and His Work,* ed. Allen Tate (New York: Delacorte, 1966), 42.

107. Daniel Ferrer notes that "the simplest set of instructions (the one that is at the basis of traditional philology) is generally not formulated in so many words"—i.e., anything that isn't crossed out comes with the expectation "include this" while "an erasure, a crossing out, or a *deleatur* on the margin" express "don't include this." He goes on to comment that some of Joyce's other visual ways of marking up his texts, like his "notorious coloured crayons," are slightly less easy to interpret, "Reflections on a Discarded Set of Proofs," *Genetic Studies in Joyce,* ed. Sam Slote (Amsterdam: Rodopi, 1995), 49–63.

108. Albert J. Frank, "Genetic Versus Clear Texts: Reading and Writing Emerson," *Documentary Evidence* 9.4 (1987): 5–9, 8.

109. McKenzie also discusses the printing and capitalization of the epigraph, and he makes a suggestion about the school edition of Congreve's plays that Wimsatt and Beardsley were likely using (edited by Nettle and Case). D. F. McKenzie, *Bibliography and the Sociology of Texts* (London: The British Library, 1986), 10–19.

110. Hershel Parker, *Flawed Texts and Verbal Icons: Literary Authority in American Fiction* (Chicago: Northwestern University Press, 1984), 214.

111. As John Bryant puts it, rather vividly, "a kind of janitorial closet out of which established texts are issued, buff and pretty, for others to interpret elsewhere in the full light of day, but a closet nonetheless where ideas themselves go darkly to die," *Melville Unfolding: Sexuality, Politics, and the Versions of Typee* (Ann Arbor: University of Michigan Press, 2008), 7.

112. W. W. Greg, *The Editorial Problem in Shakespeare: A Survey of the Foundations of the Text* (Oxford: Clarendon, 1942), x.

113. Edward Mendelson, Editor's Preface, *Collected Poems* 11–15, 11.

114. Fredson Bowers's description of the goal of textual criticism, to which he adds that "any revision" should also be included, *Principles of Textual Criticism* (San Marino: Huntington Library, 1972), 50.

115. Hans Walter Gabler, "A Tale of Two Texts," *Woolf Studies Annual* 10 (2004): 1–30, 5–6.

116. This point is discussed by Antoine Compagnon in *Literature, Theory, and Common Sense,* trans. Carol Cosman (Princeton: Princeton University Press, 2004), 56.

117. An early indication of this came in Peter Shillingsburg's 1991 article "Text as Matter, Concept, and Action": he asks whether the emphasis placed on versioning and process texts by Michael Warren, Paul Eggert, and Donald Reiman should be read as "an accommodation of structuralism" and a departure from the positivist traditions of New Bibliography, "Text as Matter, Concept, and Action," *Studies in Bibliography* 44 (1991): 31–82, 37.

118. Jerome McGann, *A Critique of Modern Textual Criticism.*

119. Robert Darnton, "What Is the History of Books?" *Daedalus* 111.3 (1982). Reprinted in *The Kiss of Lamourette: Reflections in Cultural History* (London: Norton, 1990), 107–135, 110.

120. The best-known modification, and the one that Darnton himself discusses, is by Thomas R. Adams and Nicholas Barker, published as "A New Model for the Study of the Book," in *A Potencie of Life: Books in Society,* ed. Nicholas Barker (London: British Library, 1993). See Robert Darnton, " 'What Is the History of Books?' Revisited," *Modern Intellectual History* 4.3 (2007): 495–508, 502.

121. Jerome McGann also describes "social-text editing" as a third alternative to "the Anglo-American critical eclecticism culminating in the Greg-Bowers school, and the European genetic methods developed by a line of German and French scholars of the mid and late century." "From Text to Work: Digital Tools and the Emergence of the Social Text," *Romanticism on the Net* 41–42 (2006), http://www.erudit.org/revue/ron/2006/v/n41-42/013153ar.html.

122. D. F. McKenzie, *Bibliography and the Sociology of Texts,* 28.

123. See de Selicnourt's introduction, in his *Wordsworth: The Prelude* xlvii–liii.

124. H. T. M. van Vliet, review of *Literarische Handschriften: Einführung in die "critique génétique"* by Almuth Grésillon, *Text* 14 (2002): 338–343, 338.

125. See Francois Dosse's *History of Structuralism,* vol. 2, trans. Deborah Glassman (Minneapolis: University of Minnesota Press, 1997), 367–369.

126. Cited in the introduction to Deppman, Ferrer, and Groden, eds., *Genetic Criticism,* 8. Daniel Ferrer argues that "the text is not produced by the author, but the author is produced by the text." Ferrer, "Production, Invention, and Reproduction."

127. Susan Stanford Friedman, "Spatialization: A Strategy for Reading Narrative," *Narrative* 1.1 (1993): 12–23, 18.

128. Laurent Jenny and Richard Watts, "Genetic Criticism and Its Myths," 198.

129. Paul Frank Bowman, "Genetic Criticism," *Poetics Today* 11.3 (1990): 627–646.

130. Antoine Compagnon, Introduction, *Romanic Review* 86.3 (1995): 393–401, 394.

131. Most of these were purchased, but Leonard Woolf also donated part of the original manuscript of *The Voyage Out.* See Ruth Gruber, *Virginia Woolf: The Will to Create as a Woman* (New York: Carroll and Graf, 2005), 161.

132. This is the self-narrated institutional history available in brief form on the center's web site, "History of the Rare Books Collection," http://www.hrc.utexas.edu /collections/books/info/.

133. Christine Froula, *To Write Paradise: Style and Error in Pound's Cantos,* 4.

134. Phillip Herring, *Joyce's Ulysses Notesheets in the British Museum* (Charlottesville: University Press of Virginia, 1972); Clive Driver, *Ulysses: The Manuscript and First Printings Compared* (London: Faber and Faber, 1975); Mark Schorer, *Sons and Lovers: A Facsimile of the Manuscript* (Berkeley: University of California Press, 1978); Louise De-Salvo, *Virginia Woolf's First Novel: A Voyage in the Making* (London: Macmillan, 1980).

135. See Michael Groden's reflections on the volumes in "Perplex in the Pen—and in the Pixels," *Journal of Modern Literature* 22.2 (1999): 225–244.

136. See Hans Walter Gabler's discussion of his method in "The *James Joyce Archive*: A Publisher's Gift to Joyce Studies," *Genetic Joyce Studies,* Summer 2002, http://www .antwerpjamesjoycecenter.com/JJAGabler.htm.

137. See Geoffrey Hartman, *Wordsworth's Poetry, 1787–1814,* 2nd ed. (New Haven: Yale University Press, 1971), xvii. The term *self-corrupting* was then used by Cynthia Chase and others as a summary of Hartman's position. See Cynthia Chase, "The

Accidents of Disfiguration," *Decomposing Figures: Rhetorical Readings in the Romantic Tradition* (Baltimore and London: John Hopkins University Press, 1986), 13–31, 21. Wayne Koestenbaum, "The Waste Land: T. S. Eliot's and Ezra Pound's Collaboration on Hysteria," *Twentieth Century Literature* 34.2 (1988): 113–139, 115.

138. Philippe Lejeune, "Autogenesis: Genetic Studies of Autobiographical Texts," 210. Richard Ellmann, "The First *Waste Land*," in *Eliot in His Time,* ed. A. Walton Litz (Princeton: Princeton University Press, 1973), 51–66, 63.

139. Finn Fordham, *I Do I Undo I Redo: The Textual Genesis of Modernist Selves* (Oxford: Oxford University Press, 2010), 26–27. Fordham's study illustrates the growing interest in genetic criticism among Anglophone critics. His own work focuses specifically on the relationship between processes of composition and formulations of selfhood during modernism, rather than on revision or composition in general.

140. Edmund Gosse, *Aspects and Impressions* (London and New York: Cassell, 1922), 47.

141. This is Richard Sieburth's description, but he admits reliance on Ronald Bush's thorough description of Pound's drafting process, *Ezra Pound: The Pisan Cantos* (New York: New Directions, 2003), xxxvi.

142. George Bornstein, *Material Modernism: The Politics of the Page* (Cambridge: Cambridge University Press, 2001). For the discussion of Yeats, see especially 46–50.

143. In his notes on "On First Looking into Chapman's Homer," *The Complete Works of John Keats,* vol. 1, ed. H. Buxton Forman (New York: Thomas Y. Crowell, 1817), 46.

144. See Franco Moretti, "Conjectures on World Literature," *New Left Review* 1.54 (January–February 2000), and available online, http://www.newleftreview.org/A2094.

145. The classic formulation is McKerrow's. R. B. McKerrow, *Prolegomena for the Oxford Shakespeare* (Oxford: Oxford University Press, 1939).

146. The genetic critic Pierre-Marc de Biasi describes the moment of *bon à tirer* (literally "good enough to be pulled") as "the decisive moment when what had been in a pliable and mobile manuscript state up to that point becomes fixed in the frozen shape of a published text," "What Is a Literary Draft? Toward a Functional Typology of Genetic Criticism," *Yale French Studies* 89 (1996): 26–58, 37. Commenting on the ubiquity of this metaphor, Dirk Van Hulle compares Goethe's description in *Dichtung und Warheit* of the moment when his text became "a solid mass, like water in a container on the verge of freezing, which by the smallest agitation is suddenly turned into ice" ("eine solide Masse, wie das Wasser im Gefäss, das eben auf dem Punkte des Gefrierens steht"). Rather than focusing on any particular kind of publication as the determining moment at which a text is fixed, I suggest that we view *all* forms of representation on paper—from early typescripts to late editions—as instances of fixity or arrest. See Dirk Van Hulle, "The Limited Edition Unlimited: Samuel Beckett's Fugal Artefact," *Variants 4* (2005): 133–150, 133.

2. Henry James's Perfectionism: Problems of Substitution

1. The introduction discusses some of these remarkable metaphors for revision as re-representation: they include retraversing a snowy field, cut paper applied to a shadow on the wall, and an aging brood of children in "superannuated garments." Henry James, preface, *The Golden Bowl,* v–xxv, xvi.

2. Edmund Gosse claimed that James had tried to cultivate the theatrically necessary qualities of "brevity and directness" for five years. He recalled visiting James after the "fiasco of *Guy Domville*," and being told, "At all events, I have escaped forever from the foul fiend Excision!" "Henry James," in *Aspects and Impressions* (London: Cassell, 1922), 17–54, 34.

3. Michael Anesko, *Friction with the Market* (Oxford and New York: Oxford University Press, 1986), 144.

4. The phrase is used in an unpublished letter to Howard Sturgis, August 5, 1914. I discuss the letter in more detail later in the chapter.

5. Published posthumously after being edited by Percy Lubbock as Henry James, *The Ivory Tower* (London: W. Collins, 1917) and *The Sense of the Past* (London: W. Collins, 1917).

6. Philip Horne, *Henry James and Revision*, 2–3.

7. See Michael Millgate, *Testamentary Acts* (Oxford: Clarendon, 1992), 90.

8. See the stimulating but brief discussion in Horne's final chapter, "Last Words," *Henry James and Revision*, 315.

9. Leon Edel discusses James's solution to his writing cramp in "Withdrawal from London," in Edel, ed., *Henry James: Letters,* vol. 4, 1895–1916 (Cambridge: Belknap-Harvard University Press, 1984), 4.

10. Leon Edel, introduction, *The Europeans: A Facsimile of the Manuscript*, ed. Leon Edel (New York: Howard Fertig, 1979), x, xii.

11. A. S. Byatt, "A Note on the Text," in Henry James, *The Bostonians* (New York: Random House, 2001), xxv.

12. See S. P. Rosenbaum's detailed reading of the differences, "'The Spoils of Poynton': Revisions and Editions," *Studies in Bibliography* 19 (1966): 161–174, 166.

13. Jay S. Spina and Joseph Spina have prepared a searchable PDF version of the two texts, showing deleted material in struck-out green and added material in underline brown font. http://www2.newpaltz.edu/~hathawar/WatchandWardVariorum.pdf.

14. Horne comments "but they had been," citing the letter to Ticknor, January 30, 1885 (Berg MS), 37.

15. Albert Frank Gegenheimer, "Early and Late Revisions in Henry James's 'A Passionate Pilgrim,'" *American Literature* 23.2 (May 1951): 233–242, especially 237–238.

16. Anthony J. Mazzella, "The New Isabel," reprinted in the Norton Critical Edition, Henry James, *The Portrait of a Lady,* ed. Robert D. Bamberg (New York: Norton, 1975), 597–619, 598.

17. Letter to Mrs. Dew-Smith, November 12, 1906, in Philip Horne ed., *Henry James: A Life in Letters* (London: Penguin, 1999), 442–443.

18. Henry James, *The American* (Boston: Houghton Mifflin, 1877), 19.

19. Henry James, *The American* (New York: Scribner's, 1907), 16.

20. The Norton Critical Edition prints a useful list of variants between the New York Edition texts (which it reprints) and the 1881 text in an appendix, 493–575.

21. See Norton Critical Edition 46.14–15 and appendix, 499.

22. F. O. Matthiessen, "The Painter's Sponge and Varnish Bottle," *Henry James: The Major Phase* (London: Oxford University Press, 1944), 152–186, 159.

23. See Norton Critical Edition, 237.43–238.6 and appendix, 534.

24. See Daniel N. Roselli, "Max Beerbohm's Unpublished Parody of Henry James," *Review of English Studies* 22.85 (1971): 61–63, 61.

25. W. H. Auden, "The Sea and the Mirror."

26. W. H. Auden, "The Art of Poetry No. 17," interview with Michael Newman, *Paris Review* 57 (1974).

27. Leon Edel, *Henry James: The Middle Years, 1882–1895* (Philadelphia and New York: Lippincott, 1962), 18.

28. Henry James, *The Portrait of a Lady* (Oxford: Oxford University Press, 1997).

29. Sharon Cameron has argued that Isabel's calculations about her future are self-reflexively pointless, for "recognition leads not to revelation but rather to psychic blackout," *Thinking in Henry James* (Chicago: University of Chicago Press, 1989), 61.

30. H. L. Jackson, *Marginalia: Readers Writing in Books* (New Haven and London: Yale University Press, 2001), 260–261.

31. William Makepeace Thackeray, *Vanity Fair,* ed. Peter Shillingsburg (New York: Norton, 1994), 6.

32. Recollected by John Berryman in "The Art of Poetry No. 16," interview with Peter A. Stitt, *Paris Review* 53 (Winter 1972).

33. This is the first sense of *prick*, according to the *Oxford English Dictionary (OED)*. The fourth sense includes some notions relating to writing, including "to write out changes in figures," but this is now listed as *"hist."* "prick, v." *The Oxford English Dictionary,* 2nd ed., 1989. *OED Online,* Oxford University Press, September 10, 2006, http://dictionary.oed.com.ezp2.harvard.edu/cgi/entry/50188418.

34. Charles Darwin, *The Expression of the Emotions in Man and Animals* (reprinted New York and Oxford: Oxford University Press, 1998), 310.

35. Charles Darwin, *The Expression of the Emotions in Man and Animals,* 321.

36. Julie Rivkin, "Revision and 'The Middle Years,'" 479. John Carlos Rowe argues that James repeatedly figures homoeroticism through "male characters' shared interests in literature," *The Other Henry James* (Durham and London: Duke University Press, 1998), 108.

37. Philip Roth, *The Ghost Writer* (New York: Farrar, Strauss, and Giroux, 1979), 116.

38. Joyce Carol Oates, "The Madness of Art: Henry James's 'The Middle Years,'" *New Literary History* 27.2 (1996): 259–262, 262.

39. Henry James, preface, *The Golden Bowl,* v–xxv, xvi.

40. In Jakobson's terms, he would be both addresser and addressee; in Darnton's communications circuit, he occupies both the first and last position, as author and reader.

41. "Thrift" is Foucault's term: "the author is a certain functional principle by which, in our culture, one limits, excludes, and chooses." Michel Foucault, "What Is an Author?" *Book History Reader,* 225–230, 230.

42. Gregory Vlastos, *Studies in Greek Philosophy* vol. 2 (Princeton: Princeton University Press, 1995), 188.

43. "The Middle Years" (1893) was first published in the May volume of *Scribner's Magazine.* Collected in bound volumes as vol. 12 of *Scribner's Magazine,* 609–620, 620.

44. Henry James, "The Middle Years," New York Edition, vol. 16 (New York: Scribner's, 1909), 97.

45. The first entry for *something* in the *OED* is "Some unspecified or indeterminate thing (material or immaterial)." "something, n. 1ᵃ." *Oxford English Dictionary,* 2nd ed., 1989. *OED Online,* Oxford University Press, September 10, 2006, http://dic tionary.oed.com.ezp2.harvard.edu/cgi/entry/50230631.

46. Henry Wadsworth Longfellow, *The Courtship of Miles Standish, Longfellow: The Complete Poetical Works,* ed. Horace E. Scudder (Boston and New York: Houghton Mifflin, 1893), 164–184, 167.

47. Edmund Gosse, *Aspects and Impressions,* 47.

48. Letter to Edmund Gosse, August 25, 1915, in Leon Edel, ed., *Henry James: Letters,* vol. 4, 776–778, 776.

49. J. Stephen Murphy argues that James realized the idea of a collected works was self-defeating, for the edition "runs the risk of turning that work into a physical object, designed to sit on a shelf, like an author's bust." In "Revision as a 'Living Affair' in Henry James's New York Edition," *Henry James Review* 29.2 (2008): 163–180, 170.

50. Letter to Mrs. Cadwalader Jones, October 23, 1902, in Edel, ed., *Henry James: Letters,* vol. 4, 245–247.

51. Leon Edel, *Henry James: A Life* (New York: Harper and Row, 1985), 456.

52. Sarah Campbell begins by arguing that James's practice blurs normal distinctions between "written" and "oral" and gives a useful history of the literature trying to relate James's late style to his practice of dictation. See "The Man Who Talked Like a Book, Wrote Like He Spoke," *Interval(le)s* 2.2–3.1 (Fall 2008–Winter 2009): 163–173, 167. And yet this argument is hardly intuitive, as Doris Grumbach points out. She quotes Edel and then adds, "I would have thought that the opposite would be true, that speaking one's prose would make it simpler, less prolix, more unadorned," in *Extra Innings: A Memoir* (New York: Norton, 1993), 289.

53. Letter to James B. Pinker, June 12, 1900, quoted by Horne, *Henry James: A Life in Letters,* 40.

54. Letter to William James, April 13, 1904, quoted by Horne, *Henry James: A Life in Letters,* 16.

55. From the long letter sent to Scribner's about the New York Edition, July 30, 1905, in Edel, ed., *Henry James: Letters,* vol. 4, 368.

56. Letter to Pinker, April 7, 1906, quoted by Horne, *Henry James: A Life in Letters,* 18.

57. In the first edition, the first chapter of *The Golden Bowl* is 5,586 words. For the New York Edition, I count twelve revisions to accidentals (six to spelling), and eight small substantive revisions, including the addition of a "he," a plural to singular "thought," "precisely" to "exactly" and "break" to "dissipate." The substantive revisions account for 0.14 percent of the text. In *The American,* which was 3,661 words in the first book edition, there are a small number of revisions to accidentals (mostly spelling, e.g., "gray" to "grey") and then a large number (around 230) of substantive revisions, accounting for 6.3 percent in total.

58. Henry James, *The Outcry* (New York: Scribner's, 1911). James had composed the play in 1909, but it was not to be performed until after his death in 1917. It is published in Leon Edel, ed., *The Complete Plays of Henry James* (New York and Oxford: Oxford University Press, 1990).

59. Virginia described having tea with Henry James the previous afternoon in a letter to Violet Dickinson, Sunday, August 25, 1907. In Mitchell A. Leaska, ed., *The Virginia Woolf Reader* (San Diego: Harcourt Brace, 1984), 344.

60. Theodora Bosanquet's interesting study, first published in 1920, has been recently reissued. She pays particular attention to James's relationship with his Remington typewriter, noting that its click became a spur to composition, *Henry James at Work,* ed. Lyall H. Powers (Michigan: University of Michigan Press, 2006), 35.

61. After completing the second installment of *The Princess Casamassima,* for example, James complained that he had "never yet become engaged in a novel in which, after I had begun to write and send off my MS., the details had remained so vague." See David Mark Fogel's "Note on the Texts" appended to Henry James, *Novels 1886–1890* (New York: Library of America, 1989). Rachel Isara has recently examined James's habit of serial publication, weighing his stated ambivalence against the "subtle formal pressures" that it imposed on his art. By the 1890s, he was telling correspondents that production "means production of the little *book,* pure & simple—independent of any antecedent appearance." "'Rather Rude Jolts': Henry James, Serial Novels, and the Art of Fiction," *Henry James Review* 31.2 (Spring 2010): 188–206, 198.

62. See the very long letter that James wrote in August 1900 to William Dean Howells on this subject. In Leon Edel, ed., *Henry James: Letters,* vol. 4, 1895–1916, 157–163.

63. In the preface to *The Sense of the Past,* Lubbock had only this to say: "The notes on the course which the book was to follow were dictated when he reached the point where the original draft broke off. These notes are given in full; their part in Henry James's method of work is indicated in the preface to 'The Ivory Tower.'"

64. Percy Lubbock, *The Craft of Fiction* (New York: Scribner's, 1921). Lubbock's "post-Jamesian" theory of the novel is discussed in some detail by Nicholas Dames in "Wave-Theories and Affective Physiologies: The Cognitive Strain in Victorian Novel Theories," *Victorian Studies* 46.2 (2004): 206–216.

65. See Henry James, "The Death of the Lion," *The Complete Tales of Henry James,* vol. 9, 77–118, 118.

66. Henry James, *The Ivory Tower,* 278.

67. Henry James, *The Ivory Tower,* 338.

68. Ezra Pound, "The Notes to 'The Ivory Tower,'" recast from an article printed in *The Future* magazine in 1918, and published in *The Literary Essays of Ezra Pound* (New York: New Directions, 1968), in the section on Henry James, 295–338, 336.

69. "Collins List" advertises that the two novels are published "today," in the *Times Literary Supplement,* Thursday, September 6, 1917, 423.

70. Georges Gusdorf, "Conditions and Limits of Autobiography," in *Autobiography: Essays Theoretical and Critical,* trans. and ed. James Olney (Princeton: Princeton University Press, 1980), 28–48, 38.

71. Percy Lubbock, Preface, *The Middle Years,* by Henry James (London: W. Collins, 1917). The preface is also printed in the first American edition (New York: Scribner's, 1917), but was not reprinted in most subsequent editions of the text. The excerpted, unedited version appeared in *Scribner's Magazine,* October 1917 (465–476) and November 1917 (608–615).

72. The typescript is classified as b MS Am 1237.9.
73. See Virginia Woolf, "The Old Order," *Times Literary Supplement,* London, Thursday, October 18, 1917, 497–498.
74. For convenience's sake, I give references in parentheses to Frederick Dupee's widely available edition of *The Middle Years, Henry James: Autobiography,* 547–599. Dupee prints Lubbock's text unaltered, but without the preface.
75. Tony Tanner, *Henry James and the Art of Nonfiction* (Athens: University of Georgia Press, 1995), 72.
76. Unpublished letter to Howard Sturgis, August 5, 1914. I quote from Percy Lubbock's typed transcript (in the Houghton Library), which provides the same text as Paul Fussell. Edel prints a slightly different text in his biography, plumping for "fiat" instead of "feat" and "making for *meaning*" rather than "making and meaning." The source of the difference between the two texts is unclear to me.
77. Theodora Bosanquet, diary entry for Saturday, August 8, 1914. In Bosanquet papers at Houghton Library.
78. Letter to Edmund Gosse, October 8, 1914, from Lubbock's typescript transcription in Houghton Library.
79. Letter to William Roughead, September 30, 1914, quoted in Leon Edel, *The Selected Letters of Henry James* (New York: American Book-Stratford, 1955), 220.
80. Letter to Rhoda Broughton, August 1914, quoted in Leon Edel, *Henry James: Letters,* vol. 4, 713. Paul Fussell makes the claim that "for the modern imagination that last summer has assumed the status of a permanent symbol for anything innocently but irrecoverably lost," *The Great War and Modern Memory* (New York and London: Oxford University Press, 1975), 24.
81. David C. Greetham, *Theories of the Text,* 190.
82. See Edward Mendelson, "Revision and Power: The Example of W. H. Auden," 111.
83. Herbert Butterfield's 1931 work is itself a response to the war: when he speaks of "how crooked and perverse the ways of progress are, with what willfulness and waste it twists and turns," he sounds almost like the Eliot of "Gerontion" and *The Waste Land.* Herbert Butterfield, *The Whig Interpretation of History* (London: G. Bell and Sons, 1959).
84. From letter to Rhoda Broughton, quoted above.
85. Letter to Hugh Walpole, quoted by Roslyn Jolly, *Henry James: History, Narrative, Fiction* (Oxford: Oxford University Press, 1993), 211.
86. Virginia Woolf, "Mr. Bennett and Mrs. Brown," *The Captain's Death Bed and Other Essays* (London: Hogarth, 1950), 90–111, 110.

3. Excision and Textual Waste

1. This comment was actually made in the preface to a volume containing *Daisy Miller* and other short stories, Henry James, *Daisy Miller, Pandora, The Patagonia, and Other Tales* (New York: Scribner's, 1909), xv.
2. Henry James, preface, *The Tragic Muse* (New York: Scribner's, 1908), v–xxii, x.
3. Jacques Normand's report for Eugène Fasquelle. See Christine Cano, *Proust's Deadline* (Urbana and Chicago: University of Illinois Press, 2006), 53.

4. Pound made this comment in his *Paris Review* interview, as a way of elaborating the difficulty he was having with the later *Cantos*. He agreed, "Okay, I am stuck." Ezra Pound, "The Art of Poetry No. 5," interview with Donald Hall, *Paris Review* 28 (1962), in *The Paris Review Interviews, IV,* ed. Salman Rushdie (New York: Picador, 2009), 49–78, 75.

5. Mark McGurl, *The Program Era* (Cambridge: Harvard University Press, 2009), 295.

6. The second figure is from the article "Rough Crossings: The Cutting of Raymond Carver," *New Yorker,* December 24, 2007.

7. S. E. Gontarski notes that Beckett replaced Krapp's fellow drinkers with the phrase "Not a soul," while the park filled with "Quite a number of people I got to know then" became "Deserted spot it was" and then "Hardly a soul," "Crapp's First Tapes: Beckett's Manuscript Revisions of 'Krapp's Last Tape,' " *Journal of Modern Literature* 6.1 (1977): 61–68, 67. On Bim and Bom, see the entry in C. J. Ackerley and S. E. Gontarski, eds., *The Grove Companion to Samuel Beckett* (New York: Grove, 2004), 56–57.

8. T. S. Eliot, "American Language and Literature" (1953), in *To Criticize the Critic and Other Writings* (New York: Farrar, Straus, and Giroux, 1965), 43–60, 58.

9. "Revoked . . . referentiality" is Geoffrey Hartman's phrase. For the other descriptions, see Sharon Cameron, *Choosing Not Choosing: Dickinson's Fascicles* (Chicago: University of Chicago Press, 1992), 3–4.

10. Helen Vendler describes the earlier version as "winsome," *Dickinson: Selected Poems and Commentaries* (Cambridge: Harvard University Press, 2010), 173–174. See also her discussion of "I'll tell you how the Sun rose," 64–65.

11. On "The Sisters," see L. J. Morrissey, "Joyce's Revision of 'The Sisters': From Epicleti to Modern Fiction," *James Joyce Quarterly* 24.1 (Fall 1986): 33–54. Jana Giles makes some similar observations in "The Craft of 'A Painful Case': A Study of Revisions," *European Joyce Studies* 7: *New Perspective on Dubliners,* ed. Mary Power and Ulrich Schneider (Atlanta: Rodolphi, 1997): 195–210.

12. See the "Dubliners (1914)" entry in A. Nicholas Fargnoli and Michael Patrick Gillespie, *James Joyce A to Z: The Essential Reference Guide to His Life and Writings* (Oxford: Oxford University Press, 1996), 60–61.

13. H. D., *End to Torment* (New York: New Directions, 1979), 40.

14. Hugh Kenner, *The Pound Era,* 174.

15. See Hugh Kenner on the reception of Imagism, *The Poetry of Ezra Pound* (New York: Millwood, 1947), 58.

16. F. S. Flint, "Imagisme," *Poetry,* March 1913, 198–200.

17. Ezra Pound, "Vorticism," *Fortnightly Review,* September 1, 1914, 467.

18. In its first publication in *Poetry* magazine, this poem was formatted in an unusual way, with the clusters "The apparition," "of these faces," "in the crowd," "Petals," "on a," "wet black bough" separated with extra spaces, and more extended spaces before the punctuation marks.

19. Hugh Kenner observes that Imagism often produced parataxis. " 'In a Station of the Metro' is not formally a sentence; its structure is typographic and metric." Hugh Kenner, *The Pound Era,* 186–187.

20. Daniel Albright, *Quantum Poetics* (Cambridge: Cambridge University Press, 1997), 136.

21. Hilda Doolittle, *Collected Poems, 1912–1944,* ed. Louis L. Martz (New York: New Directions, 1986), 309. The line is printed in the 1913 *Poetry* version.

22. Steven G. Yao, note 41, *Translation and the Languages of Modernism: Gender, Politics, Language* (New York: Palgrave Macmillan, 2002), 264. David Ayers discusses this poem in relation to the Greek original in *Modernism: A Short Introduction* (Oxford: Blackwell, 2004), 3–5.

23. Hugh Kenner, *The Pound Era,* 191.

24. Daniel Albright compares Pound's difficulty to that of Anton Webern in *Six Bagatelles,* asking, "Is it possible to write a longer piece that has the quality of taciturnity, of visuality, of incisive starkness of being?" *Untwisting the Serpent: Modernism in Music, Literature, and Other Arts* (Chicago: University of Chicago Press, 2000), 68–69.

25. Marianne DeKoven, *Rich and Strange: Gender, History, Modernism,* 6. This definition is quoted by Susan Stanford Friedman as "parataxis" 6 in "Definitional Excursions: The Meanings of Modern/ Modernity/ Modernism," 496.

26. Ronald Schuchard explains that Eliot made this comment while teaching his "Introduction to Contemporary Literature Course" at Harvard in 1933, "Burbank with a Baedeker, Eliot with a Cigar: American Intellectuals, Anti-Semitism, and the Idea of Culture," *Modernism/modernity* 10.1 (2006): 1–26, 24.

27. S. Foster Damon, *Amy Lowell: A Chronicle, with Extracts from Her Correspondence* (Boston: Houghton, 1935), 208.

28. Linda W. Wagner cites John Peale Bishop's comment in "*The Sun Also Rises:* One Debt to Imagism," *Journal of Narrative Technique* 2.2 (1972): 88–98, 88.

29. Letter to Thomas Hardy, quoted in Peter Howarth, *British Poetry in the Age of Modernism* (Cambridge: Cambridge University Press, 2005), 181.

30. Donald Davie, *Ezra Pound: Poet as Scultpor* (London: Routledge, 1965), 86.

31. Pound is translating Propertius 3.1.8.

32. In a letter of 1932, "I wonder how far the *Mauberley* is merely a translation of the *Homage to S.P.,* for such as couldn't understand the latter," *The Letters of Ezra Pound, 1907–1941,* 239.

33. Ezra Pound, "The Art of Poetry No. 5," 61.

34. Letter to Felix Schelling, 1922, quoted in Humphrey Carpenter, *A Serious Character: The Life of Ezra Pound* (Boston: Houghton Mifflin, 1998), 370.

35. John Jenkins Espey, *Ezra Pound's "Mauberley": A Study in Composition* (Berkeley: University of California Press, 1955), 13.

36. Ezra Pound, "Vorticism," 468.

37. This is Hadley Hemingway's memory, quoted in Milton A. Cohen, *Hemingway's Laboratory: The Paris "in our time"* (Tuscaloosa: University of Alabama Press, 2005), 16.

38. Ernest Hemingway, *A Moveable Feast* (New York: Scribner's, 1964), 12.

39. Ernest Hemingway, "The Art of Fiction No. 21," interview with George Plimpton, 29.

40. Ernest Hemingway, *A Moveable Feast,* 202.

41. Frederic Svoboda, *Hemingway and The Sun Also Rises: The Crafting of a Style* (Lawrence: University Press of Kansas, 1983), 4, 9, 31, and 44–45.

42. Ernest Hemingway, *The Sun Also Rises: A Facsimile Edition,* ed. Matthew J. Bruccoli (Detroit: Omnigraphics, 1990), vol. 1, 46.
43. Ernest Hemingway, *The Sun Also Rises: A Facsimile Edition,* vol. 1, 52–54.
44. Manuscript of *The Sun Also Rises,* Hemingway library, 6.41. Also Ernest Hemingway, *The Sun Also Rises: A Facsimile Edition,* vol. 2, 590.
45. Ernest Hemingway, *A Moveable Feast,* 184.
46. Fitzgerald's letter is quoted by Bruccoli, in Hemingway, *The Sun Also Rises,* x–xii.
47. Valerie Eliot, ed., *The Waste Land: A Facsimile and Transcript of the Original Drafts Including the Annotations of Ezra Pound,* 13.
48. Letter quoted by William Balassi, "The Trail to *The Sun Also Rises:* The First Week of Writing," *Hemingway: Essays of Reassessment,* ed. Frank Scafella (New York and Oxford: Oxford University Press, 1991), 33–51, 34.
49. Lawrence Rainey, "Eliot among the Typists: Writing *The Waste Land,*" *Modernism/modernity* 12.1 (2005): 27–84, 51.
50. William Balassi, "The Trail to *The Sun Also Rises:* The First Week of Writing," 34.
51. William Balassi, "The Trail to *The Sun Also Rises:* The First Week of Writing," 48.
52. Hershel Parker, "Fiction and the Manuscripts," *Hemingway: Essays of Reassessment,* 17–33, 22.
53. Wayne Koestenbaum, "The Waste Land: T. S. Eliot's and Ezra Pound's Collaboration on Hysteria," *Twentieth Century Literature* 34.2 (1988): 113–139, 115.
54. Vincent Sherry, *The Great War and the Language of Modernism,* 217.
55. Eliot made this claim in 1938, in the essay "On a Recent Piece of Criticism," *Purpose,* April–June 1938. See Helen Gardner, *"The Waste Land: Paris 1922,"* *Eliot in His Time,* ed. A. Walton Litz (Princeton: Princeton University Press, 1973), 67–94, 77.
56. T. S. Eliot, "Ezra Pound," *Poetry Chicago,* September 1946. Quoted by Helen Gardner, *"The Waste Land: Paris 1922," Eliot in His Time,* 68–69.
57. Included in a letter: Ezra Pound to T. S. Eliot, December 24, 1921, in *The Letters of T. S. Eliot,* vol. 1, ed. Valerie Eliot (New York: Harcourt Brace, 1988), 497–499.
58. Wayne Koestenbaum, "The Waste Land: T. S. Eliot's and Ezra Pound's Collaboration on Hysteria," 113–139. Jean-Michel Rabaté makes a sensible modification when he notes that Pound is representing himself as a midwife ("sage homme" is the masculinization of the French *sage-femme*) rather than an impregnator. "In fact Pound merely laments his own impotence, or the fact that his masturbatory writing has prevented him from producing really *modern* creations, such as *Ulysses* or *The Waste Land.* In the second half of the short poem, the narrator—the hapless E.P. revived from Mauberley—laments his own ineffectuality by dwelling on superabundance as waste. *The Ghosts of Modernity* (Orlando: University Press of Florida, 1996), 198–199.
59. See Geoffrey Hartman, *Wordsworth's Poetry, 1787–1814,* xvii.
60. Cecelia Tichi, *Shifting Gears: Technology, Literature, Culture in Modernist America,* 71. Tichi also suggests that "The poem itself offers no alternative world and no possibility of redemption, not even implicitly"; I argue for the opposite claim.
61. Richard Ellmann, "The First *Waste Land,*" *Eliot in His Time,* 51–66, 63.
62. Wayne Koestenbaum, "The Waste Land: T. S. Eliot's and Ezra Pound's Collaboration on Hysteria," 115.

63. Marjorie Perloff, *Poetics of Indeterminacy: Rimbaud to Cage* (Princeton: Princeton University Press, 1981), 173.

64. Maud Ellmann, *The Poetics of Impersonality: T. S. Eliot and Ezra Pound* (Cambridge: Harvard University Press, 1987), 93.

65. Herbert Butterfield, *The Whig Interpretation of History*, 11–22.

66. The first judgment is Richard Ellmann's in "The First *Waste Land*," 53; the second Hugh Kenner's in "The Urban Apocalypse," 35.

67. Once again, this pithy formulation is Hugh Kenner's, in Kenner, ed., *T. S. Eliot: A Selection of Critical Essays* (Englewood Cliffs, NJ: Prentice Hall, 1969), 2–3.

68. Letter from T. S. Eliot to Ezra Pound, January 1922, *Letters, 1907–1941*, 236.

69. Richard Badenhausen, *T. S. Eliot and the Art of Collaboration* (Cambridge: Cambridge University Press, 2004), 76.

70. Unpublished letter to Virginia Woolf, dated "Friday" 1923, in the Berg Collection at the New York Public Library.

71. In a letter to Richard Aldington, November 15, 1922, cited in Valerie Eliot, ed., *The Waste Land: A Facsimile*, xxv.

72. These comments were quoted by Theodore Spencer in a lecture at Harvard, cited in Valerie Eliot, ed., *The Waste Land: A Facsimile*, 1.

73. In "The Frontiers of Criticism," *On Poetry and Poets* (New York: Farrar, Strauss, and Cudahy, 1957), 121.

74. T. S. Eliot, "The Art of Poetry No. 1," 69.

75. See the letters of July 19 and September 30, 1914. Richard Badenhausen discusses these metaphors in relationship to Eliot's desire to form collaborations, 11–12.

76. John Haffenden, "Vivien Eliot and *The Waste Land:* The Forgotten Fragments," *P. N. Review* 175, 33.5 (2007): 18–23, 23.

77. See also the note to a letter to Virginia Woolf from May 7, 1924, which makes use of the phrase "sparkish wits." Vivienne's lines ran "But see, where Fresca in her boudoir sits,/ Surrounded by a court of sparkish wits," Valerie Eliot, *The Letters of T. S. Eliot*, vol. 2, *1923–1925*, 411.

78. Lawrence Rainey, "Eliot among the Typists: Writing *The Waste Land*," 53–54.

79. Quoted by Valerie Eliot, *The Waste Land: A Facsimile*, 130.

80. James E. Miller, *T. S. Eliot: The Making of an American Poet, 1888–1922* (University Park: Pennsylvania State University Press, 2005), 366.

81. Pound was not convinced that there was any connection between the two texts. In a letter from January 1922, he was firm to the point of dogma: "I do *not* advise printing 'Gerontion' as preface. One don't [*sic*] miss it *at* all as the thing now stands. To be more lucid still, let me say that I advise you NOT to print 'Gerontion' as prelude." Letter, January 1922, *The Letters of Ezra Pound, 1907–1941*, 237. Eliot's letter, beginning "Cher maître" and asking whether he *should* use "Gerontion" is printed on the previous page.

82. T. S. Eliot, "The Art of Poetry No. 1," 58.

83. See Helen Gardner, *The Composition of Four Quartets* (New York: Oxford University Press, 1978), 180–181.

84. See E. Martin Browne, *The Making of T. S. Eliot's Plays* (Cambridge: Cambridge University Press, 1969), 219–220.

85. Andrew J. Kappel, "Complete with Omissions: The Text of Marianne Moore's *Complete Poems,*" 132.

86. T. S. Eliot, "Note to the Revised Edition," *Anabasis: A Poem by St.-John Perse,* 3rd ed. (New York: Harcourt Brace, 1949), 13–14. The first edition is *Anabasis: A Poem by St.-John Perse* (London: Faber and Faber, 1930).

87. T. S. Eliot, *Anabasis,* 64 and 65. The allusion is to "Gerontion," "multiply variety with a wilderness of mirrors."

88. Quoted in Richard Badenhausen, *T. S. Eliot and the Art of Collaboration,* 189.

89. "Only once does that early work speak in the great manner," W. B. Yeats, ed., *The Oxford Book of Modern Verse, 1892–1935* (Oxford: Oxford University Press, 1936), xxii.

90. Henry James, *In the Cage* (Chicago and New York: Herbert S. Stone, 1898), 1.

91. "Remarkable as it seems to us, Eliot was planning to issue the poem without Part IV," Lawrence Rainey, "Eliot among the Typists," 40, 51.

92. Marshall McLuhan argues that Eliot's four-part structure draws on the traditions of scriptural exegesis, "Pound, Eliot and the Rhetoric of *The Waste Land,*" *New Literary History* 10.3 (1979): 557–580, 562.

93. William Carlos Williams, *The Autobiography of Williams Carlos Williams* (New York: Random House, 1951), 174.

94. When discussing a passage from the facsimile edition *not* in the final poem, I give the page number in Valerie Eliot's edition and then, after a colon, her line numbers. I use the verso page number, which is the facsimile reproduction; Valerie Eliot's typed version is on the recto. In discussion of the published 1922 text, I use Eliot's line numbers.

95. T. S. Eliot, "The London Letter," *Dial,* July 1921.

96. As Jean-Michel Rabaté has argued in his reading of the poem's peculiar obstetrics, the "disjunctive nature of Pound and Eliot's collaboration," their mutual blind spots, produce certain "textual ghosts," *The Ghosts of Modernity,* 200–202.

97. Tita Chico, "Privacy and Speculation in Early Eighteenth-Century Britain," *Cultural Critique* 52 (2002): 40–60, 41.

98. Valerie Eliot, Editorial Notes, *The Waste Land: A Facsimile and Transcript of the Original Drafts,* 127.

99. Hugh Kenner, "The Urban Apocalypse," 29. Kenner suggests that Eliot's understanding of Dryden's project and prosody was strongly influenced by his reading of Mark Van Doren's book *John Dryden,* which he reviewed for the *TLS* in May 1921.

100. Suzanne Raitt, "The Rhetoric of Efficiency in Early Modernism," *Modernism/modernity* 13.1 (2006): 835–851. Tim Armstrong considers revision in both James and Eliot in relation to Horace Fletcher's prescriptions for an efficient body. Tim Armstrong, *Modernism, Technology and the Body: A Cultural Study* (Cambridge: Cambridge University Press, 1998), 42–74.

101. Georges Lechartier, "The Program and Cost of Post-War Reconstruction in France," *Proceedings of the Academy of Political Science in the City of New York* 12.1 (July 1926): 312–315, 312.

102. On the carbon copy of the typescript. See Valerie Eliot, *The Waste Land: A Facsimile,* 40.

103. "pot-pourri, n.'" *The Oxford English Dictionary,* 2nd ed., 1989. *OED Online,* Oxford University Press, September 10, 2007, http://dictionary.oed.com.ezp2.harvard .edu/cgi/entry/50185492.

104. T. S. Eliot, *Knowledge and Experience in the Philosophy of F. H. Bradley* (New York: Columbia University Press, 1989), 54.

105. T. S. Eliot, "Tradition and the Individual Talent" (1919), in *Selected Prose,* 37–44, 38.

106. Terry Eagleton, *Marxism and Literary Criticism* (London: Routledge, 1976), 14.

107. Kenneth Asher, *T. S. Eliot and Ideology* (Cambridge: Cambridge University Press, 1995), 160.

108. Michael Oakeshott, *Experience and Its Modes* (Cambridge: Cambridge University Press, 1933), 111.

109. Jacob Korg, "Modern Art Techniques in *The Waste Land,*" *Journal of Aesthetics and Art Criticism* 18.4 (1960): 465–463, 458.

110. Frank Kermode, introduction, in T. S. Eliot, *The Waste Land and Other Poems,* ed. Frank Kermode (New York: Penguin, 2003), xxi.

111. David Tomlinson, "Eliot and the Cubists," *Twentieth-Century Literature* 26.1 (1980): 64–81, 79. Eliot described the exhibition as "the most interesting event in London at this moment."

112. G. Thomas Tanselle, "The Editorial Problem of Final Authorial Intention," 190–191.

113. In *Four Quartets,* completed more slowly, and with much more authorial control, the process was reversed. Eliot composed each individual poem in Pound's five parts, replicating even the diminished fourth of "Death by Water," but then superimposed his own symmetrical four-part structure over this. "And the end of all our exploring/ Will be to arrive where we started/ And to know the place for the first time."

4. Joyce and the Illogic of Addition

1. Richard Ellmann, *James Joyce,* 545.

2. Frank Budgen, *James Joyce and the Making of Ulysses,* quoted by Michael Groden in *Ulysses in Focus* (Gainesville: University Press of Florida, 2010), 58.

3. See Philip Herring, *Joyce's Ulysses Notesheets in the British Museum* (Charlottesville: University Press of Virginia, 1972), referenced against the 1934 Random House edition (not the easiest of choices for most readers). The first of these phrases is noted by Herring on 125, and was slotted in to "Nausicaa" (13.32); the second is from "Eumaeus," inserted at 16.332–333.

4. Andrew J. Kappel, "Complete with Omissions: The Text of Marianne Moore's *Complete Poems,*" 126.

5. Ezra Pound, letter to John Quinn, January 24, 1917, *The Letters of Ezra Pound,* 157.

6. N. Katherine Hayles, "Postmodern Parataxis: Embodied Texts, Weightless Information," *American Literary History* 2.3 (1990): 394–421, 399.

7. David Lodge discusses these associations at length in *The Modes of Modern Writing* (London: Edward Arnold, 1977), 88–93.

8. Hans Walter Gabler, *Ulysses: A Critical and Synoptic Edition*, vol. 3, 1440. Subsequent parenthetical references are to episode and line numbers in the clear text, unless otherwise stated, printed on the recto of Gabler's synoptic edition. In the *James Joyce Archive*, ed. Michael Groden, this is vol. 20, *Ulysses: "Circe" and "Eumaeus," A Facsimile of Placards for Episodes 15–16* (New York: Garland, 1978), 363.

9. Roman Jakobson, "Two Aspects of Language and Two Types of Aphasic Disturbances," first published in 1956, in *On Language*, ed. Linda Waugh and Monique Monville-Burston (Cambridge: Harvard University Press, 1990), 115–133.

10. David Lodge, *The Modes of Modern Writing*, 78–9.

11. References to Gabler's edition. The word *paraheliotropic* is interleaved on the third copy of placard proofs, *JJA* 21, *Ulysses: "Ithaca" & "Penelope": A Facsimile of Placards for Episodes 17–18* (New York and London: Garland, 1978), 19. See the original reading in "Penelope" on the placards in the same volume, 285.

12. See Graeme Hirst and Vanessa Wei Fang, "Changes in Style in Authors with Alzheimer's Disease," *English Studies* 93.3 (2012): 357–370.

13. Jonathan Arac, "Bounding Lines: *The Prelude* and Critical Revision," in *Poststructuralist Readings of English Poetry*, ed. Richard Machin and Christopher Norris (Cambridge: Cambridge University Press, 1987), 227–247, 227.

14. See, for example, the long passage beginning "A posse of Dublin metropolitan police" and ending "Dr. Pippi" in the "Cyclops" episode, which was added in proof and takes up most of page 294, all of 295, and two lines of 296 in the first book edition. Clive Driver, *Ulysses: The Manuscript and First Printings Compared*. Ronan Crowley notes that Joyce left an instruction on the first setting of the October 1 *Placard* 34, *"Insérez ici le passage sur les deux feuilles en manuscrit sans interrompre le paragraph,"* "Proof^Finder: Placards," *Genetic Joyce Studies* 8 (Spring 2008), http://www.antwerpjamesjoycecenter.com/GJS8/Proofpercent5Efinder/Placards .jsp.

15. Michael Groden, *Ulysses in Progress*, 8.

16. In a 1962 *Paris Review* interview with Donald Hall. See Ben D. Kimpel and T. C. Duncan Eaves, "Major Form in Pound's *Cantos*," *Iowa Review* 15.2 (1985): 51–66.

17. Ezra Pound, *The Cantos of Ezra Pound* (New York: New Directions, 1970), 3.

18. I have found Christine Cano's discussion of the organic metaphors used by Proust's early critics and readers to be extremely useful.

19. In an earlier article, she suggests: "The nineteenth century literary organicism that subtly informs genetic criticism posits organic form as a normative model, a model from which the excrescence-riddled text manifestly deviates." Christine Cano, "Genetic Aberrations: The Two Faces of Proust," 43.

20. Dirk Van Hulle discusses the balance between addition and removal. During the summer of 1922, "Proust kept adding passages to the typescripts of La Prisonnière," including the description of Bergotte's death, and a dictated passage comparing the "melting" of bourgeois names to Albertine's description of molded ice cream. A few months later he wrote, "from 648 to 898 nothing, I have deleted everything. So we jump from 648 to chapter 2 of Albertine disparue." See Dirk Van Hulle, *A Genetic Study of Late Manuscripts by Joyce, Proust, and Mann* (Ann Arbor: University of Michigan Press, 2004), 57–59.

21. The comment of the Pléiade editors, cited by Christine Cano, 110.

22. These appear to be the last words that Virginia Woolf ever wrote, scrawled horizontally up the side of the second of her two suicide notes to Leonard, dated March 28, 1941. The note is reprinted in facsimile in *Leave The Letters Till We're Dead: The Letters of Virginia Woolf,* ed. Nigel Nicholson, vol. 6 (London: Hogarth, 1980), 488.

23. Daniel Albright, "Virginia Woolf as Autobiographer," *Kenyon Review* 6.1 (1984): 1–17, 1.

24. Letter to Robert McAlmson, October 1921, quoted by Alyssa J. O'Brien in "The Molly Blooms of 'Penelope': Reading Joyce Archivally," *Journal of Modern Literature* 24.1 (2000): 7–24, 10.

25. See Hans Walter Gabler, "Afterword," 1876.

26. Donald H. Reiman, "'Versioning': The Presentation of Multiple Texts," *Romantic Texts and Contexts* (Columbia: University of Missouri Press, 1987), 167–180, 167.

27. D. F. McKenzie, *Bibliography and the Sociology of Texts,* 48–49.

28. See Hans Walter Gabler's discussion of his method in "The *James Joyce Archive:* A Publisher's Gift to Joyce Studies," *Genetic Joyce Studies* (Summer 2002), http://www .antwerpjamesjoycecenter.com/JJAGabler.htm.

29. Michael Groden, *Ulysses in Focus,* 90.

30. The research problems that this poses are considerable. In non-open shelf access libraries, it is difficult to call up as many volumes as are needed to perform comparative genetic work. Moreover, because the numbers of volumes are not printed on the spines, they are also liable to misclassification. In terms of holdings, Stanford has 18 of the 63 volumes; Columbia and Chicago have only the index.

31. John Haffenden, "Vivien Eliot and *The Waste Land:* The Forgotten Fragments," *P. N. Review* 175, 33.5 (2007): 18–23, 23.

32. Michael Groden, "The National Library of Ireland's New Joyce Manuscripts: An Outline and Archive Comparisons," *Joyce Studies Annual* 14 (2003): 5–17.

33. The one condition is access; at the moment, these new materials have not been reproduced, and can be examined only in the National Library archives.

34. James Joyce, *Ulysses,* "Episode IV," *The Little Review* 5.2 (June 1918): 39–52, 50.

35. Paul Vanderham notes that he also altered a description of the Dead Sea as "Dead: an old woman's: the grey sunken [cunt] of the world" to "the grey sunken belly," "Ezra Pound's Censorship of *Ulysses,*" *James Joyce Quarterly* 32.3–4 (1995): 583–595, 585.

36. Letter to John Quinn, April 3, 1918, cited by Paul Vanderham, 584.

37. Jean-Michel Rabaté, *The Ghosts of Modernity,* 197.

38. Hugh Kenner, *Ulysses* (Baltimore and London: Johns Hopkins University Press, 1987), 45.

39. See *JJA* 12, *Ulysses: Notes & "Telemachus"—"Scylla and Charybdis,"* 281.

40. James Joyce, *Ulysses,* "Episode VIII," *The Little Review* 5.9 (January 1919): 27–50, 42.

41. Michael Groden cites this passage as an example of the "initial style" but without commenting on the fact that it was added only *after* the initial period of composition (15–16).

42. "But makes them polite" is added on the first set, *JJA* 19, *Ulysses: "Sirens," "Cyclops," "Nausicaa," & "Oxen of the Sun," A Facsimile of Placards for Episodes 11–14,* 276; "That squinty one is delicate" on the second, 284.

43. Suzanne Henke finds that "Bloom's reaction to Gerty's deformity may be self-indulgent, but it is far from callous," *Joyce's Moraculous Sindbook* (Columbus: Ohio State University Press, 1978), 167.

44. From the 1921 essay on Marvell, reprinted in T. S. Eliot, *Selected Prose of T. S. Eliot,* ed. Frank Kermode (New York: Harcourt Brace Jovanovich, 1975), 161–171, 170.

45. Daniel R. Schwarz, *Reading Joyce's Ulysses* (New York: St. Martin's, 1987), 236.

46. Charles Dickens, *Little Dorrit* (Oxford: Oxford World's Classics, 1999), 561.

47. Mark Osteen, *The Economy of Ulysses: Making Both Ends Meet* (Syracuse: Syracuse University Press, 1995), 251.

48. Franco Moretti, *Signs Taken for Wonders: On the Sociology of Literary Forms,* 2nd ed., trans. Susan Fischer, David Forgacs, and David Miller (London: Verso, 2005), 207.

49. Quoted by Jeri Johnson, "Joyce and Feminism," *The Cambridge Companion to James Joyce,* 196–212, 206.

50. See Gregory Castle's discussion of the passage, "Colonial Discourse and the Subject of Empire in Joyce's 'Nausicaa,'" in *Joyce: Feminism/ Post/Colonialism,* ed. Ellen Carol Jones (Amsterdam and Atlanta: European Joyce Studies, 1998), 115–144, 125.

51. It looks to me as if "cotton wool" is two words in the manuscript, but Driver's collation doesn't pick this up, and all the published versions have "cottonwool," which seems like a more artificial commodity. Gabler II.752; 13.148–158.

52. Cf. Alexander Pye, criticizing female novel readers: "the susceptibility of the female votary of the circulating library, is proverbial," *A Commentary Illustrating the Poetic of Aristotle* (London: John Stockdale, 1792), 145.

53. In a letter to Frank Budgen. Paul Saint-Amour discusses this description as part of Joyce's interest in parody and intellectual property, *The Copywrights: Intellectual Property and the Literary Imagination,* 169–170.

54. Garry Leonard, "Power, Pornography, and the Problem of Pleasure: The Semerotics of Desire and Commodity Culture in Joyce," *James Joyce Quarterly* 30.4 (1993): 615–667, 661.

55. Derek Attridge, "Literature as Deviation," *Peculiar Language: Literature as Difference from the Renaissance to James Joyce* (Ithaca: Cornell University Press, 1988), 172–180.

56. Joyce described it as "the ugly duckling of the book and therefore, I suppose, my favourite," Richard Ellmann, *James Joyce,* 500.

57. Richard Madtes was one of the first to identify the "accretive" pattern of Joyce's revisions: "Joyce and the Building of Ithaca," *ELH* 31.4 (1964): 443–459, 444.

58. Placard proofs strike out the original balance and replace it with "1.1.6" (97), which is crossed out again in the page proofs and replaced with "0.16.6" (186). Joyce also added the detail "In Memoriam Patrick Dignam" on the page proofs.

59. See *JJA* 21, Ulysses, *"Ithaca" & "Penelope": A Facsimile of Placards for Episodes 17–18,* 86–7, and *JJA* 27, Ulysses: *"Eumaeus," "Ithaca," and "Penelope," A Facsimile of Page Proofs for Episodes 16–18,* 182.

60. Michael Groden, *Ulysses in Progress,* 191.

61. *JJA* 27, Ulysses: *"Eumaeus," "Ithaca," and "Penelope," A Facsimile of Page Proofs for Episodes 16–18,* 150.

62. As various critics have observed, "massproduct" is perhaps also a pun, suggesting a secular communion, e.g., John Gifford with Robert J. Seidman, *Ulysses Annotated: Notes for James Joyce's Ulysses* (Berkeley: University of California Press, 2008), 571.

63. Robert Martin Adams, *Surface and Symbol: The Consistency of Joyce's Ulysses* (Oxford: Oxford University Press, 1962), 82.

64. Fritz Senn, "'Ithaca': Portrait of the Chapter as a Long List," in Andrew Gibson, ed., *Joyce's "Ithaca"* (Amsterdam: Rodopi, 1996), 31–76, 72–73.

65. Virginia Woolf, "Mr. Bennett and Mrs. Brown," 101.

66. Mark Osteen, *The Economy of Ulysses*, 407.

67. Richard Madtes points out, "obvious as this sounds, it can easily be forgotten," "Joyce and the Building of Ithaca," 453.

68. Quoted by Theodore Spencer, introduction to *Stephen Hero*, 8.

69. Derek Attridge, *Joyce Effects* (Cambridge: Cambridge University Press, 2000), 83.

70. Mark Osteen suggests that "Eumaeus" might, on one level, be read as "not realist but 'hyperrealist', its subversion of narrative credit, identity, and truth creating an infinite regress of reproduction, of fleeting and modulating difference," before adding "And yet most readers detect something genuine in 'Eumaeus' beneath the play of counterfeits" (Osteen, *The Economy of Ulysses* 372).

71. Virginia Woolf quoting Bennett, "Mr. Bennett and Mrs. Brown," 90.

72. I do not agree that the outcome of this irrelevance is to subvert the possibility that language represents reality. Cordell D. K. Yee, *The World According to James Joyce: Reconstructing Representation* (London: Associated University Presses, 1997), 47.

73. Declan Kiberd, *Ulysses and Us: The Art of Everyday Life in Joyce's Masterpiece* (New York: Norton, 2009), 276.

74. Hugh Kenner sees this as a feature of the second half of the novel as a whole, but it is particularly problematic in "Penelope," *Ulysses*, 70.

75. Jonathan Quick, "Molly Bloom's Mother," *ELH* 57.1 (1990): 223–240, 223.

76. During his marriage, Bloom has clearly learned something about Molly's girlhood in Gibraltar. "All the way from Gibraltar. Forgotten any little Spanish she knew. Wonder what her father gave for it. Old style. Ah yes! of course. Bought it at the governor's auction."

77. George Bornstein, looking at the Gabler edition, argues that "an extraordinary number of the swarming details" added in revision "recapitulate major hybridities of the entire novel," *Material Modernism,* 138. In a sense this is true, but these "hybridities" are all Molly's: as I discuss, this is her early life that Bloom knows little of.

78. Attridge makes the interesting brief comment in "Molly's Flow: The Writing of 'Penelope'" that these postponed resolutions were "a stylistic feature increased during the process of composition by Joyce's insertions," *Joyce Effects,* 98.

79. "His soul swooned slowly as he heard the snow falling faintly through the universe and faintly falling, like the descent of their last end, upon all the living and the dead." James Joyce, "The Dead," *Dubliners,* ed. Hans Walter Gabler (New York and London: Garland, 1993), 336–384, 384.

80. Hugh Kenner scans out the rhythm, *Ulysses,* 147.

81. Pericles Lewis, *The Cambridge Introduction to Modernism* (Cambridge: Cambridge University Press, 2007), 175.

82. Michael Groden, *Ulysses in Focus,* 198.

83. For this common enough pro-closure position, see Peter Michelson, *Speaking the Unspeakable: A Poetics of Obscenity* (Albany: State University of New York Press, 1993), 180; Suzette A. Henke, *James Joyce and the Politics of Desire* (New York: Routledge, 1990), 160–161; Jesse Matz, *The Modern Novel: A Short Introduction* (Oxford: Blackwell, 2004), 41.

84. James Wood, "The Smallness of the 'Big' Novel: Human, All Too Inhuman," review of *White Teeth* by Zadie Smith, *The New Republic,* July 24, 2000.

85. John Updike, *Rabbit Run* (New York: Knopf, 1960).

86. John Neary compares the technique explicitly to Joyce, saying that "just as Joyce has to do with Leopold Bloom, Updike must convince us that this ordinary, literate but not literary man has such a luxurious consciousness." *Something and Nothingness: The Fiction of John Updike and John Fowles* (Carbondale: Southern Illinois University Press, 1992), 54.

87. Mark McGurl, *The Program Era,* 298.

88. Bret Easton Ellis, *Glamorama* (New York: Vintage, 2000), 179.

89. Patrick Bateman lists what he and other people wear with a high degree of object repetition (e.g., "silk tie," "linen suit," "wool and cashmere sports coat") but pointed differentiation of brand, so "He's wearing a silk tie by Bill Blass . . . I'm wearing a lightweight linen suit with pleated trousers, a cotton shirt, a dotted silk tie, all by Valentino Couture . . ." Bret Easton Ellis, *American Psycho* (New York: Vintage, 1991), 30–31.

90. Bob Perelman, "Parataxis and Narrative: The New Sentence in Theory and Practice," *American Literature* 65.2 (1993): 313–324, 313.

91. See Perelman's longer chapter on parataxis in *The Marginalization of Poetry* (Princeton: Princeton University Press, 1996), 62.

92. Fredric Jameson, *The Cultural Logic of Late Capitalism* (Durham, NC: Duke University Press, 1991), 25.

93. Walter Benjamin, "The Work of Art in the Age of Mechanical Reproduction," *Illuminations,* trans. Harry Zohn, ed. Hannah Arendt (New York: Schocken, 1968), 217–251.

94. "shore, v. 1" is "to prop" and "to lift up"; "shore, v. 2" is "to threaten"; "shore, v. 3" is "to scour" but is obsolete; "shore, v. 4" is "to run aground." *Oxford English Dictionary,* 2nd ed., 1989; online version, June 2011.

95. I have found the explanation by Luciano Floridi in the *Stanford Encyclopedia of Philosophy* to be helpful, and the term "implode" is his. "Semantic Conceptions of Information," *The Stanford Encyclopedia of Philosophy* (Spring 2011), ed. Edward N. Zalta, http://plato.stanford.edu/archives/spr2011/entries/information-semantic/.

96. Bar-Hillel and Carnap (1953) quoted by Luciano Floridi, "Philosophical Conceptions of Innovation," in *Formal Theories of Information: From Shannon to Semantic Information Theory,* ed. Giovanni Sommaruga (Berlin: Springer, 1998), 13–54, 42. The book covers much of the same material as the *Encyclopedia* article.

97. This is Philip Herring's theory, advanced in an article that attempts "to test the verisimilitude of Molly Bloom." "Towards an Historical Molly Bloom," *English Literary History* 45.3 (1978): 501–521.

98. Jonathan Quick makes the first suggestion in "Molly Bloom's Mother." The editors of *Ulysses Annotated* cite Henry Raleigh's discussion of Lunita as a prostitute, 612–613. They admit that it is unclear what Bloom knows and doesn't know about this part of his wife's background; the statement "he hadnt an idea about my mother till we were engaged otherwise hed never have got me so cheap" is not explained.

99. Kenner argues that *Ulysses* was "the decisive English-language book of the century," inspiring both *The Waste Land* and Pound's *revisions* of the early *Cantos*. Hugh Kenner, *Joyce's Voices* (Berkeley: University of California Press, 1978), xii.

5. "I Am Dead": Autobiography Revisited

1. Once again, this description is from the preface to *The Golden Bowl*, xiii.

2. Sigmund Freud, *Beyond the Pleasure Principle,* ed. and trans. James Strachey (London: Hogarth, 1920), 18.

3. Cathy Caruth, *Unclaimed Experience* (Baltimore: Johns Hopkins University Press, 1996), 59.

4. Daniel Capp's study *The Poetry of Shell Shock* (Jefferson, NC: McFarland, 2005) provides examples of repetition in the soldier poets' war poetry. Maud Ellmann discusses *The Waste Land* as "an obsessive ceremonial, because it re-inscribes the horrors it is trying to repress"; borrowing from Freud, she argues that the poem in fact repeats the horrors it tries to neutralize, 179–180.

5. T. S. Eliot, "Hamlet," *Selected Prose*, 45–49, 49.

6. Martin Löschnigg, "Autobiography," *Routledge Encyclopedia of Narrative Theory,* ed. David Herman, Manfred Jahn, and Marie-Laure Ryan (Abingdon and New York: Routledge, 2005), 34–36, 35.

7. Max Saunders's recent *Self-Impression: Life Writing, Autobiografiction, and the Forms of Modern Literature* (Oxford: Oxford University Press, 2010) examines the ways in which fiction, autobiography, biography, and various disguised or compound forms ("autobiografictions") influenced each other in the early twentieth century. In particular, he diagnoses a contradiction between two commonly held views, 1) "the classic New Critical view (initiated by the modernists themselves) that modernist impersonality requires a rejection or abjuring of biography," and 2) "the account of the modernist autobiographical novel, especially the *Künstlerroman*" (12).

8. Avrom Fleishman, *Figures of Autobiography: The Language of Self-Writing in Victorian and Modern England,* 391.

9. In the holograph draft, the first sentence runs " 'If it's a fine day tomorrow,' said Mrs. Ramsay. 'But you'll have to be up with the lark,' she added." In an article on negation in the novel, Roberta Rubenstein links this to Woolf's improving mood as she worked on the novel and argues that the novel's overall structure is *"yes/no/yes,"* "I meant *nothing* by the Lighthouse: Virginia Woolf's Poetics of Negation," *Journal of Modern Literature* 31.4 (2008): 36–53. Page references to the novel are to Virginia Woof, *To the Lighthouse,* ed. Mark Hussey (Orlando: Harcourt, 2005), 7. Ann Banfield also addresses the question of time and incompletion, arguing that "the problem of the future structures all of *To the Lighthouse*" and noting that the title completes

the original proposition "if it's fine tomorrow," "Tragic Time: The Problem of the Future in Cambridge Philosophy and *To the Lighthouse*," *Modernism/modernity* 7.1 (2000): 43–75, 54–55.

10. In her diary entry for Friday, December 8, 1939, Woolf defines her own mixed emotions about the social excitement of London as "ambivalence as Freud calls it," continuing "I'm gulping up Freud," *Diary*, vol. 5, 249.

11. Parenthetical page references to "A Sketch of the Past," *Moments of Being*, ed. Jeanne Schulkind. Virginia Woolf did not undergo analysis herself; according to Alix Strachey's account, this was because of fears that it might reduce her creativity. This, of course, is another way of equating novel-writing and analysis. See Stephen Frosh, "Psychoanalysis in Britain: 'The Rituals of Destruction,'" in *A Concise Companion to Modernism*, ed. David Bradshaw (Oxford: Blackwell, 2003), 116–137, 128.

12. Elena Gualtieri, for example, argues that "Rather than remaining fixed at some point in her daughter's past, Julia's invisible presence accompanied Woolf well into her adult life until she was exorcised by the writing of *To the Lighthouse*." *Virginia Woolf's Essays: Sketching the Past* (New York: St. Martin's, 2000), 99.

13. Maud Ellmann, *Nets of Modernism*, 63.

14. The first remark is in a diary entry for April 18, 1926, *The Diary of Virginia Woolf*, vol. 3, 76. The second is quoted by James Haule from a letter of May 15, 1927, to Ottoline Morrell. See James M. Haule, "'Le temps passé' and the Original Typescript: An Early Version of the 'Time Passes' Section of *To the Lighthouse*," *Twentieth Century Literature* 29.3 (Fall 1983): 267–311, 269.

15. James M. Haule, "'Le Temps passe,'" 271.

16. Maud Ellmann, "The Name and the Scar," *A Portrait of the Artist as a Young Man: A Casebook*, ed. Mark Wollaeger (Oxford and New York: Oxford University Press, 2003), 143–180, 154.

17. Philippe Lejeune's essay "Autogenesis: Genetic Studies of Autobiographical Texts" is published in Deppman, Ferrer, Groden, eds., *Genetic Criticism: Texts and Avant-Textes*, 193–217, and republished in *On Diary*, ed. Jeremy D. Popkin and Julie Rak, 213–236. The latter volume contains a number of other important genetic analyses of diaries, including "Composing a Diary" and "How Anne Frank Rewrote the Diary of Anne Frank."

18. Philippe Lejeune, "How Do Diaries End?" republished in *On Diary*, 187–200, 191.

19. Suzanne Bunkers has argued, "any diary that has been edited for publication, whether by a family member, an academic editor, a scholarly press, or a mass-market publishing house, bears the unmistakable marks of the editor(s) as well as the diarist," "Whose Diary Is It, Anyway?" *a/b: Auto/Biography Studies* 17.1 (2002): 11–27, 15.

20. Lynn Bloom calls these kinds of diaries "public documents" (as opposed to "truly private diaries") because they are more coherent and less cryptic, "artfully shaped to accommodate an audience" (28). I would prefer a more nuanced discrimination: these diaries hypostasize their own readership (as an unpublished novel does), but they were not actually brought *into public* by their authors, and should be distinguished from self-published diaries, like Alan Clark's *Diaries: In Power*, or Joyce Carol Oates's *Journal*. Lynn Z. Bloom, "'I Write for Myself and Strangers':

Private Diaries as Public Documents," in *Inscribing the Daily,* ed. Suzanne L. Bunkers and Cynthia A. Huff (Amherst: University of Massachusetts Press, 1996), 23–26.

21. "finish, v.¹," *The Oxford English Dictionary,* 2nd ed., 1989. *OED Online,* Oxford University Press, September 10, 2009, http://dictionary.oed.com.ezp1.harvard.edu /cgi/entry/50084997. These senses are listed as 1a and 4a.

22. Felicity Nussbaum, "Towards Conceptualizing Diary," *Studies in Autobiography,* ed. James Olney (Oxford: Oxford University Press, 1988), 128–140, 137.

23. Georges Gusdorf, "Conditions and Limits of Autobiography," in *Autobiography: Essays Theoretical and Practical,* ed. James Olney (Princeton: Princeton University Press, 1980), 29–48, 39.

24. Liz Stanley and Helen Dampier discuss the edited and reworked diary of Johanna Brandt-Warmelo, paying particular attention to "'important temporal disjunctures'" between the manuscript and published diary. "Simulacrum Diaries: Time, the 'moment of writing' and the Diaries of Johanna Brandt-Van Warmelo." *Life Writing* 3 (2006): 25–52.

25. Sybille Bedford, *Quicksands* (New York: Counterpoint, 2006), 247.

26. Graham Greene, *A Sort of Life* (New York: Simon and Schuster, 1971), 11.

27. Jacques Derrida, "The Deaths of Roland Barthes," *The Work of Mourning,* ed. and trans. Pascale-Anne Brault and Michael Naas (Chicago: University of Chicago Press, 2001), 31–68, 64–65.

28. Paul de Man, *The Rhetoric of Romanticism* (New York: Columbia University Press, 1984), 77.

29. Laura Marcus, *Auto/biographical Discourses: Theory, Criticism, Practice* (Manchester and New York: Manchester University Press, 1994), 210.

30. Paul M. Zall discusses the textual history briefly in *Benjamin Franklin's Humor* (Lexington: University Press of Kentucky, 2005), 4.

31. The first edition of *Speak, Memory* was published in the United Kingdom in 1951. In the United States, it was published in 1954 as *Conclusive Evidence.* Vladimir Nabokov, *Speak, Memory* (London: Victor Gollancz, 1951); and revised as *Speak, Memory: An Autobiography Revisited* (New York: Putnam, 1966).

32. Damian Walter Davies argues that the *Confessions* become more autobiographical over time, and suggests that De Quincey's understanding of autobiography as a mode was influenced by his reading in manuscript of *The Prelude.* "Thomas de Quincey: *Confessions of an English Opium-Eater,*" in *A Companion to Romanticism,* ed. Duncan Wu (Oxford: Blackwell, 1999), 269–276.

33. By modern standards, there are six editions of *Leaves of Grass* but "since 1891–2 it has been customary to refer to nine," according to the editors of the 1980 variorum edition.

34. Laura Marcus makes this argument most convincingly in *Auto/biographical Discourses: Theory, Criticism, Practice,* 13.

35. Charles Darwin, "Autobiography," in *The Life and Letters of Charles Darwin,* ed. Francis Darwin (London: John Murray, 1887), vol. 1, 26–82, 27.

36. Francis Darwin penned a short prefatory note to the text. Like Percy Lubbock, he also commented on the need "to make a few corrections of obvious verbal slips."

37. This was necessary in part because Trollope had a full-time job. He describes keeping a writing diary of the number of pages written each day as a check against idleness, *Autobiography of Anthony Trollope* (New York: Dodd and Mead, 1912), 103.

38. Letter to Mrs. Mill, February 1855. For a full description of the writing process of the *Autobiography,* see Albert William Levi, "The Writing of Mill's *Autobiography,*" *Ethics* 61.4 (July 1951): 284–296, 291.

39. This is Levi's conclusion (295); he also notes that the text was the product of "three different epochs in Mill's life and that the work was done respectively in the years 1854, 1861, and 1869."

40. Stephen Gill, "'Affinities Preserved': Poetic Self-Reference in Wordsworth," *Studies in Romanticism* 24.4 (1985): 531–549, 537.

41. Eugene Stelzig, "Some Notes on Romantic Subjectivity in the Context of German and English Romanticism," in *Sensus Communis: Contemporary Trends in Comparative Literature,* ed. János Riesz, Peter Boerner, and Bernard Scholz (Tübingen: Gunter Narr, 1986), 357–386, 362.

42. Jonathan Arac, "Bounding Lines: *The Prelude* and Critical Revision," 32.

43. William Wordsworth, *The Prelude,* ed. Ernest de Selincourt, 72–73.

44. Susan Wolfson, "The Illusion of Mastery: Wordsworth's Revisions of the 'Drowned Man of Esthwaite,' 1799, 1805, 1850," *PMLA* 99.5 (1984): 917–935, 928.

45. See de Selincourt's introduction, xlvii–liii.

46. Barbara Herrnstein Smith, *Poetic Closure: A Study of How Poems End* (Chicago: University of Chicago Press, 1968), 250.

47. Leslie Stephen, *The Mausoleum Book,* ed. Alan Bell (Oxford: Clarendon, 1977).

48. Leslie Stephen, "Autobiography," *Hours in a Library,* vol. 3 (New York: G. P. Putnam, 1894), 237–270, 237.

49. Virginia Hyman, "Concealment and Disclosure in Sir Leslie Stephen's *Mausoleum Book,*" *Biography* 3.2 (1980): 121–131, 121.

50. I give parenthetical directions to the relevant pages in Bell's edition, for ease of reference.

51. Laura, who was not Julia's biological child, is omitted from the list, but the memoir does dwell on her at some length—one example of its tendency to self-justification rather than tight focus on its subject. Louise DeSalvo discusses this in *Virginia Woolf: The Impact of Childhood Sexual Abuse on Her Life and Work* (Boston: Beacon Press, 1989).

52. Cited by Frédérique Amselle, who discusses Woolf's own genre confusions at the beginning of "A Sketch of the Past," where Nessa is cited as the motivating force behind the project of memoir writing, *Virginia Woolf et les écritures du moi: le journal et l'autobiographie* (Montpellier: Presses Universitaires de la Méditerranée, 2008), 46.

53. The note for 1882, for example, recounts: "25 January Adeline Virginia born," before continuing "At Easter, I went with Herbert Stephen to St. Ives."

54. See Jules Paul Seigel, "*Jenny*: The Divided Sensibility of a Young and Thoughtful Man of the World," *Studies in English Literature, 1500–1900* 9.4 (Autumn 1969): 677–693, 677.

55. See Leslie Stephen, *The Mausoleum Book,* ed. Alan Bell, 96.

56. Adam Parkes, *Kazuo Ishiguro's The Remains of the Day: A Reader's Guide* (New York: Continuum, 2001), 35.
57. Quentin Bell, *Virginia Woolf: A Biography,* 2nd ed. (London: Pimlico, 1996), 62.
58. Oscar Wilde, *The Importance of Being Earnest and Other Plays,* ed. Peter Raby (Oxford: Oxford University Press, 1998), 288.
59. Diary entry for November 28, 1928, *The Diary of Virginia Woolf,* vol. 3, 208. Woolf goes on to note that "I used to think of him & mother daily; but writing The Lighthouse, laid them in my mind. [*sic*]" As "A Sketch of the Past" shows, this was, at best, a temporary reprieve.
60. It is a curious historical fact that these two major writers—perhaps the most important modernist prose writers in English—share the same dates, 1882–1941. When she heard of Joyce's death, Woolf did note, perhaps fatefully, "Then Joyce is dead—Joyce about a fortnight younger than I am," *Diary,* vol. 5, 352–353, and remembered her first reading of *Ulysses,* published just before *Jacob's Room.*
61. Quoted by Theodore Spencer, introduction to *Stephen Hero,* 8.
62. D. H. Lawrence provides one point of comparison: he produced four separate drafts on the way to *Sons and Lovers,* the second of which survives. It has now been published by Helen Baron as a separate text titled *Paul Morel,* and once again displays very little verbal overlap with the final novel. Helen Baron, ed., *Paul Morel* (Cambridge: Cambridge University Press, 2003). Baron's introduction lays out the textual history.
63. Joyce Carol Oates, "Jocoserious Joyce," *Critical Inquiry* 2.4 (1976): 677–688, 677.
64. Joseph Prescott, "James Joyce's 'Stephen Hero,'" *Journal of English and Germanic Philology* 53.2 (1954): 214–223, 218.
65. On the difference between Emma Clery and E. C., see Bonnie Kime Scott, "Emma Clery: A Young Woman Walking Proudly through the Decayed City," *Women in Joyce,* ed. Suzette Henke and Elaine Unkeless (Urbana: University of Illinois Press, 1982).
66. Theodore Spencer adds, "he was aiming at economy," introduction, *Stephen Hero,* 11.
67. Franco Moretti considers the fifth chapter, "this slowdown, this anticlimax," as a failure, and *Portrait* as a sort of dead branch on the genetic stemma: "far from preparing *Ulysses, Portrait* delayed it," *The Way of the World: The Bildungsroman in European Culture,* trans. Albert Sbragia (London: Verso, 1987), 243–245.
68. Susan Stanford Friedman, *Joyce: The Return of the Repressed* (Ithaca: Cornell University Press, 1993), 27–50.
69. Quoted by Maud Ellmann, "The Name and the Scar," 170. Ellmann discusses the same passage in *The Nets of Modernism,* 5, noting the deictic "here" and the "knot"/"not" pun.
70. Edward Garnett, reader's report for Duckworth, *"Dubliners" and "A Portrait of the Artist as a Young Man": A Casebook,* ed. Morris Beja (London: Macmillan, 1973), 74–75, 75.
71. Michael Levenson, "Stephen's Diary in Joyce's Portrait—The Shape of Life," *English Literary History* 52.4 (Winter 1985): 1017–1035, 1017 and 1019.
72. Several critics have observed that chiasmus is a major figure in the novel, beginning with Hans Walter Gabler's "The Seven Lost Years of *A Portrait of the Artist as a*

Young Man," Approaches to Joyce's Portrait, ed. Thomas F. Staley and Bernard Benstock (Pittsburgh: University of Pittsburgh Press, 1976), 25–60. See Christine Froula, "Modernity, Drafts, Genetic Criticism: On the Virtual Lives of Joyce's Villanelle, *Yale French Studies* 89 (1996): 113–129, 119.

73. James Joyce, *A Portrait of the Artist as a Young Man,* 249, 251, and 252.

74. Woolf comments in her essay "Modern Novels" that *Ulysses,* which she was reading in *The Little Review,* "promises to be a far more interesting work" than *Portrait.* Her opinion in turn of *Ulysses* was at best mixed; James Heffernan discusses in detail at the Yale Modernism Lab, "Woolf's Reading of Joyce's *Ulysses,* 1918–1920," http://modernism.research.yale.edu/wiki/index.php/Woolf<#213>s_Reading_of_Joyce<#213>s_Ulysses,_1918-1920.

75. This was not in fact the *original* beginning of the memoir, as Georgia Johnston notes. Originally, Woolf had written "If life is a bowl which has a base, it mist stand for me up n two memories" [*sic*], 285.

76. Virginia Woolf, *A Passionate Apprentice: The Early Journals, 1897–1909,* ed. Mitchell Leaska (London: Hogarth, 1990), 115.

77. After Stella's death, the diary starts to fall apart. Joanne Campbell Tidwell cites the brevity of an entry from October 1897, that reads simply "Hamlet" and explains, "what follows is the startling departure of the lingual self she has been developing. After Stella's death, few entries reach 100 words. Most are only a few lines, and Virginia begins skipping days," *Politics and Aesthetics in the Diary of Virginia Woolf* (New York: Routledge, 2008), 15.

78. Virginia Woolf, "Reminiscences," *Moments of Being,* ed. Jeanne Schulkind, 25–59, 53.

79. The first remark is in a diary entry for April 18, 1926, *The Diary of Virginia Woolf,* vol. 3, 76. The second is quoted by James Haule from a letter of May 15, 1927, to Ottoline Morrell. James M. Haule, " 'Le temps passé' and the Original Typescript: An Early Version of the 'Time Passes' Section of *To the Lighthouse,*" 269.

80. Virginia Woolf, Holograph draft of *To the Lighthouse,* ed. Susan Dick (Toronto: University of Toronto Press, 1982), 176.

81. James M. Haule, " 'Le Temps Passé' and the Original Typescript," 288.

82. Virginia Woolf, *To the Lighthouse,* 135. The English edition adds "in May" to "in marriage."

83. Alan Warren Friedman, *Fictional Death and the Modernist Enterprise* (Cambridge: Cambridge University Press, 1995), 207.

84. Stella actually died on July 19, 1897. The version printed by Schulkind is a very rough draft and would undoubtedly have been corrected before publication.

85. "Reminiscences," like the *Mausoleum Book,* is addressed to the next generation—specifically, Vanessa's as yet unborn first son, Julia—and so Woolf writes of "your mother" (53).

86. Only the last of these dates has an entry in the actual diary. On November 15, 1940, Woolf notes that "I plunged into the past this morning; wrote about father; & then we walked in top boots & trousers through the flood." *The Diary of Virginia Woolf,* vol. 5, 338–339.

87. Anna Snaith, *Virginia Woolf: Public and Private Negotiations* (New York: Palgrave, 2000), 140.

88. Paul Fussell, *The Great War and Modern Memory,* 24.

89. BL 61973, 96.

90. Georgia Johnston, "Virginia Woolf Revising Roger Fry into the Frames of 'A Sketch of the Past,'" *Biography* 20.3 (1997): 284–301, 284. The phrase "diary approach" is borrowed from Gail Griffin's article "Braving the Mirror: Virginia Woolf as Autobiographer," *Biography* 4.2 (1981): 108–118.

91. Diary entry for February 8, 1926. Virginia Woolf, *The Diary of Virginia Woolf,* ed. Anne Olivier Bell and Andrew McNeillie, vol. 3, 1925–1930 (London: Hogarth, 1977), 58.

92. Diary entry for August 17, 1938, *The Diary of Virginia Woolf,* vol. 5, 162.

93. Virginia Woolf, *Between the Acts* (London: Hogarth, 1941), 78.

94. This is itself revised from the A.5d ms, which reads "Why do I shirk the task, not so very hard to a professional like myself, of ~~filling this boy in and wafting him with whatever substance [unclear reading] he has acquired~~ this boy from the boat to my bed sitting room at Hyde Park Gate."

95. Virginia Woolf, *The Pargiters: The Novel-Essay Portion of The Years,* ed. Mitchell A. Leaska, 8, 14.

96. Mark Hussey develops this idea in the introduction to his edition of the novel by arguing that Woolf not only needed to bridge two different narrative forms, but to "whitewash or gloss over the deeper social and political issues," *The Years* (Orlando: Harcourt, 2008), liii.

97. Jane Goldman's verdict, echoed by many, in *The Cambridge Introduction to Virginia Woolf* (Cambridge: Cambridge University Press, 2006), 24.

98. Phyllis McCord, "'Little Corks That Mark a Sunken Net': Virginia Woolf's 'Sketch of the Past' as a Fictional Memoir," *Modern Language Studies* 16.3 (1986): 247–254, 250.

99. Tyrus Miller, *Late Modernism: Politics, Fiction, and the Arts between the World Wars* (Berkeley: University of California Press, 1999).

100. Richard Ellmann adds that by the late 1930s Joyce had lost interest in *Ulysses,* but one day allowed himself to ask Beckett if anyone in Dublin read it. See Ellman, *James Joyce,* 712.

101. Jay Winter focuses in *Sites of Memory, Sites of Mourning* (Cambridge: Cambridge University Press, 1995) on the "traditionalism" of many of the mourning practices and kinds of collective consolation popular in the immediate aftermath of the war.

102. Ford Madox Ford, *The Good Soldier* (New York: John Lane, 1915), 256.

103. Ronald Bush, "'Unstill, Ever Turning': The Composition of Ezra Pound's *Drafts and Fragments.*" *Text* 7 (1994): 397–423, 397.

104. Jerome McGann, *The Textual Condition,* 129–152. In *Black Riders,* McGann gives more details of the appearance and production of the first two volumes, *A Draft of XVI. Cantos* (1925) and *A Draft of the Cantos 17–27* (1928).

105. Samuel Beckett, *Krapp's Last Tape and Other Dramatic Pieces* (New York: Grove, 1994), 12.

6. Revision, Late Modernism, and Digital Texts

1. T. S. Eliot, "The Use of Poetry and the Use of Criticism," in *Selected Prose*, ed. Kermode, 79–96, 84. Edward Lobb gives the classic account of the romantic origins of Eliot's nominally antiromantic positions in *T. S. Eliot and the Romantic Critical Tradition* (London: Routledge, 1981).

2. I am grateful to J. H. Prynne for introducing me to McFarland's work in a lecture at Cambridge University in 2000. The modern specialization of knowledge in academia, where even closely related fields are distinct fields of knowledge is used as a main example (11–33). Thomas McFarland, *Shapes of Culture* (Iowa City: University of Iowa Press, 1987).

3. The passage that Lonoff has marked, with "six surgically precise black lines," is the ending that Zuckerman understands to be "describing Dencombe's death." Philip Roth, *The Ghost Writer*, 114–15.

4. Daniel Bell, *The Cultural Contradictions of Capitalism* (New York: Basic Books, 1976), 46.

5. For a comprehensive discussion, see Robin Schulze, *Becoming Marianne Moore: The Early Poems, 1907–1924* (Berkeley: University of California Press, 2002), 474. The earlier article, "Textual Evolution: Marianne Moore, the Text of Evolution, and the Evolving Text," *Text* 11 (1998): 270–305, considers Darwin's theory of evolution as a model for the oscillations and environmental adaptation of Moore's texts over time.

6. Andrew J. Kappel, "Complete with Omissions," 144.

7. Mark McGurl, *The Program Era*, 244.

8. Robert Lowell, "The Art of Poetry No. 3," interview with Frederich Seidel, *Paris Review* 25 (1961).

9. Wendy Bishop, "Contracts, Radical Revision, Portfolios, and the Risks of Writing," *Power and Identity in the Creative Writing Classroom: The Authority Project*, ed. Anna Leahy (Clevedon: Multilingual Matters, 2005), 109–120, 109.

10. Joyce Carol Oates, "The Art of Fiction No. 72," *Paris Review* 74 (Fall–Winter 1978).

11. Vladimir Nabokov, *Pale Fire* (New York: Vintage, 1989).

12. Allen Ginsberg, "The Art of Poetry No. 8," *Paris Review* 37 (Spring 1966).

13. Philip Larkin, "What's Become of Wystan?" *Spectator*, July 15, 1960: 104–105.

14. Edward Mendelson, Editor's Preface, *Collected Poems* 11–15, 11.

15. The classic formulation is McKerrow's. R. B. McKerrow, *Prolegomena, The Oxford Shakespeare* (Oxford: Oxford University Press, 1939).

16. Adam Kirsch sums up the position concisely, "For the other camp—which includes Mr. Mendelson—Early Auden is still a genius, but Later Auden is an even bigger genius," before suggesting that there are personal investments at stake, "It's appropriate that Mr. Mendelson should defend the Later Auden, since it was the Later Auden who in 1972 plucked him from the ranks of academia to be his literary executor. Mr. Mendelson, now a professor at Columbia University, is still best known for his work with Auden's literary remains," "Auden's N.Y. Households, From Slum to Sublime" (review of Edward Mendelson's *The Later Auden*), *New York Observer*, May 2, 1999.

17. Edward Mendelson, "Revision and Power: The Example of W. H. Auden," 103.
18. Edward Mendelson, "Revision and Power: The Example of W. H. Auden," 104–105.
19. Stephen James, "Revision as Redress? Robert Lowell's Manuscripts," *Essays in Criticism* 46.1 (1996): 28–51, 46.
20. Zachary Leader, *Revision and Romantic Authorship*, 14.
21. Auden kept the stanzas in editions up to and including his *Collected Shorter Poems, 1930–1944*.
22. The typescript that he sent to the magazine (in the Berg collection) contains two stanzas that had been heavily crossed out, but which are still legible (beginning "No promises can stay/ The ruling of the court"), as well as a cancelled dedication to Thomas Mann.
23. An image of the page is scanned as a JPG file, as an example of "The author's unauthorized annotations," http://www.swarthmore.edu/library/auden/library3.html.
24. John Haffenden quotes Charles Osborne, who claims that Auden made similar changes on other friends' copies of his work, *W. H. Auden: The Critical Heritage* (London: Routledge, 1997), 30.
25. Quoted in John Haffenden, *W. H. Auden,* 28–29.
26. Orwell criticized Auden in the essay "Inside the Whale," written in 1939 and published in 1949. John Haffenden cites the relevant passages, *W. H. Auden: The Critical Heritage,* 29.
27. See Stephen Burt, "'September 1, 1939' Revisited, or, Poetry, Politics, and the Idea of the Public," *American Literary History* 15.3 (Fall 2003): 533–559; and Nicholas Jenkins, "Either *Or* or *And:* An Enigmatic Moment in the History of 'September 1, 1939,'" *Yale Review* 90.3 (July 2002): 22–39.
28. Reprinted in W. H. Auden, *Collected Poems,* 15–16. And yet, before being deleted the poem has been revised in ways that made it *more* rhetorical: emphasizing the triad of "Yesterday," "Today," "Tomorrow"; strategically capitalizing "the Mover"; and going straight from the slightly negative depiction of mass public action, "The beautiful roar of the chorus under the dome," and "the sudden forest of hands," to the next stanza, "Tomorrow, for the young, the poets exploding like bombs."
29. Reprinted in Auden, *Collected Poems,* 15.
30. W. H. Auden, Author's Foreword, 1965, reprinted in Auden, *Collected Poems,* 16.
31. Edward Mendelson, *The Later Auden* (London: Faber and Faber, 1999), 477.
32. *The English Auden,* 144–146, 145. This reading is also printed in W. H. Auden, *Look, Stranger!* (London: Faber and Faber, 1936) and its American parallel, W. H. Auden, *On This Island* (New York: Random House, 1937).
33. "Through the Looking Glass," in Auden, *Collected Poems,* 107–108, 107.
34. Revision to "Spain, 1937," made between the poem's first publication as "Spain," and its book publication in 1940.
35. The poem was first published in the *Criterion* in July 1993. Auden made the change for the 1966 *Collected Shorter Poems, 1927–1957* (London: Faber and Faber, 1966).
36. "Certainly praise: let song mount again and again," original reading from *Journey to a War* (London: Faber and Faber, 1939); new reading introduced for *Collected Shorter Poems, 1930–1944* (1950).

37. "Underneath an Abject Willow," original reading from Auden, *Look, Stranger!*
38. "Fleeing from short-haired mad executives," original reading from *Look, Stranger!* New reading introduced for the 1945 *The Collected Poetry*.
39. "Its leading characters are wise and witty," original reading in *Journey to a War;* new reading introduced for the 1966 *Collected Shorter Poems, 1927–1957.*
40. "A nondescript express in from the South," original reading in the magazine publication *New Writing* (Spring 1939); "distracts" introduced for first book publication, *Another Time* (1940).
41. "No one, not even Cambridge, was to blame," original reading in *New Writing* (Spring 1939) but, unlike the previous revision, retained for the 1940 *Another Time.* New reading introduced for the *Collected Shorter Poems, 1927–1957.*
42. "He was their servant (some say he was blind)," the first reading is in all editions from until *Selected Poems* (1968).
43. "As evening fell the day's oppression lifted," original reading in *Journey to a War* and maintained up to and including *Collected Shorter Poems, 1930–1944* (1950); second reading introduced for *W. H. Auden: A Selection by the Author* (London: Penguin, 1958) and the American version, *The Selected Poetry of W. H. Auden* (New York: Modern Library, 1959).
44. "Who needs their names? Another genus built," original reading in *Journey to a War* and maintained until the *Collected Shorter Poems, 1927–1957.* New reading introduced for the *Selected Poems* (London: Faber and Faber, 1968).
45. "On and on and on," this transposition was made for the first book publication, *Nones* (New York: Random House, 1951); the original reading in magazine publication, *Atlantic* CLXXX.5 (November 1947): 62, and *Phoenix Quarterly* 1.3 (Autumn 1948): 21.
46. Perhaps appropriately, given his own lifelong passion for correction, this revision, along with several others, appears in the poem "At The Grave of Henry James," beginning "The snow, less intransigeant than their marble." The original reading is maintained from the magazine publication to *Collected Shorter Poems, 1927–1957,* and the new "worlds" for the posthumous *Collected Poems.*
47. "I can imagine quite easily ending up," original reading from *London Magazine* 1.3 (April 1954), retained through the 1966 *Collected Shorter Poems, 1927–1957.*
48. Anyone wanting a simple, well-presented guide to Auden's changes would be advised to look at W. D. Quesenbery's guide, *Auden's Revisions*, which painstakingly collates the many British and American editions—my knowledge of this edition history is deeply indebted to this guide. As he explains, some of these editions are difficult to get hold of, and Auden himself "did not commit to a strict chronological order on the basis of either composition or publication."
49. Happily enough, it begins "About suffering they were never wrong/ The Old Masters," and ends with "Young Men late in the night/ Toss on their beds."
50. James Fenton, "Auden at Home," *New York Review of Books*, April 27, 2000.
51. This notebook, which belongs to the Berg Collection, has been published in facsimile, with an introduction by Nicholas Jenkins, *W. H. Auden: Poems 1927–1929*, ed. Patrick Lawlor (Harcourt Brace, New York Public Library, 1989), 57–58.

52. W. H. Auden, *Collected Poetry* (New York: Random House, 1945), 72 and 134–135.

53. Humphrey Carpenter's verdict, *W. H. Auden: A Biography* (Oxford: Oxford University Press, 1992), 365–366.

54. Allen Ginsberg, *Howl: Original Draft Facsimile, Transcript, and Variant Versions, Fully Annotated by the Author with Contemporaneous Correspondence, Account of First Public Reading, Legal Skirmishes, Precursor Texts, and Bibliography* (New York: Harper Collins, 1995). The original edition, now available in a small format facsimile, is *Howl and Other Poems* (San Francisco: City Lights Books, 1956).

55. "Author's Preface: Readers Guide," 1986, xi–xii.

56. Bill Morgan also cites the publication of the Harper and Row *Collected Poems, 1947–1980,* "Lines Drawn in the Sand: The Life and Writings of Allen Ginsberg," http://www.lib.unc.edu/rbc/beats/ginsberg.html.

57. Bill Savage argues that "This physical resemblance (with the light-police-blue-cover of *Howl* being, of course, more colorful than the muted browns of *The Waste Land*) asserts a canonical continuity, a connection between the generation-defining poems of the Modernists and the Beats," in "Allen Ginsberg's 'Howl' and the Paperback Revolution," republished online, http://www.poets.org/viewmedia.php/prmMID/20201.

58. Jack Kerouac, "Essentials of Spontaneous Prose," *Evergreen Review* 2.5 (Summer 1958): 72–73.

59. John Tytell, "On Burroughs's Work: A Conversation with Allen Ginsberg," *Partisan Review* 41.2 (1974): 253–262, 255.

60. Allen Ginsberg, "The *Dharma Bums* Review," *Deliberate Prose: Selected Essays, 1952–1995* (New York: Harper Collins, 2000), 342–348.

61. See Luc Sante's article in the *New York Times,* "On the Road Again," August 19, 2007, http://www.nytimes.com/2007/08/19/books/review/Sante2-t-1.html.

62. Allen Ginsberg, "Feb. 29, 1958," *Journals Mid-Fifties, 1954–1958* (New York: Harper Collins, 1995), 427.

63. Some of Ginsberg's recordings of the poem from 1956 to the 1995 performance at the Knitting Factory in New York can be heard here: http://writing.upenn.edu/pennsound/x/Ginsberg.php.

64. See Jonah Raskin, *American Scream: Allen Ginsberg's "Howl" and the Making of the Beat Generation* (Berkeley: University of California Press, 2005), 23–24.

65. Marjorie Perloff, "A Lost Batallion of Platonic Conversationalists: 'Howl' and the Language of Modernism," *The Poem That Changed America: "Howl" Fifty Years Later,* ed. Jason Shinder (New York: Farrar Straus, 2006), 24–43, 9.

66. Conrad Aiken, "The Art of Poetry No. 9," *Paris Review* 42 (Winter–Spring 1968). Elizabeth Bishop, "The Art of Poetry No. 27," *Paris Review* 80 (Summer 1981).

67. In a television interview in March 1959, quoted by Alex Goody, *Technology, Literature and Culture* (Cambridge: Polity, 2011), 117.

68. Thomas J. Travisano, *Midcentury Quartet: Bishop, Lowell, Jarell, Berryman and the Making of a Postmodern Aesthetic* (Charlottesville: University of Virginia Press, 1999), 109.

69. See Marjorie Perloff, *Frank O'Hara: Poet among Painters* (Chicago: University of Chicago Press, 1998), 116.

70. John Berryman, "The Art of Poetry No. 16," *Paris Review* 53 (Winter 1972).

71. In an article in the *Christian Science Monitor,* Matthew Shaer concludes that this would have been a bad thing for Proust and his readers: "so he reaches out to Jeff Bezos. Amazon happily makes the changes—and sends out new editions of 'In Search of Lost Time' to all its customers. And in the process, a great work of literature is tinkered and noodled to death." "Amazon sometimes issues patches for Kindle e-books. Is that a good thing?" May 11, 2010.

72. Lou Burnard, "Does Genetic Criticism Have a Future without Digital Forensics?" Presentation given at *ITEM* January 31, 2011, and text published at http://louburnard .wordpress.com/.

73. Steve Kolowich, "Archiving Writer's Work in the Age of E-Mail," *Chronicle of Higher Education,* April 10, 2009, http://chronicle.com/article/article-content/22770/.

74. Matthew Kirschenbaum, "Approaches to Managing and Collecting Born-Digital Literary Materials for Scholarly Use," White Paper to the New Office of Digital Humanities, May 2009.

75. Patricia Cohen, "Fending off Digital Decay, Bit by Bit," *New York Times,* March 15, 2010, http://www.nytimes.com/2010/03/16/books/16archive.html.

76. Robert Creeley claimed in 1968 that he did not do much revision—"I *do* work in this fashion of simply sitting down and writing, usually without any process of revision," "The Art of Poetry No. 10," *Paris Review* 44 (Fall 1968). If this continued when he began composing on a computer, his archive might prove less interesting for genetic critics than that of other writers.

77. See Michael Hancher, "Littera Scripta Manet: Blackstone and Electronic Text," *Studies in Bibliography* 54 (2001): 115–132. Matthew Kirschenbaum discusses Hancher's work as part of his own argument that scholars have paid far too much attention to the "fluidity and fungibility" of electronic text, without attending to the various ways in which it can be permanent—and permanently retrieved. Matthew G. Kirschenbaum, *Mechanisms: New Media and the Forensic Imagination* (Cambridge: Massachusetts Institute of Technology Press, 2008).

78. Matthew Kirschenbaum, *Mechanisms: New Media and the Forensic Imagination,* 197–199.

79. Dirk Van Hulle, "The Dynamics of Incompletion: Multilingual Manuscript Genetics and Digital Philology," *Neohelicon* 36.2 (2009): 451–461, 452–453.

80. Matthew G. Kirschenbaum, *Mechanisms: New Media and the Forensic Imagination,* 200.

81. Doug Reside, "'No Day but Today': A Look at Jonathan Larson's Word Files," April 22, 2011, http://www.nypl.org/blog/2011/04/22/no-day-today-look-jonathan-larsons -word-files.

82. Michael Pietsch describes his work in the "Editor's Note," David Foster Wallace, *The Pale King* (New York: Little Brown, 2011), 5–9, 5.

83. David Foster Wallace can be heard reading at http://www.lannan.org/lf/rc/event/david -foster-wallace/.

84. In the *Paris Review* blog, March 4, 2011, http://www.theparisreview.org/blog/2011 /03/04/staff-picks-comparing-backbones-jennifer-egan<#213>s-journalism/.

85. In the novel, this passage is on pages 400–401.

86. Letter from T. S. Eliot to Ezra Pound, January 1922, in *The Letters of Ezra Pound, 1907–1941,* 236.
87. Samuel Beckett, *Waiting for Godot* (New York: Grove, 1970), 29.
88. Readers who come to classic literary texts online may find less information about edition histories—and possibly less accurate texts—than their predecessors; Google Books, for example, has a way of ordering or tracking editions of a text other than through identifying vague relation. Instead of existing in discrete, easily demarcated and dated stages or forms, digital texts occupy a continuous, fluid present.
89. See the discussion of different kinds of self-rereading in chapter 1, p. 27.
90. On the continuity between manuscripts and early printed books, see Mary C. Erler, "Devotional Literature," in *The Cambridge History of the Book in Britain: Vol. 3, 1400–1557,* ed. Lotte Hellinga and J. B. Trapp (Cambridge: Cambridge University Press, 1999), 495–524, and on the use of color, 509. In *The Gutenberg Galaxy* (Toronto: University of Toronto Press, 1962), Marshall McLuhan comes back several times to the fact that "book format long retained the characteristics of manuscript appearance," 208.
91. Hellinga discusses this list of faults and describes the additions that More made for the next version as "substantial," "Printing," *The Cambridge History of the Book: Volume 3, 1400–1557,* 65–108, 89.
92. David Greetham, *Textual Scholarship: An Introduction* (New York and London: Garland, 1992), 75. Is it not rather that "finished product" has meaning only within print culture?
93. Jessica Bruder discusses the typewriter phenomenon in "Click, Clack, Ding, Sigh!" an article published on March 30, 2011, in the *New York Times.* Identifying the typewriter first with Williamsburg, she goes on to describe "type-ins" held across the country and writers' joy in the simplicity of the typewriter ("typewriters are only good for one thing"), reading this as a "renaissance" rather than nostalgia.

Works Cited

Acheson, James and Romana Huk, eds. *Contemporary British Poetry: Essays in Theory and Criticism*. Albany: State University of New York Press, 1996.

Ackerley, C. J. and S. E. Gontarski, eds. *The Grove Companion to Samuel Beckett*. New York: Grove, 2004.

Ackroyd, Peter. *T. S. Eliot: A Life*. New York: Simon and Schuster, 1984.

Adams, Robert Martin. *Surface and Symbol: The Consistency of Joyce's Ulysses*. Oxford: Oxford University Press, 1962.

Adams, Thomas R. and Nicholas Barker. "A New Model for the Study of the Book." *A Potencie of Life: Books in Society*. Ed. Nicholas Barker. London: British Library, 1993. 5–43.

Aiken, Conrad. "The Art of Poetry No. 9." Interview with Robert Hunter Wilbur. *Paris Review* 42 (Winter–Spring): 1968.

Alamargot, Denis and Lucile Chanquoy. *Through the Models of Writing*. Norwell, MA: Kluwer, 2001.

Albright, Daniel. *Quantum Poetics: Yeats, Pound, Eliot, and the Science of Modernism*. Cambridge and New York: Cambridge University Press, 1997.

———. *Untwisting the Serpent: Modernism in Music, Literature, and Other Arts*. Chicago: University of Chicago Press, 2000.

———. "Virginia Woolf as Autobiographer." *Kenyon Review* 6.1 (1984): 1–17.

Amselle, Frédérique. *Virginia Woolf et les écritures du moi: le journal et l'autobiographie*. Montpellier: Presses Universitaires de la Méditerranée, 2008.

Anesko, Michael. "Collected Editions and the Consolidation of Cultural Authority: The Case of Henry James." *Book History* 12 (2009): 186–208.

———. *Friction with the Market*. Oxford and New York: Oxford University Press, 1986.

Arac, Jonathan. "Bounding Lines: *The Prelude* and Critical Revision." In *Poststructuralist Readings of English Poetry*. Ed. Richard Machin and Christopher Norris. Cambridge: Cambridge University Press, 1987. 227–247.

Armstrong, Tim. *Modernism, Technology and the Body: A Cultural Study*. Cambridge: Cambridge University Press, 1998.

Attridge, Derek. *Joyce Effects*. Cambridge: Cambridge University Press, 2000.

———. "Joyce's Pen." In *Joyce, Penelope and the Body*. Ed. Richard Brown. Amsterdam: Rodolphi, 2006. 47–62.

———. *Peculiar Language: Literature as Difference from the Renaissance to James Joyce*. Ithaca: Cornell University Press, 1988.

———, ed. *The Cambridge Companion to James Joyce*. Cambridge: Cambridge University Press, 2004.

Auden, W. H. *Another Time*. London: Faber and Faber, 1940.

———. *Collected Poems*. Ed. Edward Mendelson. New York: Random House, 1976.

———. *Collected Shorter Poems, 1930–1944*. London: Faber and Faber, 1950.

———. *Collected Shorter Poems, 1927–1957*. London: Faber and Faber, 1966.

———. *Forewords and Afterwords*. Ed. Edward Mendelson. New York: Random House, 1973.

———. *Journey to a War*. London: Faber and Faber, 1939.

———. *Juvenilia: Poems, 1922–1928*. Ed. Katherine Bucknell. Princeton: Princeton University Press, 1994.

———. *Look, Stranger!* London: Faber and Faber, 1936.

———. *Nones*. New York: Random House, 1951.

———. *On This Island*. New York: Random House, 1937.

———. *Spain*. London: Faber and Faber, 1937.

———. *Selected Poems*. London: Faber and Faber, 1938.

———. *Selected Poems*. London: Faber and Faber, 1968.

———. *Selected Poetry of W. H. Auden*. New York: Modern Library, 1958.

———. *The Collected Poetry of W. H. Auden*. New York: Random House, 1945.

———. *The Dyer's Hand*. London: Faber and Faber, 1963.

———. *W. H. Auden: A Selection by the Author*. London: Penguin, 1958.

Austin, J. L. *How to Do Things with Words*. Cambridge: Harvard University Press, 1975.

Ayers, David. *Modernism: A Short Introduction*. Oxford: Blackwell, 2004.

Balassi, William. "The Trail to *The Sun Also Rises:* The First Week of Writing." In *Hemingway: Essays of Reassessment*. Ed. Frank Scafella. New York: Oxford University Press, 1991.

Balliet, Conrad. "The History and Rhetoric of the Triplet." *PMLA* 80.5 (1965): 528–534.

Banfield, Ann. "Tragic Time: The Problem of the Future in Cambridge Philosophy and *To the Lighthouse*." *Modernism/modernity* 7.1 (2000): 43–75.

Barker Nicholas, ed. *A Potencie of Life: Books in Society*. London: British Library, 1993.

Barry, Peter. *Contemporary British Poetry and the City*. Manchester: Manchester University Press, 2000.

Barthes, Roland. *L'Aventure Sémiologique*. Paris: Seuil, 1985.

———. "The Death of the Author" (1968). *Image, Music, Text*. London: Fontana, 1977.

Bate, Jonathan. *John Clare: A Biography*. New York: Farrar, Strauss and Giroux, 2003.

————. *The Genius of Shakespeare.* London: Picador, 1997.

Beach, Joseph Warren. *The Making of the Auden Canon.* Minneapolis: University of Minnesota Press, 1957.

Beach, Sylvia. *Shakespeare and Company.* Lincoln: University of Nebraska Press, 1991.

Beckett, Samuel. *Krapp's Last Tape and Other Dramatic Pieces.* New York: Grove, 1986.

————. *Waiting for Godot.* New York: Grove, 1970.

————. *Worstward Ho.* New York: Grove, 1983.

Bedford, Sybille. *Quicksands.* New York: Counterpoint, 2006.

Beegel, Susan F. *Hemingway's Craft of Omission: Four Manuscript Examples.* Ann Arbor: University of Michigan Press, 1988.

Beja, Morris, ed. *"Dubliners" and "A Portrait of the Artist as a Young Man": A Casebook.* London: Macmillan, 1973.

Bell, Alan. Introduction. In *The Mausoleum Book.* By Leslie Stephen. Oxford: Clarendon, 1977.

Bell, Daniel. *The Cultural Contradictions of Capitalism.* New York: Basic Books, 1976.

Bell, Quentin. *Virginia Woolf: A Biography.* Vol. 1, 1882–1912. London: Hogarth, 1972.

Bell, Susan. *The Artful Edit.* New York: Norton, 2008.

Benjamin, Walter. "The Work of Art in the Age of Mechanical Reproduction." In *Illuminations.* Trans. Harry Zohn. Ed. Hannah Arendt. New York: Schocken, 1968. 217–251.

Berryman, John. "The Art of Poetry No. 16." Interview with Peter A. Stitt. *Paris Review* 53 (Winter 1972).

Birnbaum, Robert. "Birnbaum v. Joyce Carol Oates." *The Morning News,* February 3, 2005, http://www.themorningnews.org/archives/personalities/birnbaum_v_joyce_carol_oates.php.

Bishop, Elizabeth. "The Art of Poetry No. 27." Interview with Elizabeth Spires. *Paris Review* 80 (Summer 1981).

————. *The Complete Poems, 1927–1979.* New York: Farrar, Strauss, and Giroux, 1983.

Bishop, Wendy. "Contracts, Radical Revision, Portfolios, and the Risks of Writing." In *Power and Identity in the Creative Writing Classroom: The Authority Project.* Ed. Anna Leahy. Clevedon: Multilingual Matters, 2005. 109–120.

Bloom, Lynn Z. "'I Write for Myself and Strangers': Private Diaries as Public Documents." In *Inscribing the Daily.* Ed. Suzanne L. Bunkers and Cynthia A. Huff. Amherst: University of Massachusetts Press, 1996.

Blotner, Joseph Leo. *Faulkner: A Biography.* Jackson: University Press of Mississippi, 2005.

Booth, Alison. *Greatness Engendered: George Eliot and Virginia Woolf.* Ithaca: Cornell University Press, 1992.

Booth, Wayne. *The Rhetoric of Fiction.* Chicago: University of Chicago Press, 1983.

Bornstein, George. *Material Modernism: The Politics of the Page.* Cambridge: Cambridge University Press, 2001.

————, ed. *Representing Modernist Texts: Editing as Interpretation.* Ann Arbor: University of Michigan Press, 1991.

Bosanquet, Theodora. *Henry James at Work.* Ed. Lyall H. Powers. Ann Arbor: University of Michigan Press, 2006.

Boswell, James. *Boswell's Life of Johnson.* London: H. Baldwin, 1799.

Bourdieu, Pierre. *The Rules of Art: Genesis and Structure of the Literary Field.* Trans. Susan Emanuel. Stanford: Stanford University Press, 1996.

Bowers, Fredson. *On Editing Shakespeare.* Philadelphia: University of Pennsylvania Library, 1955.

——. *Principles of Textual Criticism.* San Marino: Huntington Library, 1972.

——. *Textual and Literary Criticism.* Cambridge: Cambridge University Press, 1966.

Bowman, Paul Frank. "Genetic Criticism." *Poetics Today* 11.3 (1990): 627–646.

Bradbury, Malcolm and James McFarlane. "The Name and Nature of Modernism." In *Modernism, 1890–1930.* Ed. Malcolm Bradbury and James MacFarlane. Sussex: Harvester, 1976.

Bromwich, David. *Skeptical Music: Essays on Modern Poetry.* Chicago: University of Chicago Press, 2001.

Browne, E. Martin. *The Making of T. S. Eliot's Plays.* Cambridge: Cambridge University Press, 1969.

Bruccoli, Matthew J. *Ernest Hemingway, The Sun Also Rises: A Facsimile Edition.* Detroit: Omnigraphics, 1990.

Bruder, Jessica. "Click, Clack, Ding, Sigh!" *New York Times,* March 30, 2011.

Bryant, John. *Melville Unfolding: Sexuality, Politics, and the Versions of Typee.* Ann Arbor: University of Michigan Press, 2008.

——. *The Fluid Text: A Theory of Revision and Editing for Book and Screen.* Ann Arbor: University of Michigan Press, 2002.

Bunkers, Suzanne. "Whose Diary Is It, Anyway?" *a/b: Auto/Biography Studies* 17.1 (2002): 11–27.

Burnard, Lou. "Does Genetic Criticism Have a Future without Digital Forensics?" http://louburnard.wordpress.com/.

Burt, Stephen. "'September 1, 1939' Revisited, or, Poetry, Politics, and the Idea of the Public." *American Literary History* 15.3 (2003): 533–559.

Bush, Ronald. *The Genesis of Pound's Cantos.* Princeton: Princeton University Press, 1976.

——. ed. *T. S. Eliot: The Modernist in History.* Cambridge: Cambridge University Press, 1991.

——. "'Unstill, Ever Turning': The Composition of Ezra Pound's *Draft and Fragments.*" *Text* 7 (1994): 397–422.

Butler, Judith. *Gender Trouble: Feminism and the Subversion of Identity.* New York: Routledge, 1990.

Butterfield, Herbert. *The Whig Interpretation of History.* London: G. Bell, 1959.

Byatt, A. S. "A Note on the Text." In *The Bostonians.* By Henry James, New York: Random House, 2001.

Byron, Lord George Gordon. *Byron's Letters and Journals.* Vol. 7, Ed. Leslie A. Marchand. Cambridge: Harvard University Press, 1978.

Cameron, Sharon. *Choosing Not Choosing: Dickinson's Fascicles.* Chicago: University of Chicago Press, 1992.

——. *Thinking in Henry James.* Chicago: University of Chicago Press, 1989.

Campbell, Sarah. "The Man Who Talked Like a Book, Wrote Like He Spoke." *Interval(le)s* 2.2–3.1 (Fall 2008–Winter 2009): 163–173.

Cano, Christine M. "Genetic Aberrations: The Two Faces of Proust." *Textual Practice* 17.1 (2003): 41–60.

——. *Proust's Deadline: The Temporality of Writing and Publishing.* Urbana: University of Illinois Press, 2006.

Capp, Daniel. *The Poetry of Shell Shock.* Jefferson, NC: McFarland, 2005.

Carpenter, Humphrey. *A Serious Character: The Life of Ezra Pound.* Boston: Houghton Mifflin, 1988.

——. *W. H. Auden: A Biography.* Oxford: Oxford University Press, 1992.

Caruth, Cathy. *Unclaimed Experience: Trauma, Narrative, and History.* Baltimore: Johns Hopkins University Press, 1996.

Castle, Gregory. "Colonial Discourse and the Subject of Empire in Joyce's 'Nausicaa.'" In *Joyce: Feminism/Post/Colonialism.* Ed. Ellen Carol Jones. Amsterdam and Atlanta: European Joyce Studies, 1998.

Chase, Cynthia. "The Accidents of Disfiguration." In *Decomposing Figures: Rhetorical Readings in the Romantic Tradition.* Baltimore and London: Johns Hopkins University Press, 1986.

Chico, Tita. "Privacy and Speculation in Early Eighteenth-Century Britain." *Cultural Critique* 52 (2002): 40–60.

Cohen, Milton A. *Hemingway's Laboratory: The Paris "in our time."* Tuscaloosa: University of Alabama Press, 2005.

Cohen, Patricia. "Fending Off Digital Decay, Bit by Bit." *New York Times,* March 15, 2010.

Coleridge, Samuel Taylor. *Selected Poems by Samuel Taylor Coleridge.* Ed. William Empson and David Pirie. New York: Routledge, 2002.

—— and William Wordsworth. *Lyrical Ballads 1798 and 1800.* Ed. Michael Gamer and Dahlia Porter. Peterborough: Broadview Press, 2008.

Compagnon, Antoine. Introduction. *Romanic Review* 86.3 (1995): 393–401.

——. *Literature, Theory, and Common Sense.* Trans. Carol Cosman. Princeton: Princeton University Press, 2004.

Cook, E. T. and Alexander Wedderburn, eds. *The Complete Works of John Ruskin.* Vol. 15. London: George Allen, 1904.

Creeley, Robert. "The Art of Poetry No. 10." Interview with Lewis MacAdams and Linda Wagner-Martin. *Paris Review* 44 (Fall 1968).

Crook, Stephen. "Auden on the Record." *The W. H. Auden Society Newsletter* 6 (1990).

Crowley, Ronan. "Proof^Finder: Placards." *Genetic Joyce Studies* 8 (2008).

Crystal, David. "Repair." *A Dictionary of Language and Phonetics.* 6th ed. Oxford: Blackwell, 2008.

Culler, Jonathan. *On Deconstruction: Theory and Criticism after Structuralism.* Ithaca: Cornell University Press, 1982.

Dahl, Christopher C. "Virginia Woolf's *Moments of Being* and Autobiographical Tradition in the Stephen Family." *Journal of Modern Literature* 10 (1983): 175–196.

Dames, Nicholas. *The Physiology of the Novel: Reading, Neural Science, and the Form of Victorian Fiction.* Oxford: Oxford University Press, 2007.

——. "Wave-Theories and Affective Physiologies: The Cognitive Strain in Victorian Novel Theories." *Victorian Studies* 46.2 (2004): 206–216.

Damon, S. Foster. *Amy Lowell: A Chronicle, with Extracts from Her Correspondence.* Boston: Houghton, 1935.

Darnton, Robert. *The Kiss of Lamourette: Reflections in Cultural History.* London: Norton, 1990.

———. "What Is the History of Books?" *Daedalus* 111.3 (1982). Reprinted in *The Kiss of Lamourette: Reflections in Cultural History.* London: Norton, 1990. 107–135.

———. "'What Is the History of Books?' Revisited." *Modern Intellectual History* 4.3 (2007): 495–508.

DaRosa, Marc. "Henry James, Anonymity, and the Press: Journalistic Modernity and the Decline of the Author." *Modern Fiction Studies* 43.4 (1997): 826–859.

Darwin, Charles. "Autobiography." *The Life and Letters of Charles Darwin.* Ed. Francis Darwin. Vol. 1. London: John Murray, 1887. 26–82.

———. *The Expression of the Emotions in Man and Animals.* New York and Oxford: Oxford University Press, 1998.

Davie, Donald. *Ezra Pound: Poet as Sculptor.* London: Routledge, 1965.

Davies, Damian Walter. "Thomas de Quincey: *Confessions of an English Opium-Eater.*" In *A Companion to Romanticism.* Ed. Duncan Wu. Oxford: Blackwell, 1999. 269–276.

De Biasi, Pierre-Marc, "What Is a Literary Draft? Toward a Functional Typology of Genetic Criticism." *Yale French Studies* 89 (1996): 26–58.

DeKoven, Marianne. *Rich and Strange: Gender, History, Modernism.* Princeton: Princeton University Press, 1991.

Delany, Paul. "Who Paid for Modernism?" In *The New Economic Criticism.* Ed. Martha Woodmansee and Mark Osten. London: Routledge, 1999.

De Man, Paul. *The Rhetoric of Romanticism.* New York: Columbia University Press, 1984.

Deppman, Jed, Daniel Ferrer, and Michael Groden, eds. *Genetic Criticism: Texts and Avant-Textes.* Philadelphia: University of Pennsylvania Press, 2004.

Derrida, Jacques. "Freud and the Scene of Writing." In *Writing and Difference.* Trans. Alan Bass. Chicago: University of Chicago Press, 1978.

———. *Of Grammatology.* Trans. Gayatri Chakravorty Spivak. Baltimore and London: Johns Hopkins University Press, 1974.

———. "Signature, Event, Context." *Limited Inc.* Trans. Samuel Weber and Jeffrey Mehlman. Evanston: Northwestern University Press, 1988. 1–24.

———. "The Word Processor." *Paper Machine.* Trans. Rachel Bowlby. Stanford: Stanford University Press, 2005.

———. *The Work of Mourning.* Ed. and trans. Pascale Anne-Brault and Michael Naas. Chicago: University of Chicago Press, 2001.

DeSalvo, Louise. *Virginia Woolf's First Novel: A Voyage in the Making.* London: Macmillan, 1980.

———. *Virginia Woolf: The Impact of Childhood Sexual Abuse on Her Life and Work.* Boston: Beacon Press, 1989.

De Selincourt, Ernest. *Wordsworth: The Prelude or Growth of a Poet's Mind.* Oxford: Clarendon, 1928.

Dettmar, Kevin J. H. and Stephen Watt, eds. *Marketing Modernisms: Self-Promotion, Canonization, and Rereading.* Ann Arbor: University of Michigan Press, 1996.

Dick, Susan, ed. *Omnium Gatherum: Essays for Richard Ellmann*. Gerrards Cross, Buckinghamshire: C. Smythe, 1989.

Dickens, Charles. *Little Dorrit*. Oxford: Oxford World's Classics, 1999.

Doolittle, Hilda (H. D.). *Collected Poems, 1912–1944*. Ed. Louis L. Martz. New York: New Directions, 1986.

———. *End to Torment*. New York: New Directions, 1979.

Dosse, Francois. *History of Structuralism*. Vol. 2. Trans. Deborah Glassman. Mineapolis: University of Minnesota Press, 1992.

Doyno, Victor. *Writing Huck Finn: Mark Twain's Creative Process*. Philadelphia: University of Pennsylvania Press, 1991.

Dragunoiu, Dana. "Hemingway's Debt to Stendahl's *Armance* in *The Sun Also Rises.*" *Modern Fiction Studies*, 46 (2000): 868–892.

Driver, Clive. *Ulysses: The Manuscript and First Printing Compared*. London: Faber and Faber, 1975.

Dupee, Frederick W. Introduction. In *Henry James: Autobiography*. Princeton: Princeton University Press, 1983.

Dutton, Dennis. *The Art Instinct: Pleasure, Beauty, and Human Evolution*. New York: Bloomsbury, 2009.

Eble, Kenneth, ed. *The Europeans: A Facsimile of the Manuscript*. New York: Howard Fertig, 1979.

Edel, Leon. *Henry James: A Life*. New York: Harper and Row, 1985.

———, ed. *Henry James: Letters*. Vol. 4. 1895–1916. Cambridge and London: Harvard University Press, 1984.

———. *Henry James: The Master (1901–1916)*. Philadelphia: Lippincott, 1972.

Eliot, George. "Silly Novels by Lady Novelists." 1856. In *George Eliot: Selected Essays, Poems and Other Writings*. Ed. A. S. Byatt and Nicholas Warren. London: Penguin 1990. 140–164

Eliot, Simon. "The Business of Victorian Publishing." In *The Cambridge Companion to the Victorian Novel*. Ed. Deirdre David. Cambridge: Cambridge University Press, 2001. 37–60.

Eliot, T. S., trans. *Anabasis: A Poem by St.-John Perse*. London: Faber and Faber, 1930. 3rd ed. *Anabasis: A Poem by St.-John Perse*. New York: Harcourt Brace, 1949.

———. "A Talk on Dante." *Kenyon Review* 14.2 (1952).

———. *Collected Poems 1909–1962*. New York: Harcourt Brace, 1963.

———. "Ezra Pound." *Poetry Chicago*, September 1946.

———. *Inventions of the March Hare*. Ed. Christopher Ricks. London: Faber and Faber, 1996.

———. *Knowledge and Experience in the Philosophy of F. H. Bradley*. New York: Columbia University Press, 1989.

———. *Literary Essays*. Norfolk, CT: New Directions, 1954.

———. *On Poetry and Poets*. London: Faber and Faber, 1957.

———. *Selected Essays*. 3rd ed. London: Faber and Faber, 1951.

———. *Selected Prose*. Ed. Frank Kermode. New York: Harcourt Brace Jovanovich, 1975.

———. "The Art of Poetry No. 1." Interview with Donald Hall. *Paris Review* 21 (1959): 47–70.

——. *The Sacred Wood: Essays on Poetry and Criticism.* London: Methuen, 1920.

——. *To Criticize the Critic and Other Writings.* New York: Farrar, Straus, and Giroux, 1965.

Eliot, Valerie, ed. *The Letters of T. S. Eliot.* London: Faber and Faber, 1988.

——, ed. *The Waste Land: A Facsimile and Transcript of the Original Drafts Including the Annotations of Ezra Pound.* New York: Harcourt Brace, 1971.

Ellis, Bret Easton. *American Psycho.* New York: Vintage, 1991.

——. *Glamorama.* New York: Vintage, 2000.

Ellmann, Maud. "The Name and the Scar." In *A Portrait of the Artist as a Young Man: A Casebook.* Ed. Mark Wollaeger. Oxford and New York: Oxford University Press, 2003. 143–180.

——. *The Nets of Modernism.* Cambridge: Cambridge University Press, 2010.

——. *The Poetics of Impersonality: T. S. Eliot and Ezra Pound.* Cambridge: Harvard University Press, 1987.

Ellmann, Richard. *James Joyce.* 1959. Rev. ed. New York: Oxford University Press, 1982.

——. "The First *Waste Land.*" In *Eliot in His Time.* Ed. A. Walton Litz. Princeton: Princeton University Press, 1973.

Erler, Mary C. "Devotional Literature." In *The Cambridge History of the Book in Britain: Volume III, 1400–1557.* Ed. Lotte Hellinga and J. B. Trapp. Cambridge: Cambridge University Press, 1999. 495–515.

Espey, John Jenkins. *Ezra Pound's "Mauberley": A Study in Composition.* Berkeley: University of California Press, 1955.

Fargnoli, A. Nicholas and Michael Patrick Gillespie. *James Joyce A to Z: The Essential Reference Guide to His Life and Writings.* Oxford: Oxford University Press, 1996.

Fenton, James. "Auden at Home." *New York Review of Books* April 27, 2000.

Ferrer, Daniel. "Production, Invention, and Reproduction: Genetic vs. Textual Criticism." In *Reimagining Textuality: Textual Studies in the Late Age of Print.* Ed. Elizabeth Loizeaux and Neil Fraistat. Madison: University of Wisconsin Press, 2002. 48–59.

——. "Reflections on a Discarded Set of Proofs." *Genetic Studies in Joyce.* Ed. Sam Slote. Amsterdam: Rodopi, 1995. 49–63.

—— and Michael Groden. "Post-Genetic Joyce." *Romanic Review* 86.3 (1995): 501–512.

Finkelstein, David and Alistair McCleery. *Book History Reader.* London and New York: Routledge, 2002.

Fleishman, Avrom. *Figures of Autobiography: The Language of Self-Writing in Victorian and Modern England.* Berkeley: University of California Press, 1983.

Flint, F. S. "Imagisme." *Poetry,* March 1913, 198–200.

Ford, Ford Madox. *The Good Soldier.* New York: John Lane, 1915.

Fordham, Finn. *I Do I Undo I Redo: The Textual Genesis of Modernist Selves.* Oxford: Oxford University Press, 2010.

Foucault, Michel. "What Is an Author?" *Book History Reader.* New York: Routledge, 2006. 225–231.

Fowler, Alastair. *How to Write.* Oxford: Oxford University Press, 2006.

Frank, Albert J. "Genetic Versus Clear Texts: Reading and Writing Emerson." *Documentary Evidence* 9.4 (1987): 5–9.

Freud, Sigmund. "A Note upon the 'Mystic Writing Pad.'" 1925. *The Penguin Freud Library*. Vol. 2, *On Metapsychology. The Theory of Psychoanalysis*. London: Penguin, 1984. 428–434.

——. *Beyond the Pleasure Principle*. Ed. and trans. J. Strachey. In *The Standard Edition of the Complete Psychological Works of Sigmund Freud*. Vol. 18. London: Hogarth, 1920.

Friedman, Allen Warren. *Fictional Death and the Modernist Enterprise*. Cambridge: Cambridge University Press, 1995.

Friedman, Ellen G. "Breaking the Master Narrative: Jean Rhys's *Wide Sargasso Sea*." In *Breaking the Sequence: Women's Experimental Fiction*. Ed. Ellen Friedman and Miriam Fuchs. Princeton: Princeton University Press, 1989.

Friedman, Susan Stanford. "Definitional Excursions: The Meanings of Modern/ Modernity/ Modernism." *Modernism/modernity* 8.3 (2001): 493–513.

——. *Joyce: The Return of the Repressed*. Ithaca: Cornell University Press, 1993.

——. *Mappings: Feminism and the Cultural Geographies of Encounter*. Princeton: Princeton University Press, 1998.

——. "Spatialization: A Strategy for Reading Narrative." *Narrative* 1.1 (1993): 12–23.

——. "The Return of the Repressed in Women's Narrative." *Journal of Narrative Technique* 19 (1989): 141–156.

Frosh, Stephen. "Psychoanalysis in Britain: 'The Rituals of Destruction.'" In *A Concise Companion to Modernism*. Ed. David Bradshaw. Oxford: Blackwell, 2003.

Froula, Christine. *Groundwork for an Edition of The Cantos of Ezra Pound*. PhD diss., University of Chicago, 1977.

——. "Modernity, Drafts, Genetic Criticism: On the Virtual Lives of Joyce's Villanelle." *Yale French Studies* 89 (1996): 113–129.

——. "Reading Modernism, After Hugh Kenner (1923–2003): Hugh Kenner's Modernism and Ours." *Modernism/modernity* 12.3 (2005): 471–475.

——. *To Write Paradise: Style and Error in Pound's Cantos*. New Haven: Yale University Press, 1984.

Fussell, Paul. *The Great War and Modern Memory*. New York and London: Oxford University Press, 1975.

Gabler, Hans Walter. "A Tale of Two Texts." *Woolf Studies Annual* 10 (2004): 1–30.

——. "The *James Joyce Archive*: A Publisher's Gift to Joyce Studies." *Genetic Joyce Studies* Special Issue (Summer 2002).

——. "The Seven Lost Years of *A Portrait of the Artist as a Young Man*." In *Approaches to Joyce's Portrait*. Ed. Thomas F. Staley and Bernard Benstock. Pittsburgh: University of Pittsburgh Press, 1976. 25–60.

——, ed. *Ulysses: A Critical and Synoptic Edition*. New York: Garland, 1984.

Gardner, Helen. *The Composition of Four Quartets*. New York: Oxford University Press, 1978.

Gatrell, Simon. *Hardy the Creator: A Textual Biography*. Oxford: Clarendon, 1988.

Gee, Sophie. *Waste and Restoration: The Politics of Discarding from 'Paradise Lost' to the 'Dunciad.'* PhD diss., Harvard University, 2002.

Gegenheimer, Alfred Frank. "Early and Late Revisions in Henry James's 'A Passionate Pilgrim.'" *American Literature* 23.2 (May 1951): 233–242.

Genette, Gérard. *Figures III.* Paris: Seuil, 1972.

Gibson, Andrew, ed. *Joyce's "Ithaca."* Amsterdam: Rodopi, 1996.

Gifford, John. With Robert J. Seidman. *Ulysses Annotated: Notes for James Joyce's Ulysses.* Berkeley: University of California Press, 2008.

Gigante, Denise. *Life: Organic Form and Romanticism.* New Haven: Yale University Press, 2009.

Giles, Jana: "The Craft of 'A Painful Case': A Study of Revisions." In *European Joyce Studies 7: New Perspective on Dubliners.* Ed. Mary Power and Ulrich Schneider. Atlanta: Rodolphi, 1997.

Gill, Stephen. "'Affinities Preserved': Poetic Self-Reference in Wordsworth." *Studies in Romanticism* 24.4 (1985): 531–549.

Ginsberg, Allen. *Howl and Other Poems.* San Francisco: City Lights Books, 1956.

——. *Howl: Original Draft Facsimile, Transcript, and Variant Versions, Fully Annotated by the Author with Contemporaneous Correspondence, Account of First Public Reading, Legal Skirmishes, Precursor Texts, and Bibliography.* New York: Harper Collins, 1995.

——. *Deliberate Prose: Selected Essays, 1952–1995.* New York: Harper Collins, 2000.

——. "The Art of Poetry No. 8." Interview with Thomas Clark. *Paris Review* 37 (Spring 1966).

——. *Journals Mid-Fifties, 1954–1968.* New York: Harper Collins, 1995.

Goldman, Jane. *The Cambridge Introduction to Virginia Woolf.* Cambridge: Cambridge University Press, 2006.

Gontarski, S. E. "Crapp's First Tapes: Beckett's Manuscript Revisions of 'Krapp's Last Tape.'" *Journal of Modern Literature* 6.1 (1977): 61–68.

Goody, Alex. *Technology, Literature and Culture.* Cambridge: Polity, 2011.

Gosse, Edmund. "Henry James." In *Aspects and Impressions.* London: Cassell, 1922.

Gould, Warwick, "Writing the Life of the Text: The Case of W. B. Yeats." *Miscellanea: A Journal of English and American Studies* 30 (2004): 9–34.

Greene, Graham. *A Sort of Life.* New York: Simon and Schuster, 1971.

Greetham, D. C. *Textual Scholarship: An Introduction.* New York and London: Garland, 1992.

——. *Theories of the Text.* Oxford: Oxford University Press, 1999.

Greg, W. W. *The Editorial Problem in Shakespeare: A Survey of the Foundations of the Text.* Oxford: Clarendon, 1942.

Griffin, Gail. "Braving the Mirror: Virginia Woolf as Autobiographer." *Biography* 4.2 (1981): 108–118.

Groden, Michael. "The National Library of Ireland's New Joyce Manuscripts: An Outline and Archive Comparison." *Joyce Studies Annual* 14 (2003).

——. "Perplex in the Pen—and in the Pixels." *Journal of Modern Literature* 22.2 (1999): 225–244.

——. *Ulysses in Focus.* Gainesville: University Press of Florida, 2010.

——. *Ulysses in Progress.* Princeton: Princeton University Press, 1977.

Gruber, Ruth. *Virginia Woolf: The Will to Create as a Woman.* New York: Carroll and Graf, 2005.

Grumbach, Doris. *Extra Innings: A Memoir.* New York: Norton, 1993.

Gualtieri, Elena. *Virginia Woolf's Essays: Sketching the Past.* New York: St. Martin's, 2000.

Gusdorf, Georges. "Conditions and Limits of Autobiography." Trans. James Olney. In *Autobiography: Essays Theoretical and Critical.* Ed. James Olney. Princeton: Princeton University Press, 1980.

Haffenden, John. "Vivien Eliot and *The Waste Land:* The Forgotten Fragments." *P. N. Review* 175, 33.5 (2007): 18–23.

———, ed. *W. H. Auden: The Critical Heritage.* London: Routledge, 1997.

Hancher, Michael. "Littera Scripta Manet: Blackstone and Electronic Text." *Studies in Bibliography* 54 (2001): 115–132.

Hartman, Geoffrey. *Wordsworth's Poetry, 1787–1814.* 2nd ed. New Haven: Yale University Press, 1971.

Haugen, Kristine. *Richard Bentley: Poetry and Enlightenment.* Cambridge, MA: Harvard University Press, 2011.

Haule, James M. "'Le Temps passé' and the Original Typescript: An Early Version of the 'Time Passes' Section of *To the Lighthouse.*" *Twentieth Century Literature* 29.3 (Fall 1983): 267–311.

Hay, Louis. "Does 'Text' Exist?" Trans. Matthew Jocelyn and Hans Walter Gabler. *Studies in Bibliography* 41 (1988).

Hayles, Katherine N. "Postmodern Parataxis: Embodied Texts, Weightless Information." *American Literary History* 2.3 (1990): 394–421.

Heffernan, James. "Woolf's Reading of Joyce's *Ulysses,* 1918–1920." Available online at the Yale Modernism Lab. http://modernism.research.yale.edu/wiki/index.php/Woolf's _Reading_of_Joyce's_Ulysses,_1918-1920.

Hellinga, Lotte. "Printing." In *The Cambridge History of the Book: Volume 3, 1400–1557.* Cambridge, UK: Cambridge University Press, 1999.

Hemingway, Ernest. *A Moveable Feast.* New York: Scribner's, 1964.

———. *The Sun Also Rises.* Manuscript. Hemingway Library, Boston.

———. *The Sun Also Rises.* 1926. London: Arrow, 1994.

Henke, Suzanne. *James Joyce and the Politics of Desire.* New York: Routledge, 1990.

———. *Joyce's Moraculous Sindbook.* Columbus: Ohio State University Press, 1978.

Heinzelman, Kurt. *Make It New: The Rise of Modernism.* Austin: Harry Ransom Research Center, 2003.

Herring, Philip. *Joyce's Ulysses Notesheets in the British Museum.* Charlottesville: University Press of Virginia, 1972.

———. "Towards an Historical Molly Bloom." *ELH* 45.3 (1978): 501–521.

Hirst, Graeme and Vanessa Wei Fang. "Changes in Style in Authors with Alzheminer's Disease." *English Studies* 93.3 (2012): 357–370.

Horne, Philip., ed. *Henry James: A Life in Letters.* London: Penguin, 1999.

———. *Henry James and Revision: The New York Edition.* Oxford: Clarendon, 1990.

Housman, A. E. "The Application of Thought to Textual Criticism." *Proceedings of the Classical Association* 18 (August 1922).

Howarth, Peter. *British Poetry in the Age of Modernism.* Cambridge: Cambridge University Press, 2005.

———. Review of *Revisiting The Waste Land,* by Lawrence Rainey. *Modern Philology* 104 (2006): 280–285.

Huyssen, Andreas. *After the Great Divide.* Bloomington: Indiana University Press, 1986.

Hyman, Virginia. "Concealment and Disclosure in Sir Leslie Stephen's *Mausoleum Book.*" *Biography* 3.2 (1980): 121–131.

Ihara, Rachel. "'Rather Rude Jolts': Henry James, Serial Novels, and the Art of Fiction." *Henry James Review* 31.2 (2010): 188–206.

Jackson, H. L. *Marginalia: Readers Writing in Books.* New Haven and London: Yale University Press, 2001.

Jakobson, Roman. "Two Aspects of Language and Two Types of Aphasic Disturbances." In *On Language.* Ed. Linda Waugh and Monique Monville-Burston. Cambridge: Harvard University Press, 1990. 115–133.

James, Henry. *In the Cage.* Chicago and New York: Herbert S. Stone, 1898.

———. Preface. In *The Reverberator and Other Tales.* New York: Scribner's, 1908.

———. Preface. In *The Tragic Muse.* New York: Scribner's, 1908.

———. *Selected Letters.* Ed. Leon Edel. Cambridge: Belknap, Harvard University Press, 1987.

———. *Daisy Miller, Pandora, The Patagonia, and Other Tales.* New York: Scribner's, 1909.

———. "The Death of the Lion." In *The Complete Tales of Henry James.* Ed. Leon Edel. Philadelphia: Lipincott, 1962. 77–118.

———. "The Figure in the Carpet." In *The Complete Tales of Henry James.* Ed. Leon Edel. Vol. 9. Philadelphia: Lipincott, 1964. 273–315.

———. *The Golden Bowl.* New York: Scribner's, 1909.

———. *The Ivory Tower.* Ed. Percy Lubbock. London: W. Collins, 1917.

———. "The Middle Years." *Scribner's Magazine,* May 1893.

———. "The Middle Years." 1895 text. In *Tales of Henry James.* Ed. Christof Wegelin and Henry B. Wonham. New York: Norton, 2003.

———. "The Middle Years." In The New York Edition. Vol. 16. New York: Scribner's, 1909. 211–228.

———. *The Middle Years.* Ed. Percy Lubbock. London: W. Collins, 1917.

———. *The Outcry.* New York: Scribner's, 1911.

———. *The Outcry* (play). In *The Complete Plays of Henry James.* Ed. Leon Edel. New York; Oxford: Oxford University Press, 1990.

———. *The Sense of the Past.* London: W. Collins, 1917.

James, Stephen. "Revision as Redress? Robert Lowell's Manuscripts." *Essays in Criticism,* 46.1 (1996): 28–51.

Jameson, Fredric. *Postmodernism, or, The Cultural Logic of Late Capitalism.* Durham: Duke University Press, 1991.

———. "The Existence of Italy." In *Signatures of the Visible.* New York: Routledge, 1992. 155–230.

Jenkins, Nicholas. "Either *Or* or *And:* An Enigmatic Moment in the History of 'September 1, 1939.'" *Yale Review* 90.3 (2002): 22–39.

Jenny, Laurent and Richard Watts. "Genetic Criticism and Its Myths." *Yale French Studies* 89 (1996): 9–25.

Johnson, Jeri. "Joyce and Feminism." In *The Cambridge Companion to James Joyce,* Derek Attridge, ed. Cambridge: Cambridge University Press, 1990. 196–212.

Johnson, Samuel. *A Dictionary of the English Language.* Dublin: W. G. Jones, 1768.

Johnston, Georgia. "Virginia Woolf Revising Roger Fry into the Frames of 'A Sketch of the Past.'" *Biography* 20.3 (1997): 284–301.

Joyce, James. *A Portrait of the Artist as a Young Man.* Ed. Chester G. Anderson. New York: Penguin, 1985.

——. *Dubliners* (1914). Ed. Hans Walter Gabler with Walter Hettche. New York and London: Garland, 1993.

——. *Finnegans Wake* (1939). New York: Viking, 1951.

——. *Stephen Hero.* Ed. Theodore Spencer. New York: New Directions, 1955.

——. *The James Joyce Archive.* Ed. Michael Groden et al. 63 Volumes. New York and London: Garland, 1977–1979.

——. *Ulysses.* Paris: Shakespeare and Company, 1922.

——. *Ulysses: A Critical and Synoptic Edition.* Ed. Hans Walter Gabler with Wolfhard Steppe and Claus Melchior. New York and London: Garland, 1984.

——. *Ulysses,* "Episode IV." *The Little Review* 5.2 (June 1918): 39–52.

——. *Ulysses,* "Episode VIII." *The Little Review* 5.9 (January 1919): 27–50.

——. *Ulysses: The Manuscript and First Printings Compared.* Annot. Clive Driver. London: Faber and Faber, 1975.

Kappel, Andrew. "Complete with Omissions: The Text of Marianne Moore's *Complete Poems.*" In *Representing Modernist Texts: Editing as Interpretation.* Ed. George Bornstein. Ann Arbor: University of Michigan Press, 1991. 125–156.

Kealey, Tom. *The Creative Writing MFA Handbook: A Guide for Prospective Graduate Students.* New York: Continuum, 2007.

Keats, John. Letter to John Taylor. February 27, 1818. In *The Complete Poetical Works and Letters of John Keats.* Ed. Horace E. Scudder. Boston and New York: Houghton Mifflin, 1899.

——. "On First Looking into Chapman's Homer." In *The Complete Works of John Keats.* Ed. H. Buxton Forman. Vol. 1. New York: Thomas Y. Crowell, 1817.

Kenner, Hugh. *Joyce's Voices.* Berkeley: University of California Press, 1978.

——. *The Mechanic Muse.* New York and Oxford: Oxford University Press, 1987.

——. *The Poetry of Ezra Pound.* New York: Millwood, 1947.

——. *The Pound Era.* Berkeley and Los Angeles: University of California Press, 1971.

——. *The Sense of an Ending: Studies in the Theory of Fiction.* Oxford: Oxford University Press, 1966.

——, ed. *T. S. Eliot: A Selection of Critical Essays.* Englewood Cliffs, NJ: Prentice Hall, 1969.

——. *Ulysses.* Baltimore: Johns Hopkins University Press, 1987.

Kermode, Frank. Introduction. In *The Waste Land and Other Poems.* By T. S. Eliot. Ed. Frank Kermode. New York: Penguin, 2003.

——. "The Urban Apocalypse." In *Eliot in His Time.* Ed. A. Walton Litz. Princeton: Princeton University Press, 1973. 22–49.

Kerouac, Jack. "Essentials of Spontaneous Prose." *Evergreen Review* 2.5 (Summer 1958): 72–73.

Kiberd, Declan. *Ulysses and Us: The Art of Everyday Life in Joyce's Masterpiece.* New York: Norton, 2009.

Kimpel, Ben D. and T. C. Duncan Eaves. "Major Form in Pound's 'Cantos.'" *Iowa Review* 15.2 (1985): 51–66.

Kirsch, Adam. "Auden's N.Y. Households, From Slum to Sublime." Review of Edward Mendelson, *The Later Auden. New York Observer,* May 2, 1999.

Kirschenbaum, Matthew G. "Approaches to Managing and Collecting Born-Digital Literary Materials for Scholarly Use." White Paper to the New Office of Digital Humanities (May 2009).

———. *Mechanisms: New Media and the Forensic Imagination.* Cambridge: Massachusetts Institute of Technology Press, 2008.

Koestenbaum, Wayne. "The Waste Land: T. S. Eliot's and Ezra Pound's Collaboration on Hysteria." *Twentieth Century Literature* 34.2 (1988): 113–139.

Kolowich, Steve. "Archiving Writer's Work in the Age of E-mail." *Chronicle of Higher Education,* April 10, 2009.

Korg, Jacob. "Modern Art Techniques in *The Waste Land.*" *Journal of Aesthetics and Art Criticism* 18.4 (1960): 465–463.

Landor, Walter Savage. *Letters of Walter Savage Landor.* Ed. Stephen Wheeler. London: Duckworth, 1899.

Larkin, Philip. "What's Become of Wystan?" *Spectator,* July 15, 1960: 104–105.

Lawlor, Patrick, ed. *W. H. Auden: Poems, 1927–1929.* New York: New York Public Library, 1989.

Lawrence, D. H. *Paul Morel.* Ed. Helen Baron. Cambridge: Cambridge University Press, 2003.

Leader, Zachary. *Revision and Romantic Authorship.* Oxford: Clarendon, 1996.

Leaska, Mitchell A., ed. *The Virginia Woolf Reader.* San Diego: Harcourt Brace, 1984.

Lechartier, Georges. "The Program and Cost of Post-War Reconstruction in France." *Proceedings of the Academy of Political Science in the City of New York* 12.1 (1926): 312–315.

Lee, Hermione. *Virginia Woolf.* New York: Vintage, 1999.

Lejeune, Philippe. "How Do Diaries End?" *Biography* 24.1 (2001): 99–112.

———. *On Diary.* Ed. Jeremy D. Popkin and Julie Rak. Honolulu: University of Hawaii Press, 2009.

Leonard, Garry. "Power, Pornography and the Problem of Pleasure: The Semerotics of Desire and Commodity Culture in Joyce." *James Joyce Quarterly* 30.4 (1993): 615–667.

Lernout, Geert. "Controversial Editions: Hans Walter Gabler's *Ulysses.*" *Text* 16 (2006): 229–241.

———. "From Varieties of Genetic Experience to Radical Philology." In *Genetic Criticism and the Creative Process: Essays from Music, Literature, and Theater.* Ed. William Kinderman and Joseph E. Jones. Rochester: University of Rochester Press, 2009. 19–34.

———. "Genetic Criticism and Philology." *Text* 14 (2002): 53–75.

Lesser, Zachary. *Renaissance Drama and the Politics of Publication: Readings in the English Book Trade.* Cambridge: Cambridge University Press, 2004.

Levenson, Michael. "Stephen's Diary in Joyce's Portrait—The Shape of Life." *English Literary History* 52.4 (1985): 1017–1035.

Levi, Albert William. "The Writing of Mill's *Autobiography.*" *Ethics* 61.4 (July 1951): 284–296.

Lewis, Pericles. *The Cambridge Introduction to Modernism.* Cambridge: Cambridge University Press, 2007.

Lewis, Wyndham. "Long Live the Vortex." *Blast* 1 (June 1914).

Litz, Walton A., ed. *Eliot in His Time.* Princeton: Princeton University Press, 1973.

Lobb, Edward. *T. S. Eliot and the Romantic Critical Tradition.* London: Routledge, 1981.

Locke, John. *An Essay Concerning Human Understanding.* Ed. Peter H. Nidditch. Oxford: Clarendon, 1975.

Lodge, David. *The Modes of Modern Writing.* London: Edward Arnold, 1977.

London, Jack. *The Sea-Wolf.* Oxford: Oxford University Press, 2000.

Longfellow, Henry Wadsworth. *The Courtship of Miles Standish. Longfellow: The Complete Poetical Works.* Ed. Horace B. Scudder. Boston and New York: Houghton Mifflin, 1893.

Lorimer, W. L. "Lectio Difficilior." *Classical Review* 48.5 (1934): 171–173.

Löschnigg, Martin. "Autobiography." In *Routledge Encyclopedia of Narrative Theory.* Ed. David Herman, Manfred Jahn, and Marie-Laure Ryan. Abingdon and New York: Routledge, 2005. 34–36.

Lounsbury, Thomas R. *The Life and Times of Tennyson.* New Haven: Yale University Press, 1915.

Lowell, Robert. "The Art of Poetry No. 3." Interview with Frederich Seidel. *Paris Review* 25 (1961).

Lubbock, Percy. *The Craft of Fiction.* New York: Scribner's, 1921.

———. Preface. In *The Middle Years.* By Henry James. London: W. Collins, 1917.

Lukács, Georg. *Realism in Our Time: Literature and the Class Struggle.* New York: Harper and Row, 1962.

Madtes, Richard. "Joyce and the Building of Ithaca." *ELH* 31.4 (1964): 443–459.

Malone, Edmund. Preface. *The Plays and Poems of Shakespeare in Ten Volumes.* London: H. Baldwin, 1790.

Marcus, Laura. *Auto/biographical Discourses: Theory, Criticism, Practice.* Manchester and New York: Manchester University Press, 1994.

Marcus, Leah. *Unediting the Renaissance: Shakespeare, Marlowe, Milton.* London: Routledge, 1996.

Matthiessen, F. O., ed. Henry James, *Stories of Writers and Artists.* New York: New Directions, 1944.

———. "The Painter's Sponge and Varnish Battle." *Henry James: The Major Phase.* London: Oxford University Press, 1944.

Matz, Jesse. *The Modern Novel: A Short Introduction.* Oxford: Blackwell, 2004.

Mazzella, Anthony J. "The New Isabel." In *The Portrait of a Lady.* Ed. Robert D. Bamberg. New York: Norton, 1975. 597–619.

McCarthy, Patrick A. "A Warping Process." In *Work in Progress: Joyce Centenary Essays.* Ed. Richard F. Peterson, Alan M. Cohn, Edmund L. Epstein. Carbondale: Southern Illinois University Press, 1983. 47–57.

McCord, Phyllis. "'Little Corks That Mark a Sunken Net': Virginia Woolf's 'Sketch of the Past' as a Fictional Memoir." *Modern Language Studies* 16.3 (1986): 247–254.

McFarland, Thomas. *Shapes of Culture.* Iowa City: University of Iowa Press, 1987.

McGann, Jerome. *A Critique of Modern Textual Criticism.* Chicago and London: University of Chicago Press, 1983.

——. *Black Riders: The Visible Language of Modernism.* Princeton: Princeton University Press, 1993.

——. "From Text to Work: Digital Tools and the Emergence of the Social Text." *Romanticism on the Net* 41–42 (2006). http://www.erudit.org/revue/ron/2006/v/n41-42/013153ar.html.

——. *The Textual Condition.* Princeton: Princeton University Press, 1991.

McGurl, Mark. *The Program Era.* Cambridge: Harvard University Press, 2009.

McIntyre, Clara F. "The Later Manner of Mr. Henry James." *PMLA* 27.3 (1912): 354–371.

McKenzie, D. F. *Bibliography and the Sociology of Texts.* London: The British Library, 1986.

McKerrow, R. B. *Prolegomena, The Oxford Shakespeare.* Oxford: Oxford University Press, 1939.

McLuhan, Marshall. *The Gutenberg Galaxy.* Toronto: University of Toronto Press, 1962.

——. "Pound, Eliot and the Rhetoric of *The Waste Land.*" *New Literary History* 10.3 (1979): 557–580.

McWhirter, David, ed. *Henry James's New York Edition: The Construction of Authorship.* Stanford: Stanford University Press, 1995.

Mendelson, Edward. "Revision and Power: The Example of W. H. Auden." *Yale French Studies* 89 (1996): 103–112.

——, ed. *The English Auden: Poems, Essays, and Dramatic Writings, 1927–1932.* New York: Random House, 1977.

——. *The Later Auden.* London: Faber and Faber, 1999.

——. " 'We Are Changed by What We Change': The Power Politics of Auden's Revisions." *Romanic Review* 86.3 (1995): 527–535.

Michelson, Peter. *Speaking the Unspeakable: A Poetics of Obscenity.* Albany: State University of New York Press, 1993.

Miller, James E. *T. S. Eliot: The Making of an American Poet, 1888–1922.* University Park: Pennsylvania State University Press, 2005.

Miller, Tyrus. *Late Modernism: Politics, Fiction, and the Arts between the World Wars.* Berkeley: University of California Press, 1999.

Millgate, Michael. *Testamentary Acts.* Oxford: Clarendon, 1992.

Moore, Marianne. *Complete Poems.* New York: Macmillan, 1967.

Moretti, Franco. "Conjectures on World Literature." *New Left Review* 1.54 (January–February 2000). http://www.newleftreview.org/A2094.

——. *Signs Taken for Wonders: On the Sociology of Literary Forms.* 2nd ed. Trans. Susan Fischer, David Forgacs, and David Miller. London: Verso, 2005.

——. *The Way of the World: The Bildungsroman in European Culture.* Trans. Albert Spragia. London: Verso, 1987.

Morgan, Bill. "Lines Drawn in the Sand: The Life and Writings of Allen Ginsberg." http://www.lib.unc.edu/rbc/beats/ginsberg.html.

Morrisson, Mark. *The Public Face of Modernism: Little Magazines, Audience, and Reception, 1905–1920.* Madison: University of Wisconsin Press, 2001.

Morrissey, L. J. "Joyce's Revision of 'The Sisters': From Epicleti to Modern Fiction." *James Joyce Quarterly* 24.1 (Fall 1986): 33–54.

Moya, Elena. "Brick Lane's Monica Ali Aims to Finish New Book by Summer." Reuters. February 13, 2008. http://in.reuters.com/assets/print?aid=INIndia-31929320080213.

Murphy, J. Stephen. *Revision and the Making of Modernism.* PhD Diss. University of California, Berkeley, 2008.

———. "Revision as a 'Living Affair' in Henry James's New York Edition." *Henry James Review* 29.2 (2008): 163–180.

Nabokov, Vladimir. *Pale Fire.* New York: Vintage, 1989.

———. *Speak Memory.* London: Victor Gollancz, 1951.

———. *Speak Memory: An Autobiography Revisited.* New York: Putnam, 1966.

Nagy, Gregory. *Homer's Text and Language.* Champaign: University of Illinois Press, 2004.

Neary, John. *Something and Nothingness: The Fiction of John Updike and John Fowles.* Carbondale: Southern Illinois University Press, 1992.

Netanel, Neil. *Copyright's Paradox.* Oxford: Oxford University Press, 2008.

Nohrnberg, Peter. *The Book the Poet Makes: Collection and Re-Collection in W. B. Yeats's The Tower and Robert Lowell's Life Studies.* Cambridge: Department of English and American Language and Literature, distributed by Harvard University Press, 1994.

Nussbaum, Felicity. "Towards Conceptualizing Diary." In *Studies in Autobiography.* Ed. James Olney. Oxford: Oxford University Press, 1988. 128–140.

Oakeshott, Michael. *Experience and Its Modes.* Cambridge: Cambridge University Press, 1933.

Oates, Joyce Carol. "Birnbaum v. Joyce Carol Oates." *The Morning News,* February 3, 2005.

———. "The Art of Fiction No. 72." Interview with Robert Phillips. *Paris Review* 74 (Fall–Winter 1978).

———. "Jocoserious Joyce." *Critical Inquiry* 2.4 (1976): 677–688.

———. "The Madness of Art: Henry James's 'The Middle Years.'" *New Literary History* 27.2 (1996): 259–262.

O'Brien, Alyssa. "The Molly Blooms of 'Penelope': Reading Joyce Archivally." *Journal of Modern Literature* 24.1 (2000): 7–24.

Orwell, George. "Inside the Whale." In *W. H. Auden: The Critical Heritage,* John Haffenden, ed. London: Routledge, 1997.

"Our Boston Literary Letter." Review of *The American,* by Henry James. *Republican,* May 31, 1877.

Oxford English Dictionary. 2nd ed. Oxford: Oxford University Press, 1989. *OED Online.* Oxford University Press.

Oxford Latin Dictionary. 1647. Oxford: Clarendon, 2006.

Parker, Hershel. "Fiction and the Manuscripts." In *Hemingway: Essays of Reassessment.* Ed. Frank Scafella. New York: Oxford University Press, 1991.

———. *Flawed Texts and Verbal Icons: Literary Authority in American Fiction.* Chicago: Northwestern University Press, 1984.

Parkes, Adam. *Kazuo Ishiguro's The Remains of the Day: A Reader's Guide.* New York: Continuum, 2001.

Perloff, Marjorie. "'A Lost Battalion of Platonic Conversationalists': 'Howl' and the Language of Modernism." In *The Poem That Changed America: "Howl" Fifty Years Later.* Ed. Jason Shinder. New York: Farrar Straus, 2006. 24–43.

———. "Collage and Poetry." In *Encyclopedia of Aesthetics*. Ed. Michael Kelley. New York: Oxford University Press, 1998. Vol. 1. 348–347.

———. *Frank O'Hara: Poet among Painters*. Chicago: University of Chicago Press, 1998.

———. *Poetics of Indeterminacy: Rimbaud to Cage*. Princeton: Princeton University Press, 1981.

Perelman, Bob. "Parataxis and Narrative: The New Sentence in Theory and Practice." *American Literature* 65.2 (1993): 313–324.

———. *The Marginalization of Poetry*. Princeton: Princeton University Press, 1996.

Pethica, James. "A Note on the Texts." In *Yeats's Poetry, Drama, and Prose*. Ed. James Pethica. New York: Norton, 2000. xxi–xxiv.

Pound, Ezra. "Make It New." In *Literary Essays of Ezra Pound*. Ed. T. S. Eliot. Norfolk, CT: New Directions, 1954.

———. "Praefatio Ad Lectorem Electum." 1910. In *The Spirit of Romance*. New York: New Directions, 1968.

———. *Selected Letters, 1907–1941*. Ed. D. D. Paige. New York: New Directions, 1950.

———. *Selected Poems, 1908–1959*. London: Faber and Faber, 1975.

———. "The Art of Poetry No. 5 ." Interview with Donald Hall. *The Paris Review* 28 (1962).

———. *The Cantos of Ezra Pound*. New York: New Directions, 1970.

———. *The Letters of Ezra Pound, 1907–1941*. Ed. D. D. Paige. New York: Harcourt Brace, 1950.

———. *The Literary Essays of Ezra Pound*. New York: New Directions, 1968.

———. "The Serious Artist, IV." *New Freewoman* 1.11 (November 15, 1913): 213–214.

———. "Vorticism." *Fortnightly Review,* September 1, 1914.

Prescott, Joseph. "James Joyce's 'Stephen Hero.'" *Journal of English and Germanic Philology* 53.2 (1954): 214–223.

Price, Leah. "Introduction: Reading Matter." *PMLA* 121.1 (2006): 9–16.

——— and Pamela Thurschwell, eds. *Literary Secretaries/ Secretarial Culture*. Aldershot: Ashgate, 2005.

"Printers Flatter Typewriters." *Typewriter Topics: The Office Equipment Magazine* 7.4 (December 1907): 266.

Pugliatti, Paola. "Textual Perspectives in Italy: From Pasquali's Historicism to the Challenge of 'Variantistica' (and Beyond)." *Text* 11 (1998): 155–188.

Pye, Alexander. *A Commentary Illustrating the Poetic of Aristotle*. London: John Stockdale, 1792.

Quesenbery, W. D. *Auden's Revisions*. http://audensociety.org/Audens_Revisions_by_WD _Quesenbery.pdf.

Quick, Jonathan. "Molly Bloom's Mother." *ELH* 57.1 (1990): 223–240.

Rabaté, Jean-Michel. *The Ghosts of Modernity*. Orlando: University Press of Florida, 1996.

Raine, Craig. *T. S. Eliot*. Oxford: Oxford University Press, 2006.

Rainey, Lawrence S., ed. *A Poem Containing History: Textual Studies in The Cantos*. Ann Arbor: University of Michigan Press, 1997.

———. "Eliot among the Typists: Writing *The Waste Land*." *Modernism/modernity* 12.1 (2005): 27–84.

———. *Institutions of Modernism*. New Haven: Yale University Press, 1998.

———. *Revisiting The Waste Land*. New Haven: Yale University Press, 2005.

—— and Louis Menand. Introduction. In *The Cambridge History of Literary Criticism VII: Modernism and the New Criticism*. Ed. A. Walton Litz, Lawrence Rainey, and Louis Menand. Cambridge: Cambridge University Press, 2000. 1–16.

Raitt, Suzanne. "The Rhetoric of Efficiency in Early Modernism." *Modernism/modernity* 13.1 (2006): 835–851.

Ranous, Dora Knowlton. *Good English in Good Form*. New York: Sturgis and Walton, 1916.

Raskin, Jonah. *American Scream: Allen Ginsberg's "Howl" and the Making of the Beat Generation*. Berkeley: University of California Press, 2005.

Rasula, Jed. "Make It New." *Modernism/modernity* 17.4 (2010): 713–733.

Reiman, Donald H. *Romantic Texts and Contexts*. Columbia: University of Missouri Press, 1987.

Reside, Doug. "'No Day but Today': A Look at Jonathan Larson's Word Files." April 22, 2011. http://www.nypl.org/blog/2011/04/22/no-day-today-look-jonathan-larsons-word -files.

Ricks, Christopher. *Allusion to the Poets*. Oxford: Oxford University Press, 2002.

——. *Decisions and Revisions in T. S. Eliot*. London: The British Library and Faber and Faber, 2003.

——, ed. *Inventions of the March Hare: Poems, 1909–1917*. By T. S. Eliot. London: Faber and Faber, 1996.

Rivkin, Julie. "Doctoring the Text." In *Henry James's New York Edition: The Construction of Authorship*. Ed. David McWhirter. Stanford: Stanford University Press, 1995.

——. *False Positions: The Representational Logics of Henry James's Fiction*. Stanford: Stanford University Press, 1996.

——. "Revision and 'The Middle Years.'" In *Tales of Henry James*. Ed. Christof Wegelin and Henry B. Wonham. 470–479.

Robertson, Randy. *Censorship and Conflict in Seventeenth Century England: The Subtle Art of Division*. University Park: Pennsylvania State University Press, 2009.

Roselli, Daniel N. "Max Beerbohm's Unpublished Parody of Henry James." *Review of English Studies* 22.85 (1971): 61–63.

Rosenbaum, S. P. "'The Spoils of Poynton': Revisions and Editions." *Studies in Bibliography* 19 (1966): 161–174.

Rosenfeld, Natania. *Outsiders Together: Virginia and Leonard Woolf*. Princeton: Princeton University Press, 2000.

"Rough Crossings: The Cutting of Raymond Carver." *New Yorker,* December 24, 2007.

Roth, Philip. *The Ghost Writer*. New York: Farrar, Strauss, and Giroux, 1979.

Rowe, John Carlos. *The Other Henry James*. Durham and London: Duke University Press, 1998.

Rubenstein, Roberta. "'I meant *nothing* by the Lighthouse': Virginia Woolf's Poetics of Negation." *Journal of Modern Literature* 31.4 (2008): 36–53.

Saint-Amour, Paul. *The Copywrights: Intellectual Property and the Literary Imagination*. Ithaca: Cornell University Press, 2003.

Sante, Luc. "On the Road Again." *New York Times,* August 19, 2007.

Saunders, Max. *Self-Impression: Life-Writing, Autobiografiction, and the Forms of Modern Literature*. Oxford: Oxford University Press, 2010.

Savage, Bill. "Allen Ginsberg's 'Howl' and the Paperback Revolution." http://www.poets.org/viewmedia.php/prmMID/20201.

Scafella, Frank, ed. *Hemingway: Essays of Reassessment.* New York and Oxford: Oxford University Press, 1991.

Schuchard, Ronald. "Burbank with a Baedeker, Eliot with a Cigar: American Intellectuals, Anti-Semitism, and the Idea of Culture." *Modernism/modernity* 10.1 (2006): 1–26.

Schulkind, Jeanne. Editor's Note. In *Moments of Being.* 2nd ed. London: Hogarth, 1985.

Schulman, Grace. "Conversation with Marianne Moore." *Quarterly Review of Literature* 16.1–2 (1969): 154–171.

Schulze, Robin. "Textual Evolution: Marianne Moore, the Text of Evolution, and the Evolving Text." *Text* 11 (1998): 270–305.

Schwartz, Mimi. "Revision Profiles: Patterns and Implications." *College English* 45.6 (1983): 549–558.

Schwarz, Daniel. *Reading Joyce's Ulysses.* New York: St. Martin's, 1987.

Scott, Bonnie Kime. "Emma Clery: A Young Woman Walking Proudly Through the Decayed City." In *Women in Joyce.* Ed. Suzette Henke and Elaine Unkeless. Urbana: University of Illinois Press, 1982.

Seigel, Jules Paul. "*Jenny*: The Divided Sensibility of a Young and Thoughtful Man of the World." *Studies in English Literature, 1500–1900* 9.4 (1969): 677–693.

Shaer, Matthew. "Amazon Issues Patches for Kindle E-Books. Is that a Good Thing?" *Christian Science Monitor,* May 11, 2010.

Shakespeare, William. *King Lear: A Parallel Text Edition.* Ed. René Weis. 2nd ed. Harlow, England: Longman/Pearson, 2010.

Shelley, Percy Bysshe. "A Defence of Poetry." In *Essays, Letters from Abroad, Translations and Fragments.* Ed. Mary Shelley. Philadelphia: Lea and Blanchard, 1840.

Sheringham, Michael. "Autobiographical (In)fidelity: Virginia Woolf's 'A Sketch of the Past.'" *Imaginaires: Revue du Centre de Recherche sur l'Imaginaire dans les Littératures de Langue Anglaise* (1996): 109–118.

Shillingsburg, Peter. *From Gutenberg to Google.* Cambridge: Cambridge University Press, 2006.

———. "Text as Matter, Concept, and Action." *Studies in Bibliography* 44 (1991): 31–82.

Simic, Charles. "The Art of Poetry no. 90." Interview with Mark Ford. *Paris Review* (Spring 2005).

Singer, Jefferson A. and Peter Salovey. *The Remembered Self: Emotion and Memory in Personality.* New York: Free Press, 1993.

Singer, S. W. Preface. In *The Dramatic Works of William Shakespeare.* London: Bell and Daldy, 1856.

Skelton, Robin. *Poetry of the Thirties.* Harmondsworth: Penguin, 1964.

Slote, Sam and Luca Crispi, eds. *How Joyce Wrote Finnegans Wake: A Chapter-by-Chapter Genetic Guide.* Madison: University of Wisconsin Press, 2007.

Smith, Barbara Herrnstein. *Poetic Closure: A Study of How Poems End.* Chicago: University of Chicago Press, 1968.

Smith, Stan. *The Cambridge Companion to W. H. Auden.* Cambridge: Cambridge University Press, 2004.

Snaith, Anna. *Virginia Woolf: Public and Private Negotiations.* New York: Palgrave, 2000.

Sommaruga, Giovanni, ed. *Formal Theories of Information: From Shannon to Semantic Information Theory.* Berlin: Springer, 1998.

Spencer, Theodore. Introduction. In *Stephen Hero.* By James Joyce. New York: New Directions, 1955.

Spender, Stephen. "Remembering Eliot." In *T. S. Eliot: The Man and His Work.* Ed. Allen Tate. New York: Delacorte, 1966.

Spitzer, Leo. *Linguisics and Literary History: Essays in Stylistics.* New York: Russell and Russell, 1962.

Spooner, Henry. *Wealth from Waste.* London: George Routledge and Sons, 1918.

Sproles, Karyn J. *Desiring Women: The Partnership of Virginia Woolf and Vita Sackville-West.* Toronto: University of Toronto Press, 2006.

St Clair, William. "Publishing, Authorship, and Reading." In *The Cambridge Companion to Fiction of the Romantic Period.* Ed. Richard Maxwell and Katie Trumpener. Cambridge: Cambridge University Press, 2008. 22–46.

———. *The Reading Nation in the Romantic Period.* Cambridge: Cambridge University Press, 2004.

Stanley, Liz and Helen Dampier. "Simulacrum Diaries: Time, the 'Moment of, Writing' and the Diaries of Johanna Brandt-van Warmelo." *Life Writing* 3 (2006): 25–52.

Stelzig, Eugene. "Some Notes on Romantic Subjectivity in the Context of German and English Romanticism." In *Sensus Communis: Contemporary Trends in Comparative Literature.* Ed. János Riesz, Peter Boerner, and Bernard Scholz. Tübingen: Gunter Narr, 1986. 357–386.

Stephen, Leslie. "Autobiography." *Hours in a Library*, vol. 3. New York: G. P. Putnam, 1894.

———. *The Mausoleum Book.* Ed. Alan Bell. Oxford: Clarendon, 1977.

———. *The Mausoleum Book.* Manuscript. BL MS 57920–57922. British Library, London.

Stewart, Garrett. "Metallusion: The Used, the Renewed, and the Novel." *Modern Language Quarterly* 65.4 (2004): 583–604.

Stillinger, Jack. *Coleridge and Textual Instability: The Multiple Versions of the Major Poems.* Oxford: Oxford University Press, 1994.

———. *Multiple Authorship and the Myth of Solitary Genius.* Oxford: Oxford University Press, 1991.

Svoboda, Frederic. *Hemingway and The Sun Also Rises: The Crafting of a Style.* Lawrence: University Press of Kansas, 1983.

Swinburne, Algernon Charles. *The Swinburne Letters.* Ed. Cecil Y. Lang. New Haven: Yale University Press, 1959. Vol. 2, 1869–1875.

Talbot, F. A. *Millions from Waste.* Philadelphia: Lippincott, 1920.

Tanner, Tony. *Henry James and the Art of Nonfiction.* Athens: University of Georgia Press, 1995.

Tanselle, G. Thomas. "The Editorial Problem of Final Authorial Intention." *Studies in Bibliography* 29 (1976): 167–211.

Thackeray, William Makepeace. *Vanity Fair.* Ed. Peter Shillingsburg. New York: Norton, 1994.

"The Homer Multitext Project." *The Center for Hellenic Studies.* Harvard University. http:// chs.harvard.edu/wa/pageR?tn=ArticleWrapper&bdc=12&mn=1169.

"The Malady of Revision." In *The Atlantic Monthly* 85.507 (January 1900): 1401–1.

"The Translators to the Reader." In *The Holy Bible: An Exact Reprint Page for Page of the Authorized Version, Published in the Year MDCXI.* Oxford: Samuel Collingwood, 1833.

Tichi, Cecelia. *Shifting Gears: Technology, Literature, Culture in Modernist America.* Chapel Hill: University of North Carolina Press, 1987.

Tomlinson, David. "Eliot and the Cubists." *Twentieth-Century Literature* 26.1 (1980): 64–81.

Tomlinson, Tim. *The Portable MFA in Creative Writing.* Cincinnati, OH: Writers' Digest Books, 2006.

Travisano, Thomas J. *Midcentury Quartet: Bishop, Lowell, Jarell, Berryman and the Making of a Postmodern Aesthetic.* Charlottesville: University of Virginia Press, 1999.

Trollope, Anthony. *Autobiography of Anthony Trollope.* New York: Dodd and Mead, 1912.

Tidwell, Joanne Campbell. *Politics and Aesthetics in the Diary of Virginia Woolf.* New York: Routledge, 2008.

"Typewriter or Pen?" *The Author: A Monthly Magazine for Literary Workers* 3 (1891): 65–66.

Tytell, John. "On Burrough's Work: A Conversation with Allen Ginsberg." *Partisan Review* 41.2 (1974): 253–262.

Updike, John. *Rabbit Run.* New York: Knopf, 1960.

Valéry, Paul. "Note et digression." In *Introduction à la méthode de Léonard de Vinci.* Paris: Gallimard, 1992.

Van Hulle, Dirk. "A Darwinian Change in European Editorial Thinking." *European Studies* 26 (2008): 21–43.

———. *A Genetic Study of Late Manuscripts by Joyce, Proust, and Mann.* Ann Arbor: University of Michigan Press, 2004.

———. *Joyce's Know-How, Beckett's Nohow.* Miami: University of Florida Press, 2008.

———. "The Dynamics of Incompletion: Multilingual Manuscript Genetics and Digital Philology." *Neohelicon* 36.2 (2009): 451–461.

———. "The Limited Edition Unlimited: Samuel Beckett's Fugal Artefact." *Variants 4* (2005): 133–150.

Van Mierlo, Wim. Introduction. In *Variants 6. Textual Scholarship and the Material Book.* Ed. Wim Van Mierlo. New York: Rodopi, 2007.

———. Review of *Genetic Criticism: Textes and Avant-Textes,* by Jed Deppman, Daniel Ferrer, and Michael Groden. *Textual Cultures* 1.2 (2006): 162–168.

van Vliet, H. T. M. Review of *Literarische Handschriften: Einführung in die "critique génétique,"* by Almuth Grésillon. *Text* 14 (2002): 338–343.

Varendonck, J. *The Psychology of Day-Dreams.* London: George Allen and Unwin, 1921.

Vendler, Helen. *Dickinson: Selected Poems and Commentaries.* Cambridge: Harvard University Press, 2010.

———. *The Art of Shakespeare's Sonnets.* Cambridge: Harvard University Press, 1999.

Vlastos, Gregory. *Studies in Greek Philosophy.* Vol. 2. Princeton: Princeton University Press, 1995.

"Vorticism the Latest Cult of Rebel Artists; It Goes a Step Further Than Cubism and Futurism, and Is Sponsored by Brzeska, Epstein and Others. Its Official Mouthpiece Is a Cerise Magazine Called Blast." *New York Times,* August 9, 1914.

Wagner, Linda W. "*The Sun Also Rises:* One Debt to Imagism." *Journal of Narrative Technique* 2.2 (1972): 88–98.

Wagner-Martin, Linda, ed. *A Historical Guide to Ernest Hemingway*. New York and Oxford: Oxford University Press, 2000.

Wallace, David Foster. *The Pale King*. Ed. Michael Pietsch. New York: Little Brown, 2011.

Walsh, Marcus. *Shakespeare, Milton, & Eighteenth-Century Literary Editing: The Beginnings of Interpretive Scholarship*. Cambridge: Cambridge University Press, 1997.

Walsh, William. *Introduction to John Keats*. London and New York: Methuen, 1981.

Ward, Harry Parker. "Author's Changes." *The College Annual Guide: A Book of Information and Suggestions Intended for Use by the Business Manager and Editor-in-Chief*. Columbus: Champlin, 1914. 85–86.

Warner, William Beatty. *Licensing Entertainment: The Elevation of Novel Reading in Britain, 1684–1750*. Berkeley and Los Angeles: University of California Press, 1994.

Wilbur, Richard. *Conversations with Richard Wilbur*. Ed. William Butts. Jackson: University Press of Mississippi, 1990.

Wilde, Oscar. *The Importance of Being Earnest and Other Plays*. Ed. Peter Raby. Oxford: Oxford University Press, 1998.

Williams, Carlos Williams. *The Autobiography of Williams Carlos Williams*. New York: Random House, 1951.

Willis, John H. *Leonard and Virginia Woolf as Publishers: The Hogarth Press, 1917–41*. Charlottesville: University of Virginia Press, 1992.

Wilson, Edmund. *Axel's Castle: A Study in Imaginative Literature of 1870–1930*. New York and London: Charles Scribner's Sons, 1931.

———. "The Fruits of the MLA." *New York Review of Books*, October 10, 1968.

Wimsatt, W. K. and Monroe C. Beardsley. *The Verbal Icon: Studies in the Meaning of Poetry*. Lexington: University of Kentucky Press, 1954.

Wiseman, Timothy. *Clio's Cosmetics: Three Studies in Greco-Roman Literature*. Bristol: Phoenix Press, 2003.

Wisor, Rebecca. "Versioning Virginia Woolf: Notes Towards a Post-Eclectic Edition of *Three Guineas*." *Modernism/modernity* 16.3 (2009). 497–535.

Wolfson, Susan J. "The Illusion of Mastery: Wordsworth's Revisions of the 'Drowned Man of Esthwaite,' 1799, 1805, 1850." *PMLA* 99.5 (1984): 917–935.

Wood, James. "The Smallness of the 'Big' Novel: Human, All Too Inhuman." Review of *White Teeth* by Zadie Smith. *New Republic* (July 24, 2000): 41–46.

Woolf, Virginia. *A Passionate Apprentice: The Early Journals, 1897–1909*. Ed. Mitchell Leaska. London: Hogarth, 1990.

———. *A Room of One's Own*. 1928. London: Penguin, 1945.

———. "A Sketch of the Past." 1941. In *Moments of Being*. Ed. Jeanne Schulkind. 2nd ed. London: Hogarth, 1985.

———. *A Writer's Diary*. San Diego: Houghton Mifflin Harcourt, 2003.

———. *Between the Acts*. London: Hogarth, 1941.

———. "De Quincey's Autobiography." In *Collected Essays*. Ed. Leonard Woolf. Vol. 4. London: Hogarth, 1967. 1–7.

———. "I Am Christina Rossetti." In *Collected Essays*. Vol. 4. London: Hogarth, 1967. 54–60.

———. *Melymbrosia: A Novel*. Ed. Louise DeSalvo. San Francisco: Cleis, 2002.

———. "Mr. Bennett and Mrs. Brown." In *The Captain's Death Bed and Other Essays.* London: Hogarth, 1950. 90–111.

———. "Reminiscences." In *Moments of Being.* Ed. Jeanne Schulkind. 2nd ed. London: Hogarth, 1985.

———. *Roger Fry: A Biography.* London: Hogarth, 1940.

———. *The Diary of Virginia Woolf.* Ed. Anne Olivier Bell. London: Hogarth, 1977.

———. *The Letters of Virginia Woolf.* Ed. Nigel Nicholson. Vol. 6. London: Hogarth, 1980.

———. "The Old Order." *Times Literary Supplement.* Thursday, October 18, 1917, 497–498.

———. *The Pargiters: The Novel-Essay Portion of The Years.* Ed. Mitchell A. Leaska. London: Hogarth, 1977.

———. "The Tale of Genji." 1925. In *The Essays of Virginia Woolf.* Ed. Andrew McNeillie. Vol. 4. London: Hogarth, 1994. 264–268.

———. *The Waves.* 1931. Oxford: Oxford University Press, 1998.

———. *The Years.* 1937. Orlando: Harcourt, 2008.

———. *Three Guineas.* 1938. New York: Harcourt, 2006.

———. *To the Lighthouse.* 1927. Orlando: Harcourt, 2005.

———. *To the Lighthouse.* Holograph Draft. Ed. Susan Dick. Toronto: University of Toronto Press, 1982.

Wordsworth, William. Preface. In *The Excursion, Being a Portion of "The Recluse," A Poem.* London: Longman, Hurst, Rees, Orme, and Brown, 1814.

———. *The Prelude: Or, Growth of a Poet's Mind (Text of 1805).* Ed. Ernest de Selincourt. Oxford: Clarendon, 1926.

Yao, Steven G. *Translation and the Languages of Modernism: Gender, Politics, Language.* New York: Palgrave Macmillan, 2002.

Yeats, W. B., ed. *The Oxford Book of Modern Verse, 1892–1935.* Oxford: Oxford University Press, 1936.

———. "The Second Coming." *Dial,* November 1920.

Zall, Paul M. *Benjamin Franklin's Humor.* Lexington: University Press of Kentucky, 2005.

Zwerdling, Alex. "Mastering the Memoir: Woolf and the Family Legacy." *Modernism/ modernity* 10.1 (2003): 165–188.

Acknowledgments

I have received generous help at every stage of this book's genesis. Of course, all the imperfections of the final form are mine. My first thanks are to some inspiring teachers.

Daniel Albright's exhaustive knowledge of modernism made the book more comparative. Leah Price taught me to think critically about rereading, as well as rewriting, and was herself a model reader of early drafts. Werner Sollors introduced me to the study of modern manuscripts; more precisely, he showed me that the modernist period was also the golden age of the typewriter. Neil Hopkinson sowed the seeds of an interest in textual criticism when I was an undergraduate in Classics at Cambridge.

Most of this book was written during my three years as an Assistant Professor at Stanford, and I am grateful to the entire department for providing a supportive atmosphere for research. Franco Moretti helped me to think critically about length transformations; Alex Woloch read every chapter with inimitably close focus; Claire Jarvis was unfailingly generous as a revisionary interlocutor; Gavin Jones and Michelle Karnes offered many kinds of good advice, practical and intellectual; Nick Jenkins shared ideas about Auden; Andrew Goldstone, Joshua Landy, Saikat Majumdar, and Karen Zumhagen-Yekplé provided expert suggestions about the modernist context; John Bender, Terry Castle, and Jennifer Summit were excellent colleagues; and Alyce Boster provided every kind of help imaginable, with great kindness. Thank you, too, to the students in my three graduate classes on textual criticism and book history at Stanford and Oxford: you helped me to explain myself more clearly. I am also grateful to the many close friends who discussed these ideas with me informally over the years: Sally Connolly, Marcella Frydman, Eric Idsvoog, Josh King, Amelia Klein, Jason Manoharan, Maia McAleavey, Timothy Michael, Julie Orlemanski, Will Poole, Clare Pollard, Josh Rothman, Namwali Serpell, Jeff Severs, and Dan Shore. As a graduate student, when I was beginning to develop an interest in these questions, I received mentorship and stimulating advice from J. D. Connor, Marjorie Garber, Lisa New, Peter Nohrnberg, and Peter Sacks. Others who read, audited, and wisely advised at the early stages include James Stephen Murphy and Mark Hussey, with whom I participated in a panel on revision at the Modernist Studies Association Conference; Jonathan Arac; Steven Connor; Colin MacCabe; the members of the Bibliographical Society of America, who elected me as a New Scholar in 2008; Peter Collister; John Plotz; and Susan Halpert in the Houghton Library.

More recently, I have benefited from another new set of conversations with colleagues in England: I am deeply grateful to Ron Bush, David Bradshaw, Laura Marcus, Craig Raine, and Wim Van Mierlo for their acute advice as the project approached its inevitably unsatisfactory final form. The anonymous readers for Harvard University Press made valuable suggestions about both the style and my conceptual framing and I thank them for their careful reports. Lindsay Waters offered me excellent advice about the direction of the project, and it has been a delight to work with him and his supremely efficient assistant, Shan Wang.

For permission to print an image from the digital file of the *Rent* manuscript, I am grateful to Doug Reside at the New York Public Library and the Larson family. I thank the Woolf Estate and the Society of Authors for permission to reproduce an image of the manuscript of "A Sketch of the Past," the Houghton Library at Harvard for providing an image from the typescript of *The Middle Years*, and Faber and Faber for permission to reproduce images of the manuscripts and typescripts of *The Waste Land*.

My deepest thanks are to my parents and to Ian Martin. He has seen many discarded branches on this genetic tree and has been endlessly and unstintingly generous throughout my work on revision.

Index

Addition(s): Pope and arbitrary editorial addition, 20; distinguished from substitution and excision, 15; and overwriting, 15–16; and Henry James, 86, 93–94; general problem of in modernism, 147–155; and aphasia, 150–151; types of, 151–154; representing editorially, 155–158; to Leopold Bloom's mind, 158–163; tonal problems of, 163–174; to Molly Bloom in *Ulysses*, 174–185; elongated postwar sentence and, 185–192; indeterminacy and, 189–192.

Aiken, Conrad, 125, 255

À La recherche du temps perdu (Proust), 101, 153–154

Albright, Daniel, 107

Ali, Monica, 2, 4

Allusion, 4; in *The Waste Land*, 131–132; self-allusion in Eliot, 127, in Woolf, 221–226

American, The (James), 66, 67–69, 85, 87

Anabasis (St.-John Perse, trans. T. S. Eliot), 126–127

Anesko, Michael, 63

"Annus Mirabilis" (Dryden), 138

Anti-intentionalism, 50

Antirevisionism, 29, 31–32, 242, 250–251

Aphasia, 150–151; at the end of "Ithaca," 174; in trauma, 231; "divine aphasia," 266–267

Arac, Jonathan, 152, 205

Armstrong, Tim, 141

Asher, Kenneth, 144

Attridge, Derek, 43, 167, 175, 182

Auden, W. H.: revisions of, 7, 70; typewriter and, 39, 40; Mendelson and, 49–50; revisedness and, 241–249

Austen, Jane, 28

Authorial intention. *See* Intentionalism

Autobiography/Autobiographies: *The Middle Years* and, 91–97; revision in, 193–196; Woolf and, 197–198; diary and aspect and, 199–202; posthumous nineteenth-century, 202–206; Leslie Stephen and, 206–215; Joyce and, 215–220; "A Sketch of the Past" and, 220–235

"Backbone" (Wallace), 260–265

Badenhausen, Richard, 124, 127

Balassi, William, 118–119

Banfield, Ann, 301n9

Beach, Sylvia, 42–43; economic sacrifices of, 268
Beardsley, Monroe C., 46, 47, 48
Beckett, Samuel, 103, 234, 236
Bedford, Sybille, 201
Beebohm, Max, 70
"Beginners" (Carver), 103
Bell, Alan, as editor of the *Mausoleum Book*, 207–212
Bell, Quentin, 213
Benjamin, Walter, 189
Bentley, Richard, 26–27
Berryman, John, 256
Biasi, Pierre-Marc de, 284n145
Bishop, Elizabeth, 240, 255
Bloom, Leopold, 158–163, 184–185
Bloom, Molly, 174–185, 191–192
Blushing, 75–76
Bon à tirer, 8, 284n145
Booth, Wayne, 18
Bornstein, George, 52, 59, 299n77
Bosanquet, Theodora, 86, 91–92, 96
Bowers, Fredson, 25, 49
Bowman, Frank, 54
Bridges, Robert, 48–49
Briscoe, Lily, 197
Brod, Max, 200
Broughton, Rhoda, 98
Browne, E. Martin, 126
Browning, Browning, 3, 31
Bruder, Jessica, 313n92
Bryant, John, 6, 273n22, 282n109
Budgen, Frank, 147
Bunkers, Suzanne, 302n19
"Burbank with a Baedeker: Bleistein with a Cigar" (Eliot), 109
"Burial of the Dead, The" (Eliot), 129, 131, 135–138
Burt, Stephen, 245
Bush, Ron, 235
Butterfield, Herbert, and Whiggish history, 100, 123, 289n83
Byron, Lord George Gordon, 29, 37, 279n54

Cameron, Sharon, 103, 286n29
Campbell, Sarah, 84, 287n52
Cano, Christine, 101, 154, 296n19

Cantos (Pound): opportunity and constraints in revision and, 6; Froula's dissertation on, 22; doctoral studies of manuscripts, 55; addition and lists, 152–153; autobiography and, 235–236
Caruth, Cathy, 194–195
Carver, Raymond, 103, 267
"Chapman's Homer" (Keats), 27, 30
Chico, Tita, 132
Clarke, Cowden, 30
Cohen, Patricia, 257–258
Coleridge, Samuel Taylor, 29, 30, 152; T. S. Eliot on, 237; Charles Lamb on, 279n67
Collaborators, shaping meaning and, 58, and *The Waste Land*, 127
Compagnon, Antoine, 54
Completion: of autobiography, 199–202, 235; Stephen and, 207
Compression, 85–87, 101. *See also* Excision; Minimalism
Computer, 45, 254–260, 261, 263–265
Conrad, Joseph, 37
Conversational repair, 14
Copyright, 25, 28
Corruption, versus revision, 23–24, 26–27; self-corruption in Wordsworth's *Prelude*, 57, 122; in digital archives, 257–259
Cost, of revision, 5, 40–42, 44–45
Cotgrave, John, 26
Cubism, 145
Cultural forms and shapes, 238
Cunningham, Michael, 1

Daily Mirror, 133
Dampier, Helen, 201
Darnton, Robert, 51, 58
Darwin, Charles, 75–76, 203
Darwin, Francis, 203
Davie, Donald, 111
"Dead, The" (Joyce), 183–185
"Death by Water" (Eliot), 129, 130
"Death of the Lion, The" (James), 70
De Biasi, Pierre-Marc, 284n145
Delany, Paul, 43
De Man, Paul, 11, 202
Dencombe, 33, 71–82, 193–194, 268
Derrida, Jacques, 9, 202, 281n93

De Selincourt, Ernest, 16–17, 52, 205–206
Detail, addition of, 174–185
Diary, autobiography and, 199–202, 231–232; *Cantos* and, 235; O'Hara, and 256
Dickinson, Emily, 103–104
Dictation, James and, 83–84, 86–87, 288n63
Digital texts: Track Changes function and, 254–260; *The Pale King* and, 260–265; revision of, 267–268
Doctor Hugh, 73–78, 79–81, 194
Dowell, John, 235
Dryden, John, 138
Dubliners (Joyce), 104; closure in, 183; 217

Eagleton, Terry, 40, 144
Edel, Leon, 65, 71–72, 84, 97
Editing: classical, 19–20; final-intentionalist, 49–50; genetic criticism and, 50–56; social-text, 50–56; distance from practice of literary criticism in 20c university, 46; Percy Lubbock and, 88–97; excision, and 110; *The Sun Also Rises* and, 117–118; *The Waste Land* and, 120–146; David Foster Wallace and, 260–265
Editors: A. E. Housman, 19; Richard Bentley, 26–27; Percy Lubbock, 88–97; F. Scott Fitzgerald, 117–118; Ezra Pound, 105–108, 121–123, 131–143, 158; T. S. Eliot, 126; Edward Mendelson, 242–245; Michael Pietsch, 260–263.
Editions, 27–28, 31–32
Edwardian writers, 174–175
Efficiency, 41–42, 90
Eliot, George, 37
Eliot, Simon, 36
Eliot, T. S.: on history, 5; textual stemma and, 22; intentionalism and, 46–47; Imagism and, 103; ellipsis and, 109–110; textual waste and, 120–124; Pound and, 141–146; addition and, 190; on Hamlet, 195; on revision, 237–238; Ginsberg and, 251–252, 254; on typewriter, 254–255; revisions of, 266
Ellipsis, 108–113

Ellis, Bret Easton, 185–188
Ellmann, Maud, 122, 197, 199, 301n4
Ellmann, Richard, 122
Elongated sentence, 185–192
Emendation, 19
Epistle, as autobiography, 208
Espey, John, 113
"Eumaeus" (Joyce), 149–150, 167, 299n70
Europeans, The (James), 65
Excision: James and, 62–63; overview of, 101–103; Imagism and, 103–108; ellipsis and, 108–113; *The Sun Also Rises* and, 113–120; in *The Waste Land*, 120–124; Eliot and Pound and, 141–146; wastefulness of, 266. *See also* Compression; Minimalism
Excursion, The (Wordsworth), 31
Extension. *See* Addition(s)
Extrinsic revision, 18

Facsimile editions, 7; publication of modernist manuscripts during 1970s, in 55–56; *The Europeans* and, 65; *The Waste Land* and, 120, 122, 125; *James Joyce Archive*, 157–158; *To the Lighthouse* and, 221–222; Audens's notebooks and, 249; "Howl" and, 250–254
Fairfax, Gwendolen, 213
Faulkner, William, 37–38
Fenton, James, 249
Ferrer, Daniel, 53–54, 282n105
Feuillerat, Albert, 153
Finishing. *See* Completion
Finnegans Wake (Joyce), 44
"Fire Sermon, The" (Eliot), 127–128, 129, 132–138, 141–142
Fitzgerald, F. Scott, 117–118
Fleishman, Avrom, 195–196
Flint, F. S., 106
Fordham, Finn, 58
Form(s): genesis of text and, 5; cultural, 238
Foucault, Michel, 25
Foul proofs, 38
Four Quartets (Eliot), 127, 295n113
Fowler, Alastair, 2
Frank, Anne, 200
Franklin, Benjamin, 202

Freud, Sigmund, "The Mystic Writing
  Pad" and, 45; trauma and repetition
  compulsion, and 194–195
Friedman, Alan, 223
Froula, Christine, 6, 22, 36, 55–57, 273n23
Fry, Roger, 226–227
Fussell, Paul, 98, 289n80

Gabler, Hans Walter, 50, 56, 155, 156–157,
  158
"Game of Chess, A" (Eliot), 129
Gegenheimer, Albert, 65–66
Genetic complexity, 5
Genetic criticism, 52–59
Genette, Gerard, 220
Ghost Writer, The (Roth), 77, 238–239
Gibson, Andrew, 173
Gide, André, 200
Gill, Stephen, 204–205
Ginsberg, Allen, 56, 242, 249–254
Glamorama (Ellis), 187–188
Golden Bowl, The (James), Preface to 4, 33,
  62, 90, 193; finishing 84–85
Gordan, John, 54
Gosse, Edmund, 58, 82–83, 98, 285n2
Graham, Jorie, 267
Graves, Robert, 240
Greene, Graham, 201
Greetham, David, 13, 99, 269
Greg, W. W., 49
Grésillon, Almuth, 54
Groden, Michael, 53–56, 152, 157, 158,
  281n91
Grumbach, Doris, 287n52
Gualtieri, Elena, 302n12
Gubar, Susan, 35, 279n66
Gusdorf, Georges, 91, 201

Haffenden, John, 125, 157, 245
Hancher, Michael, 258
Harmsworth, Alfred, 133
Hartman, Geoffrey, 57, 122
Haugen, Kristine, 26
Haule, James, 198
Hay, Louis, 52–53
Hayles, N. Katherine, 148
H. D., 105, 107–108

"He Do the Police in Different Voices"
  (Eliot), 130
Hemingway, Ernest, 38, 102, 110, 113–120
Herring, Phillip, 155
Hills, Jack, 230
Hills, Stella Stephen, 212–214, 220–224
Hogarth Press, 43, 44
"Homage to Sextus Propertius" (Pound),
  111–112
Hopkins, Gerard Manley, 48–49
Horizontal revision (Tanselle), 18; in Woolf
  224, 232
Horne, Philip, 64
Housman, A. E., 19
"Howl" facsimile, 56, 242, 249–254
Hugh, Doctor, 73–81, 194
"Hugh Selwyn Mauberley" (Pound),
  112–113
Hunt, Leigh, 59
Hussey, Mark, 307n96
Huyssen, Andreas, 40–41
Hyman, Virginia, 207
Hypotaxis, 148
Hyptertext editions, 17, 54

Iceberg principle, 113–114, 119
Idealism (Plato), 79
Imagism, 34, 103–108, 110–111, 151
"In a Station of the Metro" (Pound),
  106–107, 111
Instability, textual, 6
Intentionalism, 45–56, 57
"In the Cage" (Eliot), 129
Inverse Relationship Principle, 190–191
Irving, John, 7
Isara, Rachel, 288n61
"Ithaca" (Joyce), 150, 167–174, 176, 191–192
Ivory Tower, The (James), 88–89

Jackson, H. L., 74
Jakobson, Roman, 150–151
James, Henry: revisions of, 4, 64–71;
  meaning of revision and, 26; on early
  texts, 33; on revision, 33, 237; market
  economy of modernism and, 41; genetic
  criticism and, 58; overview of, 62–64;
  and "The Middle Years," 71–83, 91–97;

post-New York Edition revision and, 83–91; dictation and, 83–84; meliorism and, 97–100; textual waste and, 101; autobiography and, 193; Gosse on, 285n2; on production, 288n61

James, Stephen, 242

Jameson, Frederic, 34, 189

Jarrell, Randall, 255

Jenkins, Nicholas, 245

Jenny, Laurent, 28–29, 54

Johnson, Samuel, 26

Johnston, Georgia, 231

Joyce, James: opportunity and constraints in revision and, 6; and revision to *Ulysses*, 15, 16, 42–43, 163–174; typewriter and, 43; market economy of modernism and, 44; intentionalism and, 46; papers of, 55–56; excision and, 101–102; minimalism and, 104; addition and, 147–151, 152; archival excess and, 155–158; Leopold Bloom revisions and, 158–163; and Molly Bloom additions, 174–185; elongated sentence and, 185–192; autobiography and, 215–220; revisions of, 265–266; Woolf on, 305n60

Juxta, 17, 67–68

Kappel, Andrew, 35–36, 126, 147–148

Kazin, Alfred, 187

Keats, John: on revision, 3; revision of, 27–28, 30; papers of, 28; Bornstein and, 59

Kemble, Fanny, 272n9

Kenner, Hugh, 138, 159, 192

Kerouac, Jack, 242, 250–251, 255

Kiberd, Declan, 178

King Lear (Shakespeare), 23–24

Kipling, Rudyard, 105

Kirsch, Adam, 308n16

Kirschenbaum, Matthew, 257, 259, 312n76

Koestenbaum, Wayne, 120, 121, 122

Korg, Jacob, 145

Krapp's Last Tape (Beckett), 103, 236

Lamb, Charles, 34–35, 279n67

Landor, Walter Savage, 31, 278n54

Laredo, Lunita, 192

Larkin, Philip, 242

Late modernism: revision and, 237–241; Auden and, 241–249; Ginsberg and, 249–254

Lawrence, D. H., 38

Leader, Zachary, 14, 30, 242–243

Leaska, Mitchell, 233

Lejeune, Philippe, 58, 199, 200–201

Leonard, Garry, 166–167

Lesser, Zachary, 23

"Letter, The" (Auden), 248–249

Levenson, Michael, 218, 219–220

Lewis, Pericles, 184

Linotype, 37, 43

Lish, Gordon, 103

"Little Gidding" (Eliot), 126

Lodge, David, 150

London, Jack, 280n82

Löschnigg, Martin, 195

Lowell, Amy, 110

Lubbock, Percy, 88–89, 91–93, 96, 288n63

"Lycidas" (Milton), 34–35

Madtes, Richard, 167–168, 172, 175

Malone, Edmund, 27

Marcus, Laura, 202

Market economy, of modernism, 40–42, 44–45

Martz, Louis, 108

Material Modernism (Bornstein), 52

Matthiessen, F. O., 78

Mausoleum Book (Stephen), 206–215

Mazzella, Anthony, 66

McCord, Phyllis, 233

McFarland, Thomas, 238

McGann, Jerome: on "lost originals", 13; on aims textual criticism, 19–20; on fine-press publishing, 43; on Yeats, 44; on sociology of texts and, 50–51; on Pound, 36, 236

McGurl, Mark, on creative writing 7, 240; on minimalism, 102; on Joyce Carol Olates, 187

McKenzie, D. F., on Wimsatt and Beardsley, 48, 282n107; on sociology of texts, 51–52; on *Ulysses*, 156–157

McLuhan, Marshall, 130, 312n89

Meliorism, 97–100, 142; textual meliorism
and *The Waste Land*, 123
Memoir. *See* Autobiography/
Autobiographies
Menand, Louis, 45
Mendelson, Edward, 49–50, 242–243, 246,
308n16
Metaphor: authorial revision and, 24; in
James's works, 34, 69–70, 75, 85, 99; in
Imagism, 107; hypotaxis and, 148;
metonymy and, 81, 150
Metonymy, 113, 148, 150
"Middle Years, The" (short story), 4, 63,
71–86,, 193–194
Middle Years, The (autobiography), 87–89;
Houghton typescript of, 91–97; 1914
and, 97–100.
Mill, J. S., 204
Miller, Tyler, 233–234
Milton, John, 26–27, 34–35
Minimalism, 102, 104–105. *See also*
Compression; Excision
Modernism and modernists: revision and,
2–3, 7–8, 266–267; difficulty and, 16,
239; poetics, 32–36; print culture,
36–39; perverse market economy of,
40–45; New Criticism and, 45–46;
Pound and, 143; addition and, 147–148;
late modernism, 233–234, 238. *See also*
Late modernism
Moments of Being (Woolf), 231
Monotype, 37, 43
Moore, Marianne, 17–18, 35–36, 126,
147–148, 239–240
More, Thomas, 269
Moretti, Franco, distant reading and,
59–60; on Joyce, 163, 217
Morgan, Bill, 250
Moveable Feast, A (Hemingway), 113–114
"Mr. Bennett and Mrs. Brown" (Woolf),
177–178
Murdoch, Iris, 151
Murphy, J. Stephen, 287n49

Nabokov, Vladimir, 7, 202–203
"Nausicaa" (Joyce), 156, 158, 161, 163–167,
184, 189
Neary, John, 186, 300n86

New Bibliography, 14, 45–49, 282n115
New Criticism, 45–50, 252
New sentence, 188–189
New writing, 239
New York Edition (James), 3–4, 63–64,
67–69
Noel, Jean-Bellemin, 53
Nussbaum, Felicity, 201

Oakeshott, Michael, 144
Oates, Joyce Carol: on revision, 1, 240–241;
on "The Middle Years," 77, 80; McGurl
on, 187; on Joyce, 215
Objections to revision, 29, 31–32
O'Hara, Frank, 255–256
Oliphant, Margaret, 211–212
On This Island (Auden), 244–245
Orwell, George, 245
Osteen, Mark, 163, 174–175, 299n70
Outcry, The (James), 87–88

Page proofs, 38–39; of *Ulysses*, 155,
168–172, 191–192; Woolf and, 227
Pale Fire (Nabokov), 241
Pale King, The (Wallace), 260–265
Pamela (Richardson), 23
Paradise Lost (Milton), 26–27
Parataxis, James and, 86; extension and,
109; metonymy, and 148; in *Ulysses*,
182–185; Perelman on, 188–189
Pargiters, The (Woolf), 233
Parker, Hershel, 48, 119
Parkes, Adam, 212
"Passionate Pilgrim, A" (James), 65–66
"Penelope" (Joyce), 178–185, 189
Perelman, Bob, 188–189
Perloff, Marjorie, 122, 142, 252
Perpetual copyright, 28
Personal computer, 45, 258–259, 261,
263–265
Pietsch, Michael, 260–265
Plate proofs, 38
"Poetry" (Moore), 239
Pope, Alexander, 20, 138
Portrait of a Lady, The (James), 66–67,
Portrait of the Artist as a Young Man, A
(Joyce), 2, 175, 206, 215–220

Poster, Mark, 267

Pound, Ezra: "make it new" and, 4–5; opportunity and constraints in revision and, 6; Froula on, 22, 36,, 56–57 273n23; on future work, 33; mining metaphor of, 34; revision of, 36; typewriter and, 39; papers of, 55; on efficiency, 90; Imagism and, 105–107, 108; excision and, 110–113; *The Waste Land* and, 121–124, 128, 130, 135–140; Eliot and, 141–146; addition and, 148, 152–153; *Ulysses* and, 158–159; autobiography and, 235–236; Rabaté on, 292n58

Prelude (Wordsworth), 16–17, 30–31, 52, 152, 204–206

"Pricking lights," 75, 167, 286n33

Print culture, 26, 36–45, 267, 268–269

Propertius, Sextus, 7

Proust, Marcel: textual waste and, 101; addition and, 153–154; van Hulle on, 296n20

Publishing: technological improvements in, 5–9, 31–32, 37, 39–40, 43, 254–260; modernist print culture, 36–45; process for, 38–39; digital culture and, 256–257.

Quick, Jonathan, 179

Rabaté, Jean-Michel, 159, 292n58, 294n96

Rabbit Run (Updike), 185–187

Rainey, Lawrence, on market economy of modernism, 6, 41, 44–45; on *The Waste Land*, 52, 118, 125, 129

Raitt, Suzanne, 141

Rasula, Jed, 272n15

Recension, 19, 276n25

Recluse, The (Wordsworth), 31

Reiman, Donald, 156

Repetition compulsion, 53, 194–195, 220

Reside, Doug, 259

Revisedness: overview of, 237–241; Auden and, 241–249; Ginsberg and, 249–254; digital texts and, 254–260; *The Pale King* and, 260–265

Revision(s): of twenty-first-century writers, 1–2; metaphoric extensions of term, 14; three types of, 15–16; intrinsic and

extrinsic, 18; history of, 19–25; distinguished from editing, 25–26, 110; romanticism's objections to, 29, 31–32; meliorism and, 98–100, 144; self-parody in, 127, 162; wastefulness of, 42, 266–267; as feature of print culture, 267

Rhythmical patterns, 183–184

Richards, Grant, 215

Richards, I. A., 48–49

Ricks, Christopher, 4

Rivkin, Julie, 34, 76

Romanticism and romantics: views on revision, 3; modernism and, 25–35

Room of One's Own, A (Woolf), 35

Rosenbach Manuscript, 155–156, 158

Rossetti, Christina, 211

Roth, Philip, 77, 238–239

Roughead, William, 98

Ruskin, John, 38, 280n78

St. Clair, William, 28, 31–32

Saint-Amout, Paul, 298n53

Saunders, Max, 113, 195, 301n7

Schuchard, Ronald, 110

Schwarz, Daniel, 162

Schwartz, Mimi, 15

Sense of the Past, The (James), 88–89

Sentence, elongated, 185–192

Shade, John, 241

Shakespeare, William, 23–25, 27, 186

Shapes, cultural, 238

Shelley, Percy Bysshe, 29, 237–238

Sherry, Vincent, 120–121

Shillingsburg, Peter, 50, 277n30, 282n115

Simic, Charles, 1–2

"Sisters, The" (Joyce), 104, 217

"Sketch of the Past, A" (Woolf), 18, 154, 197, 198, 206, 220–221, 223–235

Smith, Barbara Herrnstein, 206

Snaith, Anna, 228

Social-text editing, 50–52, 283n120

Spencer, Theodore, 215, 293n72

"Spring and Fall" (Hopkins), 48–49

Stanford Friedman, Susan, 53, 216, 217

Stanley, Liz, 201

St. Clair, William, 28, 31–32

Stead, C. K., 127

Stelzig, Eugene, 205

Stemma, textual, 19–25
Stephen, Leslie, 206–215, 218
Stephen, Stella, 199, 212–214, 220–223, 224
Stephen Hero (Joyce), 175, 215–220;
    extrinsic revision and, 18
Stillinger, Jack, 30
Sturgis, Howard, 97–98
Substitutive revision, 15–16, 238
Sun Also Rises, The (Hemingway), 102,
    113–120
"Super-position," 110, 111, 142
Svoboda, Frederic, 114
"Sweeney Among the Nightingales"
    (Eliot), 128
Swinburne, Algernon Charles, 37
Systematization, 234

Tanner, Tony, 97
Tanselle, Thomas, 9, 18, 145
Taylor, Gary, 23
Technology: improvements in publishing,
    5–9, 31–32, 37, 43; issues faced by
    twentieth-century revisers, 32; track
    changes and, 254–260. *See also*
    Typewriter
Tennyson, Alfred, Lord: Browning on, 31;
    revision of, 37; James on, 93–98; Kemble
    on, 272n9
Textual criticism: overview of, 13–18;
    history of, 19–25; intentionalism and,
    48; genetic criticism and, 56–57
Textual instability, 6
Textual stemma, 19–25
Textual waste: overview of, 101–103;
    Imagism and, 103–108; ellipsis and,
    108–113; *The Sun Also Rises* and,
    113–120; in *The Waste Land*, 120–124;
    Eliot and Pound and, 141–146
Thackeray, William Makepeace, 37, 75
"Through the Looking Glass" (Auden),
    246–247
Tichi, Cecelia, 122, 274n31
Ticknor, Benjamin, 65
Tidwell, Joanne Campbell, 306n77
To the Lighthouse (Woolf), 3, 196–198,
    221–223, 234
Track Changes function, 258–259, 261,
    263–265, 268

"Tradition and the Individual Talent,
    The" (Eliot), 144
Trauma, repetition of, 194–195
Trollope, Anthony, 203–204, 303n37
Typewriter: visual difference and, 39–40;
    Joyce and, 43; James and, 83–84; as
    compositional tool, 254–256; 1891 article
    on, 280n76; Bruder on, 313n92

Ulysses (Joyce): revision to, 6, 15, 16, 42–43,
    149–151; non-authorial error introduced
    to, 22; Gabler edition, 155–158; Bloom's
    expanding mind, 158–163; Gerty
    additions to 163–167; Molly Bloom
    additions to, 174–185; elongated
    sentence and, 185–192; inverse relation-
    ship principle and, 190–192
Updike, John, 185–187, 257

Valéry, Paul, 39
Vanderham, Paul, 158–159
Van Hulle, Dirk, 259, 277–278n42,
    284n145, 296n20
Van Vliet, H. T. M., 52–53
Verbs, in Imagism, 107–108
Vertical revision, 18
Vigneron, Robert, 153–154
Vlastos, Gregory, 79

Wallace, David Foster, 260–265
Warner, William, 23
Warren, Michael, 23
Waste, textual. *See* Textual waste
Waste Land, The (Eliot): excision and, 102;
    textual waste in, 120–124; self-
    corruption and, 122; structure of,
    129–132; tension between Pound and
    Eliot,123–140; Eliot's own revisions to,
    141–146, 266; facsimile of, 251–252, 254;
    simultaneous history in, 143–146
Weis, René, 276n27
Williams, William Carlos, 131
Wilson, Edmund, 32
Wimsatt, W. K., 46, 47, 48
Wolfson, Susan, 205
Wood, James, 185

Woolf, Leonard, 43, 200
Woolf, Virginia: revisions of, 3; extrinsic
  revision and, 18; reaction to "Lycidas"
  manuscript, 34, 35; Hogarth Press and,
  43–44; market economy of modernism
  and, 44–45; James and, 86; on *The
  Middle Years*, 92; addition and, 154,
  177–178; on Edwardian writers, 174;
  autobiography and, 196–198, 220–235;
  To the Lighthouse, 196–199, 221–224;
  Leslie Stephen and, 214–215; "A
  Sketch of the Past," 223–224; on Joyce,
  305n60
Wordsworth, William, 30–31, 152,
  204–206; revision in the *Prelude*, 16–17,
  30–31; de Selicourt on, 52; Hartman on,

57, 122; the *Prelude* as autobiography,
  203–204
World War I, 97–100; Henry James on,
  97–100; excision and, 102; Hemingway
  and, 115; waste and, 141; neuroses and,
  194–195; in *To the Lighthouse*, 222
World War II: Woolf and, 228, 232

Yao, Steven, 108
Years, The (Woolf), 233, 263, 272n11
Yeats, W. B.: publishing of, 44; Bornstein
  on, 59; on revision, 75; on T.S. Eliot,
  128; Closure in, 206; Auden on,
  243–244
Yee, Cordell, 177

www.ingramcontent.com/pod-product-compliance
Lightning Source LLC
Chambersburg PA
CBHW021830090426

42811CB00032B/2097/J